In 1778, when the expected war finally broke [illegible]
long serving First Lord of the Admiralty, had to [illegible] resources to match the French fleet not only in the Channel but in other theatres of war such as the West Indies, the Mediterranean and the Indian Ocean. In addition, the Royal Navy had to protect Britain's extensive maritime commerce, covering the large inbound and outbound convoys on which the country's economy depended. This book is a study of the men who led and the men who managed, both afloat and ashore, the Channel Fleet.

In 1778 it was commanded by Admiral Augustus Keppel; third in command was a member of the Board of Admiralty, Vice Admiral Hugh Palliser. On 27 July it engaged the French fleet commanded by d'Orvilliers. The battle was inconclusive, both sides claiming the victory. During the battle Palliser's flagship suffered particularly. At the time, no issue arose between Keppel and Palliser as to the course of the battle, but when, in late October, the latter came ashore he was shown a newspaper that suggested that he was to blame for Keppel's failure to continue the battle. He was furious, but Keppel refused to sign a statement clearing Palliser's name. The dispute escalated; Palliser demanded Keppel's court martial but he was acquitted, as was Palliser himself when he in his turn was court-martialed. The navy's officer corps was profoundly divided, and it caused lasting damage.

After Sandwich, the most important naval administrator was the outspoken Sir Charles Middleton, the Comptroller of the Navy. He was responsible for two key innovations – the coppering of ships hull's which protected them against damaging marine growths and significantly increased their speed, and the introduction of the cannonade, a lighter cannon of shorter range but greater hitting power. Middleton enjoyed a close relationship with Richard Kempenfelt who was arguably the ablest sea officer on either side. With Lord Howe, Kempenfelt was responsible for the introduction of a new system of signalling. He won a striking victory when attacking a heavily defended French convoy in 1781 but tragically died in 1782 when his flagship the *Royal George* sank at her moorings at Spithead. Throughout the war the French and Spanish planned the invasion of southern England. The enormous Combined Fleet appeared first in the Channel in 1779, but although causing a panic when it arrived off Plymouth, it was suffering from an epidemic of smallpox and abandoned the attempt.

In 1782, with the fall of Lord North's ministry, Sandwich left the Admiralty. Vilified by nineteenth century writers, his reputation has been largely restored by more recent historians.

Quintin Barry is a retired solicitor and employment judge. He has also held a variety of offices in both public and private sectors including the NHS and local radio. Following a lifelong interest in history, he is the author of a number of books on military and naval history. These include an acclaimed two volume history of the Franco-Prussian War of 1870-1871, a history of the Austro-Prussian War of 1866, and the first modern history of the Russo-Turkish War of 1877-1878. He has made a particular study of the life and career of Helmuth von Moltke. Among his recent naval books are: *The War in the North Sea 1914-1918*, *Far Distant Ships: The Blockade of Brest 1793-1815*, and *Crisis at the Chesapeake: The Royal Navy and the Struggle for America 1775-1783*.

From Ushant to Gibraltar

The Channel Fleet 1778-1783

Quintin Barry

Helion & Company Limited

Helion & Company Limited
Unit 8 Amherst Business Centre
Budbrooke Road
Warwick
CV34 5WE
England
Tel. 01926 499619
Email: info@helion.co.uk
Website: www.helion.co.uk
Twitter: @helionbooks
Visit our blog at http://blog.helion.co.uk/

Published by Helion & Company 2022
Designed and typeset by Mach 3 Solutions Ltd (www.mach3solutions.co.uk)
Cover designed by Paul Hewitt, Battlefield Design (www.battlefield-design.co.uk)

Cover: Relief of Gibraltar by Earl Howe, 11 October 1782, oil on canvas by Richard Paton (National Maritime Museum, Greenwich, London)

ISBN 978-1-915070-39-5

British Library Cataloguing-in-Publication Data.
A catalogue record for this book is available from the British Library.

For details of other military history titles published by Helion & Company Limited, contact the above address, or visit our website: http://www.helion.co.uk

We always welcome receiving book proposals from prospective authors.

Contents

List of Plates

List of Maps

Acknowledgements

This is another book in which I have been able to make extensive use of the immensely valuable resource of the publications of the Navy Records Society. The correspondence of many of the leading actors in the story of the Channel Fleet between 1778 and 1783 casts a revealing light on the way decisions were taken and their consequences.

I should also like to record my thanks to my publisher Duncan Rogers, hugely supportive as always; to Andrew Bamford, once again a patient, sympathetic and proactive editor; to George Anderson, for the maps; and to Tim Readman, who read the book in draft.

Introduction

The American Revolution had been in progress for some three years when war broke out between Britain and France in 1778. Thereafter, Britain faced the most serious threat of invasion since 1588. At the same time, hostilities began in other theatres of war – in the West Indies, the Mediterranean and the Indian Ocean – while there immediately developed a grave threat to British maritime commerce. The demands which all these made on the Royal Navy subjected it to greater stress than perhaps at any other time in its history. Later, after Spain had entered the war, Lord Sandwich, the First Lord of the Admiralty, was to reflect that Britain had never previously faced the two Bourbon powers 'thoroughly united, their naval force unbroken, and having no other war or object to draw off their attention and resources'.[1] He went on to observe that Britain, on the other hand, had no friend or ally to which she could look for assistance; apart from Portugal, those who should be her allies were actively engaged in supplying the enemy with the means of equipping their fleets.

This book is a study of the men who led and the men who managed, both afloat and ashore, the most important unit of the navy, the Channel Fleet, or Western Squadron as it was sometimes known, during this time of the greatest peril. At sea, Rear Admiral Richard Kempenfelt was, until his untimely death in 1782 when his flagship the *Royal George* sank at her moorings at Spithead, outstanding. Ashore, his friend Sir Charles Middleton (later Lord Barham), Comptroller of the Navy from 1778, was one of the most effective administrators the Royal Navy ever possessed, even if his abrasive personality sometimes led him to be shockingly outspoken.

Lord North, the Prime Minister, though an astute politician, was not a great war leader, and the prime movers in the Cabinet when it came to consider British strategy were usually Sandwich and Lord George Germain, the Secretary of State for the American colonies. Both men were, throughout almost the whole of their time in office, subject to sustained and bitter personal attacks in Parliament and the Press.

1 G.R. Barnes and J.H. Owen (eds), *The Private Papers of John, Earl of Sandwich* (London: Navy Records Society, 1936), Vol.III, p.170.

As an enterprise, the Georgian navy was both enormous and hugely complex. Although lacking any adequate form of communication system, it functioned to an extraordinary level of effectiveness. It was able to build, maintain and man a vast number of warships, and operate them against the background of a tradition of victory which none of its opponents could begin to match. In 1778, however, its officer corps could not be regarded as a band of brothers. A spirit of faction prevailed; among many, Sandwich was not popular, but, as has been said, 'if the admirals did not like Sandwich, they liked each other even less'.[2] A number were opposed to the government's policy in North America, and some senior officers refused to serve against the colonists. On the other hand, there is no doubt that over a long career in office Sandwich showed a remarkable aptitude for picking able collaborators.

The dissensions within the navy were to come dramatically to a head after the Battle of Ushant on 27 July 1778. Following this, a violent dispute erupted between the commander-in-chief of the Channel Fleet, Admiral the Hon. Augustus Keppel, and Rear Admiral Sir Hugh Palliser, his third in command, which ultimately led to the court martial of both men. The consequence was the polarisation of opinion within the navy to such an extent that it materially reduced its effectiveness. It was to be many years before the legacy of the dispute entirely wore off.

During the course of the war many of the greatest names in British naval history would make their mark. Some of them were in command of fleets or squadrons, such as Howe, Hughes Rodney and the brothers Hood; other, rising stars such as Jervis (later Lord St Vincent), Cornwallis, Keith, Duncan, Nelson and Collingwood distinguished themselves in command of individual ships. But throughout the war the Royal Navy was fighting against the odds; Sandwich was entitled, shortly before he left office in 1782, to write in his own defence that 'much more has been done than could have been expected, considering our losses by the hand of God and the unnatural combinations against us among the Powers of Europe'.[3]

2 R.J.B. Knight, 'The Royal Navy's Recovery after the Early Phase of the American Revolutionary War' in George J. Andreopoulos and Harold E. Selesky (eds), *The Aftermath of Defeat* (New Haven: Yale University Press 1994), p.17.

3 Barnes and Owen (eds), *Private Papers of John, Earl of Sandwich*, Vol.IV, p.301.

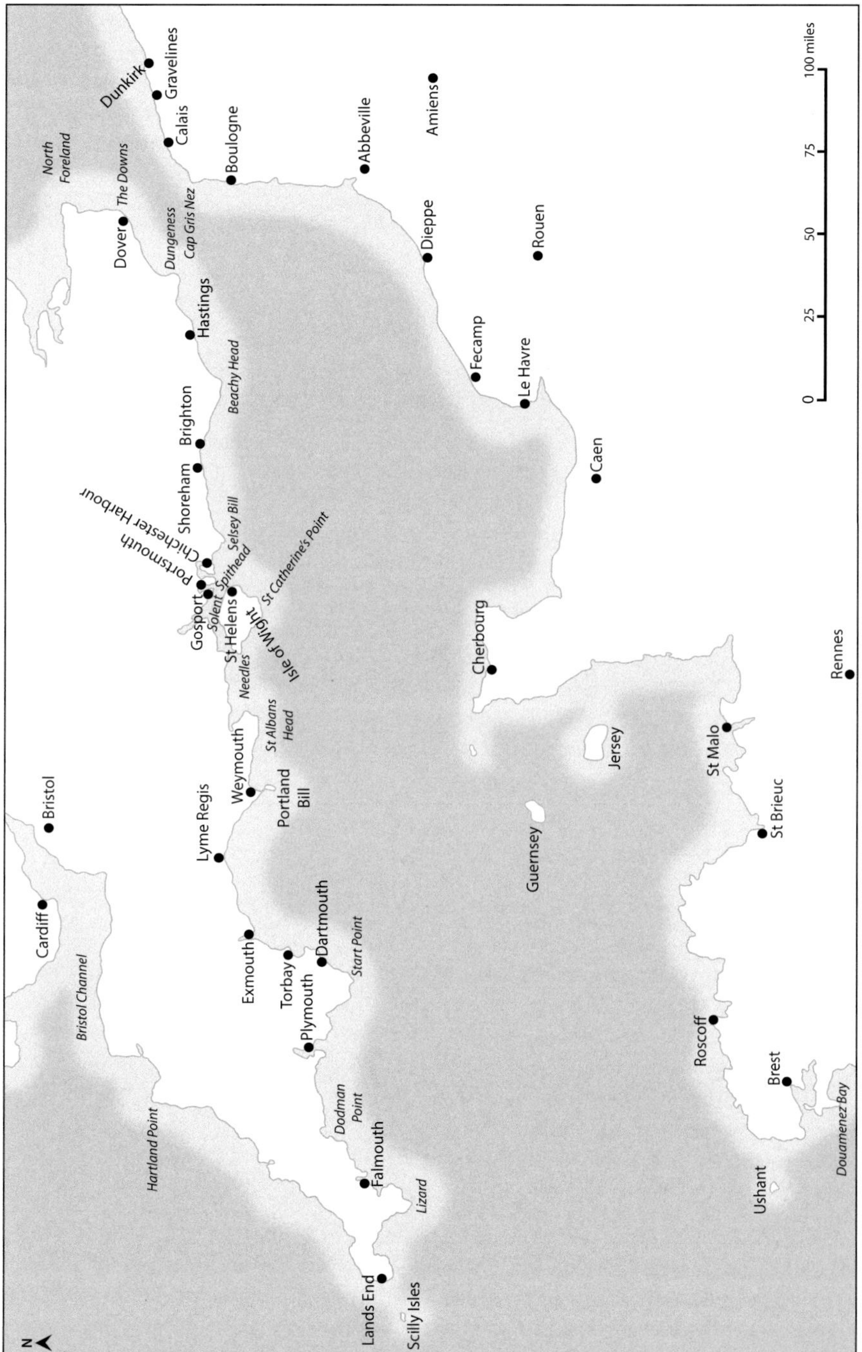

The English Channel.

Western Approaches.

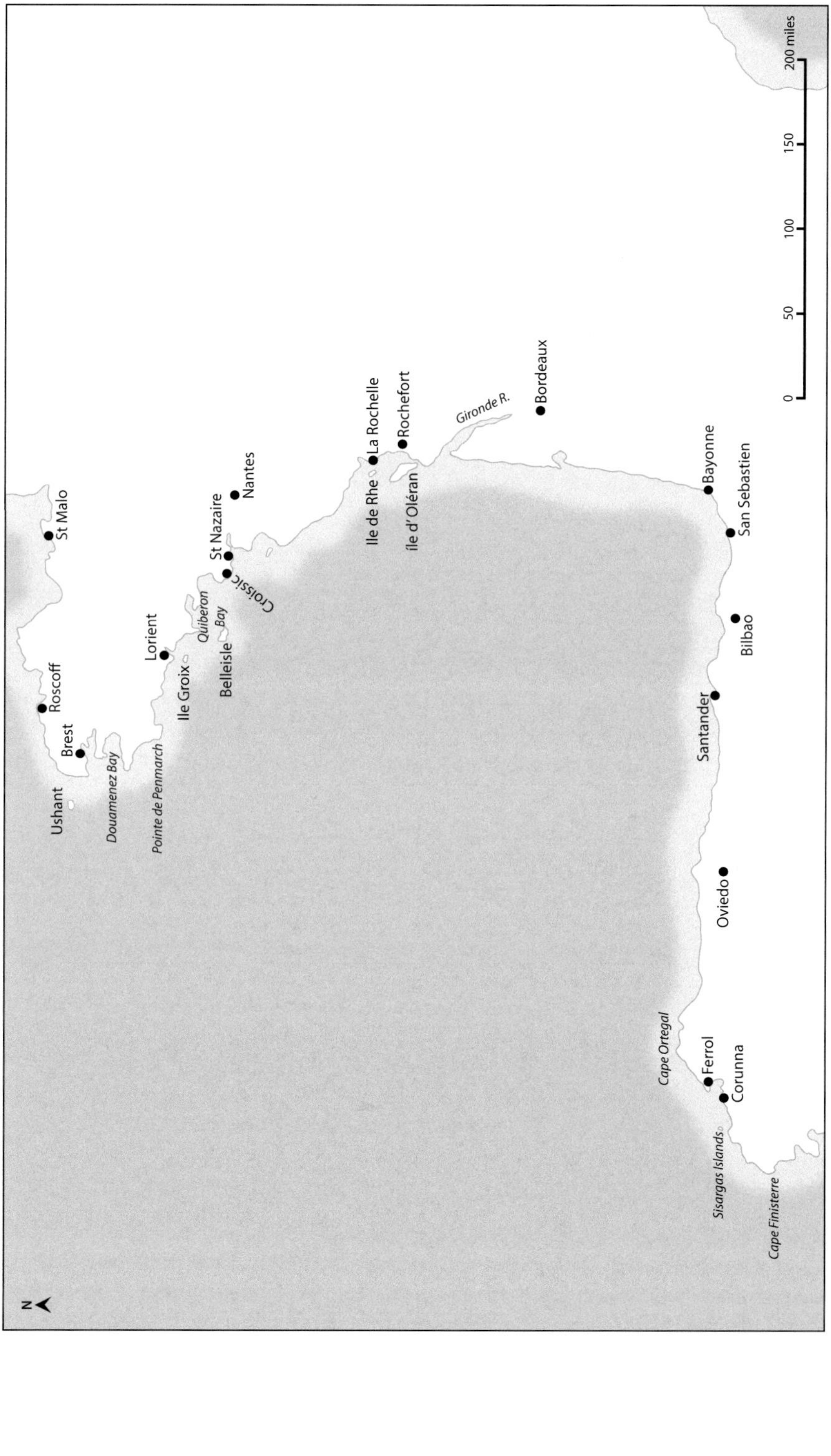

The Bay of Biscay.

1

Sandwich as First Lord

In 1771 John Montagu, fourth Earl of Sandwich, had been active in British politics for more than a quarter of a century. Throughout that time the office of state which he most desired to hold had been that of First Lord of the Admiralty, ever since he had joined the Board in 1744 as a young man of 26. Although taking a great personal interest in the navy, he had no particular naval connections other than through his great great-grandfather, the distinguished first Earl of Sandwich who was killed in action at Solebay in 1671.

Sandwich had inherited his title at the age of 10; he took his seat in the House of Lords in 1740 at the age of 22. A classicist, he was a cultured young man who had, after leaving Cambridge at the age of 21, taken a grand tour to Europe and the Near East. This voyage established his reputation as a serious scholar. In 1741 he married Dorothy Fane. He was, by the standards of the English nobility of the time, by no means wealthy, and nor was his wife; financial difficulty haunted him for much of his life. The marriage, which produced five children, was at first happy, but by 1751 his wife was showing the first signs of severe mental illness which led to their separation in 1757. A great deal of scandalous gossip was written about his mode of life, though more recent biographers have demonstrated how exaggerated this was. In 1762 he began living with Martha Ray; she was only 17 at the time, but their relationship 'represented the nearest he could get to the happy marriage he had lost forever'.[1] It ended tragically with her murder in 1779 by an unstable young man who had fallen in love with her; this, Sandwich wrote, had 'robb'd him of all comfort in this world'.

Sandwich was ambitious, in an age when that was not an attribute that was always highly regarded, and a lack of money was an undoubted hindrance. When he entered the House of Lords he joined the political group led by the Duke of Bedford, which was part of the Whig opposition to Sir Robert Walpole. Sandwich soon gained a reputation as an effective speaker in the Upper House; it was when the Duke of Bedford became First Lord that Sandwich joined him as a member of

1 N.A.M. Rodger, *The Insatiable Earl* (New York: W.W. Norton, 1993), p.6.

the Board. They were greatly assisted by the recruitment of Rear Admiral George Anson, newly returned from his round-the-world expedition. With a French war to contend with, the Board would frequently have to do without Anson's services from time to time, since he would be expected to have a command at sea.

'John, Earl of Sandwich', engraving by John Corner. (NYPL)

The new Board inherited an unsatisfactory situation: 'There was an impression of drift, complacency and inertia in both the internal discipline and the civil administration of the Navy, which the new Admiralty were determined to do something about'.[2] One matter, which concerned Anson in particular, was the need for a redesign of British warships, and the measures introduced included the first of the 74-gun ships that would become the standard ship of the line. Much attention was paid to the design of French warships, many of the features of which were adopted. Another major concern with which Anson was naturally especially concerned was the fleet's efficiency at sea. An important reform introduced by the new Board was to provide for a new rank of 'rear admiral without distinction of squadron'; holders of this rank became known as 'yellow admirals'. This device enabled the Admiralty to promote able captains over the heads of elderly and unsuitable officers who were compensated with the new rank in their retirement.

Although it was the Cabinet which effectively took most of the key strategic decisions, the Admiralty was responsible for the adoption as a basic principle of the Western Squadron, cruising off the mouth of the Channel, where it could both cover trade convoys entering and leaving and also watch the French base at Brest. It was an important development that had in the past been strongly advocated by Admiral Vernon:

2 Rodger, *Insatiable Earl*, p.22.

> The principle of a Western Squadron was one of the most valuable and enduring legacies of Bedford's Admiralty, and in one shape or another it formed the core of Britain's naval strategy for a century and more. The practical application of the policy, however, always aroused disagreement, and did so between members of the board.[3]

With the passage of time, the Duke of Bedford began to reduce his commitment to the work of the Admiralty, and accordingly Sandwich took an increasing role in its management, in which he worked closely with Anson. His reputation as a skilful young politician was enhanced by his handling of a brief crisis involving a number of government supporters for whom no office had been found. As a result he was chosen in 1746 to lead the British delegation to the discussions taking place at Breda intended to bring the War of the Austrian Succession to an end. The government was divided over this; Pelham, effectively the Prime Minister, was inclined to favour peace. On the other hand his brother, the Duke of Newcastle, headed a group that wished the war to continue, believing that major prizes were to be won especially in Canada. Bedford and his supporters formed part of this latter group. In practice, therefore, Sandwich's task was to conduct negotiations which a significant part of the government intended should not be successful. He had a difficult task in seeking to maintain his working relationships with all those concerned, since he was effectively receiving instructions from several quarters that were entirely inconsistent. In spite of this, he managed to ensure that for the best part of the year the talks went nowhere. 1747, however, was unfavourable for Britain and her Dutch allies, and the government began to move away from Newcastle's belligerent stance. In February 1748 Sandwich was appointed to lead the British delegation to a fresh peace conference at Aix la Chapelle; just at this point, the Dutch, on whom Sandwich and the British government had been counting for effective support in continuing the war, disclosed that their military and financial situation was on the point of collapse, and his task now was to negotiate a settlement on the best terms that he could get. This he succeeded in doing; Newcastle, though, who was the Secretary of State responsible for overseeing the peace talks, was extremely discontented, and did his level best to scupper the deal that had been done. In October 1748, however, the treaty was finally signed, and Sandwich was able to return to his work at the Admiralty.

Meanwhile a complex set of manoeuvres had ensued, intended to result in Sandwich's appointment as Secretary of State for the Northern Department in succession to Lord Chesterfield; in the end, Bedford moved to that post, and Sandwich became First Lord of the Admiralty, while still abroad on his diplomatic duties. He was entirely content to leave Anson in virtually sole charge while he was away, telling him that he should consider himself as in effect at the head of

3 Rodger, *Insatiable Earl*, p.35.

the Admiralty. He had complete confidence in the admiral and when he returned they worked extremely well together. In this period Sandwich instituted a series of visitations to the dockyards, which enabled the identification of a great many abuses; however, although very many orders were in consequence issued to the Navy Board, which was responsible for the management of the dockyards, most of these remained unexecuted.[4]

Sandwich was not though, to enjoy a lengthy term of office as First Lord. He had incurred the enmity of the Duke of Newcastle over the ending of the war; the Duke, who had now become reconciled to his brother, was also hostile to Bedford. The brothers calculated that if Sandwich were removed from office, Bedford would resign. As a result, Sandwich was in 1751 accordingly dismissed and, as expected, his patron's resignation followed. His fall was summarised by Nicholas Rodger: 'So long as he was useful to great men, he was favoured and advanced, but when he had served his purpose he was expended as a pawn in a political gambit'.[5]

Out of office, Sandwich returned to private life where he endured profound unhappiness. Sadly, his wife's mental health was already beginning to fail, and in 1755 they parted. He remained in the political wilderness for a dozen years. At the end of that time, it appeared that opportunity offered when it was proposed that he be sent as ambassador to Madrid; but before he could take up the post the Grenville ministry, in April 1763, offered him the post of First Lord. He remained at the Admiralty only until August, when on the death of Lord Egremont a further Cabinet reshuffle created a vacancy in the office of Secretary of State for the Northern Department, to which Sandwich was appointed. This post carried with it responsibilities now exercised by the Home Secretary, and when the Cabinet decided to take the hugely unpopular course of prosecuting John Wilkes for seditious libel, Sandwich became involved in the conduct of the affair. It had involved Wilkes' arraignment before the House of Commons, with the object of depriving him of his Parliamentary privilege; then, on Sandwich's suggestion, a separate charge of publishing an obscene libel was brought before the House of Lords in November 1763. This had its effect; Wilkes was expelled from the House of Commons and subsequently convicted on both the charges of obscene libel and seditious libel, and imprisoned. To the general public, Wilkes appeared as a victim of the government's persecution, and it was at Sandwich's door that was laid the blame for this.

Sandwich held office as Secretary of State from 1763 until 1765. The editor of his diplomatic correspondence, Frank Spencer, summed up his two years in office:

> As Secretary of State, Sandwich did little more than follow the general lines of policy laid down by tradition and Grenville's economy. He did

4 Rodger, *Insatiable Earl*, p.67.
5 Rodger, *Insatiable Earl*, p.68.

> nothing to improve Britain's international position but he did not worsen it, and it is hard to see what more he could have done under the circumstances. It is impossible to conduct a rigorous economy campaign and weaken the navy, as Grenville did, and yet run the risks of a firm and active foreign policy.[6]

By July 1765 King George III had become disenchanted with the Grenville ministry, and in that month he removed it from office, replacing it with an administration led by the Marquis of Rockingham. Sandwich did not expect the new government to last very long. Its effective leader was the king's uncle, the Duke of Cumberland, though his position as a royal duke meant that he must remain in the background. He died in October 1765. The ministry was not a strong one. Among its significant supporters were two distinguished admirals, Sir Charles Saunders and Augustus Keppel. It lingered on until the following year when it was succeeded by the administration led by the Duke of Grafton; William Pitt, now Earl of Chatham, was its central figure, as Secretary of State. A further reshuffle of this government at the end of 1766 led to Sandwich becoming joint Postmaster General, a modest and undemanding enough post, in which he was uncomfortable. This ministry remained in office until June 1770, at which point the King invited Lord North to form a government. North was a masterly manager of the House of Commons, and he was able to put together a ministry that, as it turned out, had considerable staying power.

In December of that year, Sandwich took office as Secretary of State for the Southern Department, on the occasion of the resignation of Lord Weymouth over North's handling of the Falklands crisis. The First Lord of the Admiralty at this time was the elderly but highly respected Admiral Sir Edward Hawke. Under his stewardship the navy had undoubtedly declined; Augustus Hervey, never a man to understate a case, wrote that it was 'a ruined service … I have the particulars of many instances of neglect very alarming to this country, but when ignorance and obstinacy are predominant at that board, it is of little consequence to represent'.[7] In the middle of an ongoing crisis that might lead to the outbreak of war, it was considered inappropriate to try to remove Hawke, but once that had passed, North felt able to do so, and turned to Sandwich, who thus took office as First Lord of the Admiralty for the third time.

Sandwich brought to the post the experience of a quarter of century at the top of British politics, as well as a profound understanding of the way in which the eighteenth-century Royal Navy worked, as well as all of its limitations. On the debit side, his previous career, his political connections, his character and his use

6 George Martelli, *Jemmy Twitcher* (London: Jonathan Cape, 1962), p.67.

7 Rodger, *Insatiable Earl*, p.129.

of patronage all meant that he came with the kind of baggage that would be readily seized upon by his enemies.

Throughout his lengthy term of office Sandwich was subject to constant pressure – from the King, who had strong views as to what should be done and often expressed them very forcefully, from the Cabinet, which constantly sought to limit expenditure on the navy, from a frequently hostile House of Commons, and from applicants aggressively seeking appointments; but he had learnt how to deal effectively with all of these problems.

Sandwich was a complex and many faceted character whom history generally for very many years treated unfairly. Until at least the middle of the twentieth century, historians ascribed to him not only all manner of personal failings but also grave errors in the course of his public service. Sir Geoffrey Callender, a historian who regarded patriotism as more important than an objective search for truth, felt able to write of Sandwich that he was

> [A] clever man with great industry and aptitude for business, but a man of evil and immoral life; a man without scruples, without ideals; a man who degraded his high office, and subordinated the lasting interests of his country to the transient needs of a Parliamentary majority. There is no need to credit his inventive faculties with all the horrid devices that sapped the navy of its strength … These abuses had occurred before. But Sandwich systematised them. He revived the old devices for defrauding the service and added new tricks of his own.[8]

This grave perversion of the truth was matched by the *Cambridge Modern History*, which described Sandwich as 'a man entirely without nautical experience and far too much engrossed by his pleasures to concern himself with the disagreeable details of administration'.[9] Callender, at least was prepared to testify to Sandwich's industry and ability.

Other, sounder historians nevertheless also accepted the view of Sandwich promoted by his enemies. Sir John Knox Laughton, the editor of *The Barham Papers*, dismissed Sandwich's tenure of office as First Lord by focusing on his use of patronage: 'It is not too much to say that by no one has the patronage of the First Lord been so abused as it was by Sandwich, and that by that abuse the Navy was reduced to the lowest pitch'.[10] This position was followed by Admiral James, who

8 Geoffrey Callender, *Sea Kings of Britain: Keppel to Nelson 1760-1850* (London: Longmans Green, 1939), p.7.

9 A.W. Ward et al (eds), *The Cambridge New Modern History* (Cambridge: Cambridge University Press, 1907), Vol.VI, p.444.

10 Sir John Knox Laughton (ed.), *The Barham Papers* (London: Navy Records Society, 1910), Vol.II, p.viii.

wrote of Sandwich's tenure of the Admiralty that 'it was a long story of administrative jobbery and corruption'.[11]

Calumnies of this kind were shown as entirely false by the publication in the 1930s by the Navy Records Society of four volumes of Sandwich's correspondence. Their publication did much to sweep away the narrative put about by Sandwich's Whig opponents; J.H. Broomfield wrote: 'In place of the dissolute, corrupt and incompetent figure of Whig legend, there is now seen an able, determined administrator, frustrated in his attempts to restore the strength of a neglected fleet by the apathy and personal ambition of fellow ministers'.[12]

Broomfield went on to examine the reasons for the undoubted fact that among many naval officers Sandwich was extremely unpopular. He concluded that there was ample evidence to show that it was his political activity that was responsible for this, and in particular his creation of a small but influential personal following. In the House of Commons, in addition to the three Huntingdon seats which he controlled, he was also able to make use of the Admiralty seats, filling these with a number of his followers such as Captain Lord Mulgrave, Captain Hugh Palliser, Captain Charles Phipps and Captain Maurice Suckling. They proved to be men of marked ability and a valuable support both to Sandwich and the administration, but they were not selected in the usual way of the eighteenth century:

> Those whom he attached to himself in this way were all relative nonentities by eighteenth century standards. They were not of particularly distinguished birth, they had no record of Parliamentary service nor of any considerable administrative experience and they were all comparatively junior men in their profession. On the other hand, it is clear that Sandwich chose them with care, for all proved to be seamen of outstanding ability and to be equally successful as administrators. Ability, however, was not an accepted eighteenth century yardstick, and the competence of these men did little to endear them to the hearts of Sandwich's opponents.[13]

Following a sympathetic biography in 1969 by George Martelli, the appearance in 1993 of the surpassing biography by Nicholas Rodger wholly rehabilitated Sandwich's reputation. Not only did he demolish the opinions of Sandwich held by such as Callender, by restoring his reputation as an outstanding naval administrator in a comprehensive analysis of his years as First Lord of the Admiralty, but he also provided a convincing portrait of a profoundly intelligent and cultured man of his time.

11 Rear Admiral W.M. James, *The British Navy in Adversity* (London: Longmans Green, 1933), p.16.

12 J.H. Broomfield, 'Lord Sandwich at the Admiralty Board: Politics in the British Navy, 1771-1778' in *The Mariner's Mirror* (February 1965), p.7.

13 Broomfield, 'Lord Sandwich at the Admiralty Board', p.9.

A rather different view was expressed by an American historian, John A. Tilly, who approached Sandwich's career from the point of view of his naval strategy. He considered him a competent administrator, but went on to write that 'an objective evaluation of Sandwich's Admiralty must conclude that it was conscientious but abysmally inept ... Neither Sandwich nor any of his subordinates ever produced a coherent scheme for fighting a naval war'.[14]

Looking at the way in which he was perceived by his contemporaries, it is undoubtedly true, as was apparent to politicians and sea officers alike, that the First Lord had in his hand the opportunity to bestow considerable benefit, as Professor Richard Pears pointed out:

> The opportunities for naval patronage were immense; the more so because the system for distributing prize-money rendered certain stations, and certain kinds of ships, much more lucrative than others, and enhanced the advantages of an independent command. A friend at the Admiralty could do much to help a captain push his fortune.[15]

Sandwich sometimes sailed close to the wind, not least in making appointments without consultation with the Cabinet, and so successfully did his Whig opponents promote their allegations of his jobbery that it even had its effect on the minds of his friends and colleagues in government. On 18 August 1777, John Robinson, the Secretary to the Treasury, wrote to Sandwich with a serious warning about the effect of appointing individuals who did not carry with them popular opinion or confidence:

> Wisdom and security to the public dictates the propriety of, nay loudly calls for, his Majesty's servants filling every command and every station with men of the greatest experience in service, acknowledged abilities, and tried conduct, carrying along with them also the opinion of the public.[16]

Broomfield, summing up Sandwich's term of office as First Lord, concluded that he was certainly not guilty of neglect or corruption, but was 'probably one of the best First Lords to sit at the board in the eighteenth century,' and that he and his colleagues did their utmost to rebuild a neglected naval force. He went on:

> It is equally clear, however, that by his political activities Sandwich left himself open to the charge that the service was being sacrificed to jobbery.

14 John A. Tilly, *The British Navy and the American Revolution* (Colombia, SC: University of South Carolina Press 1987), pp.277-278.

15 Richard Pears, *King George III and the Politicians* (Oxford: Oxford University Press, 1954), p.19.

16 Barnes and Owen (eds), *Private Papers of John, Earl of Sandwich*, Vol.I, pp.239-240.

It is not surprising therefore that he became extremely unpopular both in the navy and in the nation at large. Nor is it surprising in the light of the naval disasters of those years that for more than a century after his death the charge was considered proven against him.[17]

17 Broomfield, 'Lord Sandwich at the Admiralty Board', p.17.

2

The Admiralty

The Admiralty had been housed in Whitehall since the reign of William III, in a building that was notoriously damp and which by 1723 was seriously decayed. It was then pulled down, and a new building erected on the site. Nicholas Rodger, in his history of the Admiralty published in 1979, was extremely unimpressed by this building, writing:

> There it stands to this day, wretchedly ill proportioned and disfiguring a noble site, with its unremarkable rear view across Horse Guards where the Admiralty garden once lay, and its dingy courtyard on the other side 'deservedly veiled,' as Horace Walpole put it, by the remains of the Adam screen.[1]

If the building was unremarkable, what is particularly remarkable is the limited extent of the resources with which the Board of Admiralty and its secretariat governed the affairs of the Navy. Whereas the Navy Board had up to 9,000 employees, and even the Victualling Board in London by 1747 had 74 staff, the total staff of the Admiralty in Whitehall was less than 40. Rodger remarked that to function effectively 'the Admiralty demanded and received from its clerks a dedication highly untypical of the Georgian civil service'. For this, they enjoyed a very high level of pay and benefits.

Apart from the First Lord himself, and the naval lords on the Board, it was the Secretary of the Admiralty who exercised the most powerful influence on the Navy and its operations. The first administrator to serve with the title of Secretary of the Admiralty was Samuel Pepys, appointed in 1673 after having served on the Navy Board since 1660. He exerted far more authority than any confidential servant of the Navy who had gone before him, representing the navy in the House of Commons, of which he became a member in 1673, and enjoying the complete confidence of King Charles II. After the Glorious Revolution of 1688, Pepys'

1 N.A.M. Rodger, *The Admiralty* (Lavenham: Terence Dalton, 1979), p.63.

successors were by no means as influential as he, but as the years went by the office gradually began to assume greater and greater importance. This was particularly the case during the 40-year-long secretaryship of Josiah Burdhettt, who retired in 1742. He was succeeded by Thomas Corbett, who held office until 1751, and then by John Cleveland, who died in 1763.

The next to take office was Philip Stephens. Born in 1723, he had from the age of 16 spent 12 years in the office of the Navy Board. In 1751 Anson arranged for him to join the staff of the Admiralty. He subsequently served as Anson's secretary before he was appointed Assistant Secretary to the Board. After becoming Secretary, he entered Parliament as the member for the borough of Sandwich in 1768, which he was to represent until 1806. When Sandwich returned to office as First Lord in 1771, therefore, he inherited a Secretary who had already been in post for eight years.

In analysing the functions of the Secretary of the Admiralty, Nicholas Roger observed that 'it was a position of crucial importance, and it was almost unique in eighteenth century politics'.[2] Unlike the Under Secretaries in other departments of state, the Secretaries of the Admiralty remained in office when the Board changed, being in that respect, as the Parliamentary Commissioners described them in 1787, 'stationary officers'. This meant that they enjoyed long continuity of service, which in turn conferred on them very considerable authority. It was the Secretary who dealt with correspondence, and who decided whether to deal with it himself or refer it to the Board; he controlled the administration of the office and acted in effect as the First Lord's political manager, representing the Admiralty in the House of Commons. All this gave him an influence far greater than the apparent significance of his office. Remarkably, it was generally accepted that the Secretary was non-political, so that when in 1779 Lord Bristol delivered a fierce attack on Sandwich's administration, he was careful to except Philip Stephens from his strictures, describing him as 'the most diligent, most intelligent, and indefatigable man in business I ever knew, and for whose absence or sickness I am not at all surprised at anything that may happen to go wrong'.[3]

George Jackson filled the office of Second Secretary, although the post was not formally so described until 1783, having been previously known at various times as Assistant Secretary, Joint Secretary and Deputy Secretary. It was only after 1756 that appointments were regularly made to this post, which had been held by Philip Stephens for four years before he became Secretary. Jackson served from November 1766 until June 1782, and was in regular personal correspondence with a number of senior officers; Samuel Hood, for instance, wrote frequently to him with his candid views on a wide range of subjects.

2 Rodger, *Admiralty*, p.64.
3 Rodger, *Admiralty*, pp.66-67.

A First Lord naturally gave particular consideration to the composition of his Board of Admiralty. Within a few weeks after Sandwich had again become First Lord, he was able on the retirement of Admiral Sir Francis Holburne as a naval lord to appoint in his place Captain Augustus Hervey, who had become a good friend of his. A dashing commander, Hervey was also a notorious rake, recording in his journal an extraordinary record of his sexual activities. Hervey had been born in 1724, a grandson of the first Earl of Bristol, who had done much to establish the family as one of the great Whig dynasties of the eighteenth century. He entered the navy in 1735, joining a ship commanded by his uncle William Hervey, and was rated midshipman a year later. Thanks to his distinguished parentage, he was promoted lieutenant in September 1740, and was made post in 1747, seeing action in the Battle of Minorca in 1756 in command of the *Phoenix*. Subsequently, in command of the *Dragon*, 74, he took part in the capture of Belle Isle, and then served in the West Indies in the operations against Martinique, before serving with distinction at the siege and capture of Havana in 1762. In the following year he commanded the *Centurion*. He had entered Parliament in 1757; when he joined the Board of Admiralty, Sandwich had at first found him a valuable support, since he was at that point the only naval member. In that capacity, he gave Sandwich the benefit of his considerable naval experience, writing for instance in the spring of 1771 a detailed letter of advice in connection with the arrangement for guard ships. These were ships of the line kept in commission at each port which could be quickly mobilised to provide the nucleus of a fleet. Sandwich appreciated working with Hervey, writing in that year on 13 June during his summer tour of the dockyards:

> I believe you will find the reductions have in general been made according to your idea, and that a considerable number of landsmen are continued in the service; and I perceive it to be the opinion of many of our best officers that a ship so filled is better manned than if she had nothing but able seaman on board. I do assure you I have not been idle since I have left you, as you will perceive when I communicate to you the several observations I have made during this visitation, all of which is reduced into writing, and on which I shall be very happy if your opinion coincides with mine, and I should be greatly obliged to you for any further hints which your experience in and knowledge of naval matters may suggest.[4]

Understandably, Hervey took a particular interest in operational questions and those concerning personnel, and Sandwich took careful note of his expert advice. Although Hervey was a member of Parliament, he rarely spoke there, and at this

4 Barnes and Owen (eds), *Private Papers of John, Earl of Sandwich*, Vol.I, p.18.

time it was John Buller, a lay member of the Board, who usually spoke for the Admiralty in the House of Commons.

Hervey suffered a disappointment in 1773; a diplomatic crisis with France in that year had led to plans to send out a fleet to the Mediterranean, of which Hervey was selected to be third in command with a commodore's pendant. However, the crisis was averted and the fleet was not sent. Hervey continued in his position as a naval lord, but was increasingly afflicted by ill-health, and was consequently frequently unable to attend meetings of the Board. In addition, he was in any case becoming disenchanted with his situation there. The result of this was that the close friendship which had existed between him and Sandwich was beginning to fade. In the autumn of 1774, Hervey's older brother, the Earl of Bristol, suffered a severe stroke, which raised the probability that Hervey, his heir, would succeed to the title. This in fact occurred on 18 March 1775, and as a result Hervey found himself a very wealthy man. This prompted him to seek promotion to flag rank, and also to insist that as a peer he should not be expected to sign documents below that of other members of the Board who were commoners. By now Sandwich was coming to the conclusion that it would be better that Hervey should go. Almost inevitably, due to Hervey's aristocratic eminence, the King became involved; Sandwich wrote to him on 27 March to report on his conversation with Hervey, and the situation which had arisen:

> Ld Sandwich told Ld Bristol that he thought the King listened to the idea of a promotion, but that he did not fully explain his intention; and that upon the whole it was Lord Sandwich's opinion that if he confined himself to the single object of the flag, and agreed to vacate the Admiralty, he would prevail upon your Majesty to gratify him ...Ld Sandwich told him that he thought it would be very awkward for him to come over all the other Lords of the Admiralty to sign second, to which he answered that he could sit at the Board on no other conditions, if there was any difficulty on that point he must at once determine to quit, whether he had his flag or not.[5]

The upshot of all this was that Hervey resigned, but he was granted the promotion to rear admiral that he sought. Regrettably, the relationship between Sandwich and Hervey would thereafter steadily deteriorate to the point where it became, on Hervey's part at any rate, one of bitter enmity. His departure cleared the way for Sandwich to make a new appointment to the Board. His choice was Sir Hugh Palliser. He took office as the senior naval lord on 31 March, and was promoted to the rank of rear admiral.

5 Quoted in Michael Holmes, *Augustus Hervey: A Naval Casanova* (Bishop Auckland: Pentland Press, 1996), pp.260-261.

Hugh Palliser was born into a Yorkshire landowning family on 26 February 1723. His parents died while he was still young. At the age of 12 he joined the navy as a midshipman aboard a vessel commanded by his uncle, whom he followed to two other vessels and finally to the *Essex*. While serving aboard her he passed for lieutenant and was promoted to that rank in 1741. In February 1746 he was given his first command, the *Weasel*, and in November of that year was made post. He took command of the *Captain*, and sailed in her to the West Indies, subsequently transferring to the *Sutherland*. In early 1748 he was seriously wounded as a result of an explosion in the ship's arms chest. Thereafter he remained lame in his left leg, and for the rest of his life frequently suffered intense pain.

Later in 1748 he was posted to the *Sheerness*, 24, in which he sailed to the East Indies, where he served until bringing her back to Britain to pay off in April 1750. He was next appointed to command the *Yarmouth*, the guard ship based at Chatham, followed by a posting to the 20-gun post-ship *Seahorse*. Aboard her, he ran into difficulties with the Scottish legal system, when refusing to hand over one of his seamen accused of uttering a forged document. As a result, Palliser was himself arrested, and held for several days in Edinburgh's Tollbooth prison before the Court of Session ordered his release.

In 1755, after a spell in command of the *Bristol*, 50, he took charge of a convoy escorted by the *Seahorse* and *Nightingale* taking troops to the West Indies shortly before the outbreak of the Seven Years War. He chose to take the convoy by an unorthodox route, sailing as far south as the Tropic of Cancer, enabling the convoy to avoid the storms it might have encountered further north, and he was commended for the initiative which he had shown. When the war broke out, he was posted to the *Eagle*, 60, aboard which he fought a successful single ship action against the French East Indiaman *Duc d'Aquitaine* off Ushant on 30 May 1757. The French ship, though an Indiaman, was armed with fifty 18-pounders and had a large crew of nearly 500 men. The *Eagle* was that time sailing in company with the *Medway*, 60, but she could not get up into action, and the *Eagle* engaged the French vessel on her own, inflicting 97 shot holes in her sides, and bringing down her main and mizzen masts before she struck, having had 50 men killed.[6] The *Eagle* had herself been damaged in the engagement, and returned to Portsmouth for repairs, and Palliser next took command of the *Shrewsbury*, 74, in which he had a successful spell of service with the Channel Fleet under Anson. In 1759 he took part in the capture of Quebec, commanding the body of seamen who landed to seize the Lower Town. In the following year he went to the Mediterranean, where among other operations he captured a Danish merchant ship; at that time Denmark was neutral, but Palliser was aware that Danish ships were employed in trading for the French from the Levant, a practice to which Britain wished to put

6 William Laird Clowes, *The Royal Navy: A History from the Earliest Times* (London: Sampson Low Marston and Co, 1898), Vol.III, p.295.

an end. Before the war ended, Palliser was given command of a small squadron to recapture St John's, Newfoundland, but by the time he arrived it had already been retaken.

In 1764 Palliser was appointed as governor and commander-in-chief of the Newfoundland station, with the *Guernsey*, 50, and several frigates under his command, with the rank of commodore. A distinguished career afloat in the age of sail did not necessarily prepare an officer to be an effective administrator, but Palliser made the most of the transition to demonstrate his management skills. He soon found himself at odds with a French squadron which had been sent to protect their country's fishing grounds; he found that they had altered their maps to show an entitlement to a greater area than had been agreed upon by the terms of the Treaty of Paris of 1763. In the ensuing dispute, the British government upheld the action which he had taken. Thereafter he actively supported the Newfoundland fishing industry, which provided a source of trained seamen for the British navy, and he promoted legislation for its encouragement and support.

Palliser served in Newfoundland until 1768. In 1770 his administrative ability was recognised by his appointment as Comptroller of the Navy, effectively heading the Navy Board; he also became an Elder Brother of Trinity House. This was before Sandwich had returned to office as First Lord, but the latter at once recognised Palliser's merit, and formed a close working relationship with him. In 1773 Palliser was made a baronet, and in the following year was elected as member of Parliament for Scarborough; he was a staunch Tory. Sandwich had seen enough to know that here was the man he needed to shoulder part of the burden of managing the Admiralty, and Palliser was soon demonstrating his talent in his new role.

Captain Constantine Phipps, Sandwich's other key protégé, came from a more aristocratic background than Hugh Palliser. He was born on 19 May 1744, the eldest son of Lord Mulgrave, an Irish peer; Augustus Hervey was one of his uncles. He was educated at Eton, where he studied under the distinguished naturalist Joseph Banks. He joined the navy in January 1759 as a cadet aboard Augustus Hervey's ship *Monmouth*, 70, following him to the *Dragon*, 74, in 1761. Aboard her he served with distinction in the operations against Martinique, and in March 1762 was promoted lieutenant by Rodney. Remaining with his uncle, he took part aboard the *Dragon* in the siege and capture of Havana, in the course of which he was wounded. In November 1763 he took command of the sloop *Diligence*, 12, and then in June 1765 was appointed to the *Terpsichore*, 24. In the following year, serving as a lieutenant, he sailed aboard the *Niger* in an expedition to Newfoundland carrying Joseph Banks.

In 1767 he was posted to the *Boreas*, and in the following year he was elected to Parliament as member for Lincoln. At this time, he was an opponent of the government led by Lord North. He continued his service afloat by heading an expedition towards the North Pole in June 1773, when sailing with the *Racehorse* and the *Carcass*. Aboard the latter vessel was the young Midshipman Horatio Nelson. The expedition was accompanied by a naturalist and an astronomer. It reached the Seven Islands before being forced back by the ice. Phipps was the first to give a detailed account of the polar bear and the ivory gull, both of which he described in the book about the expedition which he published in the following year. In that year, he lost his seat as a member of Parliament; then, in September 1775 he succeeded to the title as second Baron Mulgrave on the death of his father. By now, he had caught Sandwich's attention, who wrote of him at that time: 'I know his connection with opposition is entirely at an end, and that he wants much to come into Parliament'.[7] The First Lord predicted that Mulgrave would be 'a very good acquisition for us in the House of Commons,' and in 1776 he arranged for the young captain's election as Member of Parliament for Huntingdon, one of the seats which he controlled. In December 1777 Mulgrave joined the Board of Admiralty, and in the following year became an Elder Brother of Trinity House.

Mulgrave at once justified Sandwich's confidence in him, becoming the Admiralty's principal spokesman in the House of Commons. In this capacity he represented the government in every debate on naval affairs with great skill, notwithstanding his relative youth, and carried in addition a heavy burden of administrative work. In the House he had the assistance of Palliser; the sustained attacks on Sandwich's administration of the Admiralty formed an important plank of the opposition's campaign against the North ministry, so Mulgrave was kept busy. Broomfield noted that Sandwich 'was working his group of able, but inconsiderable, dependents into the best places in the service and many more distinguished officers thought it was being done at their expense'.[8] The rewards which Sandwich was giving to his followers became the principal ground of his unpopularity with the opposition.

7 Broomfield, 'Lord Sandwich at the Admiralty Board', p.11.
8 Broomfield, 'Lord Sandwich at the Admiralty Board', p.10.

3

Admirals

The most prominent of Sandwich's naval opponents in Parliament was Vice Admiral Augustus Keppel. The second son of the Earl of Albemarle, Keppel was born on 25 April 1725 into one of the leading Whig families of the day. He first went to sea at the age of 10; at the age of 15, he joined Anson's ship *Centurion* for its round the world voyage in 1740. At the age of 17 he was promoted acting lieutenant, and he was made post in 1744, still only 19 years of age. Throughout the War of the Austrian Succession he was actively employed; after it ended, he was sent in 1749 to the Mediterranean in command of the small squadron there, with the rank of commodore, taking with him Sir Joshua Reynolds as far as Minorca. While there, Reynolds painted the first of six portraits of Keppel. Still with the rank of commodore, Keppel was next posted in command of the North American station in 1751, serving there for four years.

With the outbreak of the Seven Years War, Keppel was again constantly on active service. 1757 saw him as a member of the court martial which tried Admiral Byng; he was one of those who unsuccessfully sought a pardon for him. In 1759 he distinguished himself particularly at the battle of Quiberon Bay. In March 1761, flying his commodore's pendant aboard the *Valiant*, he led an expedition to capture Belle Isle, off the French coast. He next went as second-in-command to Sir George Pocock with the fleet sent to attack Havana; his brother the Earl of Albemarle commanded the land forces. Keppel took a major part in the operations against the fortress, which were described by David Syrett, the editor of the Navy Records Society volume devoted to the siege and capture of the place, as 'a masterpiece of planning of amphibious warfare, and of the exploitation of naval superiority'.[1] When Havana was taken, Keppel established his personal fortune when he received prize-money of £25,000.

In October 1762 Keppel was promoted to rear admiral, and later that year took command of the Jamaica station. He joined the Board of Admiralty in July 1765 as a naval lord, serving there until December 1766. He was promoted to vice admiral

1 David Syrett (ed.), *The Siege and Capture of Havana* (London: Navy Records Society, 1970), p.xxxiv.

'The Honourable Augustus Keppel, Admiral of the Blue Squadron of His Majesties Fleet'. Engraving by Edward Fisher after Joshua Reynolds. (Anne S.K. Brown Collection)

in October 1770, at which time it was understood that he should command the fleet which was mobilised against Spain during the Falklands crisis, but as it turned out the issue was resolved peacefully.

Keppel represented Chichester in Parliament from 1755 until 1761, then Windsor until 1780, and finally Surrey until 1782. He was a strong and active supporter of the Whig faction led by the Marquis of Rockingham and the Duke of Richmond, and when the Whigs left office was an influential member of the opposition in Parliament. He was sympathetic to the cause of the American colonists, and made it known that he would not accept a command against them. From the moment of Sandwich's appointment as First Lord in 1771, he was a constant critic.

At the end of 1775 he was drawn into the brouhaha that arose over Sandwich's hasty award to Palliser of the Lieutenant-Generalcy of Marines which had become vacant on the death of Admiral Sir Charles Saunders. Sandwich was unaware that Lord North had promised this to Lord Howe, who was incandescent with fury. Unsuccessful efforts by the government to resolve the affair made matters worse.

For his part, Keppel, who was above Palliser on the Navy List himself, was outraged at the latter's appointment, writing furiously on 17 December to Sandwich:

> It is much credited that Admiral Forbes is to retire from the post of General of Marines and that Rear Admiral Lord Howe is to be appointed his successor. I am not used to feel disgrace or affront; but indeed, my Lord, I must feel cold to my own honour and the ranking which I stand in his Majesty's service, if I remain silent and see one of the youngest rear admirals of the fleet promoted to Lieutenant-General of Marines, and a few days afterwards another rear admiral made General of Marines… Such a repetition of promotion to the junior admirals of the fleet cannot but dispirit every senior officer jealous of his own honour, as it tends to manifest to the whole profession the low esteem he stands in.[2]

Sandwich was unmoved, replying that the question of seniority had never arisen in the case of such appointments. This did nothing to satisfy Keppel, who wrote again to Sandwich on 27 December: 'Your lordship is pleased to reason different from myself, which by no means heals the affront or can allow me to see the senior officers of the fleet but in a neglected light … what is to follow time will discover'.[3] The upshot of all this was a tacit understanding that should war with France arise, Keppel would be appointed to command the Channel Fleet. It was a pledge which Sandwich may have given only reluctantly, but he was no doubt aware that there were in fact few other flag officers who could be considered for the post in any case.

At all events, when the time came to make the appointment, Sandwich wrote a most courteous letter to Keppel on 15 November 1776 to tell him that he had been commanded by the King to tell him that there was a probability of his having occasion to serve in command of the fleet that was equipping for sea, adding: 'I never executed my orders from my sovereign with more real satisfaction than I do the present'. Even allowing for the courtly manner of such correspondence, this was a generous letter, as was Keppel's reply: 'I must return your Lordship thanks for the very polite and obliging manner in which you have been pleased to convey to me his Majesty's intentions and distinguished mark of opinion and approbation'.[4] So great was the mistrust of Sandwich by some of his political opponents that Keppel's cousin, the Duke of Richmond, wrote to him with a grave warning that the First Lord could be setting him up to fail. Accepting that Keppel was not in a position to refuse his service, he went on to convey his concern that the command could be a poisoned chalice:

2 Barnes and Owen (eds), *Private Papers of John, Earl of Sandwich*, Vol.II, pp.202-203.
3 Barnes and Owen (eds), *Private Papers of John, Earl of Sandwich*, Vol.II, pp.204-205.
4 Barnes and Owen (eds), *Private Papers of John, Earl of Sandwich*, Vol.II, p.15.

> I cannot wish you joy of having a fleet to command, prepared by the Earl of Sandwich, with new men and officers, unacquainted with each other, to risk your reputation and the fate of your country upon, against a French and Spanish fleet who are, I fear, much better prepared ... Let me advise you to insist upon your own terms. No one can be surprised that you should suspect a minister whom you have constantly opposed, of not giving you all the help he might do to a friend, without suspecting him of treachery. If he has but a bad fleet to send out, 'tis doing Lord Sandwich no injustice to suppose he would be glad to put it under the command of a man whom he does not love. If we meet with a misfortune he hopes to get off ... I would advise you to have the condition of each ship examined by your officers ... I would determine not to trust Lord Sandwich for a piece of ropeyarn, but have the most authentic returns in due form.[5]

The choice of Keppel to command the Channel Fleet in the event of war may have been practically inevitable, but it meant that Britain's principal fleet would be in the hands of a commander who did not possess all the qualities of an outstanding leader. Sir Nathaniel Wraxall, in his contemporary memoirs, offered a downbeat view of Keppel's abilities as a commander: 'In self possession, judgment, superior maritime skill, and presence of mind; in all those endowments of a great commander which ensure victory, I have always regarded him as deficient'. Mackesy, quoting this opinion, regarded it as consistent with the picture of the admiral that appears from his correspondence, and this is certainly right.[6]

Unlike Keppel, Richard, Viscount Howe, was not an active party man in the politics of the day, but though not one of the most senior admirals he was one of the more influential naval figures, who commanded great respect in the service. Born in 1726, he served as a midshipman in Anson's squadron; his ship the *Severn* became detached from the rest of the squadron and was badly damaged in severe storms before struggling back to England in 1742. Howe became a lieutenant in 1744, and by 1746 he had made post captain. He was flag captain to Rear Admiral Charles Knowles in the West Indies, in command of the *Cornwall*, 80. After a spell ashore he took command of the *Glory*, 44, in 1751, serving on the coast of West Africa. During the Seven Years War, in command of the *Dunkirk*, 60, he saw service in North America and with the Channel Fleet. He was elected as member of Parliament for Dartmouth in 1757, and in that year took command of the French-built *Magnanime*, 74, part of the squadron under Hawke's command in operations against the Ile d'Aix and Rochefort. In the following year he conducted a number of combined operations against the French coast in command of a small squadron, and his reputation in the Navy became well established. In 1759 his

5 Quoted James, *The British Navy in Adversity*, p.121.

6 Piers Mackesy, *The War for America* (London: Longmans Green, 1964), p.203.

ship played a major part in the Battle of Quiberon Bay. For the rest of the war, Howe, as a commodore, was engaged in the blockade of the French Biscay ports. During the peace, he served for some time as a junior naval lord at the Admiralty; then, in the Rockingham administration of 1765 he became Treasurer of the Navy, resigning when that government fell. He was, however, reappointed under the Grafton administration that then took office in 1766, and remained as Treasurer until North came to power.

Howe's reputation in the navy was considerably enhanced by his deep interest in the practical aspects of his profession, not least in the matter of signalling. Of this, one historian wrote, comparing him with Rodney:

> By contrast, Lord Howe was of preeminent importance in the reform of British tactics and signalling. He was the first to separate signals and tactics, and he gave his fleet an official, printed signal book, the accompanying book of instructions being "explanatory of and relative to the signal book herewith delivered". This was as early as 1776, when he commanded on the North American station.[7]

Howe was unemployed at the start of the American war, but he soon began to aspire to play a part in resolving the crisis. When, after the bungled affair of the Lieutenant-Generalcy of Marines, he was on the point of storming off to the King to resign his commission, the matter was resolved by his being offered the command of the North American station. He was no great admirer of Sandwich, whom he plainly mistrusted, but they were able to work satisfactorily together during Howe's period in command in America, albeit that this did not produce great success.

There were a number of other admirals reasonably high on the Navy list who could possibly be considered for fleet commands. One of the most notable of these was Vice Admiral John Byron, who had had a remarkable career. At the age of 17 he sailed in 1740 as a midshipman aboard the converted East Indiaman *Wager*, 28, part of Commodore George Anson's squadron on his voyage around the world. In May 1741 the *Wager* was shipwrecked on the coast of Chile. The survivors split into two groups, one party sailing round by boat to the Atlantic coast at Rio de Janeiro, and the other party, which included Byron, heading northwards up the Pacific coast. They encountered appalling weather, and were driven back to their starting point, losing part of their number. Finally, a local chieftain guided the survivors on their northward journey, and after further privations they reached a Spanish settlement, from where they were taken as prisoners to Santiago, the capital of Chile. There they were well treated, until in 1744 they were released,

7 Brian Tunstall (ed. Nicholas Tracy), *Naval Warfare in the Age of Sail* (London: Conway Maritime Press: 1990), p.7.

Byron returning to England in 1746 as one of the only 36 of those who survived their ordeal. Byron later wrote an account of his adventures, which proved very successful.

Byron was appointed captain of the *Siren* in 1746. During the Seven Years War he commanded a squadron at Louisbourg, with a mission to destroy the fortifications there. In 1760 he defeated a French squadron at the Battle of Restigouche. In 1764 he was sent with two ships to look for a suitable site for a naval base off the South American coast, after first being directed to locate Pepys Island, which had allegedly been discovered by a pirate named Cowley in 1683. The island proved, however, to be non-existent. Thereafter, between 1764 and 1766 he took his ships on a circumnavigation of the globe. Returning to England, in 1769 he was appointed as governor of Newfoundland in succession to Hugh Palliser, a post he held for three years.

He was promoted to rear admiral in 1775, and in September of that year Sandwich offered him appointment as second-in-command on the North American station; Byron declined, writing to the First Lord to say that he would embrace the offer with 'infinite satisfaction' if his health permitted, but that in its presently impaired state he was afraid that he was not equal to the task.[8] Throughout his career Byron was noted for the appalling weather which he continually encountered, which earned him the nickname 'Foul Weather Jack'. It was a title which he was to live up to during his service in the American Revolutionary War.

Another senior admiral, who was well regarded as a solid and reliable flag officer, was Sir Robert Harland. Born in 1715, he entered the navy at the age of 14. By 1744 he was a lieutenant aboard the *Princessa* at the Battle of Toulon, and in the following year took command of the fireship *Scipio*. In 1746 he was made post captain, commanding the *Tilbury* at the Second Battle of Cape Finisterre in the following year. His next command was the *Nottingham*, 60, and aboard her he took a major part in the capture of the French *Magnanime*, 74, which had been partially dismasted in a storm and was on her way to Brest for repairs when she was sighted off Ushant by the Channel Fleet which was cruising under Hawke. The *Nottingham* was sent in chase of the Frenchman, and fought for an hour before she was supported by the *Portland*. The engagement continued for nearly six hours before the *Magnanime* struck; she was added to the British navy under her old name.[9]

Harland went on to command a number of other vessels, and finally the *Princess Louisa*, aboard which he took part in the Battle of Lagos in August 1759. He was promoted to rear admiral in 1770, and went out to command the East Indies Station in the following year, serving there until 1775. He was promoted to vice admiral on 5 February 1776.

8 Barnes and Owen (eds), *Private Papers of John, Earl of Sandwich*, Vol.I, p.75.

9 Clowes, *Royal Navy*, Vol.III, p.287.

The case of Samuel Barrington illustrates the powerful advantage for a young officer to have influence. Born in 1729, he was the younger brother of William, Second Viscount Barrington. He joined the navy in 1740 at the age of 11. He passed for lieutenant in 1745 and was confirmed in that rank in September of the following year. By now his elder brother was a member of the Board of Admiralty, and was pressing for his further promotion. This came soon, when he succeeded Palliser as master and commander of the sloop *Weazle*, in which he served until May 1747. He was then made post, at the tender age of 18, and was given command of the *Bellona*, an ex-French privateer that had been taken into the navy. Later in the year he captured a French East Indiamann, the *Duc de Chartres*. In November his career took a further step forward with his appointment to command the *Romney*, aboard which he served under both Hawke and Warren before the war ended.

In 1748 Barrington was appointed to command the newly built *Seahorse*, 24, and he served in her until 1753, when he was succeeded in command by Palliser. He then took command of the *Crown* and was sent to make a report on the forts in West Africa; next year he was assigned to the *Norwich*, sailing to North America as part of a squadron under Keppel. He returned to England in 1757, taking command in April of the new 60-gun ship *Achilles,* serving in the Channel Fleet under the command first of Hawke and then of Anson. In 1759 he captured the *Comte de St Florentine.* Soon after this Rodney hoisted his flag in the *Achilles.* Next year Barrington went with Byron to assist in the demolition of the fortifications at Louisbourg. He continued in command of the *Achilles* until 1762, for five busy years. In 1768, as tutor to the king's youngest brother, the Duke of Cumberland, he was appointed to command the frigate *Venus.* Later, during the Spanish crisis, he commanded the *Albion*, 74.

Barrington was a close friend of John Jervis, and with him travelled in Russia in 1774, and then cruised off the coast of France in the following year. He was a difficult, touchy individual, and would in due course cause Sandwich, and the King, considerable problems, but there was no doubt of his ability. He was promoted to rear admiral in January 1778.[10]

An instance of Barrington's readiness to take offence arose from his misunderstanding when Sandwich made in November 1778 a tentative offer of the post of second-in-command to Howe in North America. Barrington declined, annoyed at what he thought of as having been previously passed over in favour of a junior officer for the command in the Leeward Islands. Sandwich did his best to repair the breach, writing twice to reassure him; in his first letter he told him that he knew 'no officer in the King's Service more fit to be trusted with a Command' than Barrington. Then Sandwich wrote again to say that he had 'no object more at heart' than that of accommodating Barrington to the utmost. He added,

10 D. Bonner-Smith (ed.), *The Barrington Papers* (London: Navy Records Society, 1937), Vol.I, p.443.

presciently, that he was convinced that they would never understand one another by correspondence.[11]

At any one time there were a considerable number of naval officers in the House of Commons. Most of them tended to limit their contributions to naval affairs. The government could count on those that sat for seats controlled by the Admiralty for support against opposition attacks. Since there was no strong party affiliation in the House of Commons, individuals changed sides from time to time, either on principle or, as in the case of George Johnstone, for self-advancement. Johnstone, a self-seeking and, it must be said, a rather unpleasant individual, had a high profile throughout his career. Born in 1730, he was not appointed as lieutenant until 1755. Thereafter, his career was marked by frequent disputes; he was court-martialled for disobedience in 1757, when he was reprimanded. He was in trouble again in the following year, when he was suspended by Rear Admiral Cotes after a dispute over prize-money. Johnstone finally obtained his first command in 1760 in the sloop *Hornet*. In spite of having some influence behind him in the person of Lord Elibank, he had to wait a long time before being made post captain, which he achieved in 1762. In 1764 he was appointed as governor of West Florida, a post he held for three years. In 1768 he was elected to the House of Commons. Then, famously, he provoked and fought a duel with Lord George Germain, in which neither man was injured. Thereafter he was an outspoken if inconsistent supporter of the opposition until, in 1778, he switched sides to give his support to Lord North's administration. For this he was rewarded by becoming one of the three commissioners appointed to go to North America to negotiate with the colonists.[12]

11 Bonner-Smith (ed.), *Barrington Papers*, Vol.I, pp.450-454,

12 R.F.A. Fabel, *Bombast and Broadsides: The Lives of George Johnstone* (Tuscaloosa: University of Alabama Press, 2000), p.81.

4

Middleton and the Navy Board

When Sir Hugh Palliser, hitherto the Comptroller of the Navy, became a member of the Board of Admiralty in April 1775, Sandwich had to find a successor for what was one of the most important, and most demanding, posts in the administration of the navy. His choice fell on Captain Maurice Suckling, the uncle and mentor of Horatio Nelson. Suckling had served successfully in the West Indies, where he had made a considerable fortune in prize money. Unfortunately, he quite soon became ill, and in January 1777 found it necessary to write to Sandwich to reassure him that he was still capable of doing the job. His health continued to decline, however, and Sandwich was obliged to consider who should take over as Comptroller. The First Lord's record in choosing men of ability for the key posts on which his administration depended was remarkable, and he again made an inspired choice when, in February 1778 he sounded out Captain Charles Middleton as to his willingness to accept the post when it became vacant, as it surely must in the near future. At first, Middleton was hesitant; many years later he wrote: 'When Lord Sandwich proposed to me being Comptroller of the Navy, I… required some little time to consider it.. The truth was I felt myself unequal to the magnitude and consequence of the office and the confinement it would occasion me'.[1]

In order to obtain Middleton's acceptance, Sandwich made an approach to his family, asking Rear Admiral James Gambier, Middleton's brother-in-law, who had become Commissioner of Portsmouth dockyard, to persuade him. On 8 March, Middleton wrote to Sandwich somewhat obliquely indicating that he would accept the post. Suckling died on 14 July, and a week later the King approved Middleton's appointment. Nicholas Rodger has written that 'arguably this was the single most important decision that Sandwich took in his entire career'.[2]

The Navy Board's principal function was the civil administration of the entire navy, a responsibility of enormous complexity. The Comptroller was one of its four principal officers, and effectively its executive chairman, though formally of

1 Laughton (ed.), *Barham Papers*, Vol.III, pp.25-26.
2 Rodger, *Insatiable Earl*, p.168.

Charles Middleton, depicted in later life after he had reached flag rank and been ennobled as Baron Barham. Stipple engraving by Maria Anne Bourlier, after John Downman. (Yale Center for British Art, Paul Mellon Collection, B1977.14.9777)

the same standing as his three colleagues. These were the Surveyor, responsible for warship design; the Treasurer; and the Clerk of the Acts, who in earlier times had been known as Clerk of the King's Ships, and who was responsible for the management of the Navy Office itself. The Navy Board was an organisation very much larger than the Admiralty, to which it was nominally subordinate. Its most demanding responsibility was the management of the Royal dockyards, each of which was overseen by a Commissioner, a naval captain on half pay, though the senior officers of each dockyard actually accounted direct to the relevant officer of the Navy Board.

Sandwich's choice of Middleton as Comptroller was in many ways a surprising one. His naval career had not been particularly distinguished, and although he was obviously known to the First Lord, theirs had not been in any way a close relationship, and he did not have a high profile in the Navy. St Vincent on one occasion referred to him as 'that damned Scotch packhorse'. Middleton was born in Leith on 14 October 1726; his father was a Customs officer. He first went to sea in April 1741, as a captain's servant aboard the *Sandwich*, 90. Subsequently a midshipman aboard the *Flamborough*, 20, Middleton passed his examination for lieutenant in November 1745. His first posting thereafter was as third lieutenant of the *Chesterfield*, 44, which was not an entirely fortunate assignment; her crew mutinied while most of the officers were ashore in Sierra Leone in October 1748. When Middleton returned home in 1749, the War of the Austrian Succession had come to an end, and he was on half pay until 1752, when he became third lieutenant of the guardship *Culloden*, 74.[3]

In 1753 he went to the West Indies as second lieutenant of the *Anson*, 60. Her first lieutenant was Richard Kempenfelt, who became one of Middleton's closest friends. When he left the ship in January 1755, Middleton succeeded him as first lieutenant. His first command was the sloop *Speaker*, 12, in which he took a couple of prizes before her leaky condition ended her career in July 1757. It was in 1760 that his real opportunity to make his fortune came, when, in command of the *Emerald*, 28, he enjoyed a lucrative cruise in the Leeward Islands, taking 16 prizes by May 1761 before returning to England. His ship was deemed incapable of repair, and she was broken up. Later that year, Middleton was married to Margaret Gambier. He soon went to sea again, as captain of the *Adventure*, 32, serving in the Channel. When, in 1763, she was paid off, he went on half pay, declining the chance of commanding a brand-new frigate.

Middleton remained on half pay for the next 12 years and devoted himself to life as a gentleman farmer in Kent. He and his wife, and their close friends, were devout Evangelicals, a conviction which made him a distinct rarity in the Navy. His biographer noted that 'Evangelicalism was so deeply imprinted on Middleton's character and his conduct as a public man that in his old age his enemies thought of him as an Evangelical first and a naval administrator second'.[4] His profound religious beliefs were entirely consistent with his absolute self-confidence, and a readiness to pass judgment on others, and also a willingness to accept the huge responsibility of a demanding job; he 'was a seagoing exemplar of the famous Protestant ethic'.

3 John E. Talbott, *The Pen and Ink Sailor* (London: Frank Cass, 1998), pp.2-5.
4 Talbott, *Pen and Ink Sailor*, p.14.

After 12 years ashore, Middleton applied to Sandwich for a command, and was appointed in March 1775 to the guard ship *Ardent*, 64, conveniently moored in the Medway. Next, he was appointed as captain of the *Prince George*, 90, a guard ship at Portsmouth, and it was aboard her that he received Sandwich's first enquiry as to the Controllership. By then he had learned that the *Prince George* was to be a flagship, and that did not appeal to him, so he asked for the command of a frigate. He was appointed to the *Jupiter*, 50, a fourth rate building at Deptford, but before she was ready for sea he was appointed to the post in which he would come to exercise such a colossal influence on the history of the British Navy.

It was no doubt his boundless self-confidence, which afforded him the certainty that he was always right, coupled with his capacity for hard work, that enabled him to make the transition from sea officer to manager of the most complex, and most powerful, organisation in the public service. Rodger describes him as viewing 'the conduct of most of those with whom he had to deal with unconcealed contempt, and his own conduct with unconcealed admiration. No doubtful transaction ever shook his conviction that he was right'.[5] He spared no one the expression of his opinions – not even the First Lord escaped his admonitions, who received a letter from Middleton in 1779 that can hardly have pleased him:

> If I, my lord, who am a professional man, find myself unequal to the duties of the office I am in, with an application of twelve hours six days in the week, how is it possible that your lordship can manage yours, which is equally extensive, in three or four? Indeed, my lord, it cannot be. The two offices are so nearly connected, that I must be wilfully blind not to see the sad management that prevails at present, and the ruin that accompanies it.[6]

Rodger vigorously rejects the charge of indolence on the part of Sandwich, quoting a number of authorities to show that he 'habitually worked long hours at his desk', a fact acknowledged even by his enemies. Middleton's comments on others, whom he considered less dedicated than himself, ensured that he could never expect universal popularity, but to this he was wholly indifferent. Later First Lords would find him impossible to work with; but with Sandwich, however, he had a consistently effective relationship, due to the First Lord's remarkable patience and tolerance.

Among the qualities which enabled Middleton to make such a success of the job of Comptroller was his unrelenting determination to get his own way, and in two matters in particular this ensured his success in overcoming opposition. The first of these was the adoption of a system of copper sheathing for ships' hulls. Wooden ships were vulnerable to the growth of barnacles and seaweed on their bottoms

5 Rodger, *Insatiable Earl*, p.160.
6 Laughton (ed.), *Barham Papers*, Vol.II, pp.3-5.

which seriously impaired their speed, requiring them to be regularly docked to remove the growths. Especially in warmer waters, they were also vulnerable to the ship worm (*teredo navalis*) which ate away the underwater woodwork. In the West Indies, the problem had been met partially by the device of sheathing the ships' bottoms with several thicknesses of fir plank, which required regular renewal. In 1762 experiments began with copper sheathing. Though this was found to be successful in preventing the depredations of the ship worm, and also the marine growths, there was a serious drawback; the copper caused the galvanic corrosion of the underwater iron fittings. The very considerable advantage of covering the hull meant that a solution must be found, and it was something to which Middleton had already devoted a lot of attention. When asking to be relieved of command of the *Prince George*, he had asked that the frigate for which he had applied should be coppered. He wrote to Sandwich about the advantages this gave:

> The utility of such an improvement is so well known to your Lordship in particular, and so generally approved in the service that I have not a doubt but the next generation will see it universally adopted, and if such advantage should meet with any difference of opinion, and I should be allowed to pay the difference of expense to government, I would most readily do it, convinced of the sensible benefits the service would reap thereby.[7]

Middleton, once in office as Comptroller, espoused a system designed to keep the copper away from the ironwork. This was to coat the hull in several layers of waterproofed brown paper before the copper sheathing was applied. The technique was devised by a Liverpool shipbuilder in the back end of 1778, and Middleton quickly became convinced that here was a solution. By January 1779 he had persuaded the Commissioners of the Navy Board, and on 8 January Portsmouth dockyard was ordered to adopt this procedure on the next ship to be coppered. The Admiralty agreed, and asked the Navy Board whether ships of the line could be so treated, as well as frigates. On 27 January Middleton replied that the Navy Board was confident that this was so. Rodger sees this as an example of Middleton's own excessive self-confidence: 'Middleton's talents at self persuasion were unequalled, and after perfunctory trials he convinced himself that the problem was solved'.[8]

Having thus convinced himself, he went on to convince Sandwich. The First Lord had taken a keen interest in experiments to solve the problem of the ships' bottoms, and had kept the King informed about them. Although persuaded that the system would work, he felt it necessary that the King be consulted before the radical decision to copper the entire fleet was taken. Middleton, many years later, wrote that 'the measure to be sure was not only bold but arduous':

7 Talbott, *Pen and Ink Sailor*, p.48.

8 Rodger, *Insatiable Earl*, p.296.

> I proposed it privately to Lord Sandwich; but he hesitated and, after several conversations and assurances, mentioned it to the King. I afterwards accompanied his Lordship to Buckingham House and explained the whole process in so satisfactory a manner that he conceived it at once and ordered it to be carried into execution.[9]

Middleton added a comment on the reaction of some serving officers to the covering of the fleet: 'Admiral Barrington, amongst others, declared that the ships would sink at their anchors. They were ignorant of the means used'.

Practical experience soon showed that the decision, though bold, had been correct. Captain Walter Young, Rodney's flag captain, writing to Middleton in July 1780, gave a detailed account of the benefits:

> Your attention to the coppering reflects the greatest merit on you. It is impossible for me to describe the advantages attending it, and indeed exceed the expectation of everyone. The advantages from the helm alone is immense, as they feel them instantly, and wear in one third of the distance they ever did; it keeps them tight, and covers the neglects in your dockyards from bad caulking; increases their speed in every situation, more particularly in light winds tending to a calm, which is no small advantage in this and every fair weather country. Its greatest effect is in sailing large.[10]

The industrial task of coppering the whole fleet was immense. By early 1782 a total of 313 ships had been given copper sheathing: 82 ships of the line, 14 ships of 50 guns, 115 frigates and 102 sloops and cutters.[11] The French were a long way behind; in 1781, for example, only half of the French ships making up de Grasse's fleet in the West Indies were coppered, while the Spanish lagged still further behind, only one of their ships serving there being coppered.

Important as were the perceived benefits, the decision amounted to a huge gamble, because the technical problems were still not fully understood. The waterproofing of the paper seals was not completely reliable, and when water did get in, the corrosion of the iron bolts continued, and since coppered ships needed to be docked much less often, the defects that arose were not discovered. Rodger observed: 'It is certain that the end of the war came fortuitously for the coppering process, allowing ships to be paid off and examined at leisure which otherwise would have been driven on until they fell apart'.[12] For his part, Middleton for a

9 Laughton (ed.), *Barham Papers*, Vol.III, p.29.
10 Laughton (ed.), *Barham Papers*, Vol.I, pp.66-67.
11 Knight, 'The Royal Navy's Recovery', p.22.
12 Rodger, *Insatiable Earl*, p.298.

long time refused to accept the evidence of corrosion, and resisted the enquiry which was set up. Roger Knight has pointed out that the coppering decision was also a considerable financial gamble, adding as it did between 10 and 15 percent to the cost of every ship, which was something that Middleton, Sandwich and the King do not appear to have worried about.[13] There was one other downside aspect of coppering, which made itself felt in the early stages of the introduction of the process, and that was where a fleet consisted only partly of coppered ships, manoeuvrability was a problem, because it was only with great difficulty that they could be made to sail more slowly than the rest of the fleet.

The other key innovation for which Middleton could claim much of the credit was the introduction of the carronade, an entirely novel design of gun. It was made possible by the invention of a cylinder boring machine to bore out the barrel of the gun, enabling the production of a much lighter weapon with a truer bore. It was effective at short ranges, so much so that it was nicknamed 'the smasher'. Middleton was acquainted with Charles Gascoigne, the manager of the Carron Iron Company where the carronade was developed. He was at once persuaded of the weapon's potential. Its relatively light weight meant that it could be installed on decks that could not bear the weight of the long gun. It required a crew of only two men, compared to the 11 or 12 required to man the long cannon. It could be fired twice as quickly, and did not overheat.[14]

In early July 1779 a trial of the carronade was held at Woolwich Arsenal under the auspices of the Board of Ordnance, the body responsible for supplying guns and ammunition to the Navy and the army, but which was independent of both. From the start, the Ordnance had its doubts about the utility of the new weapon, as did Lord Mulgrave, one of Sandwich's closest naval advisers. Middleton, though, was emphatic in his belief that it must be adopted:

> They are the best improvements hitherto proposed, and if added to the guns already established on our smaller ships they will be rendered superior in force to any of the same size belonging to the enemy, without the necessity of other ways augmenting their sizes, and adding to their number of men.[15]

Middleton persuaded Sandwich of the weapon's potential, and the First Lord backed his opinion, throwing his weight behind its introduction in the face of considerable initial opposition.

This opposition came particularly from Mulgrave, whose opinion Sandwich normally respected. At the same time Walter Young, writing from the West Indies

13 Knight, 'The Royal Navy's Recovery', p.23.

14 Talbott, *Pen and Ink Sailor*, p.63.

15 Talbott, *Pen and Ink Sailor*, pp.63-64.

to Middleton in July 1780, was unable to give much account of the carronades in action, as they had been supplied to only one ship and had not been much used in the battle against de Guichen; he thought carronades might 'be made very useful in small ships as their proper ordnance; for instance, in sloops or the small 20-gun ships'.[16] Kempenfelt, writing to Middleton in March 1780, complained that sufficient trials had not been made on board a ship to assess the value of carronades. He noted the objections raised as to their limited range in particular, but was certain that the largest carronades would be 'the least exceptionable'. When the Ordnance Board conducted trials at Landguard Fort on 18 July 1780, things had not gone very well, and in October it notified the Admiralty that 'these experiments have confirmed our opinion that carronades are of little use in the Royal Navy'.[17] The Navy Board stoutly rejected this opinion, relying on the reports of practical experience in battle, and pointing out that carronades should not be compared with cannon as to range asthey were designed for short-range action.

In the end Middleton's determination prevailed. The Admiralty was persuaded, and so was the King, whom Sandwich had kept informed throughout the process of development of the carronade. So, too, were a number of captains, who urgently requested that the weapon should be supplied to their ships. Middleton's achievement had been remarkable, as described by his biographer: 'Constantly reiterating his warning that the risk of losing a major encounter at sea outweighed the dangers of innovation, he persuaded the Navy to adopt, at the height of a great war, an untried technique for preserving ships' bottoms and an untested weapon'.[18]

Middleton had an extremely low opinion of the effectiveness of the British government. He also had a very poor opinion of the Board of Admiralty; he had, though, a clear idea of the best way to improve its performance, and this was for him as Comptroller to have a seat on the Board. In 1782 he was to write to Lord Shelburne to explain why this was so:

> The advantages which a Comptroller from the nature of his office must have in point of naval knowledge is so well known, that every First Lord of the Admiralty whether Sea or Land finds it necessary to consult him on every subject of moment. Should this alteration therefore take place, it will become less material than it has been hitherto, whether the First Lord be of the sea or land, and probably better of the latter kind if a very able one of the former cannot be found.[19]

16 Laughton (ed.), *Barham Papers*, Vol.I, p.67.
17 Talbott, *Pen and Ink Sailor*, p.65.
18 Talbott, *Pen and Ink Sailor*, p.69.
19 Mackesy, *War for America*, p.485.

5

Tactics and Signalling in 1778

On both sides of the Channel the process of evolving an effective system of tactics had been lengthy, and over the years a great deal of thought had been given to how best to conduct a sea battle under sail. Modern readers are perhaps apt sometimes to take for granted the ability of wooden sailing ships to come readily into action against the enemy. In spite of the astonishing level of seamanship that had been developed over the centuries, this was in practice not at all straightforward. In particular, ships of the line were heavy, unwieldy vessels that could do nothing quickly, and managing a large number of these cumbersome weapons of war was extremely difficult. The tactical doctrines that had been gradually evolved took account of this, but gave a fleet commander only a limited number of battle options. It was for this reason that so much reverence was attached to the most important formation of all, which was the line of battle.

Once the sailing ship had replaced the oared galley as the principal weapon of sea warfare, totally different considerations determined the way in which a battle was to be fought. Gradually a primitive system of tactics began to emerge, which took account not only of the fact that the movements of a fleet were subject at all times to the direction and strength of the wind, but also to the fact that the ships' guns were largely mounted on the broadside. The first effective set of instructions issued for the management of a British fleet in line of battle came in the middle of the seventeenth century. These were issued over the signatures of the 'Generals at Sea,' Blake, Deane and Monck, at the start of the First Anglo-Dutch War. They provided the following instruction:

> As soon as they shall see the general engage, or make a signal by shooting off two guns and putting a red flag over the fore top masthead, then each squadron shall take the best advantage they can to engage with the enemy next unto them; and in order thereto all the ships of every squadron shall endeavour to keep in line with the chief unless the chief be maimed or otherwise disabled (which God forbid!) whereby the said ship that wears the flag should not come in to do the service which is requisite. Then every

> ship of the said squadron shall endeavour to keep in line with the admiral or he that commands in chief next unto him, and nearest the enemy.[1]

The experience of sea fighting during the rest of the century led to the evolution of the set of instructions issued by Edward Russell in 1691, which were first employed in the Battle of Cape Barfleur in the following year.

These instructions were revised in 1703 to give clarity to the signals to be used. These were issued by Sir George Rooke, and were subsequently republished by the Admiralty towards the end of the first quarter of the eighteenth century together with his sailing instructions under the title 'Sailing and Fighting Instructions for his Majesty's Fleet'. When Julian Corbett edited the Navy Records Society volume of *Fighting Instructions 1530-1816* in 1905, he subtitled the Fighting Instructions as 'the permanent instructions 1707-1783'. The assumption by Corbett, following that of Sir John Laughton a little earlier, was that these were firm orders from the Admiralty, and that they had the effect of limiting the initiative of fleet commanders.

However, in 1972 John Creswell pointed out that the Fighting Instructions produced by the Admiralty were not in fact unalterable orders calling for strict obedience, but were issued for the guidance of commanders in chief, upon whom lay the actual responsibility for the tactics to be employed by the fleet which they led.[2] Nonetheless, although these Fighting Instructions did not require absolute compliance, their existence and of course their source did exercise a huge influence over commanders in chief and their subordinate captains. By the middle of the eighteenth century, though, individual admirals were beginning to supplement the Fighting Instructions by the issue of Additional Instructions of their own.

Much work has been done to clarify exactly what signals and instructions applied in the many battles of the eighteenth century, and the extent to which they were understood by subordinate captains and actually executed by them. Nevertheless, the fundamental basis for the deployment of fleets remained that of the line of battle, and the instructions provided that 'if the admiral and his fleet have the wind of the enemy, and they have stretched themselves in line of battle, the van of the admiral's fleet is to steer with the van of the enemy's and there engage them'.[3] It was, of course, almost invariably a key aim, as the fleets manoeuvred, to seek the initiative by gaining the windward position.

In issuing orders to the ships under his command, an admiral was handicapped by the limited number of signals available to him. The signals in force for most of the eighteenth century were based on a set of signals first published in 1689; this was largely drafted by reference to the fighting and sailing instructions. As

1 J.S. Corbett (ed.), *Fighting Instructions 1530-1816* (London: Navy Records Society, 1905), p.100.
2 John Creswell, *British Admirals in the Eighteenth Century* (London: Allen & Unwin, 1972), p.28.
3 Creswell, *British Admirals*, p.30.

the development of signalling systems continued, the number of flags employed increased to reflect the additional instructions that were from time to time introduced. In the era of Blake, Deane and Monck, only three flags and one pendant were used, the red flag being employed in three different positions. Two decades later, the Duke of York's second revision of the signalling system required nine flags and one pendant.[4] The process of introducing additional flags continued, so that by 1782, for example, Rodney's instructions required the use of 40 flags and seven pendants. By then, however, the revolution in signalling methods had already begun with the signal book issued by Lord Howe in July 1776.

In his analysis of eighteenth century tactics, Nicholas Rodger drew attention to the tendency of British writers of the period to treat the subject of naval tactics as a branch of geometry, and he went on to distinguish theory and practice:

> Theoretical tactics were precise, rigid and complex; practical tactics were loose, untidy and simple. Theoretical tactics promised ingenious technical solutions intended to achieve crushing victory with the maximum of genius and the minimum of effort. In real tactics, everything was very simple, and very difficult.[5]

Rodger went on to describe one of the most serious problems that an individual captain would face in endeavouring to grasp what was expected of him from the signals made by his commander-in-chief:

> The signals, moreover, were conveyed by combinations of flags or pendants hoisted in specific positions, and guns fired to windward or leeward. In order to understand a signal it was necessary to have a view of the flagship from broad on the bow or quarter; in a line ahead keeping tolerable station the flagship's signals would be impossible for most of the squadron to take in.[6]

Furthermore, once an action had commenced, the sound of the guns which were an essential part of many signals could not easily be distinguished, while gun smoke obscured signals from a flagship that might be several miles off.

While British tactical doctrine, such as it was, evolved by the application of practical experience as well as the geometrical principles referred to, the French had earlier taken a more intellectual approach from the outset, and in 1697 there was

4 L.E. Holland, 'The Development of Signalling in the Royal Navy' in *The Mariner's Mirror* (February 1953), p.6.

5 N.A.M. Rodger, 'Image and Reality in Eighteenth Century Naval Tactics' in *The Mariner's Mirror* (August 2003), p.282.

6 Rodger, 'Image and Reality', p.288.

published in France a book entitled *Treatise on Naval Evolutions.* This textbook, written by Paul Hoste, covered many aspects of battle tactics, although its author modestly claimed that his exposition consisted merely of 'general reflections':

> It is in this that the art of war at sea properly consists. I feel that I have not the necessary lights to give rules the subject of so much importance, and do not propose to give precepts to Admirals of fleets, but content myself with proposing to them examples, because in matters so vast as these scarce anything can be decided in theory; it is the genius of a hero, possessing professional talent and experience, that is necessary to constitute a great Admiral.[7]

Later French writers, following Hoste's intellectual tradition, further developed his tactical theories. These included the Vicomte Bigot de Morogues, who published in 1763 his *Naval Tactics, or a Treatise on Evolutions and Signals.* In the work of Hoste, Morogues and others France had produced a body of work that went beyond the geometric concepts that Nicholas Rodger described.

For all fleets, however, the practical difficulties of effectively manoeuvring a substantial number of vessels were considerable. Ships capable of differing speeds due to design or condition, with crews of varying efficiency, commanded by captains of uneven competence, could not always respond with equal promptness to an admiral's signals, and inevitably all manoeuvres of the fleet tended to affect the precision of the line of battle. Once battle was joined, an admiral's ability to control his fleet was markedly reduced.

Nevertheless, British admirals did endeavour to follow the Admiralty's Fighting Instructions as far as they could. In the case of the unfortunate Admiral Byng at the Battle of Minorca, he is said to have had the book open in his hand as the two fleets drew together. However, he failed to order his fleet to attack as directed by Article 17 in that situation, and at his court-martial this told heavily against him. His problem, essentially, was that he brought his fleet into action at an angle to the enemy's line. Creswell remarks that there has been sympathy for Byng in that 'he suffered the death penalty merely because he was an incompetent tactician. But that he could hardly have handled his fleet worse than he did admits of no doubt'.[8]

One significant feature of naval tactics of the time concerned the possibility of the breaking of the enemy's line. In the work of Hoste, no reference is made to this, which Creswell surmises arose from the relatively loose formations of the fleets that fought during the Anglo-Dutch Wars, despite their general success in maintaining some sort of line.[9] He notes that 'there was nothing new in the idea of

7 Quoted in Creswell, *British Admirals*, p.46.

8 Creswell, *British Admirals*, p.113.

9 Creswell, *British Admirals*, p.47.

passing through an enemy's line from the lee side if there was a suitable gap,' while 'breaking the line' was a term used to describe a ship falling out of her place in her own line. When it came to be used of a deliberate manoeuvre to break through the enemy's line of battle, it conveyed the idea of 'breaking his fleet to pieces and chewing it up'. Thus, when part of Rodney's fleet passed through de Grasse's line at the battle of Les Saintes in 1782 it was hailed as a brilliant and novel tactical strike. Peter Trew's recent biography of the admiral was actually entitled *Rodney and the Breaking of the Line*.[10] The reality was somewhat different, as John Jervis, as usual able to see the wood for the trees, wrote with characteristic bluntness: 'Lord Rodney passed through the enemy's line by accident, not design, although historians have given him credit for the latter'.[11]

In his review of eighteenth century tactics, Nicholas Rodger remarked that 'the study of naval tactics was once regarded as a central aspect of naval history,' but that after the First World War it had fallen out of favour partly because 'it had been studied in a narrow, hermetic and technical manner which revolted uncommitted historians without offering anything of apparent relevance to naval officers'.[12] He was particularly severe on the work of Brian Tunstall, the author of a work on the evolution of fighting tactics between 1650 and 1850, complaining that he had excluded 'almost everything not derived from signal books'. Nevertheless, Tunstall's book, which was published posthumously, provided a comprehensive illustration of the evolution of signalling in the eighteenth century and the stage of development which it had reached in the period following the Seven Years War.

At the start of that war the then-Captain Richard Howe, commanding a squadron of small vessels off the French coast, issued a set of additional signals to his captains. These, Tunstall noted, were 'the earliest issued by the man destined to reform the whole signalling system and have a lasting influence on British naval tactics'.[13] Two years later, though still not yet a flag officer, Howe introduced an innovation by issuing a printed book of 'Additional Signals and Instructions to be observed by the Ships of War'. Then, in 1762, by now Commodore Lord Howe, he issued a printed book of signals for the use of the squadron which he was then commanding in the Basque roads. Howe's style of writing has always been regarded as frequently quite remarkably obscure; Rodger considered that 'Howe was master of an extraordinarily elaborate and elliptical style of speech and writing which was imitated by none and understood by few'. This was particularly unfortunate considering that he aimed at flexibility and simplicity. Tunstall quotes as an example of his style the ambiguity of his signal number 59, intended for use in an emergency:

10 Peter Trew, *Rodney and the Breaking of the Line* (Barnsley: Pen & Sword 2006).
11 Creswell, *British Admirals*, pp.141-142.
12 Rodger, 'Image and Reality', p.280.
13 Tunstall, *Naval Warfare in the Age of Sail*, p.105.

> When the commander-in-chief upon making the signal for line ahead or abreast, though meaning to form on the starboard tack, would nevertheless have the ship appointed to lead on the larboard tack, and that division then to lead: or on the contrary the ships of the starboard division to lead though forming on the larboard tack. The same change of divisions is meant to be made when this signal is shown with the signal for forming in two separate lines of battle.[14]

Following the end of the Seven Years War, it was in France that the greatest strides were being made in the development of naval tactics, with the publication of Morogues' book, followed by that of Bourdé de Villehuet two years later. Tunstall describes the latter as being 'rather disappointing to the historian, lacking the lavish historical examples found elsewhere, but as being more useful and practical because of its small size'.[15] Bourdé incorporated in his work a description of the numerical signalling system devised by Mahé de la Bourdonnais, who had served in the Indian Ocean during the War of the Austrian Succession. It was Tunstall's belief that his numerical signalling system 'if it had been adopted by the French navy would have been a major tactical development'. However, a rival system was adopted. This was designed by Jean Francois Cheyron, Chevalier du Pavillon, who had great personal influence with the French naval establishment. Although he and Morogues had by their work created a system of tactics far removed from that produced by the civilian mathematicians and scientists that had preceded them, they still followed Hoste in concentrating on the need for evolutions, and in substituting these for fighting, rather than emphasising the need for offensive action. Pavillon had devised a tabular system:

> He lifted French signalling out of its Seven Years War defeatist traditionalism, and put it on a new and complicated mathematical basis. Given quickness and accuracy both of reading and sending signals, the system was capable of being used to ring the changes on every possible fleet formation. In this sense it gave scope for tactical sophistications far beyond anything as yet regarded as standard in the British service.[16]

Nevertheless Tunstall, although noting that it was an advance on the existing system, concluded that it was a cul-de-sac in the development of signalling, since once the French navy turned in the direction of this reform, it became more difficult to proceed to the ultimate goal of a true numerical system. However, in spite of its extreme complexity, it was adopted first by the Brest squadron and then

14 Tunstall, *Naval Warfare in the Age of Sail*, p.117.
15 Tunstall, *Naval Warfare in the Age of Sail*, p.122.
16 Tunstall, *Naval Warfare in the Age of Sail*, p.128.

by the rest of the French navy throughout the War of American Independence, and continued in use during the French Revolutionary and Napoleonic wars.[17] Pavillon was to serve as chief of staff to d'Orvilliers in 1778.

Naturally a good deal of interest was taken in England in the work being done in France, but the first translation of Morogues' naval tactics was incomplete and entirely unsatisfactory. During the peace there was ample opportunity for an interchange of ideas between British and French naval officers. One of those who took the chance to visit France during this period was Captain Richard Kempenfelt, who spent a good deal of time travelling there. His principal interest in doing so was to make a study of French shipbuilding methods; he also visited a number of French harbours. At the same time, he became very much impressed by what he learned of the tactical studies which had been evolving in France, and the accompanying systems of signalling. He was particularly impressed with the numerical system propounded by La Bourdonnais, which had a considerable influence on his own thinking.

Richard Kempenfelt was born in 1718, the son of Magnus Kempenfelt, a member of a Swedish noble family, all of whose surviving brothers had military or naval careers. Kempenfelt senior had served in the army of James II before, in 1702, accepting service under Queen Anne, with the rank of colonel. He became in due course Lieutenant Governor of Jersey, dying in about 1727. The young Kempenfelt entered the navy at the age of 10, and saw his first action at the siege and capture of Portobello in 1739, under Admiral Edward Vernon, having previously passed his lieutenant's examination. He had evidently been a protégé of Sir Charles Wager, the First Lord of the Admiralty, and had impressed Vernon, who wrote to the First Lord on 7 October 1740: 'Your recommendations I believe you will have observed, have never been forgotten by me … Young Kempenfelt I have kept to be a midshipman in the *Burford*, and intend providing for him as you desire, having, as well as you, a regard for the worthy character of his father'.[18] Two such eminent patrons would have been of great assistance to a young man at the start of his naval career, but regrettably the elderly Wager died, and Vernon was dismissed after his famously violent dispute with the Admiralty. As a result, the progress of Kempenfelt's naval career was slower than it might have been. He was commissioned as a lieutenant in 1741, serving at first in Vernon's flagship the *Strafford*, and subsequently in the *Superb*, 60, and then the *Seahorse*, 20. Returning to England in 1746, he became first lieutenant of the *Tavistock*, 50. With the outbreak of the Seven Years War he became master and commander, aboard his first command, the 14-gun *Lightning*. He finally made post captain in January 1757 with the command of the *Elizabeth*, 64, carrying the broad pennant of Commodore Charles Steevens. Aboard her he took a distinguished part in the battles of Cuddalore and Negapatam under Vice

17 Rodger, 'Image and Reality', p.290.

18 B. McL. Ranft (ed.), *The Vernon Papers* (London: Navy Records Society, 1958), p.135.

Admiral George Pocock. In the following year he became flag captain again to Steevens, now rear admiral, aboard the *Grafton*, 70. She took part in the Battle of Pondicherry in September 1759; next year he transferred to the *Norfolk*, 74. In 1761, following Steevens' death, he became flag captain to Rear Admiral Samuel Cornish, with whom he took part in the capture of Manila. He thereafter briefly served as governor of Cavite before returning home with Cornish's dispatches. Then, back aboard the *Norfolk*, he served in the East Indies until conclusion of the peace in 1763.

Kempenfelt was on half pay throughout the peace. He was not to serve at sea again until 1778. During this period he gave close consideration to the questions of signalling and tactics, but before he could develop his own ideas Lord Howe had taken the first step to revolutionise signalling. As soon as Howe arrived to take up his command of the North American Station, Howe issued on 12 July 1776 his instructions and standing orders for the ships under his command together with his printed *Signal Book for the Ships of War*. This was in an entirely new form:

> He reduced the total number of flags to twenty one. Many of these were of new design; and in this respect he showed a strong partiality for two or three horizontal stripes. Then, under these twenty one flags he grouped all the necessary Instructions without particular regard to the flag designs with which they had been previously associated. The effect of this departure from accepted usage, this attempt to simplify and classify its contents, put the Signal Book on a new footing. It became a recognised authority; and, to make it more complete, Lord Howe supplemented it with a book of Instructions describing how the more complicated manoeuvres were to be performed.[19]

Corbett, in the first of his two books on the subject, described the sweeping change that Howe introduced as 'no mere substitution of a new set of instructions, but a complete revolution of method. The basis of the new tactical code was no longer the fighting instructions, but the signal book'.[20] It has been generally agreed that here was a major development in the history of naval tactics; Tunstall, for example, considered that 'in form, layout and typography, moreover, it has a special character which persisted throughout all Howe's later work and can be instantly recognised':

> On the one hand it marked the separation and independence of the new signalling system from all instructional matter and its supremacy over such instructions as remained. On the other, it provided a new, though

19 Holland, 'Development of Signalling in the Royal Navy', pp.7-8.

20 Corbett (ed.), *Fighting Instructions*, p.233.

> subordinate, system of instruction. Unlike the official book, Howe's book consisted partly of standing orders, partly of orders designed to make the admiral's general tactical ideas more easily understood, and partly of explanation of how certain signals were to be executed so as to standardise evolutions. The actual signals were very sparingly described.[21]

Howe's objective was to enable an admiral to control more effectively the movement of the ships under his command, and thereby to provide the opportunity of gaining a tactical advantage by concentrating the firepower of his fleet against a part only of the enemy. In this way, he intended to avoid the stalemate which so often led to an indecisive result when the opposing fleets merely formed parallel lines firing at each other. At the beginning of the century Sir Cloudesley Shovell had written:

> Experience has taught me, that where men are equally inured and disciplined to war, it is without a miracle, number that gains the victory, for both in fleets, squadrons and single ships of near equal force, by the time one is beaten and ready to retreat the other is also beaten and glad the enemy has left him. To fight, beat and chase an enemy of the same strength I have sometimes seen, but rarely have seen at sea any victory worth boasting, where the strength has been near equal.[22]

The problem was clearly understood in France as well; Morogues wrote:

> We have no longer decisive affairs at sea – that is to say such as the end of a war absolutely depends on, nor even general actions, except where both sides desire it equally. Nothing but superior tactics and manoeuvring can secure such ends, and for these the first essential is a good and simple system of signals.[23]

Captain John Jervis would famously sum up the problem when he wrote after the First Battle of Ushant to the effect that an engagement between two fleets of equal force never could produce a decisive result, unless they were equally determined to fight it out, or the commander-in-chief of one of them misconducted his line.[24]

Howe's system was continued by his immediate successor on the North American Station, Sir George Collier, but not by those who followed him,

21 Tunstall, *Naval Warfare in the Age of Sail*, p.129.

22 Quoted in John B Hattendorff, 'Sir George Rooke and Sir Cloudesley Shovell c1650-1709 and 1650-1707' in Peter le Fevre and Richard Harding (eds). *Precursors of Nelson: British Admirals of the Eighteenth Century* (London: Chatham Publishing 2000), p.64.

23 Corbett (ed.), *Fighting Instructions*, p.10.

24 Rodger, 'Image and Reality', p.292.

Admirals Byron and Arbuthnot, who reverted to the previous system of issuing Additional Instructions. However, Richard Kempenfelt had been following with close attention Howe's introduction of his new signalling system, and carried on the work when he became in due course Captain of the Fleet in the Channel Fleet in 1779. Before this, Charles Knowles, then only a lieutenant, produced in 1778 a book which included the system of numerical signals which he had developed and which he later claimed that he had given to Howe on his arrival at Newport, Rhode Island. According to Knowles, Howe afterwards introduced these signals into the Channel Fleet. Although Knowles unquestionably produced some extremely valuable tactical ideas, his recollections were only published half a century later when he was 76 years old and may not be entirely accurate. For example, he claimed to have discovered the tabular flag system with the assistance of a chessboard, but Tunstall regards that as dubious, since by that time the French system was already well-known in England. Nor is it possible to determine what influence Knowles may have had on Kempenfelt and others. His work was revised continuously during the ensuing two decades. At all events, Howe's work was next to be carried on by Kempenfelt when he went to sea as Captain of the Fleet to Sir Charles Hardy.

6

France and the French Navy

France's defeat in the Seven Years War had left the Duc de Choiseul, Louis XV's chief minister, with a burning determination to reverse its outcome. In due course the opportunity to do so would arise but not until after he had left office, and Louis XV had died. There were three principal factors that enabled the French government to contemplate going to war with Britain again and which, in due course, would lead to its outbreak in 1778.

The first of these factors became a reality before the end of the Seven Years War, when the second Family Compact between the thrones of France and Spain was signed in August 1761. It effectively united them for the purposes of war, and has been regarded as 'the starting point of the restoration of France's position in Europe,' though at first it was to bring only disasters in its train.[1] It was an alliance which was to take effect whenever either power was engaged in war, whether offensive or defensive, and Choiseul saw its maintenance as essential to France's international interests.

In February 1765 he addressed a memoir to Louis XV setting out the reasons for advocating the policy to be followed, and emphasising the crucial importance of the Family Compact; the King's policy must, he said, be 'to manage with the most scrupulous attention his system of alliance with Spain, to regard the Spanish power as a power necessary to France'. He was in no doubt of what must be regarded as the overwhelming reason for ensuring a close relationship with Spain; this was the perpetual threat which France faced from across the Channel:

> England is the declared enemy of your power and of your state, and she will be so always. Many ages must elapse before a durable peace can be established with this state, which looks forward to the supremacy in the four quarters of the globe. Only the revolution which will occur someday in America, though we shall probably not see it, will put

1 Edward S. Corwin, *French Policy and the American Alliance* (Princeton NJ: Princeton University Press, 1916), p.36.

> England back to that state of weakness in which Europe will have no more to fear of her.[2]

The second factor of crucial importance to a French government ready to face war with Britain was the revival of the navy. For this, France owed an enormous debt to Choiseul. For nine years, after he became Navy Minister as well as Foreign Minister in 1761, Choiseul bent every effort to bring about the restoration of the French navy, which had been effectively smashed to pieces in the battles of 1759. Although he gave up the Navy Ministry in 1766, he was succeeded by his cousin the Duc de Choiseul-Praslin, and they continued together the work of rebuilding, until Choiseul's fall from power in 1770.

In grasping the need to reconstruct her navy, if France was to avenge her defeat in the Seven Years War, Choiseul started with a serious difficulty, in that the available financial resources were quite inadequate for the scale of the rebuilding programme that must be launched. His solution was to make an appeal to national pride, by inviting the local Estates and other public bodies to subscribe for the building of ships. The result of this call for funds exceeded his expectation; it produced 16 ships, of which one, the *Bretagne*, was of 110 guns; the *Ville de Paris* was of 90 guns; there were two of 80 guns, six 74s, one 64 and five 54s. In addition, a huge general subscription brought in 13 million livres.[3]

Choiseul also undertook a number of other significant reforms directed towards increasing the navy's efficiency. A new classification of ships, and the standardisation of guns and other equipment, greatly simplified the arming and refitting of ships in whatever port they might be. The great naval ports of Brest and Toulon were almost completely rebuilt, and Lorient, the East India Company's port on the Bay of Biscay, was acquired to provide an additional Atlantic station between Brest and Rochefort. Choiseul also remodelled the corps of cadets which produced aspiring officers, although there remained an attitude of social superiority with which those of noble origin, the *rouges*, regarded the rest, the *bleus*. He also reformed the shore-based administration, prescribed uniforms and pay, and created a corps of naval constructors. Naval medical schools were established, and the Marine Academy was remodelled.

All these developments were closely followed in Britain; France was perceived as a constant threat in any case, but any increase in the strength of her navy touched a particularly tender spot; 'it made the French menace direct, specific, concrete and readily grasped, as French support for Jacobitism had done in the 1740s'.[4] The British scrutiny of the rebuilding of their navy was well understood by the French, and was greatly resented; it was believed that British policy was to do what

2 Corwin, *French Policy and the American Alliance*, p.40.

3 E.H. Jenkins, *A History of the French Navy* (London: Macdonald & Janes, 1973), p.142.

4 Jeremy Black, *Natural and Necessary Enemies* (London: Duckworth & Co, 1980), p.74.

it could to keep the French navy reduced, and that the principle that was applied was 'of watching our ports, of surveying our dockyards and arsenals, of spoiling our projects, our preparations, our least movements'. These words appeared in a document addressed to Louis XVI by the Comte de Broglie entitled *Conjectures Raisonnés*. Broglie was to write some five years later a crucial memoir advocating an alliance with the rebellious American colonists, asserting that 'without colonies and commerce Britain would be without a marine, and without a marine would be henceforth only a third-class power'.[5] It was widely believed in France that Britain would, if obliged to concede independence to the Americans, attempt to seize the French possessions in the West Indies together with parts of Spanish America. In this, as in most French consideration of British intentions, it was the navy that was central to the formation of policy.

Choiseul and his cousin had intended that the development of the French navy would produce 80 ships of the line. When they left office, the total was 64, together with 50 frigates and corvettes. This was an imposing force, but on its own was not large enough to take on the British Royal Navy. It was here that the Family Compact was vital; it provided that either participant could call on the other for at least 20 ships of the line and six frigates. This would have been the case, for instance, had the Anglo Spanish dispute over the Falkland Islands in 1770 led to war; when this issue was resolved peacefully, Choiseul, who had been perfectly ready to face war, was dismissed by Louis XV.

Choiseul's departure was bad news for the French navy. The new Navy Minister, de Boynes, proceeded to attempt a set of reforms of the naval administration based on a number of rigid principles. He endeavoured to organise the navy like the army, dividing ships and officers into eight brigades; he provided for the navy to be responsible for its own infantry and artillery support; he set up a naval academy at Le Havre, which threatened to undermine the status of cadets trained aboard ship; and worst of all, he attempted to reform the administration of the naval ports in such a fashion that there was a breakdown in the lines of responsibility and an ensuing struggle for power between the Intendant, the Port Commandant, the colonels commanding the marine infantry, and the head of the port officers.[6] Subsequently, he attempted to combine all these posts into one administrative body. In the course of this management upheaval, he did, however, introduce one reform that was really useful; he established a squadron of evolutions which undertook manoeuvres, giving at least some ships and their crews the opportunity to gain valuable experience in ship handling, gunnery and signalling.[7]

5 Corwin, *French Policy and the American Alliance*, p.154.

6 Jonathan Dull, *The French Navy and American Independence* (Princeton NJ: Princeton University Press, 2005), p.13.

7 Jenkins, *History of the French Navy*, pp.145-146.

When he came to the throne in 1774 Louis XVI, who had always had a genuine interest in the navy, replaced Boynes by another administrator from outside the service. Like Boynes, Antoine de Sartine had no practical experience of naval matters, but unlike him he proved a quick learner. Born in 1729, he was Lieutenant-General of the Paris police and had been effectively responsible for the city's administration since 1759: 'He became one of the most capable naval ministers in French history: a firm yet tactful leader, a prudent and courageous war minister, an innovative and meticulous administrator, a man who took particular pride in the health of his ships crews'.[8]

Sartine was greatly assisted by his decision to employ as a key member of his staff Charles Claret, Chevalier de Fleurieu, who would himself one day become Navy Minister. It fell to Sartine to reverse some of the unpopular reforms introduced by his predecessor, and he obtained the king's permission to re-establish the administration of the ports and arsenals, and to return responsibility for the navy's artillery to the army. He also abolished the Academy at Le Havre; he concluded that it was poorly located for training cruises, which normally took place in the Bay of Biscay, and that it could not produce a sufficient number of officers. In taking this step he may have been emptying the baby out with the bathwater; E.H. Jenkins certainly judged it to be a mistake, since a patent of nobility had not been required for its entrance, whereas all the aspirants recruited at each port were required to provide evidence of such status.[9] Sartine also did something about the great age of senior officers, some of whom were getting very long in the tooth; he appointed 15 new commodores in part to replace older men who were asked to retire. He did not, however, attempt a cull of the higher flag ranks.

Away from administration, Sartine's immediate task was to build up the strength of the fleet. During the four years before he took office, in order to save cost, the navy had been using up the reserves of masts, wood, hemp and other crucially important naval supplies that Choiseul and his cousin had prudently accumulated. His difficulties were also exacerbated by the budgetary restrictions which he faced. His request for an increase of 4 million livres above that which was normally allowed for variable expenses was disapproved. Sartine had run head-on into the brick wall of the determination of Turgot, the Finance Minister, to cut back royal expenditure.

Given the limitations imposed by Turgot's financial policy, it was only gradually that Sartine was able to make some inroads into the shortages of naval supplies, and he was obliged to limit naval operations to their existing very restricted level. But international events would soon begin to give him a more powerful argument in favour of increased naval expenditure. Sartine kept a close eye on what the British government was spending on the fleet, following the outbreak of hostilities

8 Dull, *French Navy and American Independence*, p.14.
9 Jenkins, *History of the French Navy*, p.147.

in North America, and in March 1775 he caused panic among the intendants of Brest, Rochefort and Toulon when addressing a request to them to know how many ships at each port could be made ready for sea.[10] He was obliged to reassure them that his enquiry did not mean that war was imminent. The replies which he received indicated that 40 ships of the line could be ready within four months. In June, he obtained 4 million livres towards existing overspending, overhauls, and the construction of smaller vessels. There was, however, little change in French naval operational activity, since there did seem at that time to be no likelihood of hostilities. The squadron of evolutions which went to sea under de Guichen in 1775 consisted of only four frigates and eight smaller vessels; in the following year, the squadron under du Chaffault comprised three ships of the line, seven frigates and a number of lesser ships.[11]

The scope of the operations carried out by the squadrons of evolution was, however, very narrow. For the scheme proposed for 1776 *Capitaine de Vaisseau* Perier de Salvert, who was the son-in-law of Morogues, produced a plan for a much more comprehensive set of operations. His recommendations were intended to produce a thorough training for war:

> His proposals included strategical operations, exercises in concentration, heavy gunfire at a hulk, squadrons manoeuvring against one another, scouting, search operations and landing operations. Nor did he forget the tactical training of young officers: "in each ship should be embarked a table five feet square, on which compass cards should be drawn for the moving of little models of ships made for the purpose, so that young officers can learn tactical manoeuvres".[12]

In spite of the budgetary restrictions imposed on the French navy, there was still a good deal for enquiring naval tourists such as Kempenfelt to see. The ships built by Choiseul formed the nucleus of a fleet that was growing steadily. Between 1766 and 1770 France and Spain had between them built more than double the number of new ships added to the British fleet, and consequently the British advantage in numbers had steadily decreased. The French had also had the benefit of a number of extremely able naval architects, and the process was beginning of building a fleet around a number of homogenous designs.[13]

The class system, and the sense among most French officers that being of the nobility, they were effectively the equal of their superiors, was something that neither Choiseul nor his successors had been able to eradicate. Admiral James

10 Dull, *French Navy and American Independence*, p.25.
11 Jenkins, *History of the French Navy*, p.147.
12 James, *The British Navy in Adversity*, p.80.
13 Richard Harding, *Seapower and Naval Warfare 1650-1830* (London: UCL Press, 1999), p.232.

quotes a passage from Troude's *Batailles Navales* which illustrated the problems which this could cause:

> Under Louis XVI the intimacy and fellowship existing between the chief and subordinate led the latter to discuss the orders which were given him. Admiral, captain, officers, midshipmen, ate together; everything was in common. They "thee-and-thou'd" each other like chums. In handling the ship the inferior gave his opinion, argued: and the chief, irritated, often preferred to yield rather than make enemies.[14]

It also appears to be the case that the treatment of the seamen had not improved:

> The system of *classes* had ceased to work. The benefits attached to it by Colbert at its creation had been whittled away or had fallen into desuetude. Pay was irregular, supplies of clothing so poor that ships' companies went half naked, hammocks often lacking, food bad. Living miserably aboard, the men had the added misery of knowing that their wives and families were starving ashore.[15]

Nevertheless, Admiral James felt able to conclude that the French fleet, although smaller than the British fleet would become when it was fully mobilised, was effectively manned and stored. This may be something of an overstatement, but it would certainly appear that a spirit of renaissance did permeate the officer corps, however much their class feeling may have adversely affected efficiency.

Alfred Mahan reviewed the ability of the French admirals from whom the government could choose to appoint to important commands:

> Although they as yet lacked practice, and were numerically too few, the French officers were well-equipped by mental resources, by instruction and reflection, to handle large fleets; and they now had large fleets to handle … No such conjunction had occurred since Tourville; none such recurred during the Revolution. The condition was unique in naval history of the sail period. To meet it, assuming an approach to equality in contending fleets, was required, first, a commander-in-chief, and then a competent body of officers. The latter the British had only in the sense of fine seamen and gallant men. In courage there is no occasion to institute comparisons between the two nations; in kind there may have been a difference, but certainly not in degree. The practical superiority of seamanship in the

14 James, *The British Navy in Adversity*, p.80.
15 Jenkins, *History of the French Navy*, p.147.

> British may be taken as a set off to the more highly trained understanding of military principles and methods on the part of their enemy.[16]

Mahan thought that for commander-in-chief, the British had only two with the qualities possessed by the French, these being Howe and Rodney. His view would not be shared by many historians, who could point to a considerable number of other able British commanders who made their reputations during the course of the war.

Mahan was right, however, in noting a considerable improvement in the quality of French naval commanders. Of these, perhaps the ablest was Louis Guillouet, Comte d'Orvilliers. Born in 1708, he joined the navy at the age of 20, becoming *capitaine de vaisseau* in 1756, *chef d'escadre* in 1764, and *lieutenant-général* (equating to vice admiral) in 1777. Luc Urbain du Bouëxic de Guichen, born in 1712, joined the navy in 1730 and reached the rank of *capitaine de vaisseau* in 1756, and *chef d'escadre* in 1776. Charles-Henri Hector d'Estaing, the youngest of the more prominent French admirals, was born in 1729, and served in the army for many years, ultimately reaching the rank of *lieutenant-général* in 1772. Meanwhile he entered the service of the French East India Company in 1759, and formally transferred to the navy in 1762, with the rank of *chef d'escadre*. Louis-Charles, Comte du Chaffault du Besné, born in 1708, joined the navy in 1725; he became a *capitaine de vaisseau* in 1754 and ten years later *chef d'escadre*. Active in the interwar years, he was made *lieutenant-général* in 1777. Jean Guillaume Toussaint Picquet, Comte de la Motte, generally referred to as La Motte-Picquet. was born in 1720, joining the navy at the age of 15. He had an active and successful career before being promoted to *capitaine de vaisseau* in 1760. He became *chef d'escadre* in 1777. François-Joseph Paul de Grasse was born in 1722, entering the French navy in 1740 after six years with the Order of Knights of St John at Malta. He reached the rank of *capitaine de vaisseau* in 1765 and that of *chef d'escadre* in 1778.

It will be apparent from the foregoing that, as with the British navy, most of the senior French commanders were of a considerable age when they were appointed to fleet command. The leading Spanish admiral was Don Luis de Córdova, who was born in 1706; his naval service began at the age of 11, and he became one of the most experienced and aggressive Spanish commanders of the eighteenth century.

Sartine's struggle for further resources continued, in parallel with the demands created by the policy of Vergennes, which was increasingly moving in the direction of practical support for the American colonists. This of course considerably strengthened the claim for additional funds to be made available for the navy. It was, therefore, the rebellion of Britain's American colonists that was the third of the key factors which pushed France inexorably towards war. The outbreak of the revolution in North America which Choiseul had foretold was now becoming a

16 Admiral A.T. Mahan, *Types of Naval Officers* (London: Sampson Low & Co, 1904), pp.195-196.

reality. The opportunity to accelerate the detachment from Britain of her colonies there was one which Vergennes, who had been Foreign Minister since 1774, considered must be grasped. He was always concerned that France's international policy should be scrupulously correct; he 'regarded the honour of the King as setting very definite limits beyond which political advantage was not to be sought'. There was one exception to this virtuous position. In a document he wrote for King Louis XVI, he made clear the reason why he was always ready to deceive Britain:

> We see lying alongside us a nation greedy, restless, more jealous of the prosperity of its neighbours than awake to its own happiness, powerfully armed and ready to strike on the instant. Let us not deceive ourselves; whatever parade the English ministers may make of their pacific intentions, we cannot count upon this disposition longer than their domestic difficulties continue.[17]

The generally held belief that Britain's international position was dependent on her retention of the American colonies led to Vergennes' conviction that their loss must substantially affect the balance of power in France's favour. That being so, he proceeded on the basis that it was not only allowable but right to take advantage of such a favourable opportunity to destroy the power that Britain had used so outrageously.

The mercantilist opinion held by so many in France that Britain would be very seriously weakened by losing her American colonies was one that was shared by many in Britain. This accounted for the ongoing determination of George III and his Cabinet to do whatever it took to defeat the revolution and return the colonies to their allegiance. On the one hand, therefore, to help achieve such a significant diminution of British power, the French government was prepared to accept the risk that it would lead to war; on the other, the British government was ready to go on increasing its military and naval commitment in North America to prevent it. Jonathan Dull considered that the French overestimate of the consequence to Britain of losing America was a 'fundamental misperception,' and that it led France to fight a war which was ruinously expensive and diplomatically unproductive.[18]

Vergennes had concluded, in August 1775, that as long as the North ministry remained in power in Britain, there was little danger that there would be a reconciliation between America and Britain which would result in their turning jointly against France and Spain. Contemplating the likely course of events, Vergennes' secretary Gerard de Rayneval wrote a paper suggesting that the Americans would proceed to seek their independence, but that unless they were given assistance, Britain would probably succeed in subjugating them. France, then, must decide

17 Corwin, *French Policy and the American Alliance*, p.63.
18 Dull, *French Navy and American Independence*, p.37.

'Meur. le Comte de Vergennes, Chevalier des Ordres du Roi, Ministre, Conseiller et Sécrétaire d'État, ayant le Départemt. des Affaires Etrangeres'. Unattributed engraving (NYPL)

what to do, in the light of the request received from the colonists for aid and supplies: 'England is the natural enemy of France, and a greedy, ambitious, unjust and treacherous enemy, the constant and cherished object of whose system is, if not the destruction of France, at least her abasement, humiliation and ruin'. If France gave the help requested, and the Americans were successful, then, de Rayneval concluded, 'the power of England will shrink and ours will expand correspondingly;' furthermore the balance of trade would change because 'her commerce will suffer an irreparable loss while ours will increase;' and it might even be that France could regain some of her lost possessions in North America.[19] Simplified in this way, the decision to assist the American colonists seemed like a 'no-brainer' to the hawks surrounding the French monarch.

The discreet provision of aid would present no problem, at least in selling arms and munitions in exchange for American produce, and money likewise could be supplied. More of a problem would be providing warships without declaring openly for the Americans and thus precipitating war. In March 1776, the receipt of an upbeat report from Bonvouloir, the agent sent to assess the situation in America by the French ambassador in London, finally made up Vergennes' mind to provide support to the colonists, and there began a struggle between the King's ministers over such a proposal; Turgot was adamantly opposed, seeking instead domestic reform and economy. He saw, correctly, the serious risk of war that might result, believing that in the long run colonies would generally detach themselves from the mother country in any case. On 2 May, the King authorised the advance of 1 million livres for the purchase of supplies for the Americans; with the commencement of the programme of secret aid the slide to war had begun; and on 12 May Turgot, having lost the battle for the King's ear, was dismissed. The temptation to do something to assist the colonists had been irresistible; but in providing support, albeit secretly and unofficially, the French were picking up the corner of a towel without knowing how long it was.

With this decision having been taken, common prudence demanded that steps to prepare the navy should be taken. At this time the French navy was far from being ready for war. As at 1 January 1777, there were 37 ships of the line in commission, an increase of 14 over the past year; but this must be set against the fact that Britain had as early as June 1776 82 ships at sea or ready to be armed, and by October had increased the number of guard ships to 35. In the spring of 1777 Sartine embarked on a massive programme of resupplying naval stores, and the dockyards increased the throughput of overhauls of ships of the line, while by the end of the year eight new frigates joined the fleet with another 12 ordered. This activity was of crucial significance in determining the stance of the French government; Jonathan Dull has written that 'the work of the ports was probably the key element in the transition from peace to war, underlying the more obvious evolution of diplomacy and naval operations'.[20] Naval expenditure was continuing to increase; for the year 1777 Sartine had asked for and received over 45 million livres, of which some 20.1 million was for the navy and 16.6 million for the colonies, with a supplemental award of 9.2 million. During the first six months of the year there was a marked increase in French patrols in the Bay of Biscay with the object of protecting commercial shipping, in response to increased British naval activity in the area aimed at intercepting American commerce.

19 Corwin, *French Policy and the American Alliance*, pp.69-70.
20 Dull, *French Navy and American Independence*, p.68.

During 1777 the British government was becoming increasingly insistent that something should be done to limit the activity of American privateers, which were being encouraged by Benjamin Franklin and his fellow Commissioners to make use of French ports. This was something that seriously concerned Vergennes, who had done his best to ensure that the American vessels enjoyed no more than the right to take refuge from adverse weather conditions. Throughout the year the issue had become increasingly acute, and by the middle of July Vergennes concluded that the situation had reached a point at which France needed to consider its position, and must resolve 'either to abandon America or to aid her courageously and effectively'.[21]

The American Commissioners kept in close touch with the French government and regularly reported home on the discussions taking place. At the beginning of 1777 they were able to report on the enthusiasm in France for the American cause: 'The hearts of the French are universally for us, and the cry is strong for immediate war with Britain. Indeed everything tends that way, but the Court has its reasons for postponing it a little longer'.[22] The French were taking care to avoid precipitating war prematurely; when refusing an American request to provide eight warships, the formal response stated: 'The sending of eight vessels to the shores of America would not change the face of affairs there. As powerfully armed as the English are in Europe they would quickly send a greatly superior squadron which would reduce the other to inaction'. To agree to the request, it was explained, France would compromise herself openly with no advantage to the Americans, since it would be a legitimate reason for war.[23] French patrols especially in the Bay of Biscay were ordered to ensure that privateers did not operate near the French coast or ports, since this would be a serious provocation. Du Chaffault was given careful instructions as to how he should act if he saw a vessel being chased by British warships. If she hoisted French colours, he should take her under his protection; otherwise he was not to meddle in any way except where the vessel was very close to the coast.

In his original programme for the expansion of the French Navy, Choiseul had set a target of 80 ships of the line. By the time of Louis XV's death in 1774 there were 66 ships of the line, together with 36 frigates and about 50 smaller vessels, so the gap between the strength of the French and British fleets had closed considerably. Many of the ships of the line, however, required overhaul and refitting, and Sartine kept up the pressure on the dockyards to make as many as possible ready for sea. Further new ships of the line were being completed, and French confidence grew. It is, however, something of an overstatement for Edward Corwin to write

21 Corwin, *French Policy and the American Alliance*, p.101.

22 William Bell Clark and William James Morgan (eds), *Naval Documents of the American Revolution* (Washington, DC: US Navy Dept, 1964), Vol.VIII, pp.516-517.

23 Clark and Morgan (eds), *Naval Documents of the American Revolution*, Vol.VIII, p.532.

that by the middle of July 1777 'the French marine had reached a plane from which substantial parity with the British marine was within easy reach'.[24] It is certainly true that many of the British ships of the line laid up in ordinary would require considerable work to make them battle ready, but the dockyard resources available for this were ultimately far greater than those available to Sartine. In the event of a naval war, however, France could and would look to the considerable Spanish navy to even the odds.

Having by July 1777 concluded that the time had come for France to decide the course it should follow, Vergennes prepared for Louis XVI a memoir on 23 July setting out the plain alternatives which must be faced. In this he argued firmly for a close alliance. As Corwin summed it up:

> The primary question, Vergennes declared, was whether France and Spain could afford to see the colonies return either directly or indirectly to British control; and that question turned on the further one, whether it was sound policy to contribute to the strength of an enemy when opportunity offered to enfeeble that enemy. England was the natural rival of the house of Bourbon. Mistress again of North America and its immense resources of all sorts, she would be a menace to the possessions of the two crowns in that part of the world.[25]

The secret aid that was being supplied to the American colonists was no longer enough, Vergennes suggested, to prevent their possible reconciliation with Britain. Open assistance meant war; but, he argued, this was probably imminent anyway. A close alliance was what was required; the European situation was in every way favourable to joint action against Britain by France and Spain. Louis accepted Vergennes' advice that same day; but he attached a critical condition: the policy outlined must be dependent on Spanish cooperation. Without this, therefore, decisive action was impossible and that meant that Vergennes must now persuade Don José Moñino y Redondo, Conde de Floridablanca, Spain's new chief minister, to fall into line. The latter's response was not altogether reassuring; he would base his policy, he said, on the Family Compact, but would also regard the interests of Spain as at least equal in importance to those of France, and for the moment he did not consider 'the abasement of England' as a key policy objective. To his mind, if it was possible to keep going the struggle between Britain and her colonies until both sides were exhausted, then well and good. France and Spain should await their moment to intervene; and in any case, the annual treasure fleets from Mexico would not begin to arrive until the following spring, and Floridablanca was not going to give Britain a chance to pounce on that.

24 Corwin, *French Policy and the American Alliance*, p.101.

25 Corwin, *French Policy and the American Alliance*, p.101.

'D. José Moñino, Conde de Floridablanca'. Engraving by Juan Carrafa after Antonio Guerrero. (NYPL)

Floridablanca had taken office in February 1777. He was a lawyer by profession. He was a supporter of the reformist policies of Carlos III, and in 1772 was appointed as ambassador to the Vatican. In this post he managed to obtain the support of Pope Clement XIV for the suppression of the Jesuits in Spain, which had taken place five years previously, and he was rewarded for this by being made a count. Once he had become chief minister, he began a thorough reform of the antiquated Spanish bureaucracy. He worked energetically to rebuild the Spanish economy, agreeing trade deals with Morocco and the Ottoman Empire. As Vergennes was finding out, Floridablanca was a hard-headed negotiator who was determined to get the best deal for Spain that he could.

During 1777 Vergennes had therefore to proceed with caution. He would continue to sustain the American colonists as far as he could without bringing about a war with Britain for which the French navy was not yet ready. In discussion with the American Commissioners in Paris, he was obliged to refuse their request for a commercial treaty. He did, though, promise further financial aid. At sea, the French units under du Chaffault, de Grasse and La Motte-Picquet were increasingly coming into contact with British patrols seeking to intercept American merchant shipping and, especially, privateers. These latter had been bringing prizes into French ports; Lord Stormont, the British ambassador, fumed at his inability effectively to limit the activities of the privateers; and had presented a series of formal protests. Vergennes acted to meet the British objections, smoothly offering assurances that orders would be given to remedy the abuses of which Stormont complained. The ambassador was far from convinced, ending a report of this that he was 'far from expecting a radical cure,'[26] and he complained of the constant duplicity and insidious policy of the French court. The situation continued to deteriorate to the point where Vergennes feared that a British declaration of war might be imminent, and he felt obliged to order that du Chaffault's patrols were strengthened. In September, British pressure finally succeeded in enforcing the departure from French ports of the privateer squadron that had been based there, and with this, and the end of the summer sailing weather, tension for the moment was reduced.[27] The continuing atmosphere of crisis did however enable Sartine successfully to obtain additional funds for the navy.

Commenting on this tortuous diplomacy, the American Commissioners smugly reported to the Committee for Foreign Affairs that the French government was professing to England 'a resolution to observe all treaties;' but that in fact 'to us it privately professes a real Friendship, wishes success to our Cause, winks at the supplies we obtain here as much as it can without giving open grounds of Complaint to England, privately affords us very essential Aids; and goes on preparing for War'.[28]

Meanwhile Vergennes was continuing to work on the Spanish government, among whose members there was a real apprehension of the threat which an independent America might offer to Spanish possessions. In his memoir of 23 July, he had endeavoured to show that such a threat was much exaggerated, but Floridablanca was not reassured. The American Commissioners, for their part, had by now abandoned their previous threat that unless France vigorously supported them, they might be forced to make a deal with the British government.

26 Clark and Morgan (eds), *Naval Documents of the American Revolution*, Vol.IX, p.393.

27 Dull, *French Navy and American Independence*, pp.80-81.

28 Clark and Morgan (eds), *Naval Documents of the American Revolution*, Vol.IX, p.633.

In December 1777 the news of Saratoga arrived in Paris. It has been suggested that its effect has been overstated, Dull writing that 'Saratoga has been assigned however an importance which it does not merit, that of having so demonstrated the capacity of the American army that France was willing to enter the war as America's ally'.[29] The French council of state had already faced the need to abandon its policy of limited involvement. It was the successful strengthening of the French navy, rather than American military success, that encouraged the government to take a bolder line. In fact, it could have been argued that taken on its own, the American victory at Saratoga demonstrated the probability that the Americans would gain their independence, and France might need to do little more than it already was doing to bring about that result. Saratoga was exactly the kind of military success that the programme of secret aid had been intended to bring about. However, the constant pressure from the American Commissioners in Paris reinforced the French desire to take on Britain at a moment of her weakness.

However, it was the Spanish navy that Vergennes required, and for a long time it seemed that he would not get it. When, after Saratoga, the decision of the French royal council to offer an alliance to the Americans was made known by France's new ambassador in Madrid, the Comte de Montmorin, to the Spanish Minister, the effect was dramatic:

> The intensity of his emotion displayed itself in both countenance and gesture. To contradict or oppose him was in vain. 'He trembled in all his body and had the greatest difficulty in the world in expressing himself. "You think," said he finally, "this moment a most auspicious one for the two crowns; I think it the most fatal for Spain; but it would be the fairest day of my life if the king would let me retire".[30]

It is difficult not to feel considerable sympathy for Floridablanca. His country was being drawn inexorably into a war for which there was, for Spain, little upside. Carlos III shared his minister's concerns; but after some days a feeling of resignation took the place of the first intemperate reaction, and Spain began to prepare a possible shopping list.

The Spanish navy that Vergennes looked to for essential support was considerable. Ossun, Montmorin's predecessor, had prepared a detailed report of its strength in January 1777, listing 59 ships of the line of which 42 were ready to be armed, with five more by June and another five by the end of the year. By the end of 1778 all 59 would be ready for sea. It was becoming evident to Vergennes, though, that he would have to wait some time before Spain was prepared to enter into hostilities.

29 Dull, *French Navy and American Independence*, p.90.

30 Corwin, *French Policy and the American Alliance*, p.159.

Vergennes continued to discuss with the American Commissioners the terms of the treaty to be entered into while awaiting Montmorin's report. Floridablanca, though, was still concerned to delay the outbreak of war as long as he could. At the same time, in the course of conversations with Stormont, the British ambassador, Vergennes became aware that in London it was already taken for granted that there was a treaty in existence. Given this, he now intended to force the pace if he could, telling Montmorin in Madrid that it would be necessary to announce the treaty by the end of April. This would be before the Spanish treasure fleet arrived. Floridablanca continued to maintain his refusal to commit himself until the publication of the treaty, and Vergennes went forward. On 7 March, Louis XVI formally approved the treaty; the French ambassador in London officially notified the British government six days later. Vergennes had been obliged to proceed without waiting for the Spanish to commit themselves to immediate war, but he proceeded in the confident belief that for 1778 the French fleet was strong enough to deal with the demands made on it, and that decisive action could be taken jointly with Spain in the following year. In taking action at this time, Vergennes believed that he had finally eliminated the possibility of any deal being made between Britain and the colonists. Furthermore, the treaty represented the clearest possible statement that France intended to ensure American independence, even at the cost of war.[31]

Once the public announcement of the American alliance had taken place, and the consequent progress towards the outbreak of war having been decisively accelerated, Sartine put in hand enhanced naval preparation. The dockyard at Toulon was ordered, following the fitting out of the first 10 ships of the line, to prepare a second squadron of seven more ships of the line; while that at Brest was ordered to begin preparation of the largest ships of the line, *Bretagne*, *Ville de Paris* and *Duc de Bourgogne*. As a precaution, the produce of the West Indies was to be convoyed to France under naval escort, and all merchant shipping was warned to proceed with caution. The stage was set, and it would not be long before hostilities began in earnest.

31 Dull, *French Navy and American Independence*, p.105.

7

Britain's Royal Navy 1763-1778

Lord Egmont, who became First Lord of the Admiralty in 1763, had faced the usual struggle to defend the Navy Estimates, but in 1765 he succeeded in obtaining approval for a long-term plan to expand the capacity of the Royal dockyards. His scheme was restricted for financial reasons to Portsmouth and Plymouth, but it got under way, although proceeding only slowly, during the 1760s. Egmont's successor, Sir Edward Hawke, was less successful in getting the votes needed to expand the dockyard scheme. Moreover, the programme of visitations of the dockyards that Egmont had begun was abandoned; and the steady decay of many of the ships laid up in ordinary was insidiously weakening the apparent strength of the Royal Navy.

When Sandwich came into office in 1771 he was entirely mindful of the difficulty which the dockyards faced in endeavouring to keep in repair the ships laid up in ordinary, writing:

> When ships are laid up in Ordinary they are divided into three Classes (exclusive of those in good condition) namely such as require small, middling, and great Repair. – Those that are nearest being brought into condition for service must naturally be first taken in hand and while they are in the Dock the others grow worse and worse, and before there is any room for them many of them successively become past repair, and must be broke up or sold; whereas were their docks sufficient, more of them would be taken in the same time, and many valuable ships saved from destruction which would in process of time fully repay the Expense of the Additional docks and other requisites.[1]

Sandwich immediately grasped that the problem was basically that of the durability of the ships of the fleet; though he was able to resume Egmont's programme of expansion of the dockyards, he wrote that 'neither this or any thing else that

1 Rodger, *Insatiable Earl*, p.133.

can be devised, will enable us to keep up the proper number, unless it is contrived to give them a greater duration than that which we have experienced of late years, nor is it in my opinion possible for any nation to keep up a fleet so built'.[2] He made these remarks in the minutes of a dockyard visitation; Sandwich had been able to resume this programme, which was essential if the true situation was to be known and kept under proper review. It was by means such as this that Sandwich made himself thoroughly familiar with the dockyards; it has been said that he knew them better than any First Lord before or since and better than the Navy Board.

From the first, Sandwich was under constant pressure to keep down naval expenditure. In September 1772 North wrote to him calling for a reduction in the number of guard ships. These were the ships of the line kept permanently in readiness, with 60 percent of their normal complement. North wished to reduce the number from 20 to 16, on the basis that 'a sudden attack is certainly not to be apprehended'. To this, Sandwich responded with a survey of the way in which the policy of maintaining a number of ships ready for service had been applied since it was first introduced at the beginning of the century. If a reduction in expenditure had to be made, he was firmly of the view that this should be made elsewhere. The King, disliking the idea of war, took the First Lord's part, believing that the readiness of the fleet was the best way to avoid it. He wrote to North in 1773:

> I cannot conclude without expressing my approbation of Lord Sandwich's plan for having the guard ships always ready for immediate service; that will, I am persuaded, prevent many wars for by that means we have ever twenty large ships ready before the enemy can equip one, consequently about the start of three months, which is an immense advantage in all military operations.[3]

Naturally, Sandwich monitored closely the intelligence which he was receiving about the state of things in France and the strength of her navy. Necessarily, the possibility of war was never far from his mind, and he exchanged correspondence with Lord Rochford on the subject in the autumn of 1772, remarking: 'I dread the consequences of too long acquiescence in suffering other great powers to take considerable strides without interfering, as I know that when our proper strength is exerted we are more considerable than any of them, France not excepted'.[4] The information reaching him about the French navy was not reassuring; a report he received in December 1772 suggested that it could in due course send to sea a fleet of 74 ships of the line and 54 frigates, most of which had been built since the end of the Seven Years War.

2 N.A.M. Rodger, *The Command of the Ocean* (London: Allen Lane, 2004), p.370.
3 Barnes and Owen (eds), *Private Papers of John, Earl of Sandwich*, Vol.I, p.4.
4 Barnes and Owen (eds), *Private Papers of John, Earl of Sandwich*, Vol.I, p.29.

North, though, continued to be averse to the kind of expenditure which increased preparation would entail. He was also concerned that making preparations of that kind might have such an effect on the minds of ministers in France and Spain as to bring war nearer. Then, as time passed and the difficulty of compelling the rebellious colonists to return to their allegiance became increasingly apparent, the government's attention was understandably focused on the commitment that must be made to the operations in North America. When the colonists took up arms against the mother country, the British government had seen no alternative but to take all necessary steps to suppress the rebellion and restore the authority of the Crown. In doing so, it saw the necessary operations in the light of a police action, requiring the use of military force; the naval component was wholly subordinate to this, consisting of logistical support to the army and the blockade of the American coast. As a result, the ministry seriously underestimated the threat that the Americans would pose at sea. It was a surprising misjudgement; not only could the Americans call on many of the thousands of their seamen who had served with the Royal Navy in the Seven Years War, but the colonies had a well-developed shipbuilding industry; it has been estimated that they had provided nearly a third of the ships in the British merchant marine. The strong and continuing maritime tradition was based not only on fishing and trade, but also on piracy, smuggling and privateering.

The steady increase in the number of smaller warships required for operations in North America gradually brought home to the Admiralty, and to the Cabinet, that the war did indeed have a much more substantial naval component than had been realised. This did not require a general mobilisation, but it drew away from home waters many of the frigates and smaller vessels that would be needed to support a fleet in a European war. The Admiralty's response to this problem was not immediate; it has been pointed out that in the first two years of the Seven Years War 42 new frigates had been ordered, but that in the period 1775 to 1778 only nine new frigates were built.[5] The commitment of so many smaller vessels to North America meant that when the Americans began increasingly to conduct an assault on British maritime trade in European waters, the navy was hard pressed to provide the necessary protection.

Nor had it proved possible effectively to interdict the supply of arms and munitions to the rebels from neutral ports in Europe. British warships were obliged to go carefully in seizing French ships suspected of carrying munitions to America for fear of precipitating war with France. For this reason, the Admiralty was perpetually on the horns of a dilemma, as Sandwich explained in a letter to Captain Digby who was to cruise in the Bay of Biscay:

5 David Syrett, *The Royal Navy in European Waters during the American Revolutionary War* (Columbia SC: University of South Carolina, 1998), p.3.

> You will be aware that bringing in a French ship upon suspicions that appear not well grounded afterwards may draw us into a war, which in our present circumstances ought by all means to be avoided; but the intercepting these large supplies that are intended for the rebels is of so much consequence that some risk must be run for so important an object. However, I have entire dependence on you not to involve us in difficulties with France unless you are convinced you are upon good grounds.[6]

Digby replied to reassure Sandwich that he strongly felt the delicacy of the business he was engaged with.

American privateering in European waters increased substantially during the closing months of 1776 and into 1777, when they were joined by American warships. Insurance rates for British merchant shipping rose sharply, and the want of sufficient small fast warships to escort convoys and to catch privateers began seriously to be felt. In October 1776 Garnier reported to Vergennes from the French embassy in London that it was estimated there that American privateers had already cost British merchant shipping £600,000 during the year:

> What is certain is that the government does not know what to do to protect its transports everywhere and also the national commerce, for which it has however great interest in not raising a clamour. Since almost all the frigates and corvettes are already at sea for this purpose, the British are of necessity beginning to use ships of the line, although they are less appropriate for this kind of service.[7]

Among those commanding a ship of the line on this service, Captain John Jervis, having returned in the *Foudroyant*, 80, from a cruise in the Bay of Biscay, wrote to Philip Stephens to describe a typical encounter. He had met with La Motte-Picquet's squadron of three ships of the line and a corvette. Civilities were exchanged; but Jervis reported of La Motte-Picquet that 'during that whole day, and part of the night, he stuck close to us, tacking and altering his course as we did'.[8] Incidents of this kind were a commonplace; it was a very combustible situation and called for a good deal of restraint and common sense on the part of the French and British commanders concerned.

The effect of American privateering activity on the coasting trade was particularly serious; a letter from Dublin in July 1777 complained: 'Our trade with Waterford, Cork, Belfast and Derry, is entirely at a stand, in consequence of the

6 Barnes and Owen (eds), *Private Papers of John, Earl of Sandwich*, Vol.I, p.254.
7 Clark and Morgan (eds), *Naval Documents of the American Revolution*, Vol.VII, p.698.
8 Clark and Morgan (eds), *Naval Documents of the American Revolution*, Vol.IX, p.464.

swarms of American privateers which infest our coast'.[9] Sandwich was obliged to refuse requests that men of war should be stationed in every port, since even if such were available it would tie them up at a time when there were so many urgent duties required of them. In some ports, though, sloops and cutters were so stationed, while others patrolled off French and Spanish ports.

By the middle of 1777 the urgent need for more smaller warships in particular was belatedly recognised, and money was made available to order new sloops and frigates, and to charter armed vessels for convoy protection. The convoy system itself for international trade was greatly enlarged, and in July the Admiralty began to plan a comprehensive system of convoys to protect the coastal trade as well.[10] By then, the forces employed were considerable. In the autumn of 1777, the cruisers regularly patrolling the Bay of Biscay were supplemented by small squadrons of ships of the line, which put to sea in response to intelligence reports received. Digby had sailed with four ships of the line and a frigate in November with the object of catching a number of rebel ships reported as preparing to put to sea. After his return, Captain Samuel Hood with four ships of the line took his place, sailing on Christmas Day 1777. He too had been ordered to proceed with great caution in order to avoid creating a major incident by a 'wanton detention'. However, he reported on his return that this had not arisen: 'I had no opportunity of exercising my judgment and discretion, having seen but three French ships on my cruise, two of which were frigates named the *Belle Poul* [sic] and *Zephyr*, and not more than six sail upon the whole, which I thought very extraordinary'.[11]

In addition to Jervis, Hood and Digby, many other officers, who would in due course take high rank in the navy in the coming war, commanded ships engaged in this difficult service off the French coast. These included Barrington, Hyde Parker, Rowley, Thomas Graves and Hughes. The Royal Navy was not lacking in men of real ability, although at the start of the war most did not have the seniority to be considered for the command of major fleets.

It has been said that the Navy's unpreparedness for a major naval war in 1777-1778 arose not so much from underfunding as from a failure promptly to mobilise the ships of the line in response to the French challenge.[12] This is only partially true; but it is the reason for the delay in ordering full mobilisation that is significant, and this was most certainly due to financial restraint. North and the members of his Cabinet were extremely cost conscious, and desired to limit expenditure where they could. Sandwich had been facing resistance from his colleagues to his call for additional mobilisation for a considerable time. In the summer of 1776, he persuaded a reluctant Cabinet to agree to an increase in the number of guard

9 Clark and Morgan (eds), *Naval Documents of the American Revolution*, Vol.IX, p.475.

10 Syrett, *European Waters*, p.9.

11 Barnes and Owen (eds), *Private Papers of John, Earl of Sandwich*, Vol.I, p.263.

12 Syrett, *European Waters*, p.11.

ships, but his request to bring forward another 12 ships of the line was refused. On 21 July, he told North that he had intelligence of a most serious nature:

> I think the last letters from Lord Stormont mentioned that 23 ships of the line are preparing at Brest, and seven at Toulon; the Spanish have at least 10 sail of the line in commission and many more in readiness to be commissioned; and I own I dread the consequences, and cannot help thinking we shall have much to answer for, if they are allowed to have a fleet of 50 sail in Europe ready to receive men, when we shall not have half that number in the same degree of preparation.[13]

Receiving a reply from North accepting that the situation did call for urgent discussion, Sandwich followed up his letter with another to North that same day, writing that 'if they have a fleet ready for service double to ours, their advantages and our danger will be such that I tremble to think of it'. If the French went on preparing their ships for receiving men and putting in hand other steps to make their fleet ready, 'they may have a fleet at sea much superior to anything we can bring against them (especially when joined by the Spaniards) for a considerable time, and if they really mean anything hostile to this country may attack us when we can resist them only with an inferior force'.[14] He could hardly have put it more plainly, and this time the Cabinet gave way, and approved the bringing forward of the additional 12 ships of the line.

On 31 October 1776 Sandwich, during the debate on the Address following the King's Speech, told the House of Lords that the assertion that Britain was left in a defenceless state at home as a result of the navy's commitments in America was ill founded: Britain had a naval force at that instant ready for sea, fully sufficient for her defence and protection. He added that Britain had the 'most ample assurances' from the courts concerned of their pacific and friendly disposition. He went on to say that if it should turn out otherwise, he was determined that the kingdom should be prepared for any event that might happen. On the same day North delivered a similar message when speaking in the House of Commons, observing that the armament going on in France which had been so 'mightily magnified' was a small one, consisting of six ships of the line and four frigates. These preparations did not, he said, import anything directly hostile, and 'the assurances of their pacific disposition were as strong as words could make them'.[15] Whether North really believed in those assurances is an open question; if he did, he was gullible in the extreme, believing what he wanted to believe. If he did not, and was affecting to do so to justify his reluctance to make available the additional resources that

13 Barnes and Owen (eds), *Private Papers of John, Earl of Sandwich*, Vol.I, pp.213-214.

14 Barnes and Owen (eds), *Private Papers of John, Earl of Sandwich*, Vol.I, pp.215-216.

15 Clark and Morgan (eds), *Naval Documents of the American Revolution*, Vol.VII, pp.718-720.

would be needed for an immediate full mobilisation, he was delinquent. It seems doubtful that Sandwich, at any rate, would have believed the assurances, and was merely following North's line.

In fact, before the end of 1776, Sandwich's constant pressure to increase the Royal Navy's preparedness had achieved a not inconsiderable result. By 1 December there had been a steady increase in manpower to a total of 45,591, which as David Syrett points out, was 'a major step towards full mobilisation'.[16] That autumn, Sandwich was writing to Howe to reassure him that he would provide him with whatever reinforcement was necessary in North America. He added, though, that 'the conduct of France and Spain is so mysterious that it is impossible to say what demands we may have for line of battleships in the course of the winter'. Two months later, he was again making much the same point to Howe: 'It is much to be wished no line of battleships be wanted in America, for such is the state of things now in Europe that, in my opinion, our safety depends upon our having a powerful fleet at home ready for service'.[17]

One of the most severe critics of the conduct of the policy conducted by the government at this time, and of Sandwich in particular, has been Sir John Knox Laughton, who did not conceal his distaste for the democratic process, writing in his introduction to *The Barham Papers:*

> One of the doubtful advantages of that system of party government, which its admirers claim as the palladium of our political liberties, is that – whichever party may be in office – the Treasury is unwilling to spend money on our armaments, knowing that, at the next election, it will be denounced as a flock of vultures who have been battening on the very vitals of the poor... During the autumn of 1777 the ministry had been warned, not only by neutral members but by the opposition, that the house of Bourbon was only waiting for an opportunity to take the part of the revolted colonists. But timely preparations would have cost money, and might have seemed to invite a war.[18]

Nevertheless, even Laughton conceded that when push came to shove in 1778, 'by the beginning of May a considerable fleet had been got together,' although he did not give the Admiralty any credit for this.

Sandwich continued his struggle for additional mobilisation. In March 1777 his concern was sharpened by his being obliged to dispatch further ships to join Howe in North America without these being replaced in home waters. At this time, he calculated that, after deducting four more under orders to sail to Howe, Britain

16 Syrett, *European Waters*, p.15.

17 Barnes and Owen (eds), *Private Papers of John, Earl of Sandwich*, Vol.I, p.170.

18 Laughton (ed.), *Barham Papers*, Vol.I, pp.xxv-xxvi.

had 32 of the line compared to 49 French and Spanish. If anything, the situation was getting worse.[19]

Though Sandwich was in this way consistently warning the Cabinet of the serious and growing threat, he was limited by the need to display in public a firm solidarity with his colleagues; he could do no more than hint at disagreement:

> His Lordship supposes that I said early in the last session, that I would undertake, at all times to have a naval force equal to cope with, or superior to, any which the united efforts of the House of Bourbon would be able to bring against us. I confess that these amount pretty nearly to my words … I am still of the same opinion, that we ought; nor do I hold myself responsible, as an official man, that we have not. I act merely ministerially, under the direction of His Majesty's councils, and can never therefore be deemed farther responsible, or bound by any engagement, than so far as I am enabled to perform it.[20]

Throughout the period 1775-1777 the tension between Sandwich, on the one hand, and North and the rest of the Cabinet on the other, had been steadily increasing. At no time, though, does Sandwich appear ever to have suggested that he might make it a resignation issue. The urgency of the First Lord's advice sharpened with the continuing lack of success in America. North, however, remained insistent on minimising expenditure, on financial grounds and because of the difficulty of obtaining Parliamentary approval. In addition, he wished nothing to be done that might threaten the peace.

A number of historians have held Sandwich to blame for the failure to mobilise, but the evidence clearly shows that it was North's reluctance to supply the necessary funds that prevented it. Even so, it would be wrong to suggest that the navy was completely unprepared. Certainly, a large number of vessels had been sent to operate in North America; but in July 1777 the *London Chronicle* was able to publish a list of no less than 28 ships of the line said to be cruising in the Channel.[21] One of the principal problems the Admiralty was facing continued to be that of manpower, and particularly the lack of experienced and reliable seamen. As early as October 1776, Philip Stephens had been writing to Howe to ask him to send back to England petty officers from the ships under his command in North America. At this time steps were being taken to increase the complement of the guard ships in the Channel so that they should be in constant readiness for the sea.

19 Nicholas Tracy, *Navies, Deterrence and American Independence* (Vancouver: University of British Columbia Press, 1988), p.143.

20 Rodger, *Insatiable Earl*, p.224.

21 Clark and Morgan (eds), *Naval Documents of the American Revolution*, Vol.IX, p.508.

Fundamentally, Lord North was no war leader, as he himself recognised. Writing to the King in 1778 (in the third person) not long after war with France had broken out, he observed:

> In critical times it is necessary that there should be one directing minister, who shall plan the whole of the operations of government, and control all the other departments of administration, so far as to make them cooperate zealously and actively with his designs even though contrary to their own. Lord North… is certainly not capable of being such a minister as he has described.[22]

It was a sound analysis of what was required to conduct a war successfully. North made plain that he perfectly understood his limitations. They continued to prevent him from taking effective control of his Cabinet to such an extent that in the following year Sandwich felt obliged to write to him to point out the consequences of his failing to do so: 'Will your lordship in this place allow me to lament the state of our Cabinet meetings, and to point out to you how absolutely necessary it is that you should take the lead among us, and not suffer any question to be agitated there that is not decided and carried into execution'.[23] The problem was that North, though an excellent political manager, and a careful financial administrator, was even in peacetime an ineffectual leader of his Cabinet. His awareness of this did not help him to exert the control for which Sandwich called.

Although he continued to display a calm assurance in public, it was impossible, by the summer of 1777, for Sandwich not to be profoundly concerned about the readiness of the navy for a war that he and others could see was becoming more and more likely. On 3 August he prepared a paper for North on its current state of preparation:

> I think it my duty at this crisis to lay before your Lordship the state of our naval force now ready for service, and to point out the necessity of immediately commissioning at least an equal number of line of battleships to replace any that may be sent away from Europe. I lay down as a maxim that England ought for her own security to have a superior force in readiness at home to anything that France and Spain united have in readiness on their side. The state of our fleet at home consists at this time in 36 ships of the line in commission and fit for service, but some men (particularly marines) are wanting to make them all complete to their establishment; and as some of these ships must always be in harbour cleaning, I should

22 Rodger, *The Command of the Ocean*, p.352.
23 Rodger, *Insatiable Earl*, p.219.

> think that upon a sudden emergency we should not be able to get more than 30 of them at once to sea.[24]

In reiterating his previous advice that if ships of the line were to be sent to America, they should at once be replaced in home waters, he emphasised that 'on the first suspicion of any evil intention on the part of France, it is obligatory on us instantly to send very considerable reinforcements to Lord Howe'. Ever since the outbreak of fighting in North America, when his ships were engaged in active operations there, Sandwich had been much more concerned with the situation that might develop in European waters.

On 25 August 1777, Palliser prepared a memorandum assessing the actual strength of the fleet in home waters. 36 ships of the line were in commission, on various duties; some of these had been ordered in for docking, while 17 were cruising on different stations. Six more ships of the line were ready to receive men. Ominously, there were only 12 frigates in commission there, two of which were under orders for America. Eleven more would be launched in the following four months. This meant, he pointed out, that a maximum of 21 would be at home, many of which would be in hand docking and repairing. Twenty more might be launched in 1778. In the event of war, there might be none immediately available to accompany the fleet. As for manning, he estimated that immediately some 12,300 men were required, 4,000 of which were to complete the complements of the ships in commission, and 3,550 to man six more ships of the line and 2,164 for the 11 new frigates.[25] Next day Sandwich wrote to North to point out that France appeared to have 44 in commission, and Spain a further 20. He ended his note with a pointed question: 'Are we now safe at home without a further armament?'

The news of Saratoga did not arrive until the middle of December, though indications had already been received of Burgoyne's lack of success. It was on 7 December that, in response to a request at a meeting of the Cabinet, Sandwich set out his thoughts on the naval war and the way it should thereafter be conducted. In this paper he set out in detail his opinion as to the strategy to be followed in America. Howe's principal objective should be to block up the American ports; at the request of Germain, he added that Howe should also cooperate with the army in attempting to seize those ports, while also destroying American shipping and generally attacking the American coasts. The key passage in his paper, though, addressed the state of the navy at home. There were, he said, 42 ships of the line in commission and ready for service; he feared that France and Spain had at least an equal number in Europe. It would take 12 months to get 25 more ships of the line ready for sea; seven were now ready to receive men, and if commissioned would be ready for sea in the spring. He thought that if these seven were at

24 Barnes and Owen (eds), *Private Papers of John, Earl of Sandwich*, Vol.I, p.236.

25 Barnes and Owen (eds), *Private Papers of John, Earl of Sandwich*, Vol.I, pp.242-244,

once taken in hand, they could be commissioned in two months. Sandwich's paper concluded that 'if we are certain that France and Spain will not take advantage of our distresses, our force at home is more than sufficient, and the public should not be burdened with that enormous expense;' on the other hand if it was to be concluded that 'they are at the bottom our inveterate enemies and are only waiting for the favourable moment to strike, then every precaution should be taken, and in particular six of the ships of the line ready to receive men should be commissioned and another six should be made ready'.[26]

Yet there was really no longer any room for serious doubt of the true situation. On 7 January Stormont reported from Paris that a treaty had been signed with the Americans. This was not yet the case, but all the indications were that this was the direction of French policy. North clung to the hope that a concession to the Americans that no further taxes would be collected from them by Parliament would induce them to make peace with Britain, but there was no sound reason for believing in the possibility.

On 20 February Stormont wrote that the French were carrying on their naval preparations 'with the utmost diligence and vigour':

> *La Bretagne*, now at Brest, a first rate man-of-war of 110 guns and reckoned one of the finest ships in the French navy, is put in commission. Great numbers of men are constantly at work building new ships and arming and equipping every ship that is fit for service. The intelligence I had some time ago, of orders sent to the Toulon squadron to join that at Brest, has been confirmed to me from several quarters.[27]

This prompted Sandwich to point out to North that if France was commissioning a ship of 110 guns, it was time to commission the *Victory* and every ship of the line that could be made fit for service. North at last reluctantly conceded at the beginning of March that preparations should go forward 'with great diligence'. Responding to this, and to the suggestion that the necessary preparations should be discussed over dinner on 7 March, Sandwich wrote to North to tell him of the size of the potential enemy forces:

> By the accounts this day received from France, it appears that the Duc de Chartres is actually at Brest taking upon him the command of the fleet, which consists of 21 ships of the line and 35 frigates; and that there are at Toulon 12 of the line and 13 frigates, making in all 33 of the line and 48 frigates in commission and ready for service. Spain has also, I believe, 32

26 Barnes and Owen (eds), *Private Papers of John, Earl of Sandwich*, Vol.I, pp.334-335.
27 Barnes and Owen (eds), *Private Papers of John, Earl of Sandwich*, Vol.I, pp.343-344.

> of the line and eight frigates, so that the House of Bourbon have in Europe an actual force of 65 of the line.[28]

Against this, Britain could only look to 41 ships of the line as immediately ready for sea, with nine others in preparation. The First Lord's immediate concern was that British trade would be at the enemy's mercy. He added that, if the Duc de Chartres was already at Brest, 'should not Admiral Keppel be at Portsmouth?'

Then, on 13 March, came the formal news of the Franco American alliance, and the die was cast. At a meeting of the Cabinet on 14 March it was agreed to recall Stormont and order a general mobilisation. Immediately, Howe was to send a substantial force of ships and troops south for the defence of the Leeward Islands. A pre-emptive strike against the French island of St Lucia, in respect of which Mulgrave had already submitted a plan to Sandwich, was accepted by the Cabinet. Howe was to send back home 10 frigates and six sloops, and Keppel was ordered to hoist his flag immediately. Two days later the Navy Board was directed to order the dockyards 'to be employed as much extra on all ships fitting, repairing, or building, as they can with advantage to forward the service', recruiting as many additional workmen as could be so engaged.[29] Ships under construction would be completed without waiting for them to be seasoned.

At their next meeting on 18 March, the Cabinet revised upwards the force which Howe was to send to the Leeward Islands. The evacuation of Philadelphia was ordered, while if the peace commissioners to be sent to New York found that they could achieve nothing, the commander-in-chief there should be prepared if he thought it necessary to evacuate the city itself. The frigates (now increased to 14 in number) and sloops to be sent back immediately to England by Howe were specified in detail. Secret instructions about the proposed attack on St Lucia went to Lieutenant General Sir Henry Clinton, commander in chief in North America, on 21 March. After a long period of paralysis on the part of the government, things were moving fast, but it would now be urgently necessary to determine the strategy to be adopted in the coming war against France and, probably, Spain.

28 Barnes and Owen (eds), *Private Papers of John, Earl of Sandwich*, Vol.I, p.349.
29 Barnes and Owen (eds), *Private Papers of John, Earl of Sandwich*, Vol.II, p 363.

8

War Strategy: Britain

Julian Corbett defined maritime strategy as meaning the principles governing a war in which the sea is a decisive factor:

> Naval strategy is but that part of it which determines the movements of the fleet when maritime strategy has determined what part the fleet must play in relation to the action of the land forces; for it scarcely needs saying that it is almost impossible that a war can be decided by naval action alone. Unaided, naval pressure can only work by a process of exhaustion. Its effects must always be slow, and so galling both to our own commercial community and to neutrals, that the tendency is always to accept terms of peace that are far from conclusive.[1]

In 1778 the British Cabinet found it difficult to apply any particular principles, because it found itself in what was, for Britain, a uniquely difficult position, in which it was obliged to meet a number of pressing dangers and to do so with inadequate resources. It was difficult to devise a coherent war plan because Britain's principal political objects were defensive in nature. One of these was the retention of the American colonies, and this was already being seen as possibly unattainable. The other principal object consisted of little more than defeating any attempt to invade the British Isles. Beyond this, it was a matter of seizing opportunities overseas as and when they arose. Even the usual object of naval strategy, to obtain and keep command of the sea, was in 1778 difficult to plan for, since Britain was for once facing a potentially much superior enemy. At best, all that could be hoped for was to achieve local, and temporary, command of the sea.

Geography, of course, played a crucial part in determining the strategic options available to Britain and France. In home waters, the location of the principal naval bases gave the British a considerable advantage. Their three main bases were at Portsmouth, Plymouth and Chatham, which meant that British fleets could be

1 Julian S Corbett, *Some Principles of Maritime Strategy* (London: Longmans Green & Co, 1911), p.15.

assembled there without being exposed to enemy action. Their other principal base was Gibraltar. The French fleet in Europe was based at Brest and Toulon, with subsidiary ports on the Bay of Biscay at Rochefort and Lorient. When Spain joined the war, France would also have access to her principal home ports at Cadiz and Cartagena. Britain could in theory station a fleet at Gibraltar to prevent the French uniting their fleets at either Brest or Toulon. Experience in past wars had also shown that it was possible, though very difficult, to blockade Brest, using the Channel ports and additional anchorages at Falmouth and Torbay.[2] The despatch of squadrons to serve in distant waters was something that the British could usually count on being able to do without interference, whereas to do so the French, on the other hand, would have to evade any British forces watching their ports.

During the Falklands crisis of 1770, William Pitt the Elder, Earl of Chatham, speaking in the House of Lords, outlined the proper strategy for the British navy in a war with France and Spain:

> The first great and acknowledged object of naval defence in the country, is to maintain such a superior naval force at home, that even the united fleets of France and Spain may never be masters of the Channel ... The second naval object with an English minister should be to maintain at all times a powerful western squadron. In the profoundest peace it should be respectable; in war it should be formidable. Without it, the colonies, the commerce, the navigation of Great Britain lie at the mercy of the House of Bourbon. The third object, indispensable as I conceive, in the distribution of our navy, is to maintain such a force in the Bay of Gibraltar as may be sufficient to cover that garrison, to watch the motions of the Spaniards, and to keep open the communication with Minorca.[3]

As has been previously noted, the concept of maintaining a powerful Western Squadron at the entrance to the Channel had been fundamental to British naval thinking for very many years. In fact, as G.S. Graham has pointed out, there was a precedent as early as the previous century, when in 1673 Charles II stationed cruisers to protect overseas trade in the Channel, and subsequently in the reigns of William III and Queen Anne a Western or Soundings Squadron was stationed there for the same purpose.[4]

In the War of the Austrian Succession, Vernon's maintenance of a strong Western Squadron in 1745 was particularly effective. It was his policy to station a powerful squadron of ships of the line at the western entrance to the Channel,

2 James, *The British Navy in Adversity*, p.81.
3 Quoted in G.J. Marcus, *A Naval History of England* (Boston: Little Brown & Co, 1961), Vol.I, p.422.
4 G.S. Graham, *Empire of the North Atlantic* (Toronto: University of Toronto Press, 1966), p.151n.

together with a smaller force under his own command in the Downs. Vernon's concept was based on historical precedent, as he explained:

> Look back to the latter end of the reign of Queen Anne, when we had well conducted Western Squadrons under the direction of experienced admirals, with a proper latitude in their orders, and it will be found that the trade was well protected by them, the enemy's privateers suppressed, and some detached to proper stations that distressed the enemy's trade at the same time; and were in the best stations with the main body, for protecting all these Kingdoms from invasions.[5]

Anson, given a sufficient fleet to constitute a strong Western Squadron in the later stages of the war, used it effectively, not least because he was largely given a free hand, and with it he won the decisive Battle of Cape Finisterre on 3 May1747. Later that year Hawke, who succeeded him in command of the Western Squadron, won another decisive victory there. In the Seven Years War, the strategy of employing a powerful Western Squadron successfully achieved the purposes so clearly outlined by Pitt in 1770. It culminated in the shattering victory of Quiberon Bay on 20 November 1759, when Hawke, defying appalling weather conditions, led the British fleet to crush the French under Conflans and thereby destroyed all possibility of an invasion of England.

Central to any effort to maintain control of the English Channel was the requirement effectively to watch the French ports on the Bay of Biscay, and in particular Brest. There was never any doubt of the need for this, but the key question was how this was to be managed. On the one hand it might be left to frigates patrolling off the French ports, which would be reinforced in case of need by all or part of the Channel Fleet. Alternatively, a close blockade could be maintained by the fleet itself, operating at sea continuously in conjunction with an inshore squadron. This would be a major strategic commitment, which might have the effect of limiting the forces that might be detached for operation in distant waters, and certainly would expose the ships of the line to the cumulative effect of damage, especially to masts and rigging, in cruising in all weathers. In the Seven Years War, the maintenance of an effective guard on French ports was by means of a distant blockade based on regular reliefs. This strategy was enunciated in 1756, in a passage which Graham considers was probably written by Anson:

> Our colonies are so numerous and so extensive that to keep a naval force at each equal to the united force of France would be impracticable with double our navy. The best defence therefore for our colonies as well as our coasts is to have such a squadron always to the westward as may in all

5 Marcus, *Naval History of England*, Vol.I, pp.267-268.

> probability either keep the French in port or give them battle with advantage if they come out.[6]

A strategy of blockade not only exposed the ships involved to a great deal of wear and tear; it was also expensive in human terms, though its cost in this respect has never been calculated. Keeping the fleet fully manned was a perpetual source of anxiety to the Admiralty. One of the first steps taken at the series of Cabinet meetings which followed the French announcement of their American alliance was to resort to the brutal and unpopular system of impressment. This was the only effective means by which sufficient seamen could be raised swiftly in a crisis. Landsmen might volunteer in reasonable numbers, while marines were permanently enrolled (though many were serving in America) but obtaining the experienced seamen essential to the fitting out of vessels for sea was a different matter:

> Thoroughbred seamen were reluctant to serve in the navy in time of war because they could always count on far higher pay in merchant ships, and on better chances of prize money in privateers. The only ways to procure them in sufficient numbers were by means of impressment, an embargo on merchant shipping, and loudly advertised bounties; and those the government hesitated to employ until the last moment lest it should seem an act of aggression and spoil the chances of peace.[7]

The delay in taking this step had already hampered the preparation of the fleet, and it would be some time before ships could approach their full complement. The Royal Navy could look with envy at the situation in France, where the *Inscription Maritime* gave the government a much swifter and more efficient means of manning the fleet.

The maintenance of a Western Squadron, therefore, could serve both defensive and offensive purposes, but at all times the need to protect British trade and to seize any opportunity of damaging enemy trade was a major element in its employment. Not only was it a crucial policy objective to ensure the security of both inbound and outbound convoys; the existence of a strong force at the entrance to the Channel enabled Britain to threaten not only French trade but also military convoys. It has been estimated that 30 percent of France's imports and 35 percent of her export trade was destined for the West Indies. The trade routes followed by Britain and France were largely determined by the prevailing winds. Westbound ships clearing from British ports worked their way south to the latitude of Madeira in order to pick up the trade winds. Ships bound for the East Indies, via the Cape, took the same course for the first part of the voyage. They were thus in a danger

6 Quoted Admiral Sir H. Richmond, *National Policy and Naval Strength* (London: Longmans, 1928), p.346.
7 Barnes and Owen (eds), *Private Papers of John, Earl of Sandwich*, Vol.II, pp.6-7.

zone until well clear of the latitude of Gibraltar, and their safety could only be assured by the adoption of a convoy and escort system. During the eighteenth century, trade with their respective overseas possessions was of vital importance to Great Britain, France, Spain and Holland.[8]

Thus, the requirement to defend British trade was an ever-present element of British naval strategy. No government could afford to allow that trade to be halted or seriously damaged, whether by enemy privateers or by regular naval forces. As the American war proceeded, as has been seen, the growing effectiveness of American privateers, and subsequently also warships, was a serious problem, and whatever strategic objectives were adopted, the need to manage and protect a convoy system was an essential part of the navy's task.

In terms of vital defensive objectives, the protection of the British Isles from invasion was all-important. When it came to it, the loss of America, or India, or even the West Indies, would not be an absolutely fatal blow to Britain; but a successful invasion certainly would. That this was so had been understood on both sides of the Channel for centuries, which is why, in the eighteenth century, the French considered a multitude of plans for a major invasion. The British navy's obligation to protect the nation's coasts required the retention of a substantial force at all times in home waters, but it could never completely guarantee their security, and the French, if they were able to slip past the British squadrons watching their ports, could always manage to reach peripheral coasts in the west and the north.[9] However, such operations could never be decisive; for the French, a war winning invasion strategy required a major landing in the south of England. For that, the French fleet must gain command of the Channel in order to protect the invasion fleet. The French must also overcome the difficulty presented by their lack of any one port sufficiently large to accommodate such a fleet, and there was little hope of effecting a descent on the British coast by surprise, due to the time taken for the invasion force to leave harbour.

With a French war obviously looming, the Cabinet had begun to look at key strategic issues following receipt of the news of Saratoga, on 18 December 1777. Both Palliser and Mulgrave attended the meeting to answer a number of pertinent questions as to what Britain could or should now do. The Cabinet already had before it Sandwich's paper of 8 December which had been endorsed 'Opinion about the naval war December 8, 1777 sent to Ld North shewing the impropriety of trusting to the promises of France and Spain, and proposing further Armaments'. After dealing with a number of questions about the ongoing situation in North America, Palliser and Mulgrave were asked if the 42 ships of the line then in commission at

8 James, *The British Navy in Adversity*, pp.83-85.

9 J.R. Jones, 'Limitations of British Sea Power in the French Wars, 1689-1815'in J. Black and P. Woodfine (eds), *The British Navy and the Use of Naval Power in the Eighteenth Century* (Leicester: Leicester University Press, 1988), p.43.

home would admit of proper detachments being made for the security of Britain's distant possessions. Their answer was emphatic: 'According to the accounts we have of the force of France and Spain in Europe, it would be unsafe to make detachments from the 42 ships'.[10]

This being the case, the strategic options available to Britain in March 1778 were severely limited. The situation facing the country and its navy was very different from that which had been the case in previous wars. In both the War of the Austrian Succession and the Seven Years War, France had been tied down in a continental war, enabling Britain to detach powerful forces for overseas operations. Now, the situation was effectively reversed; Britain was engaged in a war of increasing complexity, made even more difficult by the fact that it was being fought on the other side of the Atlantic. France, on the other hand, and Spain when and if she joined in, had no such other commitments. Plainly, therefore, Britain's strategy must be defensive. Pitt's prescription of the proper objectives of the Royal Navy did not make allowance for an extensive American commitment; although Sandwich and the Cabinet recognised that it was necessary to wind it down in the new situation, the demands it made were still going to be substantial, and the deployment of naval forces in North America interlocked with the requirement to undertake operations in the West Indies. Thus, the strategy that was evolved by the Cabinet in their meetings of March 1778 recognised Britain's limited room for manoeuvre.

The basis of the strategy now adopted by the Cabinet was a paper written by Lord Amherst, who on 19 March was effectively appointed as commander-in-chief of the army (though not actually given that title) with a seat in the Cabinet. This was apparently written as a draft of the instructions to be sent to Howe, and as such was slightly revised by Sandwich:

> The object of the war being now changed and the contest in America being a secondary consideration, our principal object must be distressing France and defending and securing our own possessions against their hostile Attempts to carry such measures into execution, the sending the Force mentioned in your instructions – for reducing and taking possession of Ste Lucia and securing the West India Islands it is hoped you will find a sufficient number of ships for effecting that very essential service. That if all the ships pointed out in our instructions cannot be assembled in time, or shall not be in proper condition for executing this important service, your Lordship will detach such a number from your fleet as you shall think adequate to the intended purpose.[11]

10 Barnes and Owen (eds), *Private Papers of John, Earl of Sandwich*, Vol.I, pp.337-339.
11 Barnes and Owen (eds), *Private Papers of John, Earl of Sandwich*, Vol.I, p.365.

Amherst was a man of good sense, integrity and a capacity to get on well with his subordinate commanders, and he impressed North with his administrative abilities. The Prime Minister considered him 'the most attentive to public economy of any military that I ever knew'. He was, though, not generally at ease with politicians, and became increasingly taciturn in his manner of expressing the advice which he gave.[12]

One issue very much in the mind of the Admiralty was the question of the French fleet fitting out in Toulon. Its purpose was unclear; if it was intended for North America it would completely alter the strategic situation at sea there; on the other hand, as had been suggested, its destination might be Brest, there to unite with the substantial fleet at anchor there. Alternatively, it was also possible that it was destined for India or the West Indies.

The urgent issue considered at the meeting of the Cabinet held on 6 April, therefore, was that of what action to take in respect of the Toulon fleet. Keppel, who had by now hoisted his flag at Portsmouth, supported Sandwich's position, which was that for the present there should be no large detachments from the Channel Fleet. This had been the basis of the First Lord's advice to the March meetings of the Cabinet, but to allow the Toulon fleet to proceed on its way unhindered would give the French the strategic initiative. Intelligence reports showed 12 ships of the line at Toulon, and at least 21 at Brest; the Spanish, it was estimated, had some 32 in Europe; the potential enemy strength was therefore some 50 percent greater than the British had immediately available.[13] Sandwich had prepared for the meeting a note which he put before the King and the Cabinet in which he made clear how dangerous it would be to divide the naval forces available until these had increased sufficiently:

> It is my opinion that there are not ships enough as yet in readiness to form a squadron fit to meet the Toulon fleet under Monsieur d'Estaing unless we would sacrifice every other intended service to this object, or to send out Admiral Keppel with a proper force to meet Monsieur d'Estaing, which however seems to me a very dangerous measure, as our own coast and Ireland would then be subject to alarm as the Brest fleet would be superior to anything that we shall have ready for sea till Admiral Keppel's return.[14]

If the numbers had not been so unfavourable, the strategic importance of being able to blockade or intercept the Toulon fleet would have been considerable; as it was, there were not the ships available to do so, and it effectively meant the

12 Mackesy, *War for America*, p.181.
13 Syrett, *European Waters*, p.25.
14 Barnes and Owen (eds), *Private Papers of John, Earl of Sandwich*, Vol.II, p.23.

abandonment of the Mediterranean. The Cabinet accepted Sandwich's view. The decision has been held by some historians to have been a serious error; among others, Admiral Mahan called it 'an unpardonable fault'.[15]

A crucially important aspect of the conduct of the naval war in home waters was the relationship between the commander-in-chief of the Channel Fleet and the First Lord. Although politically they were fundamentally opposed, in fact Keppel and Sandwich exchanged collaborative and mutually supportive letters. Keppel was no longer the dashing commander of the Seven Years War. Older, stouter, and much less fit, he approached the task of commanding the Channel Fleet with barely concealed apprehension. He was, however, at this time far from complaining about the state of those of his ships that had been on active service, whatever he may have been much later heard to say in the House of Commons. The editors of Sandwich's papers point out that at this time there was a long and friendly correspondence between Keppel and the First Lord, and there was no suggestion from the admiral that he was not being given all the support which he had a right to expect. Importantly, his letters showed that he was generous both to Palliser, who was to be his third in command, and to Mulgrave, who commanded the *Courageux*, notwithstanding that they were both members of the Board of Admiralty and hence politically aligned against Keppel in his capacity as a member of the opposition.[16]

Keppel did, though, perfectly reasonably complain of the want of frigates, due to the large number that were operating in North America. The failure to launch a large frigate building programme sooner had been a function of the financial stringency imposed on the navy. It had, however, always been a general practice to apply money during peacetime to the construction of ships of the line, which took so long to build, counting on being able to build smaller vessels such as frigates or sloops much more quickly when they were required at the start of a war. Nevertheless, since war with France had existed as a real possibility for so long, and since so many vessels were on service in North America, it was a failure of judgment to have not ordered additional frigates much sooner.

As preparations urgently continued, not all the sentiments expressed at this time were pessimistic; the King was greatly cheered to receive a message from Lord Hawke regretting that his health prevented him from offering his services but which went on to tell him that 'he thought it his duty to assure me that, whatever others might from private views declare, that he is convinced a finer or better officered and equipped fleet never was seen in this kingdom than the present'.[17] The King was pleased to be able to pass this on to Sandwich. He was spending a lot of time with the fleet, visiting first the Medway and then Portsmouth, and was

15 Admiral A.T. Mahan, *The Major Operations of the Navies in the War of American Independence* (London: Sampson Low Marston & Co, 1913), p.79.

16 Barnes and Owen (eds), *Private Papers of John, Earl of Sandwich*, Vol.II, p.4.

17 Barnes and Owen (eds), *Private Papers of John, Earl of Sandwich*, Vol.II, p.24.

pleased with what he saw, telling the First Lord that he knew very well that every effort was being used to fit out the fleet.

On 15 April, Keppel set down his thoughts and anxieties in a note on which Sandwich recorded his answers to the questions raised. It was an instructive exchange, demonstrating the commander-in-chief's lack of self-assurance. Two particularly important questions were posed. First was the issue of how far and in what degree battle was to be offered, if the Channel Fleet consisted of 25 or 30 ships of the line. To this, Sandwich replied that if the superiority of the French fleet was not very apparent, he should be ordered to give them battle. Next was a question of what should be done if the Toulon fleet joined that already in Brest roads. In that case, was the British fleet to remain at sea or to return to port for reinforcements? Sandwich replied: 'If the two fleets are joined and are superior, which will then most likely be the case, Admiral Keppel to return to St Helens for reinforcements which from time to time will be ordered to assemble at that place'.[18] Throughout his paper, Keppel displayed his concerns about meeting a superior French fleet, as well he might, since the fleet under his command represented at that time all the naval defence then available for the British Isles.

There remained a continuing anxiety about the destiny of d'Estaing and his fleet at Toulon. He finally put to sea on 13 April, but it was still not immediately clear where he was bound. His fleet consisted of 12 ships of the line and five frigates. Germain was in no doubt where he was going. As usual looking at the war solely in the context of America, he wrote bitterly on 27 April: 'I never can sufficiently lament the not having sent a fleet to Gibraltar to prevent the Toulon Squadron passing the Straits, the risk of that measure was trifling in comparison to what we may suffer by leaving such a fleet at liberty to attack us in North America, the West Indies or Newfoundland'.[19] He demanded the immediate reinforcement of Howe to prevent the fatal consequences which he said might follow from the French having an avowed superiority at sea upon the coast of North America. Sandwich did not disagree that this was probably d'Estaing's destination; but he still adamantly refused to agree to the making of a substantial detachment from the Channel Fleet, writing to Keppel on 28 April:

> There is every reason in the world to believe that he is bound for Boston, probably with an intention to attack Nova Scotia and Canada, or perhaps to fall upon Lord Howe's fleet and to cut off our army upon the American continent. However, we cannot for certain say where he is going, and therefore our dilemma is very great, particularly as we are not able to make any detachments from home consistent with the security of this island.[20]

18 Barnes and Owen (eds), *Private Papers of John, Earl of Sandwich*, Vol.II, pp.24-27.

19 Syrett, *European Waters*, p.25.

20 Barnes and Owen (eds), *Private Papers of John, Earl of Sandwich*, Vol.II, pp.36-37.

'Charles Henri Cte, d'Estaing, Chevalier des Ordes du Roy, Lieutenant Général de ses Armées, Vice Amiral de France, Né le 24 Novembre 1729'. Engraving by Coulet after the Abbe de Haisne. (Anne S.K. Brown Collection)

The Cabinet met next day to discuss the issue as a matter of urgency. Germain put before it a paper calling for immediate action:

> At least twelve ships should ... pursue and attack them in whatever station they may have taken, and even to follow them to West Indies... The remainder of the Fleet under Admiral Keppel, with the reinforcements preparing to join him, it is presumed will be sufficient for the protection of this country; but in all military operations of importance some risk

> must be run, and it is more meritorious to suffer in vigorous and necessary exertion of our force, than to remain inactive and tamely submit to the loss of detached fleets, armies and distant possessions, which must infallibly draw after it the absolute ruin of Great Britain.[21]

This time Germain's passionate argument prevailed. Even Keppel conceded that if the news of d'Estaing's destination was confirmed, a detachment must be made; and the King wrote to Sandwich on 29 April that 'if that is the case we must strengthen Lord Howe, for should his fleet and the army under his brother be destroyed, no one can answer what confusion it may not occasion at home'.[22] There was concern about the command arrangements to be made for the force to be sent to North America, since if it arrived at Halifax under a junior officer, it would pass under the command of Rear Admiral James Gambier, the senior officer there. No one seems to have had a good opinion of him, and North in particular was unwilling to see him in command. In the light of this generally held view, the command was given to Vice Admiral John Byron with the intention that he should sail at once with the ships to be sent, which he was able to do.

Given the extent to which Britain's naval resources were overstretched at this time, it was inevitable that the strategy to be followed was reactive; the French clearly held the initiative. The one aggressive move planned was the attack on St Lucia, which if successful would give the naval forces defending the British possessions in the West Indies a considerable advantage. Proposing this in March 1778, Mulgrave had suggested that the use of a considerable part of the army in North America in this way, 'at a time when the first operations must be doubtful in the opinion of the world, will have the advantage of secrecy'. St Lucia could, once taken, be easily held. 'And without considering the value of the island, the excellence and advantageous situation of its port, the best in the West Indies and which effectively commands Martinique so as to obstruct their trade and intercept their privateers, points it out as the most desirable acquisition'.[23]

Effectively now facing not only the rebellious colonists and France but also possibly Spain as well, Britain's strategy was one of attrition, at least as far as North America was concerned. There were insufficient forces to attempt both a decisive victory there and to defeat France. For Jonathan Dull there was a basic defect in endeavouring to win a war of attrition, since in both military and naval forces Britain was already gravely overstretched. Furthermore, he suggests, the strategy adopted failed to exploit the opportunities of the changed situation. Once open war with France began, the munitions, financial backing and markets for their trade, on all of which the Americans depended, might be cut off at their source

21 Syrett, *European Waters*, p.27.

22 Barnes and Owen (eds), *Private Papers of John, Earl of Sandwich*, Vol.II p38.

23 Barnes and Owen (eds), *Private Papers of John, Earl of Sandwich*, Vol.I, pp.357-358.

by blockading the French coast: 'Better still, if the French navy could be decisively defeated, Britain could then devote all her naval forces to destruction of American and French commerce'.[24] It is an intriguing theory, but for such a strategy to have succeeded everything would have had to fall right, all the time, and the chances of pulling it off would have been extremely slender.

Apart, therefore, from the attack on St Lucia, the Royal Navy would have to respond to the moves made by the French, which meant that sooner rather than later there would be a crisis in the Channel. In March, neither side was anxious to bring this on; the British fleet was obviously far from ready, while France was waiting to hear what Spain would do.

24 Dull, *French Navy and American Independence*, pp.106-107.

9

War Strategy: France

The strategy to be pursued by France would be determined by the Council of State, of which the key members were the chief minister, the Comte de Maurepas (a past navy minister), Vergennes and Sartine. It was this group that effectively controlled the decision-making, not least because of the youth and inexperience of Louis XVI. The war plans that came before the council for consideration were prepared by Sartine and his able assistant Fleurieu, but it was Vergennes who had the most powerful voice in the council's discussions. Dull described his position:

> With his balance of prudence and audacity, his firm commonsense, and his perpetual emphasis on the diplomatic consequences of military action, Vergennes would become one of the great war leaders of his century. Leaving predominance of place to Maurepas and detailed dispositions to Sartine and Fleurieu, Vergennes became the major director of French war strategy.[1]

From time to time the war minister, Montbarey, took part in decision-making, but the three remaining members of the council did not generally do so.

In order to seek a decisive victory, France would in this war have two principal options. One was to endeavour to repeat the attempt to invade the south coast of England, the strategy that in the end had led nowhere during the Seven Years War. It meant facing the Royal Navy in its home waters, close to its main bases, while France did not have the ports on the English Channel that could easily launch an invasion or, indeed, provide a base for the French battle fleet. An invasion plan must, in any case, be based on a united effort by France and Spain, and while Vergennes waited for the Spanish to make their position clear it was already apparent that no scheme of invasion could in any event be put in hand before 1779.

As with any war leader, Vergennes sought to win the war as quickly as possible, but he did not seek to crush Britain absolutely, since such a colossal shift in the

1 Dull, *French Navy and American Independence*, pp.108-109.

balance of power in Europe risked transferring to France the jealousy and suspicion aroused by the huge successes achieved by Britain in recent wars. He wished only to weaken, not destroy her, writing: 'Even if I could destroy England, I would abstain from doing so, as from the wildest folly; but there is nothing I would not do to make her alter that jealous policy which, equally harmful to her and to ourselves, is at bottom nothing but trickery'.[2]

Vergennes's instinct, therefore, was to win the war if he could by striking at Britain's trade and her colonies rather than to seek to win a decisive battle at sea as a precursor to the invasion of the British Isles. His preference was to adopt the war plan put forward by the Navy Ministry, where it was believed that a decisive victory which would destroy or fatally damage the British fleet was probably not possible. Rather than stake everything on an invasion, this strategy, which was devised by Fleurieu, aimed at keeping Britain's attention focused on home waters while striking at her elsewhere to achieve the maximum economic effect.

Vergennes was a man of his time. Eighteenth-century conflicts were essentially limited wars, and he approached the problem of defeating Britain with that in his mind. It was his belief that it was neither necessary nor desirable to launch an invasion of Britain. Since his object was merely to use the opportunity provided by the uprising of the Americans to weaken Britain, and to humiliate her in the way in which France had been humiliated at the end of the Seven Years War, he could reasonably hope that in the very different circumstances in which the two nations now met in conflict, Britain's resources might be so overstretched that she would be compelled to make peace. At that time France would then be able to dictate the terms on which the war could be ended.

A very different view of the strategy that France should follow was taken by *Maréchal* de Broglie. He was to be in command of the large force of troops that would be assembled in Normandy in order to concentrate British attention on the possibility of invasion, and thus ensure that the Channel Fleet was maintained at full strength and pinned down in home waters. De Broglie was a firm believer in the project of invading Britain, but Vergennes remained, in the spring of 1778, unpersuaded. In any case, he appears not to have been on good terms with de Broglie.[3]

Throughout the year, Vergennes remained convinced of the feasibility of the indirect route to victory, writing to Montmorin in November: 'It is at least as important to beat the English in the economic field as on the battlefield'. He repeated this view in the following February: 'If we succeed only in interrupting Britain's trade, you may depend on it that the resultant alarm and despondency will be as great as if we had landed in some part of the island'.[4]

2 A. Temple Patterson, *The Other Armada* (Manchester: Manchester University Press, 1960), pp.37-38.

3 Patterson, *The Other Armada*, p.39.

4 Patterson, *The Other Armada*, p.38.

The strategy to be adopted in 1778, therefore, was that for which d'Estaing's fleet had been prepared. Jenkins set out one view of this, suggesting the reasons why the Americas were not intended to be the principal theatre of war:

> The business of d'Estaing's fleet was first to land troops that should provide the necessary stiffening for Washington's more irregular forces – as they did. Second, it was to support land operations as far as it was able. Third, when the stormy seas forced it to leave the American coast, it was to sail to the West Indies and capture some of the British possessions there, until the return of the calmer season enabled it to resume its activities in support of the troops on the mainland.[5]

On the other hand, Dull suggested that d'Estaing might possibly succeed in taking or destroying the relatively weak battle squadron with which Howe was operating, in which case the British troops in mainland America, dependent almost entirely on food and supplies coming from Britain, could be blockaded and perhaps obliged to surrender, thus ending the war.[6] This, though, can scarcely be regarded as a realistic possibility. Even if d'Estaing did defeat Howe in this way, there can be no doubt that the British would at once react by sending a large fleet across the Atlantic, and in the result d'Estaing might himself be defeated and blockaded.

In January 1778 the Council of State took a preliminary decision to despatch the Toulon fleet to America. The most effective means of assisting the colonists to gain their independence would, it concluded, be to send d'Estaing to attack the British naval forces in North America, and thereafter possibly to be divided between Newfoundland and the West Indies. Meantime military encampments would be established along the Channel coast to compel the British to maintain naval forces to guard against invasion. The Spanish government was notified of this plan. Floridablanca declined the offer which had been made to him of 10 ships of the line to ensure the safe arrival of the Spanish treasure fleet. He did however confirm that, in the situation created by the Franco-American treaties, Spain would stand by its commitment under the Family Compact. Floridablanca, however, was determined not to be rushed, and he was not at all interested in recognising American independence. When he first heard of the negotiations between Vergennes and the Americans, he told Montmorin that it was equivalent to declaring war on England. If Spain did enter the war, he said, she would not be the first to ask for peace; before doing so, Spain 'would sell her last shirt'. As has been seen, he had reacted very badly to the first official news of the alliance.[7]

5 Jenkins, *History of the French Navy*, p.150.

6 Dull, *French Navy and American Independence*, p.109.

7 Corwin, *French Policy and the American Alliance*, p.158.

With discussions between Paris and Madrid still ongoing in the spring and early summer of 1778, it was impossible for Vergennes to make any further long-term strategic decisions. Without Spain it was apparent to him that France would probably not be capable on her own of delivering the kind of blow which would bring the war to a speedy end, which was his primary objective. Vergennes, therefore, was obliged throughout the year to continue to negotiate with the reluctant Floridablanca in order to bring him to a position in which the two allies might begin seriously to plan a joint strategy against Britain.

Reaching agreement on this was not going to be straightforward. In March Montmorin was reporting to Vergennes that the Spanish minister's view was that the Americans ought to be allowed to weaken themselves, and be left in a state of anarchy, in order that they should not be a threat to the Spanish possessions in the New World. Floridablanca refined this by subsequently suggesting that 'seeds of division and jealousy' should be sown between America and Britain, and that Canada should remain British.[8] This latter suggestion chimed perfectly with Vergennes's own ideas on the subject; here, at any rate, there would be no difficulty in reaching agreement. In November, Montmorin wrote to Vergennes outlining the current Spanish attitude:

> There is no concealing the fact that the interest they feel here in the Americans is not very tender … Spain regards United States as destined to become her enemy in no remote future, and consequently, far from allowing them to approach her possessions she would omit no precaution calculated to keep them off, and especially from the banks of the Mississippi.[9]

Montmorin was in any case dubious about the value to France of the Spanish alliance, which he considered was not worth the price to be paid for it; but Vergennes never wavered in his belief in the necessity of waiting for it.

What is not entirely clear is how far Vergennes and his colleagues had thought through their strategic situation as it would be throughout 1778, if the Spaniards did not immediately join in the war. Jonathan Dull appears to think that they considered that the despatch of d'Estaing's fleet was itself a potential winning move, although this was an extremely unlikely proposition. Yet if they did consider that this was so, it might have been better to delay d'Estaing's departure for a while, in order to get further with the negotiations with Floridablanca, and thus in this way delay the start of the war. It was certainly true, of course, that d'Estaing's arrival on the American coast would strengthen the colonists, draw British forces away from the Gulf of Mexico that might otherwise be tempted to attack the Spanish

8 Corwin, *French Policy and the American Alliance*, p.176.
9 Corwin, *French Policy and the American Alliance*, p.177.

treasure fleet, and provide a force there for operations if required. On the other hand, there was not much likelihood of the British pre-empting Spanish intervention by attacking the treasure fleet at time when it was still hoped that Spain would stay out of the war.

The negotiations with Spain were held up while Floridablanca pursued the project of a mediation of the Franco British disputes under the auspices of His Most Catholic Majesty Carlos III. To this suggestion, the British government had responded favourably, not least because it offered the prospect of keeping Spain out of joining an autumn campaign. Although it really stood no prospect of success, Vergennes was obliged to stand by while contacts were made to explore the possibilities of mediation. At the same time Floridablanca reassured Vergennes with a personal letter to the effect that while Carlos III was hopeful of peace, he was aware that negotiations might fail, and was continuing his preparations 'with the greatest activity and trusted that his nephew was doing the same'.[10] Outwardly, though, the Spanish were being careful to avoid compromising their neutrality while mediation appeared still to be a live possibility.

For the moment, therefore, France would be standing alone against Britain during the campaigning season of 1778. D'Estaing had made only slow progress since leaving Toulon, and it was not until the night of 16/17 May that he finally passed through the Straits of Gibraltar. Although it was generally assumed in Britain that his destination was indeed the American coast, it was considered unwise for Byron's fleet to depart until this had been positively confirmed; there had been a report from Paris that d'Estaing was bound for Cadiz, and a letter from Vice Admiral Robert Duff at Gibraltar suggested the same thing. This left open the question of whether the Toulon squadron really was heading for North America. Then, on 13 May news came that d'Estaing had been sighted off Algiers; after consultation with the King, Sandwich decided, without pausing to notify Germain, that he must take immediate action to halt Byron. He wrote to Weymouth to explain what had been done: 'I received his Majesty's commands today to send an express to Plymouth to stop the sailing of Admiral Byron's fleet till further orders, upon an idea that we must very soon receive certain intelligence whether M. d'Estaing is gone to Cadiz or not'.[11]

The decision to hold back Byron's fleet was confirmed next day at the Cabinet meeting, which also discussed the question of where Byron should go when he finally sailed. Keppel apparently later suggested that five ships might have been sent to reinforce Howe immediately, but the reason for not making such a move was the fact that it was not known in London whether Howe had already sent off the force to attack St Lucia in accordance with his secret orders.

10 Corwin, *French Policy and the American Alliance*, p.185.

11 Barnes and Owen (eds), *Private Papers of John, Earl of Sandwich*, Vol.II, p.58.

Uncertainty also characterised the French reaction to the news of Byron's fleet. Although his strength and destination were pretty well understood, the Council of State felt unable to risk sending a further squadron from Brest to pursue Byron, out of a fear for the security of French trade.[12] Looking back at Vergennes' strategy, it is clear that the best that could realistically have been hoped for from d'Estaing was to support the Americans, threaten Britain's possessions in the West Indies and, possibly, seriously damage Howe's fleet. He could not, however, be expected to undertake an effective blockade of the American coast in an attempt to starve the British land forces into submission. 1778, therefore, was going only to be the first act of a much longer drama.

As it was, it was clear that Byron's squadron, when it eventually sailed, would be a significant factor in d'Estaing's campaign on the other side of the Atlantic. Having been stopped in his tracks on 13 May, Byron was forced to kick his heels while the Cabinet awaited positive intelligence about d'Estaing's destination. Palliser, meanwhile, now at Portsmouth, on 14 May wrote to update Sandwich on the situation of the fleet there. He reported that Keppel had 21 fine ships, or would have if they were fully manned; as it was, seven of them were well short of their full complement. He found a growing anxiety in the fleet about its strength relative to the French: 'I find the language here begins to prevail that we are in want of ships for the present occasions. I take all opportunities to contradict it, and insist that we want only men, having many ships ready to receive them and more preparing for it'.[13]

The weather, meanwhile, was now taking a hand. For the moment the wind was dead against any fleet preparing to sail down Channel, as Keppel reported to Sandwich. His concern, not unreasonably, was that the Cabinet should make up its mind about the orders to be given so that when the wind changed to easterly the fleets could put to sea at once. Like Palliser, Keppel was anxious about the shortage of men. He was also very concerned about the prospect of invasion, writing to Sandwich on 17 May:

> I wish I could form to myself a hope that this country would very soon have a force of frigates, and that many would be in a little time with us from Lord Howe. The French are most assuredly intent upon invading England or Ireland; if they do attempt it I am certain, without frigates to oppose their embarcations, they will make their landing.[14]

12 Dull, *French Navy and American Independence*, p.115.

13 Barnes and Owen (eds), *Private Papers of John, Earl of Sandwich*, Vol.II, p.59.

14 Barnes and Owen (eds), *Private Papers of John, Earl of Sandwich*, Vol.II, pp.63-66.

10

The *Belle Poule* and the *Arethusa*

Curiously, although the Admiralty had had for a considerable time convincing intelligence of the preparations at Toulon to send d'Estaing's fleet to sea, it was not until 20 April that the frigate *Proserpine* had been sent with orders for Vice Admiral Duff, commanding at Gibraltar, to station her, together with one of his own frigates, to watch for d'Estaing on either side of the Straits. Another was sent to cruise off Brest. Since the movements of the fleet at Toulon were all important in deciding exactly what the British should do next, it seems surprising that a watch had not been kept on that port well before d'Estaing sailed. Nor was any warning sent to Howe in North America, whose most recent orders dealt with the despatch of the forces to go to the West Indies. It was only on 4 May that messages went to Howe with news that d'Estaing would not be intercepted. This information reached him on 29 June, when the West India packet arrived off the Delaware with news that on her transatlantic voyage she had been chased by a French squadron.[1]

Meanwhile Byron's fleet was now concentrated at Plymouth, awaiting sailing orders. It had been decided that when he did finally put to sea, he should steer for New York, rather than Halifax as originally intended, on the advice of Samuel Hood. This decision, which was taken by the Cabinet, was based on the mistaken belief that a convoy carrying three regiments for the defence of Halifax was already on its way there; in fact, the Admiralty had held the convoy back pending the departure of Byron's fleet. Fortunately, the misjudgement did not have any evil consequence.

During the period of waiting, Keppel sent a stream of letters to Sandwich displaying his continued anxiety about the situation of his fleet. He made plain a pronounced lack of confidence in its ability to defeat the French fleet, writing for instance on 20 May:

> The opinion your Lordship seems to entertain, that the Brest fleet ready for sea consists of twenty five ships of the line and a large number of

1 Mackesy, *War for America*, p.198.

> frigates, is so formidable in its description, under the present state of the fleet of England for home service, that it will require the most serious consideration for those entrusted with the government of this country how far the fate of England will be risked, if in a naval battle near the coast the English fleet should not be conqueror. I am not a person that will offer an opinion upon a matter of such nice importance. I hope I shall do my duty becoming an officer in every situation; and I might perhaps not be sorry, if I considered myself *only,* to give battle to the French fleet when I might not dare as a councillor to my King to advise it.[2]

It was an anxious time for all concerned, especially for Palliser and Mulgrave, who as well as serving with the fleet remained in their capacity as members of the Board of Admiralty, but if they felt any misgivings about Keppel's handling of the fleet, they forbore to make any comment to Sandwich; Palliser in fact continued to be entirely supportive of the commander in chief.

Keppel was constantly anxious about the possibility of his being made a scapegoat in the event that a wrong decision was taken about the departure of Byron's fleet. On 26 May he wrote that when reviewing his orders he could not say that he felt much satisfaction with regard to them:

> It is impossible to avoid seeing that, both in case of detaching Vice-Admiral Byron's squadron or detaining him a time that may be thought too long in the event, the blame must fall upon myself. Indeed there does appear *a positive period* for my sending him away where *the intelligence is certain*, and at which time my instructions decide positively; but suppose I have information at the time that the Brest fleet is ready to come out to sea, nearly three ships to two in force compared with the King's that will remain under my command. Is it meant that I should with seventeen or eighteen ships of the line leave it to the choice of the French to come out or not, to give battle to the fleet under my command after it is reduced by detaching Vice-Admiral Byron's Squadron?[3]

Palliser had rather more encouraging words to address to the First Lord, observing that once the fleet was manned, all would be safe, and the King and his ministers would be able to adopt what measures they pleased:

> It must be a pleasing reflection to remember that your Lordship's counsels to these ends were perfectly right; and had they been followed in time our present difficulties might have been in great part prevented, as we should

2 Barnes and Owen (eds), *Private Papers of John, Earl of Sandwich*, Vol.II, p.69.
3 Barnes and Owen (eds), *Private Papers of John, Earl of Sandwich*, Vol.II, pp.77-78.

> have been ahead of our enemies in preparation for war and thereby might possibly have prevented it.[4]

At this time, it was George III who was most convinced that d'Estaing was headed for North America, and he was repeatedly stressing this in his communications to Sandwich and North. One undated note, clearly written while positive information was still awaited, emphasised the King's belief in the need for an aggressive policy:

> I am very clearly of opinion that the moment we hear d'Estaing has passed the Gulf of Gibraltar and gone forward towards America, that Byron must follow him. Should he be returned to Toulon, then Keppel must instantly sail off Brest with such ships as he has in condition, and be joined by Byron and his squadron; and as soon as Keppel can have a reinforcement to render him equal to the rest fleet, then Byron must be detached with a sufficient force to the Gulf of Gibraltar.[5]

The frustrating period of waiting came to an end on 2 June when the *Proserpine* sailed into Falmouth Harbour. She had sighted d'Estaing inside the Straits on 16 May and Captain Sutton sent in a boat to Gibraltar with the news. He had lost the enemy that night but, in the morning, had further news of the French from a Dutch warship, and in the afternoon met the *Enterprise*, which had sighted the French off Cape Spartel. The two ships found d'Estaing at dawn on 18 May, and Sutton set his course for England, ordering the *Enterprise* to follow the French to establish their course. The two frigates met again on 21 May en route for England. Captain Sutton came ashore to report on his sighting of d'Estaing's fleet. He noted 'from the regular course the fleet steered and the great press of sail they carried I cannot help supposing it is for the West Indies'. Keppel sent Sutton to London to report in person. Reading his report, the King correctly concluded that although d'Estaing's course was south-westerly, 'it was to get in a certain track, to make the passage more secure to North America,' and he insisted that the Cabinet could not meet too soon to give Byron his sailing orders.[6]

It was nevertheless an anxious decision for the members of the Cabinet, but when they met on 5 June they concluded that on the evidence before them d'Estaing's destination must be taken as North America, and by 7 June Byron had received his orders to sail at once. The wind was against him for two days but on 9 June it changed sufficiently for him to leave Plymouth and, and he made sail for Sandy Hook.

4 Barnes and Owen (eds), *Private Papers of John, Earl of Sandwich*, Vol.II, pp.79-81.
5 Barnes and Owen (eds), *Private Papers of John, Earl of Sandwich*, Vol.II, pp.74-75n.
6 Barnes and Owen (eds), *Private Papers of John, Earl of Sandwich*, Vol.II, p 89.

Orders went to Keppel at the same time to put to sea, which he finally did on 12 June with 20 ships of the line. His orders gave him a considerable number of disparate responsibilities. He was to escort the convoy going to Gibraltar with reinforcements safely into the latitude of Ushant, and to intercept any force which might come out from Brest to attack it; he was to prevent the junction of the Brest and Toulon fleets; and he was to pursue the Brest fleet if it evaded him, and to give battle if the enemy superiority was not too great. If it was, he should return to St Helens for reinforcements. He was to seize any French ships of the line or East Indiamen that he encountered, but not to bother to take frigates unless they were watching his fleet. Any Spanish ships acting with the French should also be seized, but otherwise these were to be treated as friendly. His overall task was to protect Great Britain and Ireland. He was also responsible for the protection of British trade, and to seize or destroy any vessels belonging to the Americans or trading with them.[7]

These instructions were abundantly clear, and before he sailed Keppel wrote to Sandwich to thank him for 'the very explicit letter you have troubled yourself to write to me,' going on to remark that 'twenty English ships of the line is certainly a formidable force'.[8]

In Brest, the despatch of d'Orvillier's fleet to sea had also been delayed by uncertainty, in this case about Byron's movements. As late as June 20 it was believed that Byron was still close to Keppel; if they were intended to operate together, the Channel Fleet would be substantially superior to the fleet in Brest. At the same time Vergennes still hoped that a way could be found to make Britain responsible for commencing hostilities. Within days, that problem had been effectively solved, when on 17 June the Channel Fleet sighted two French frigates and two smaller vessels. Keppel, bearing in mind his orders, concluded that the French ships were there to reconnoitre the Channel Fleet, and he ordered that they be chased and brought to his flagship. One of the frigates, the *Licorne*, duly complied; but then next day attempted to escape. When a shot was fired across her bow, she fired a broadside at the *America*, 64, and then struck her colours.

The other frigate, the *Belle Poule*, commanded by *Lieutenant de Vaisseau* La Clocheterie, made off, accompanied by the cutter *Coureur*. They were pursued by the *Arethusa* and the *Alert* cutter, which caught up with the French ship at sunset. *Arethusa's* captain, Samuel Marshall, told La Clocheterie that he had orders to escort the *Belle Poule* to Keppel's flagship. The Frenchman point blank refused to comply; *Arethusa* then fired a shot across the bow of the *Belle Poule*, which replied with a broadside. There was little wind, and the two frigates fought broadside to broadside for some two hours, according to Marshall's report. The other ships were too far off to assist the *Arethusa*, which suffered extensive damage to

7 Martelli, *Jemmy Twitcher*, pp.138-139.

8 Barnes and Owen (eds), *Private Papers of John, Earl of Sandwich*, Vol.II, p 93.

her masts and rigging, and the *Belle Poule* set her course towards the French coast, anchoring amid the rocks of Plouascat. It had been a fiercely contested action; the *Belle Poule* lost 45 men killed and 57 wounded, and the *Arethusa* eight killed and 36 wounded.[9] Meanwhile the *Alert* had engaged the *Coureur*, and captured her.

La Clocheterie, who had put up such a vigorous fight against the *Arethusa*, became overnight a national hero, and the toast of fashionable Paris society; he was promoted to the rank of *capitaine de vaisseau*. Not only had his exploit demonstrated the skill and courage of the French navy in battle; it had also provided Vergennes with the *casus belli* that he sought, since the odds faced by the three French frigates showed that it must have been the Channel Fleet that was the aggressor. The need for restraint, therefore, was coming to an end.[10]

On 19 June the *Milford* and *Proserpine* chased and captured another French frigate, the *Pallas*. In view of the engagements which had taken place with the other French vessels, Keppel decided to detain the *Pallas*, and sent her into Portsmouth with a prize crew. It seemed clear to both Keppel and Palliser that the French frigates had been under orders deliberately to provoke a confrontation with the Channel Fleet with the object of making Britain responsible for the commencement of hostilities.

Among the papers found aboard the captured *Pallas* was a letter from Sartine ordering that 'Captain Cook, the useful navigator, was on no account to be molested'. Another, of more immediate importance to Keppel, was a list of the ships which composed the French fleet in Brest. This brought the uncomfortable news that there were as many as 27 ships of the line there ready for sea, with six more preparing, under the command of d'Orvilliers.[11] At this time Keppel had accomplished the first of the tasks assigned to him, which was to shepherd the crucially important convoy bound for Gibraltar safely out of the Channel. That done, Keppel believed that in accordance with the terms of his instructions he should return home for reinforcements, rather than risking encountering d'Orvilliers with a fleet much superior to his own. He wrote to Sandwich on 21 June to point out that the report of the size of the French fleet accorded with the indications which the Admiralty had received. That being so, he said that he was obliged by his instructions to proceed to St Helens. He went on:

> My pride might have induced me to a battle with the French fleet at all risks; but when I consider the defeat of the fleet under my command, which is always possible but more so when greatly inferior in numbers, would in all probability be attended with fatal consequences, I do not put myself in the scale against so much danger to my country, though I

9 Clowes, *Royal Navy*, Vol.IV, pp.14-15.
10 Dull, *French Navy and American Independence*, p.119.
11 James, *The British Navy in Adversity*, p.125.

> have an unhappiness upon this occasion beyond any situation I have ever before been in.[12]

Keppel was clearly uneasy about how his return would be viewed, and with good reason. The King, somewhat misunderstanding the arithmetic of the balance of forces, was outraged to read the correspondence which Sandwich passed on to him:

> I cannot conceal that I am much hurt at the resolution taken by Admiral Keppel of instantly returning to St Helens on learning that the Brest fleet amounts to 27 sail of the line. At the same time he says that 5 ships of the line have sailed, consequently that must reduce the Brest fleet to 22 sail. I fear this step will greatly discourage the ardour of the country: I therefore hope at your Cabinet meeting this day it may be settled to represent unto me the propriety of ordering the Admiral to return to his station.[13]

Privately, Sandwich and the other members of the Cabinet were also extremely displeased to receive the news of Keppel's return to St Helens, but the First Lord was careful to avoid criticising him. The relationship between Cabinet and commander-in-chief, politically opposed as they were, remained one of mutual mistrust. Keppel was constantly on the lookout for indications that he was being set up for failure by the government, which in its turn was always suspicious that the admiral was concerned principally to cause it embarrassment by stressing the inadequacy of his fleet.[14]

Sandwich, very conscious of the need to get the Channel Fleet back to sea as soon as possible, went down to Portsmouth to do what he could to hasten this. On 29 June he suggested to Keppel that in order to speed the coming into service of the reinforcements, seamen should be taken from the ships already with the fleet, but the commander-in-chief was absolutely opposed to this. Later that day Keppel wrote to Sandwich to confirm his objection to this course: 'Without taking one man from the ships, the deficiency from the numbers sending every day to the hospital will render them very weak, and make it imprudent to put the plan into operation'. He went on to stress the importance of his sailing with a force at least equal to the French, if the country was to be able 'to hope and expect a happy issue'.[15]

The First Lord was dismayed to receive this, replying on the same day to say that Keppel's letter gave him the greatest concern. Everything was being done to add at

12 Barnes and Owen (eds), *Private Papers of John, Earl of Sandwich*, Vol.II, p.98.

13 Barnes and Owen (eds), *Private Papers of John, Earl of Sandwich*, Vol.II, pp.98-99.

14 Rodger, *Insatiable Earl*, p.244.

15 Barnes and Owen (eds), *Private Papers of John, Earl of Sandwich*, Vol.II, pp.103-104.

least four ships of the line to Keppel's fleet. He sought Keppel's approval to the plan that had been put forward for manning the *Vengeance* and *Defiance*:

> Let me make it my request to you that you may aid me in this point; for if I return to London without being able to say that your fleet will be ready to sail again in a very few days, much well-founded uneasiness will appear, not only among the trading part of the nation, but with every person who has the welfare of the kingdom at heart.[16]

Following the incidents involving the *Belle Poule* and other frigates, Louis XVI formally authorised his navy to take action against British ships, and on 10 July orders went to d'Orvilliers, who had been on standby since 25 June, to put to sea. His orders, as summarised by E.H. Jenkins, were very much more cautious than the terms of the letter which Sartine had previously sent him:

> On taking over his command, d'Orvilliers had been sent a long letter by Sartine saying that the eyes of Europe would be on his fleet, that officers were to understand that the mistakes and misfortunes of the past were to be wiped out by dash in attack, that if any ship, forced on the defensive against odds, should strike before it 'reached the last extremity,' the greatest royal displeasure would fall on its commanding officer, and (recognising one of the great weaknesses of the service) that officers were to avoid disputation and obey the orders of their seniors instantly and unquestioningly.[17]

Second and third in command of the fleet were du Chaffault and the Duc de Chartres. The sailing orders were somewhat equivocal, as the letter which d'Orvilliers wrote to Sartine before sailing made clear:

> Since you leave me free to continue my cruise, I will not bring the fleet back to Brest, unless by positive orders, until I have fulfilled the month at sea mentioned in my instructions and known to all the captains. Till then, I will not fly before Admiral Keppel, whatever his strength; only, if I know him to be too superior, I will avoid a disproportionate action as well as I can; but if the enemy really seeks to force it, it will be very hard to shun.[18]

Sartine had received advice from Kerguelen, the celebrated explorer of the South Seas, and La Motte-Picquet that, until Spain joined the war, there was no point in

16 Barnes and Owen (eds), *Private Papers of John, Earl of Sandwich*, Vol.II, p.104.
17 Jenkins, *History of the French Navy*, p.151.
18 James, *The British Navy in Adversity*, p.126.

seeking a decisive action. Anchored in Brest, with de Broglie's troops in Normandy, the fleet could pin down the British fleet, while effective action was taken against British trade. D'Orvilliers, who had reported that his admirals and captains were eager to attack Keppel, put to sea on 10 July with 32 ships of the line and no less than 15 frigates. His flag was aboard the *Bretagne*, 110; du Chaffault was aboard the *Couronne*, 80, and the Duc de Chartres the *Saint Esprit*, 80. D'Orvilliers had only two three deckers, and two of his ships of the line were only 50-gun vessels. He had Pavillon as his chief of staff, and the system of signalling that he employed was based on the latter's design of 1776; it was the most comprehensive and elaborate system that had so far been used to conduct the movements of a battle fleet.[19] Two days after the fleet sailed, a frigate was sent after it giving d'Orvilliers permission to return to port if he judged it prudent. This careful afterthought was entirely justified, since in the summer of 1778 the fleet was going to sea without any immediate objective of pressing importance.

Meanwhile, from St Helens, Keppel continued to bombard Sandwich with letters recording his views of the situation. On 3 July he wrote to say that he did not 'wonder at all at the alarms of the merchants, and wishing the fleet at sea,' but when doing so he remarked that they should also hope that it was in sufficient force:

> The King's Councils have determined twenty four ships' force sufficient; I will sail when I am joined by that addition of ships. I have never lost an hour's time: I never will. My proceedings have ever been with good motives, void of fear for myself, yet full of anxiety for the King's flag and safety of his home dominions.[20]

This prompted a tart response from Sandwich: 'I have no doubt but that when you come to any real business you will give sufficient grounds for the fullest approbation of your conduct. Nothing has yet happened that has furnished with such an opportunity'. In his letter of the same day Keppel was worrying about the station that the fleet should take up; that which was best for the covering of inbound convoys was sufficiently far from Brest for the French fleet to come out and run up the Channel unobserved. But for the need to protect the convoys, a station off Brest itself was therefore desirable; as it was, the Lizard was perhaps best.[21]

Two days later Keppel was again insisting that he could not sail with less force then determined by his instructions, but that when he did so he would do his duty to the utmost. He would have liked to meet the French in mid-Channel, but he feared that they would be wiser, and keep near their own coast, 'where in the

19 Tunstall, *Naval Warfare in the Age of Sail*, p.135. For a full order of battle, see Appendix II of this work.

20 Barnes and Owen (eds), *Private Papers of John, Earl of Sandwich*, Vol.II, p.105.

21 Barnes and Owen (eds), *Private Papers of John, Earl of Sandwich*, Vol.II, pp.106-107.

event of a battle their frigates must operate very disadvantageously to the English fleet even after it had beaten the French'. Next day, Palliser wrote to Sandwich in terms which the First Lord must have found more reassuring. He had had several 'serious and confidential' discussions with Keppel. As a result, he wrote that he thought that he could safely assure the First Lord that Keppel's disposition was of 'the fairest and most honourable kind:'

> He is perfectly satisfied so far as relates to your Lordship's conduct towards him, of which he always speaks in terms of praise that is due to you. Therefore, let me beg of you to entertain the strongest dependence that when a proper opportunity offers he will acquit himself to the King and his country as becomes a man of honour, and that we shall all do our duty is as far as we are enabled.[22]

War had still not formally been declared, and Keppel's last exchange with Sandwich before he sailed raised the question of what to do with any French frigates encountered by the fleet. To this, Sandwich referred him to his former instructions to take them if they persevered in watching the fleet:

> The additional instructions which you have received lately will authorise you to take everything belonging to France that falls in your way, in case they commit hostilities against us; but for some reason or other they do not seem eager to begin, therefore it is greatly for our advantage to avoid an open rupture till our preparations are further advanced and our trade got in, and it is extremely material that we should be strong in argument that we are not the aggressors, though it will not be discreet to give up any material point to that political question.[23]

Sandwich told Keppel that the *Licorne's* conduct justified the detention of the frigates that had been taken, but that for the moment there was to be no attack on French trade, and a number of prizes which had been taken by Captain Windsor of the *Fox* were to be returned. However, these last days of peace were soon to come to an end, as each of the battle fleets completed their preparations to put to sea.

22 Barnes and Owen (eds), *Private Papers of John, Earl of Sandwich*, Vol.II, pp.110-112.
23 Barnes and Owen (eds), *Private Papers of John, Earl of Sandwich*, Vol.II, p.114.

11

The Battle of Ushant: First Phase

It has been suggested by Nicholas Rodger that the dispatch of Byron to North America was a grave error of judgment; if Howe had been left to fend for himself, which in the event he had to do anyway, and Byron's ships had remained as part of Keppel's fleet as he and Sandwich had wanted, the balance of naval power in home waters would have been transformed. Keppel, if he had met d'Orvilliers with Byron's ships as well as his own, would have had a possibly decisive superiority. If d'Orvilliers had decided not to take him on at these odds, Keppel might have blockaded him in Brest. In these circumstances 'the naval war would have taken a potentially decisive turn in Britain's favour'.[1] The reason that the Cabinet missed this chance was, Rodger considers, because its members 'could not get America out of their mind,' and as a result sent Byron across the Atlantic 'on a costly wild goose chase'. However, abandoning Howe in this way to face d'Estaing's powerful fleet without attempting to reinforce him would have been seen as a serious failure of will, and an admission that the war in America was already lost; and it would have taken a Cabinet with a stronger nerve than that of Lord North to take such a decision.

When Keppel put to sea on 9 July, his fleet was numerically inferior at first, but when it reached Plymouth on 14 July the Channel Fleet had been reinforced to 26 ships of the line. On 16 July Keppel's strength was brought up to 29 ships of the line. By the time it had taken station off Ushant on 19 July it had been joined by one further ship of the line. None of his ships carried less than 64 guns; the total number of guns in Keppel's line of battle was 2,278. Seven of his ships were three deckers: *Duke*, 90, *Queen*, 90, carrying Harland's flag, *Sandwich*, 90, *Victory*, 100, Keppel's flagship, *Prince George*, 98, *Formidable*, 98, Palliser's flagship, and *Ocean*, 90.[2] D'Orvilliers had only two three deckers, his flagship *Bretagne*, 110, and *Ville de Paris*, 90, carrying the flag of de Guichen, second in command of the centre division. The total number of guns carried by d'Orvilliers' battle line as

1 Rodger, *Insatiable Earl*, p.278.

2 For a full order of battle, see Appendix I of this work.

originally constituted was 2,198. It has been suggested, however, that there was in fact little disparity between the two fleets, because the French ships were of a better design, carried a greater weight of metal and had larger crews than their British equivalents.[3]

As he made his way down Channel, Keppel was becoming increasingly anxious about the incidence of sickness in his fleet. He wrote to Vice Admiral Lord Shuldham, commander in chief at Plymouth, asking for help, and was sent three tenders of seamen and marines. He told Sandwich on 16 July:

> I could have disposed of the whole, but his readiness pleased me so that I immediately returned him one of the tenders without breaking in upon her numbers; the others I gave to the ships in want, a few to each …The fleet in general are now complete, though I am kept in alarm for fear of the sickness increasing on board the two sickly ships – the *Courageux* and *Stirling Castle*.[4]

Given his anxiety about the manning of his fleet, his quixotic gesture in sending back one of the tenders seems decidedly odd.

Next day Keppel wrote to say that 'a battle with the French must depend on them; if they are eager, I shall endeavour to get them a little from their own coast, but I am apprehensive they will not allow me to lead them from their land'.[5] On 21 July, after having experienced a fierce gale, he wrote again to Sandwich, wondering 'at not seeing the French fleet;' if they were still out, he thought that perhaps they too had suffered damage in the severe storm, which had cost the *Victory* her main yard.

One way and another, the efforts of the French Navy Ministry and the British Admiralty had sent to sea very large fleets indeed. It has been calculated that Keppel's line of battle stretched for nine miles, and there is no doubt that the size of the fleets put a considerable strain on the rudimentary signalling systems in use.[6] It was also inevitable that even when instructions were clearly understood, and promptly initiated, manoeuvres took a long time to complete. A further consequence of the great size of the two fleets was that it was always going to be extremely difficult to gain any sort of decisive result, unless both commanders were hell bent on fighting it out regardless of the risks involved. Certainly, neither Keppel nor d'Orvilliers could possibly afford to take such a chance.

Ushant, or Ile d'Ouessant, lies a dozen miles off the French coast. It had always been a key reference point during naval wars between France and Britain, standing

3 Jenkins, *History of the French Navy*, p.151.
4 Barnes and Owen (eds), *Private Papers of John, Earl of Sandwich*, Vol.II, pp.119-120.
5 Barnes and Owen (eds), *Private Papers of John, Earl of Sandwich*, Vol.II, p.123.
6 Sam Willis, *The Struggle for Sea Power* (London: Atlantic Books 2015), p.220.

as it does at the western entrance to the English Channel. Importantly, it is only 25 miles from the entrance to Brest Roads. Ushant is a small rocky island some five miles in length and just under two miles wide. In the eighteenth century it generally had a population of somewhat less than 2,000, largely engaged in its fishing industry; in modern times that number has fallen sharply. The bare island is exposed to the full force of the south-westerly gales rolling in from the Atlantic. It is surrounded by a number of smaller islands, which together with a number of others lying between Ushant and the rock-bound coast of Brittany provide a serious hazard to vessels using the inshore waters. An important lighthouse stands at Creac'h, at the western end of the island.

Given the orders which had been issued to Keppel and d'Orvilliers, it was always likely that once at sea they would encounter each other somewhere in the vicinity of Ushant, and so it proved. Out in the Atlantic, the stormy weather had continued. The French fleet was first briefly sighted at about 1.00 p.m. on 23 July, but drifting fog obscured visibility. At this time the British fleet was working its way northward. At about 4.00 p.m. the fog lifted, and the two fleets came again in sight of each other. They were about 60 miles west of Ushant. Due to the prevailing conditions the actual composition of the French fleet was unclear to Keppel. When sighted d'Orvilliers was steering a southerly course; the wind was in the north-west, and Keppel was to windward. He signalled for line of battle, which his fleet had taken up by the evening. All afternoon the visibility had continued to be patchy; it appeared to Keppel that during this time the French fleet was 'standing from the King's fleet'. At about 7.00 p.m. d'Orvilliers then tacked, heading towards the British line, but by that time, it appeared to Keppel, to be too late to attempt to force an action, 'as action in the night is always to be avoided'. He 'brought the fleet to, with the larboard tack, leaving the option to the French'.[7] The wind, of gale force, continued west and north-west during the night. As the sun went down, the French had also been seen to be lying to, which scarcely accords with the suggestion that they were doing all they could to avoid an engagement.

During the night d'Orvilliers skilfully worked to windward. As dawn broke on 24 July, the French had moved to a position north-west of the Channel Fleet; Keppel had lost the weather gauge, but he now stood between d'Orvilliers and his base. For the moment, each of the commanders was reasonably content with his position. D'Orvilliers, though, had a problem; during the night two of his ships, the *Duc de Bourgogne*, 80, and *Alexandre*, 64, which formed part of the vanguard under du Chaffault, had become detached from the French fleet and had got into a position to leeward of the British. A third ship had also missed the signal to tack, but, correctly judging what had happened, was able to re-join the fleet. Keppel now discontinued the signal for the line of battle, and made a signal for general chase to windward. He sent chasers to threaten the two detached French ships, hoping

7 James, *The British Navy in Adversity*, p.129.

thereby that d'Orvilliers would be obliged to run down to their assistance, but the French admiral was not to be tempted in this way. In the event, the two ships made their way back to Brest, thereby reducing the two fleets to parity in terms of ships of the line.

For the next two days the wind continued in the west. Try as he might, Keppel was unable to overcome the disadvantage of his leeward position, and d'Orvilliers had no difficulty in avoiding the attempts made to bring him to action, by the simple expedient of manoeuvring further out into the Atlantic. During this time the weather continued to be too bad for the lower deck ports to be open. Keppel sent off a message to Shuldham on 24 July:

> I have been two days in sight of the French: the option of action has been with them. They are at present to windward near hull down, both fleets upon a wind steering to the south-west. The French fleet seems to sail well. The force of the two fleets forbids my separating; and therefore unless both are agreed to close I know not when it will happen. We count forty sail, great and small; whether their line consists of thirty two ships, I have never been near enough to determine.[8]

Keppel, in his desire not to lose touch with the French, had been obliged to give up his line of battle, since it was his view, which was widely shared among his captains when giving evidence at his court martial, that to do so meant that he might be out-sailed, and as a result might miss an opportunity to bring the French to action. He told his court martial that instead he determined to keep his fleet as well collected as he could, 'and near enough to assist and act with each other in case a change of wind or other favourable circumstances should enable me to force the French fleet to action'.[9]

Keppel had convinced himself that d'Orvilliers wanted to avoid a fight come what may, but this was not in fact the French admiral's attitude. He had undertaken not to retreat in the face of the Channel Fleet, but beyond that he was looking for an opportunity to engage, but only on terms that would be advantageous to his fleet. During the night of 26/27 July he sent a message to the Duc de Chartres, whose flagship the *Saint Esprit* had lost her maintopmast, that he intended to fight next day.[10] For this reason, when at dawn on 27 July the fleets came again in sight of each other, he manoeuvred cautiously in his windward position in search of just such a favourable opportunity.

8 Barnes and Owen (eds), *Private Papers of John, Earl of Sandwich*, Vol.II, p.127.

9 Thomas Blandemor (ed.), *Transcript of the Court Martial of the Hon Augustus Keppel*, (London: Wilkes & Co, 1779), p.249.

10 A H Taylor, 'The French Fleet in the Channel, 1778 and 1779' in *The Mariner's Mirror* (1938), p.277.

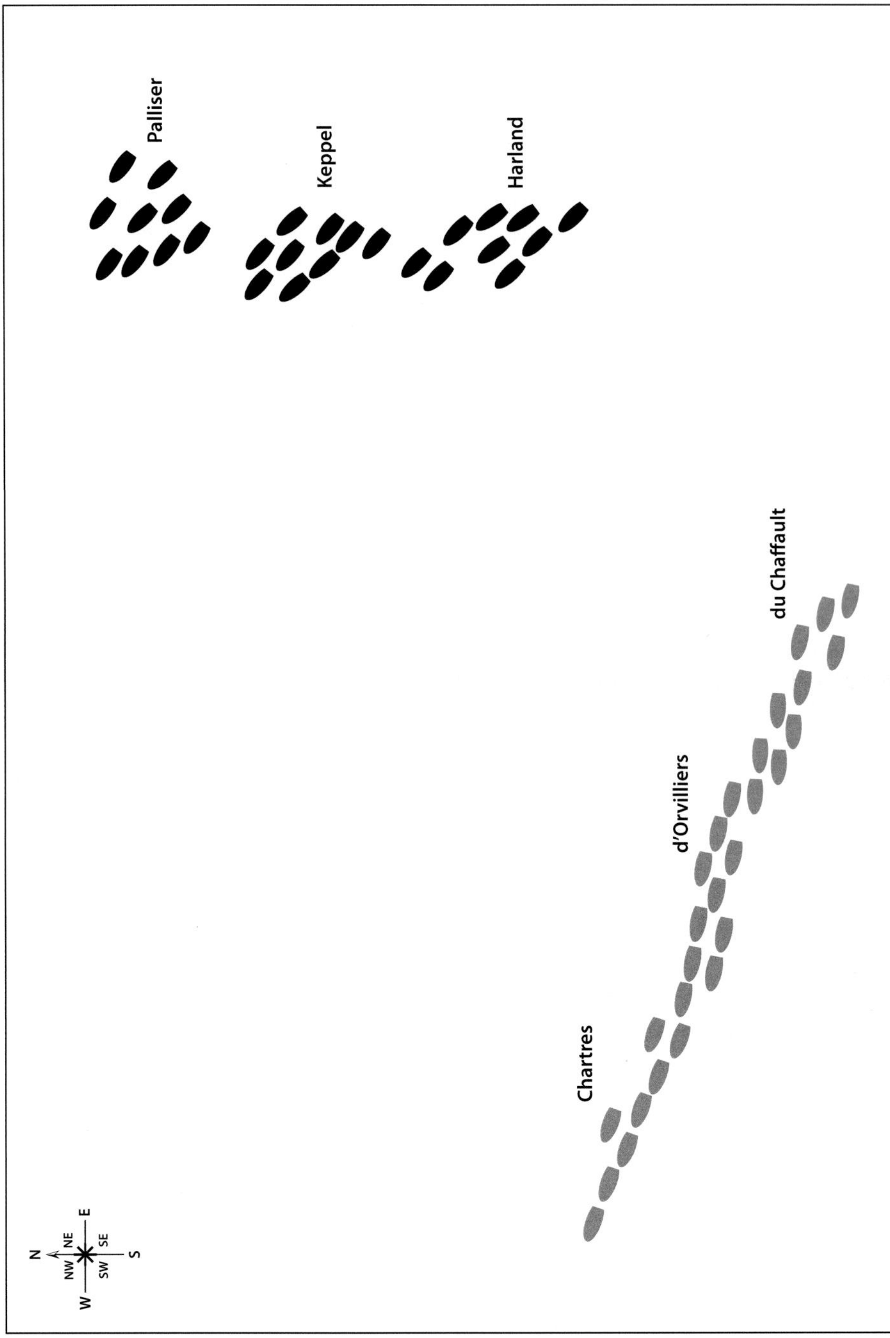

Dawn 27 July 1778. Wind south-west, both fleets on port tack; Palliser's division has dropped astern.

The fleets were, as dawn broke, some six miles or so apart, both steering west-north-west, with the French dead to windward in line ahead. One of Keppel's first decisions that morning was to hoist the signal for a general chase. This was followed at 6.00 a.m. by an order signalled direct to the seven fastest sailers of Palliser's division to chase to windward. This signal was made on the initiative of Rear Admiral John Campbell, who was serving aboard the *Victory* as Captain of the Fleet.[11] At that time the order of sailing had been effectively reversed, and Palliser's division was leading the fleet; it was sailing in bow and quarter line. In this formation in principal the ships of a fleet were almost abreast, but so disposed that if they all tacked at the same time they would take up a position in line of battle.[12] However at this juncture neither fleet was regularly formed, particularly the British; Palliser's ships, effectively on the right wing, were somewhat further from the French than the rest, and the 6.00 a.m. order was intended to bring them forward. Their position, as Palliser pointed out at his own court martial, resulted from Keppel's last order for the fleet to tack all together, which had been on the morning of the previous day. Lord Longford, captain of the *America*, 64, told Keppel's court martial: 'If the wind had continued when that signal was made to chase, and the signal had not been made, I do not believe that any part of the Vice Admiral of the Blue's division, could have come into action at all'.[13]

At about 9.00 a.m. d'Orvilliers decided that he should observe the British fleet more closely, and at the same time he wished to take steps to prevent Keppel from attacking his rear, which he suspected might be the intention. Accordingly, he ordered his fleet to wear in succession, a manoeuvre which brought it closer to the Channel Fleet. However, just as the French began this movement, the wind changed from southwest to south-southwest, which had the effect of bringing the bows of the French fleet roughly into a southerly direction. Their line was by now somewhat extended and not perfectly straight.[14]

This gave Keppel the chance to force an action. The Channel Fleet, which had been on an approximately westerly course, continued until it was astern of the French fleet, and only slightly to leeward. At 10.15 a.m. Keppel ordered his ships to tack together, which they did, forming an irregular line, although still very disordered, and following almost in the wake of the rearmost French ship. Palliser's division was now especially dispersed. Just then there was a dark rain squall, which obscured visibility for about three quarters of an hour. When the weather cleared, it seemed to d'Orvilliers that some of Palliser's ships, although in poor order, might be about to fall on his rear, and at 11.00 a.m. he ordered his fleet to go about simultaneously on the port tack, thus restoring his original course and

11 Tunstall, *Naval Warfare in the Age of Sail*, p.137.

12 Mahan, *Major Operations*, p.84.

13 Blandemor (ed.), *Court Martial*, p.222.

14 Tunstall, *Naval Warfare in the Age of Sail*, p.138.

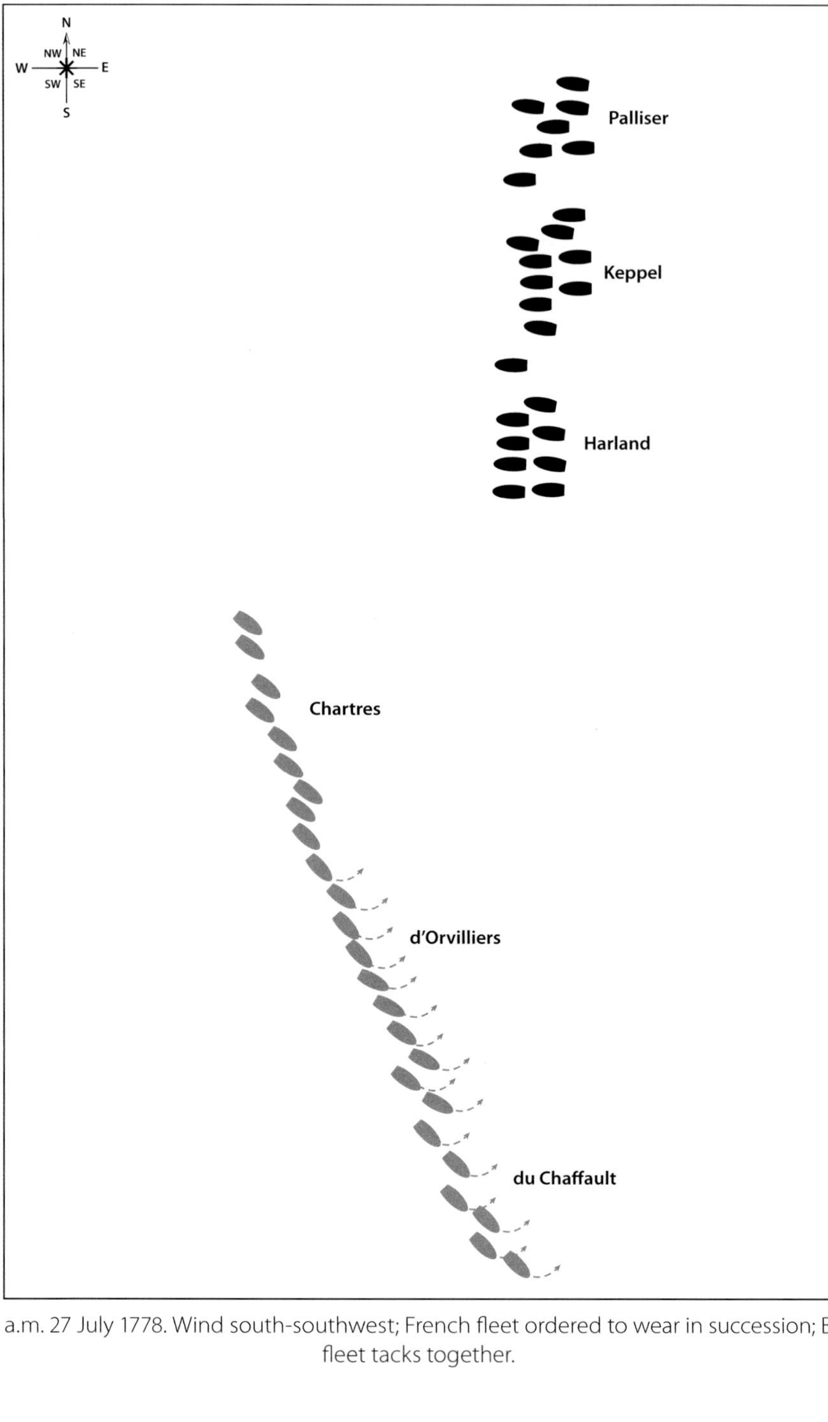

9.00 a.m. 27 July 1778. Wind south-southwest; French fleet ordered to wear in succession; British fleet tacks together.

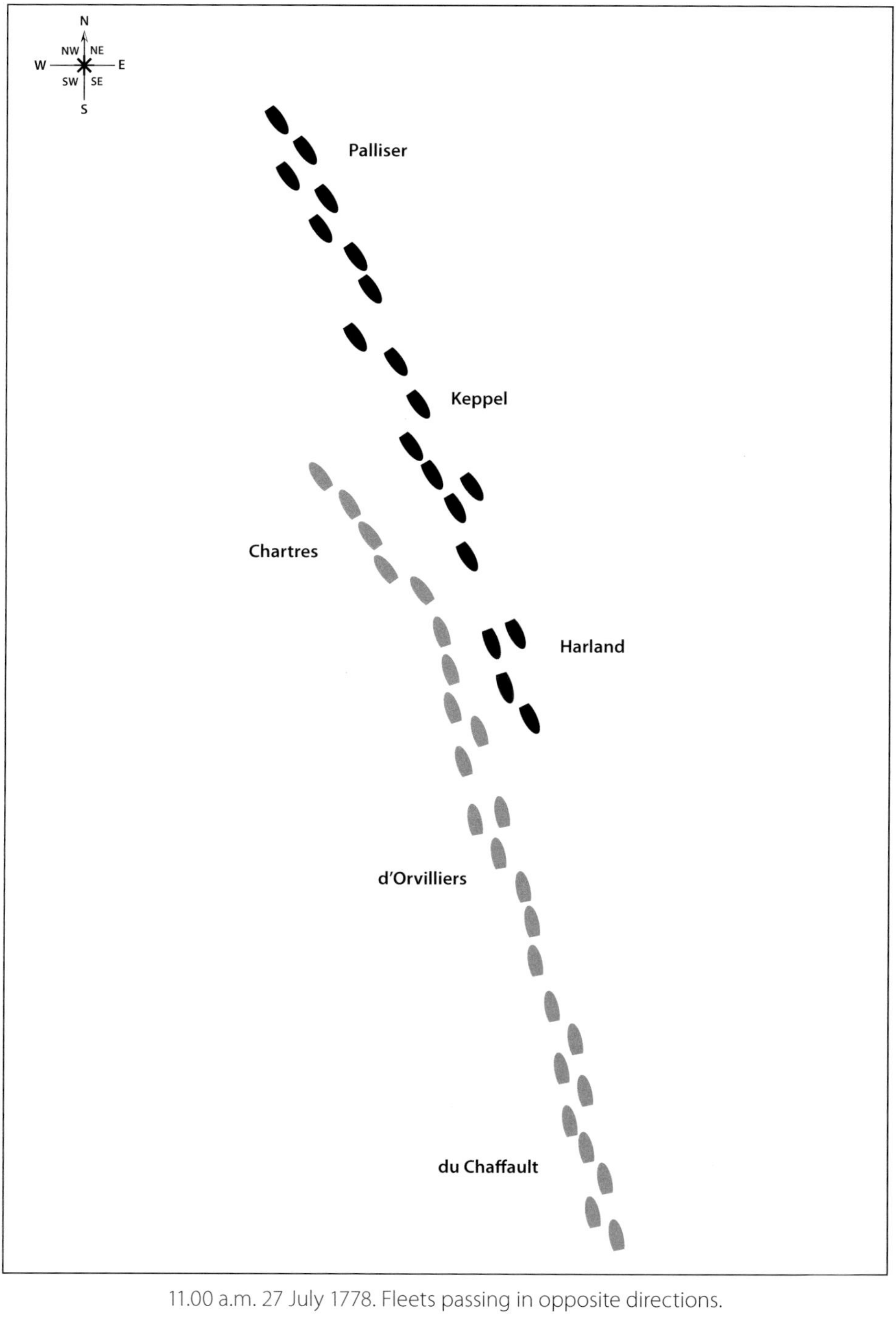

11.00 a.m. 27 July 1778. Fleets passing in opposite directions.

reversing again the order of sailing of his fleet. D'Orvilliers was now satisfied that an engagement could not be avoided; effectively his latest manoeuvre was for the French fleet to approach the British line head on, passing slightly to its windward. In this way d'Orvilliers was able to bring his entire fleet into action.[15]

By now, variations in the sailing qualities of individual ships, and the lack of battle practice on both sides, meant that neither fleet was in an orderly line. Harland, who gave evidence at the court martial strongly favourable to Keppel, observed that if the admiral had formed line of battle, he could not have brought the French to action that day. In reply to a question from Keppel, he said that when the French began firing, they did so at a great distance. Subsequently, when he came to give evidence at Palliser's court martial, he described Keppel's conduct of the action in particularly glowing terms:

> Pursuing the French in the way we did that day was a bold, and necessary, and allowable stroke of war, where nothing but risk, as it appeared, could stop the French fleet from getting off. The great decisive strokes of the day were to follow, by closing with the enemy, and fighting it out.[16]

As the two fleets closed, d'Orvilliers signalled for his ships to form a close-hauled line of battle, and the first three ships of his line began to steer slightly away from the oncoming British fleet. The remainder of the French held their course, however, and the action began on the French side with the fourth ship of the line, the *Intrépide*, 74. Firing began at about 11.20 a.m.

Mahan was of the opinion that that right up to the manoeuvres that immediately preceded the beginning of the engagement, d'Orvilliers was still trying to avoid action, and that Keppel was making the right move to force it upon him:

> It was not the time for a drill master, nor a parade. Besides, thanks to the morning signal for the leewardly ships to chase, these, forming the rear of the disorderly column in which he was advancing, were now well to windward, able therefore to support their commander if needful, as well as to attack the enemy. In short, practically the whole force was coming into action, although much less regularly than might have been desired.[17]

This view of the matter entirely adopted Keppel's answer to the first charge against him at his court martial, which had alleged 'that the French fleet was in regular line on the tack which approached the British fleet, all their motions indicating a desire to give battle'. Keppel, insisting that the French were still trying to avoid

15 Syrett, *European Waters*, p.42.
16 Tunstall, *Naval Warfare in the Age of Sail*, p.138.
17 Mahan, *Major Operations*, p.86.

action, claimed that the charge had been contradicted by the prosecutor's own witnesses.[18] He dismissed the allegation that he 'did not make the necessary preparations for fight,' by pointing out that it was self-evident that ships engaging other than in line of battle could not be 'so closely, uniformly and mutually supportive of each other' as when it was possible to form line. As to the claim that d'Orvilliers was still trying to avoid action, it has been seen that his manoeuvres were, from early on the morning of 27 July, entirely consistent with his having recognised that the time had come to fight.

Thus, it was Harland's division that began the action as it passed the French van and continued down the enemy line, followed by Keppel with the centre division and then Palliser with the rear. As a result of all the changes of course that had taken place, the British line was now still more disordered, with gaps between ships of as much as half a mile, while some of them were engaging the French much more closely than others. It has been calculated that the combined relative speed at which the two fleets were passing was about six to eight knots. Captain John Bazeley, Palliser's flag captain aboard the *Formidable*, told Keppel's court martial that in the weather of 27 July a ship might run with all her sails set between seven and nine knots.[19] Bazeley, whose evidence extended over three days, and who naturally tended to support Palliser's case, was given a very hard time by the members of the court martial, whose questions to him left little doubt of the mind set with which they approached their task. This was largely due to his firm assertion that but for the signal for the fastest ships of Palliser's division to chase to windward, the situation of the division was that it was in a proper formation to take station in a line of battle, if such an order had been given, and would have been able to have gone into action in a joint body. As it was, he said, Palliser was less well supported than Harland or Keppel, and the *Formidable* suffered greater damage.[20] This was also due in part to the fact that the *Formidable*, in order to be able to engage each of the French ships for longer as she passed down their line, deliberately slowed her progress by backing her mizzentopsail; inevitably, this meant that she received more of their fire in return.

As Harland's division and the French vanguard came together, and the firing began, almost at once Keppel made the signal to engage. Many of the ships at first had not their colours flying. The French, as they often did, fired deliberately to damage masts and rigging. Being to windward, and accordingly heeling over in the squally weather, it took a deliberate decision on their part to fire high. It was a tactic that proved effective; many British ships suffered serious damage aloft:

18 Blandemor (ed.), *Court Martial*, p.252.

19 Blandemor (ed.), *Court Martial*, p.136; Tunstall, *Naval Warfare in the Age of Sail*, p.139.

20 Blandemor (ed.), *Court Martial*, p.126.

'Sir Robert Harland Bart. Vice Admiral of the Red and Second in Command on 27 July 1778'. Mezzotint by Richard Earlom, after Nathaniel Dance. (Yale Center for British Art, Gift of Mr. and Mrs. J. Richardson Dilworth, B1973.3.19)

It was noted that when at close range they were firing langridge rather than grapeshot. When langridge (any old bits of scrap iron that could be loaded into a gun) hit a sail it tore it to bits, whereas grape only peppered it. Whether this was the French intention is as may be, but the fact was that by the time the two fleets had passed clear of each other five British ships were immobile until they could do extensive repairs.[21]

21 Creswell, *British Admirals*, p.127.

'The sea fight between Keppel and d'Orvilliers'. Engraved for Cowley's *History of England*. (Library of Congress)

As the engagement became general, thick clouds of smoke from the gunfire covered the two fleets.

As Keppel, aboard the *Victory*, passed down the French line, his ship received broadsides from six French ships before itself opening fire. It was Keppel's wish first to engage d'Orvilliers's flagship, the *Bretagne*, though why that precluded his gunners from firing at the ships he first encountered is far from clear. As it was, Keppel considered that d'Orvilliers was 'out of his station far from the centre of his line, and next, or very near, to a ship carrying a Vice Admiral's flag'.[22] If the latter

22 Blandemor (ed.), *Court Martial*, p.252.

was flying aboard one of the ships in the French centre division, it was presumably that of de Guichen, in the *Ville de Paris*. When the *Victory* reached the *Bretagne*, she delivered a broadside, before moving on to engage successively six more French ships as she passed down the line.

Harland's division, meanwhile, had reached the rear of the French fleet. He later told Keppel's court martial that as his division had passed down their line the French ships were in some confusion:

> In passing them, the van of the French fleet were not well connected with the centre, nor the centre with the rear, as to distance or connection, and though there were six to eight ships that had got up nearly close together, and formed in a body out of the centre, there were two or three of those six or eight ships, which had the appearance of confusion.[23]

Harland also thought that when the French were first firing at his ship, the *Queen*, they were at a great distance.

When Harland's division had finally passed the French rear, at 12.30 p.m. he ordered, on his own initiative, his ships to go about and follow the rear of the French fleet. At this time both the British centre and Palliser's division in the rear were heavily engaged. The latter's 10 ships were still in a scattered and irregular formation, due in large part to their fastest ships having advanced in accordance with Campbell's order to chase to windward. As a result, individual ships of Palliser's division were at times under the fire of several French ships, and sustained more serious damage, especially to their masts and rigging, than the rest of the British fleet. They were also hampered from time to time in getting a clear field of fire for their own guns.

Apart from Palliser's flagship, the *Formidable*, there was one other three decker in the rear division. This was the *Ocean*, commanded by Captain John Laforey, who described the difficulties which the ships of the rear division encountered when they began to engage in their irregular formation. He had been following the *Egmont*, 74, at the time when the *Ocean* came into action; his ship was on the *Formidable's* lee bow:

> The distance betwixt the *Formidable* and the *Egmont* was so short, that it was with difficulty I could keep betwixt them to engage, without firing upon them, and I was once very near on board the *Egmont* … From the first to the last I had difficulty even in keeping clear of the *Egmont*, but I was nearer to the *Egmont* the whole time of action, than to the Vice Admiral, which was about an hour and a half.[24]

23 Blandemor (ed.), *Court Martial*, p.264.
24 Blandemor (ed.), *Court Martial*, p.322.

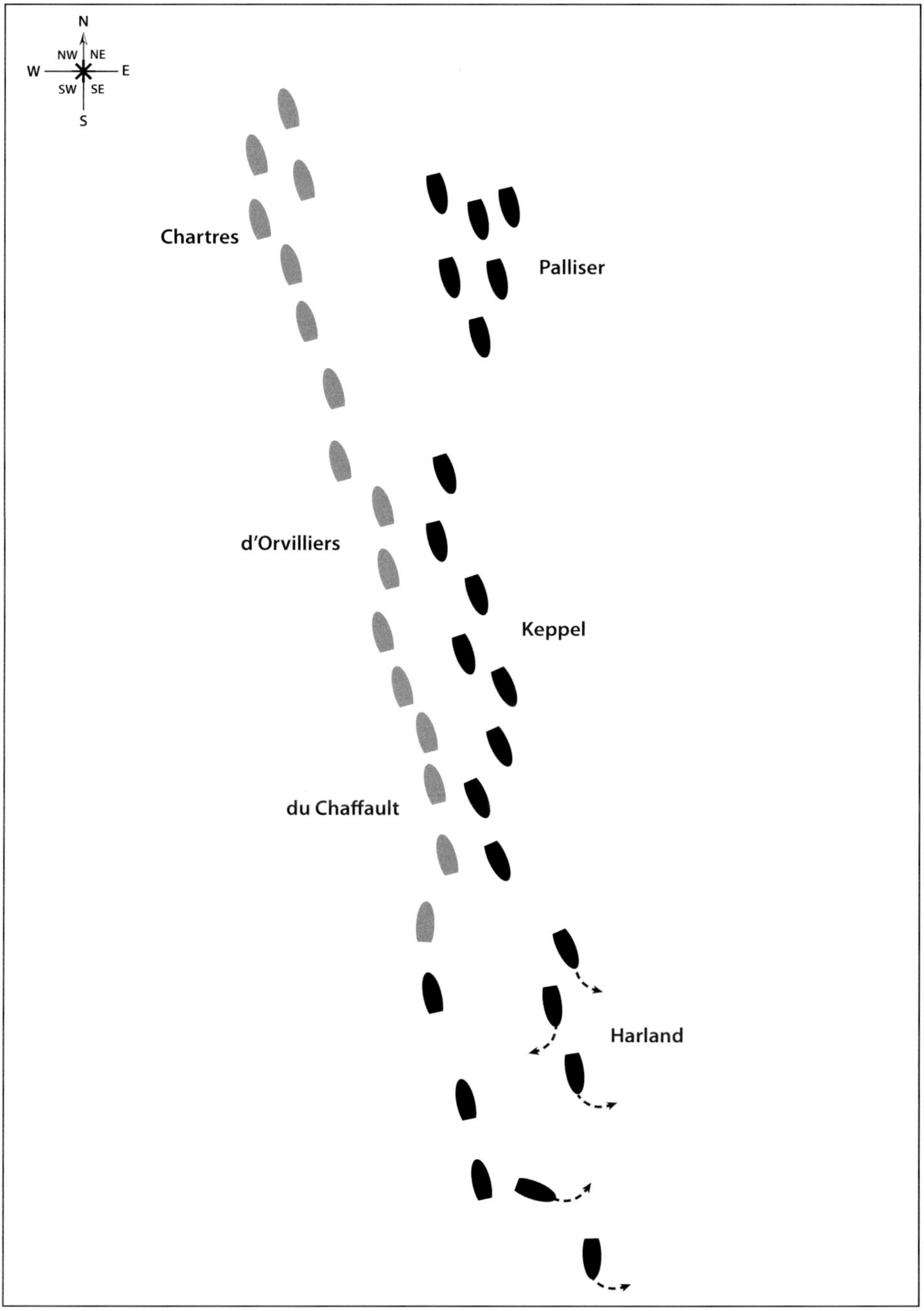

12.30 p.m. 27 July 1778. Fleets engage; Harland goes about on reaching the end of the French line.

Bazeley, in his evidence, had confirmed the confused situation of Palliser's division as it came into action.

At the time when Harland, with the van, signalled to his division to go about and follow the rear of the French fleet, visibility was seriously impaired by the clouds of powder smoke. However, d'Orvilliers probably had a clearer view of what was actually going on, and he signalled to his own van, under the Duc de Chartres, to wear in succession so as to follow the British round and fall on their rear. Chartres either did not see or did not understand the signal, but wore his ship, the *Saint Esprit*, to come under the *Bretagne*'s stern to ask d'Orvilliers for orders. The admiral told him that his intention was to pass along the British fleet from end to end to leeward, to take advantage of its disordered state. By going to leeward, showing his weather side to the enemy, he could use the lower deck guns, whereas in the state of the sea the lower ports on the lee side could not be opened.[25] Meanwhile the three ships of Chartres' division that had kept to windward were now in a bow and quarter line, having turned back on to the same course as the rest of the fleet, but remaining to windward. In the end it was Chartres himself who took the lead, and wore his ship, with the rest of the fleet following suit. Tunstall summarised the situation: 'By now, what with the confusion over signals and damage to masts and rigging, their van ships were no longer in the original order of battle and they had already fallen away to leeward of the retreating British rear'.[26] Quite why Chartres should have failed to comprehend the signal to wear in succession is far from clear; Jenkins suggests that it may have been a reluctance to break 'the sacred rigidity of the line of battle' that led to his doubts. He certainly should not have hesitated; he had on board the capable La Motte-Picquet to advise him.[27]

At the other end of the line Keppel, aboard the *Victory*, cleared the last French ship at about 1.00 p.m. He could now see Harland's division tacking to pursue the French rear. He could also see that there were a number of British ships to leeward in a state of disorder, disabled by battle damage after endeavouring to comply with Harland's order. He attempted to follow Harland round, but the *Victory's* rigging and masts had been so seriously damaged that she was unable to tack, and was obliged to wear. By the time that she did so, she was a mile or more beyond the French rear; Keppel had been unable to wear sooner because of the confusion it would have caused among the ships following him. He then ordered the rest of the fleet to wear also so as to close on the French fleet on the port tack. He also had in mind the need to protect his badly damaged ships, which seemed to be drifting away to leeward. It was about 2.00 p.m. before the *Victory* was on course to follow the French fleet; behind her came several ships of the centre division.

25 Mahan, *Major Operations*, p.90.

26 Tunstall, *Naval Warfare in the Age of Sail*, p.140.

27 Jenkins, *History of the French Navy*, p.152.

'Louis Philippe Joseph d'Orléans, Duc de Chartres, Colonel Général des Hussards'. Colour mezzotint by John Raphael Smith after Joshua Reynolds. (Anne S.K. Brown Collection)

During the engagement, the fleets had passed each other very slowly, under easy sail, and this of course contributed to the extent that they were able to inflict damage on each other. It was generally believed that the effect of the heavy exchange of fire was to make the breeze die down; Jervis of the *Foudroyant* recorded in his journal 'the wind having quite abated by the concussion of the air'.[28]

28 Creswell, *British Admirals*, p.126.

12

The Battle of Ushant: Disengagement

The crisis of the battle had now been reached. It remained to be seen whether either fleet was in a position to force a decisive result, or indeed was prepared to take any risks to achieve this. In fact, the French had probably already lost their best moment for a decisive success. D'Orvilliers had spotted the opportunity to double the rear of the British line, and had given the necessary order to Chartres, but the latter's failure promptly to carry it out had cost the French admiral the chance to take advantage of the situation. The French fleet, as a result, had not begun the movement to head southwards and pass the tail of the Channel Fleet to leeward until about 2.00 p.m.

Meanwhile Keppel, whose movements were hampered by the extent of the damage which his flagship had sustained, signalled for the frigate *Proserpine* to come under his stern. When she did so, at about 2.00 p.m., he instructed Captain Sutton to carry an order to Harland to take up a position at the head of the fleet on the larboard tack. However, before Sutton could set off with this message, Keppel was able to see that the French fleet was wearing and was now standing to the southward on the starboard tack. He could also see that it was in no sort of regular order, but as he told his court martial, he could not profit from this, not being able to collect a force sufficient to check the French movement. Accordingly, Sutton was sent off with a message for Harland to form astern of the *Victory*; Sutton reckoned that he delivered this at about 3.00 p.m., by which time Harland's division was already bearing down to take station astern of the flagship.[1]

The signal to engage had been hauled down aboard the *Victory* at 1:26 p.m., and, 15 minutes later, the signal to form line of battle at a cable's length was hoisted in its place, in an effort to get the British fleet into some sort of order.[2] The *Victory* was, at that moment, the nearest to the enemy, according to Keppel, supported by no more than three or four ships of the centre division. According to him, the *Formidable*, which had suffered particularly severely as she passed down the

1 Blandemor (ed.), *Court Martial*, p.211.

2 Tunstall, *Naval Warfare in the Age of Sail*, p.140.

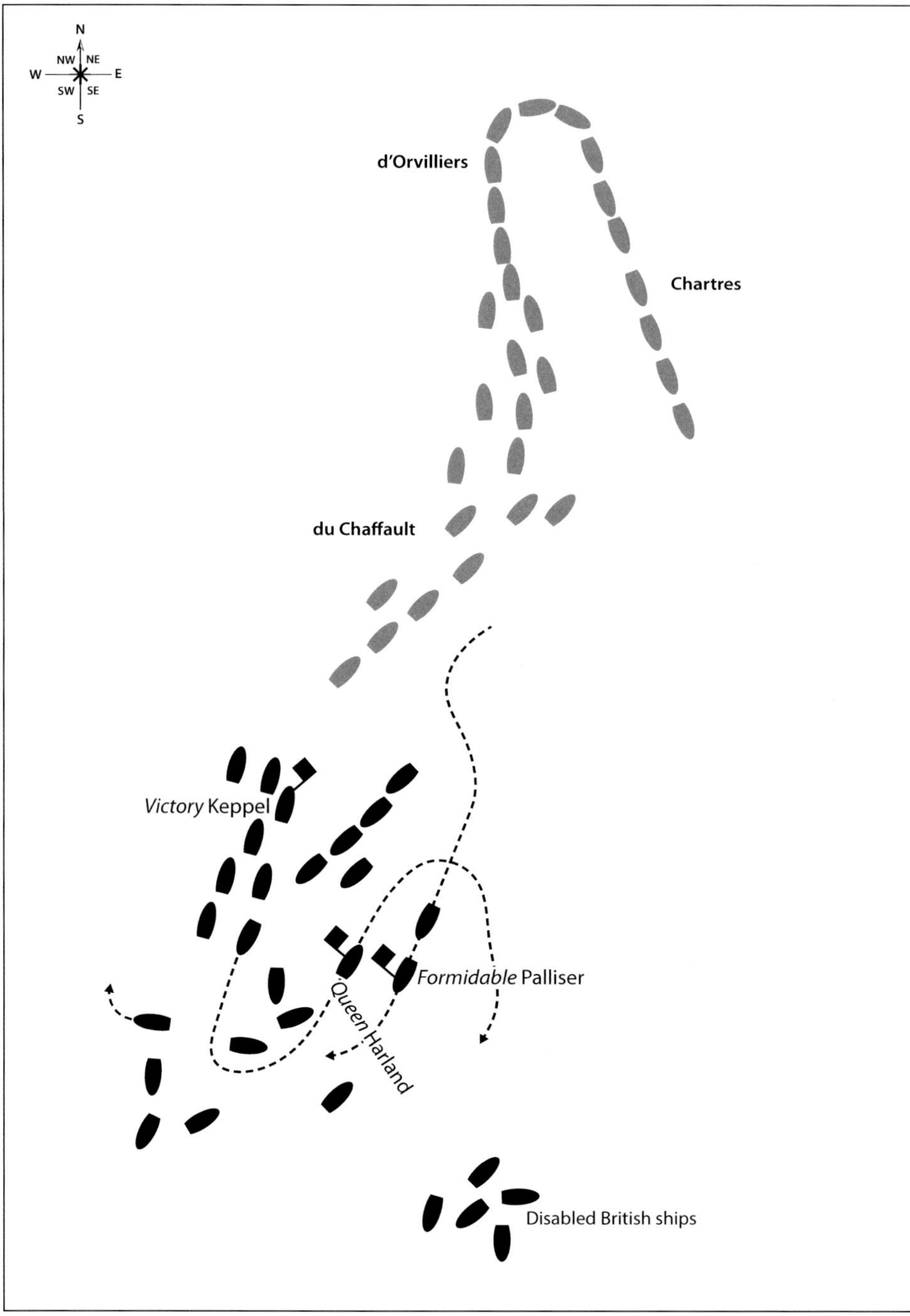

2.30 p.m. 27 July 1778. French wearing in succession after the action.

French line, was on the starboard tack, standing away from her proper station, even though the signal to form line of battle was flying. It appears that the *Formidable* was the last of the British ships to pass the tail of the French line, and then passed the *Victory* to leeward at about 2:30 p.m.

Harland was still on the larboard tack, following the French rear. His ships had suffered the least damage, and he had most of them collected with him. Keppel's message to him that he should wear and take the rear of the line was sent in order to keep the enemy in check until Palliser's division had come into line in accordance with the signal. By now the movements of the fleets had left a group of the most severely damaged British ships, apparently more or less incapable of manoeuvre, furthest to leeward to the south south-east; next came Keppel, with a number of ships of the centre and rear, while further to windward and astern was the *Formidable* with the rest of the rear division. By the time that Keppel's message had reached Harland, the latter had already begun to wear round on his own initiative, to take up a position at the rear of the Channel Fleet.

Keppel was indignant that Palliser had made no attempt to execute the order to form line of battle. The reason for this illustrated the shortcomings of the existing signal system in the Royal Navy, as outlined by Tunstall:

> At his own trial Palliser explained this by saying that, as his ship was end on to the *Victory*, he could not at first see the signal which was flying from her mizzen peak, which was the union flag and a blue flag with a red cross. Similarly he could not see the signal to wear, a blue pendant at the ensign staff.[3]

Nor could Palliser see the signal aboard the *Arethusa*, the repeating frigate, because she had been called in from her station to the *Victory*, and Captain Marshall was for the best part of an hour himself aboard the flagship.

When the *Victory* wore, she passed right round the *Formidable*. Palliser's flagship was unable, at this point, to come into line with the *Victory* due to the damage which she had suffered, particularly to her foremast. At about 3.00 p.m., Keppel signalled to wear for the second time, a manoeuvre which brought him onto the starboard tack, roughly parallel with the French, who had now reached a position about level with the British, about two miles to windward.[4] The group of badly damaged ships, which lay to the southward, no longer appeared to him to be in danger from the French fleet. Keppel's immediate concern was now that most of Palliser's division was still well to windward of the rest of the fleet.

At this point d'Orvilliers, in theory at any rate, might have had a further opportunity of catching the British at a disadvantage, separated as they were into three

3 Tunstall, *Naval Warfare in the Age of Sail*, p.140.
4 Tunstall, *Naval Warfare in the Age of Sail*, p.141.

groups. However, for the moment he contented himself by remaining to leeward, coming down slowly and forming into line, but taking no immediate steps to renew the action. Keppel, at 3.15 p.m., signalled for the ships to windward to come into his wake; it was a signal which he later contended was kept flying until 8.00 p.m. At 3.30 p.m. Keppel again signalled for the line of battle at a cable's distance. An hour later, according to Sir William Burnaby, the captain of the *Milford*, 28, he called up the frigate to take an order to Harland that he was to take up his proper station in the van. Burnaby may have been wrong about the time, since by 4.00 p.m. Harland's division had already joined the centre in the line of battle. At all events, Keppel sent him off with his message to Harland, and the latter duly complied, passing between Palliser's division and Keppel's division to take up his position at the head of the fleet.[5]

From now on, the failure of Palliser's division to come into line at the rear of the British fleet occasioned Keppel the greatest concern. He appears not to have grasped the fact that the *Formidable* had sustained so much damage that she could not keep pace with the *Victory* and the rest of the fleet; Burnaby told Keppel's court martial that 'the little sail the *Formidable* carried after the action could not possibly enable her to keep way with the *Victory*'.[6] The immediate consequence of the *Formidable*'s inability to join the line of battle was that the other ships of her division took station on her rather than on the *Victory.* Their captains gave evidence that they considered that this was the proper course to adopt in accordance with the Fighting Instructions. The rear division thus formed a separate body of ships about two miles from the rest of the British fleet.

By now the French fleet had completed their formation into line of battle. Although they made no move to close with the British, it was clear to Keppel that the existing separation of his fleet into two parts was a source of danger. At some time between 5.00 and 6.00 p.m. he again called up a frigate to transmit the orders he wanted to give. This was the *Fox*, 28, commanded by Captain Windsor. Keppel called the orders over to Windsor by megaphone, and the *Fox* then made her way, not without difficulty, to the *Formidable,* where she was cheered by the crew of Palliser's flagship. Palliser was later able to show that his recollection, and that of his officers, was that it was not until 7.30 p.m. that Windsor delivered his message and that this was much more accurate than Windsor's evidence that he delivered it two hours earlier, which in the circumstances was scarcely possible. The order which Windsor carried was for Palliser to come down into the *Victory*'s wake. According to him he added that Keppel was waiting for Palliser to do so to resume the action. According to Lieutenant Bertie, of the *Fox*, the precise terms of the order, called across to the *Formidable*, were repeated several times: 'The answer each time was, from the stern gallery, "Sir, I understand you perfectly".' Bertie

5 Blandemor (ed.), *Court Martial*, p.35.
6 Blandemor (ed.), *Court Martial*, p.39.

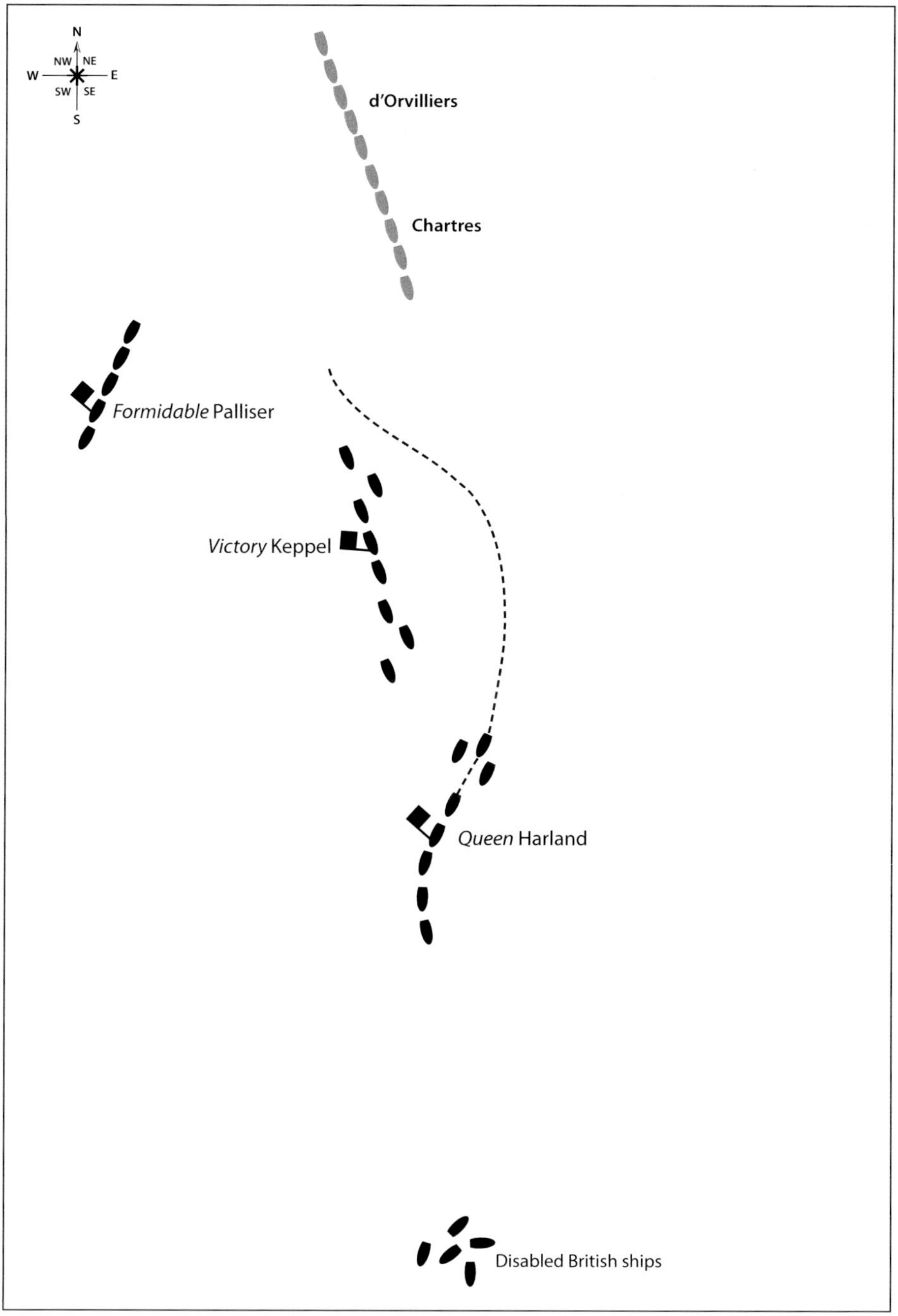

6.00 p.m. 27 July 1778. French forming line of battle to windward of the British.

thought that the reply came from Palliser himself, though he was not certain. He said that it took the *Fox* about half an hour to reach the *Formidable*.

Palliser, however, at his own court martial, insisted that he had not received the message from Windsor until 7.30 p.m., and pointed out that by then, according to the evidence given by Campbell, it was already so late that Keppel had given up all thought of re-engaging. Palliser also denied that the message referred to the *Formidable* as well as to the ships of her division, and, in particular, that it referred to Keppel waiting for him before he re-engaged. The admiral, he said, was not waiting for him, nor had he been the whole afternoon. In any case, the *Formidable* was still not in a position to comply, as she could not yet bend her foresail.[7]

Mahan observed that, Palliser having made no movement in response to this order, Keppel, 'with extraordinary – if not culpable – forbearance refrained from summoning the rear ships into line by their individual pennants'. He finally took this step at about 7.00 p.m., but by then had concluded that it was in any case too late to renew the action. The historian Sir Geoffrey Callender, one of Keppel's warmest cheerleaders, explained the admiral's reasoning:

> Before the line could be completed, darkness fell upon the sea. Not for this would Keppel have delayed his attack had he had with him half the fleet that fought at Quiberon. But the French seemed more pugnacious than usual, and his own side lacking in dash. The windward position gave him choice of time and he postponed further fighting till daybreak.[8]

In fact, as Palliser contended, Keppel was not waiting for Palliser's division, and his message that this was so was very probably an embroidery which Keppel added later.

It was not only the extensive damage suffered by the *Formidable* that caused the delay in effecting repairs; her boatswain had been killed, one of her lieutenants had been wounded, and two others were so ill that they were incapable of coming on deck. As a result, it was not until late at night that the work was completed in spite of every effort that the *Formidable's* crew could make. Palliser explained that he sent no message nor displayed a signal of distress, nor contemplated shifting his flag, because he could see no reason to do so. At his own court martial he pointed out that the reference in the Fighting Instructions to an admiral shifting his flag was merely permissive, and that to do so would have retarded the work of repair. The whole operation of shifting his flag would have taken considerable time, involving the transfer of his 'signal colours, necessaries and attendants'; it would have meant the chosen ship also laying to, as well as increasing the *Formidable's* distance from her station. He had no frigate with which to send a message to Keppel until about

7 Anon., *The Defence of Vice Admiral Sir Hugh Palliser* (London: T. Cadell, 1779), pp.46-48.

8 Callender, *Sea Kings*, p.15.

8.00 p.m., but, in any case, he thought it unnecessary, not least because Keppel's instruction to the individual ships of his division to come into line had not been accompanied by a similar instruction to the *Formidable*.[9]

During the night, d'Orvilliers came to the conclusion that he had done enough; as dawn broke on the following morning only three French ships could be seen from the deck of the *Victory*, while from the mastheads of some of the British fleet the rest of the French fleet could be seen in the south east from 15 to 20 miles distant. It was one of the least convincing elements of the charges which Keppel faced that he 'did not cause the fleet to pursue the flying enemy nor even to chase the three ships that fled after the rest'. In reality, as Keppel said, there was 'not the smallest prospect of coming up with them more especially as their ships, though certainly much damaged in their hulls, had not apparently suffered much in their masts and sails'.[10] He did order four ships to give chase, but soon abandoned the attempt. He now decided, reasonably enough, to return to England to repair his damaged ships, and the fleet duly anchored in Cawsand Bay at noon on 31 July.

D'Orvilliers might have done more, but given the strategic sense of the orders which he carried, his decision to withdraw was not unreasonable. He had certainly had the best of the battle, although his casualties were somewhat higher. He lost 161 men killed and 513 wounded which compared to the British loss of 133 killed and 373 wounded.[11] The disparity was largely due to the difference in gunnery technique. The French practice of firing to cripple the enemy's masts and rigging caused fewer casualties than the British concentration on the enemy's hulls, but it had left d'Orvilliers's fleet in a much better state to manoeuvre than that of Keppel. The battle had demonstrated the inadequacy, on both sides, of the communication provided by the existing system of signalling. Keppel's endeavours to overcome this by the use of frigates to carry orders by word of mouth meant enormous delay in carrying out the manoeuvres he intended, and the French system of communications proved little better.[12]

Thus, the battle had proved indecisive. One of the principal reasons for this was that on both sides there was a lack of experience in fighting a large-scale action involving so many ships. Many of them were only recently commissioned, with relatively untrained crews. David Syrett points out that 'no officer in either fleet had taken part in a major action since the Seven Years War and, as a result, a number of manoeuvres were conducted ineptly'.[13] Another reason was that the initial engagement was a passing action, with the fleets on parallel but opposite courses. In addition to this, the French, at any rate, came into the battle with an

9 Anon., *Defence of Vice Admiral Sir Hugh Palliser*, p.60.
10 Blandemor (ed.), *Court Martial*, p.259.
11 Mahan, *Major Operations*, p.91.
12 Tunstall, *Naval Warfare in the Age of Sail*, p.141.
13 Syrett, *European Waters*, p 44.

excessive caution; their self-confidence was limited by the record of their navy in the most recent wars.

Unsurprisingly, both sides felt able to claim the battle as a victory, as Mahan observed:

> This was simply a point of honour, for material advantage accrued to neither. Keppel had succeeded in forcing d'Orvilliers to action against his will; d'Orvilliers, by a well judged evolution, had retained a superiority of manoeuvring power after the engagement. Had his next signal been promptly obeyed, he might have passed again by the British fleet, in fairly good order, before it re-formed, and concentrated his fire on the more leewardly of its vessels.[14]

Mahan went on to point out that even after the loss of this opportunity it was still in d'Orvilliers's power to renew the fight; Keppel, 'by running off the wind, had given his opponent full opportunity to reach his fleet and to attack'. In his view, d'Orvilliers should either have attacked, or else have retreated; it was not good generalship to give the enemy time. On the other hand, having been given time to rally in this way, Keppel should have made more vigorous efforts to renew the fight. He certainly could have called Palliser's ships into line much sooner. Admiral James considered that Palliser's captains 'should have seen what was required and should have realised that by remaining with their divisional flagship they were keeping away from any chance of renewing the fight'.[15] Against this, though, it must be said that for the individual captains to act on their own judgment and go against the Fighting Instructions which bound them was asking a lot; among them there were a number of captains of marked ability, as shown by their subsequent careers.

Overall, d'Orvilliers had demonstrated the greater skill. Had he been prepared to make the attempt to exploit the advantage that his tactical nous and the fighting effectiveness of his fleet had created, he might have been able to win a decisive victory. As it was, the caution with which the French approached the engagement, certainly with lower expectations, ensured that the battle ultimately did prove indecisive; nevertheless, they could feel the greater satisfaction at its outcome. Callender, an enthusiastically partisan admirer of Keppel, mourned the disappointing result, seeing in it perhaps a greater significance than was justified:

> A victory of the Quiberon type in 1778 would have entirely changed the history of the world. It would have shut the French up in their own ports and rendered them incapable of assisting the Americans ... The French did not see things as clearly as this. But they had accepted the British

14 Mahan, *Major Operations*, p.92.

15 James, *The British Navy in Adversity*, pp.135-136.

> challenge. They had fought at sea and not been destroyed. They had struck the first blow, continued the battle while it pleased them, and at their will concluded it. Therefore, not without cause, they claimed the victory.[16]

Sam Willis trenchantly summed up the battle's outcome:

> The French had not won a crushing victory, but they had not tried to win a crushing victory … d'Orvilliers had followed his orders to the letter. He had taken his fleet out, he had fought only once, and he had prevented his fleet from being defeated while delivering a stinging slap to the enemy.[17]

In the British fleet there was a widespread feeling of disappointment, a sense that matters had not turned out as they should have done. One sailor wrote: 'the want of Attention to the Signals that were made occassioned all the confusion that happend …Its a general observation of the Officers of the fleet, that no ships could be fought better or better managed than the Enemies ships were, there line was formed very exact'.[18]

Lieutenant John Blankett, serving aboard the *Victory*, made a pointed comparison between the performance of the two fleets: 'The French behaved more like seamen, and more officer like than was imagined they would do, their ships were in very high order, well-managed, well rigged and … much more attentive to order than our own'.[19]

Another judgment came from a particularly authoritative source; 18 months after the battle, Kempenfelt, who had been a member of Palliser's court martial, reflected in a letter to Middleton on the general competence that had been displayed by the French:

> Enquire of those who were in the fleet with Mr Keppel the summer before last, if the French did not manage their ships like seamen; and as to their frigates, they showed an alertness, I have been told, not equalled by any of ours. When their signals were at any time thrown out to make sail, they were in an instant under a cloud of canvas; when they returned to their admiral, or were called to him, they run close up to his stern with all sail set, when in a moment all disappeared but the top sails. If a ship was but at a small distance, if called to the admiral, she immediately spread all her sail, even to stern sails if they would draw. This appears to be not only seamanship, but the brilliancy of it.[20]

16 Callender, *Sea Kings*, p.16.
17 Willis, *Struggle for Sea Power*, p.222.
18 Rodger, *Insatiable Earl*, p.244.
19 Rodger, *Command of the Ocean*, p.337.
20 Laughton (ed.), *Barham Papers*, Vol.I, p.311.

As his fleet made its way back to England, Keppel composed his official report to the Admiralty, claiming a victory. In this, he offered no criticism of Palliser whatever; indeed, the contrary was the case. He wrote: 'The spirited conduct of the Vice Admiral Sir Robert Harland, Vice Admiral Sir Hugh Palliser and the Captain of the Fleet, supported by their officers and men, deserves much commendation'.[21] He also wrote a private letter to Sandwich, in which he boastfully repeated the claim of victory:

> The French fleet's retiring for so many days, and the little prospect I saw of ever getting to battle in a line, determined me the moment the wind gave an opportunity to get to their rear, or any part of their line, in the best way that offered. The 27th was the first change in the wind, and my public letter relates it as minutely and truly as possible. The object of the French was at the masts and rigging, and they have crippled the fleet in that respect beyond any degree I ever before saw. That I have beat the French there cannot be a doubt, and their retreat in the night is shameful and disgraceful to them as a nation after the fair opportunity I gave them to form their line.[22]

Jervis, after the *Foudroyant* had dropped anchor in Plymouth Sound, wrote to Jackson at the Admiralty with his views on the battle, which were upbeat. In the light of what was later to come, it is noteworthy that he too made no criticism of Palliser:

> The French, I am convinced, never would have fought us, if they had not been surprised into it, by a sudden and shift of wind; and when they formed their inimitable line, after our brush, it was merely to cover their intention of flight. Four of our ships having got themselves to leeward so far as to be cut off by the enemy, if Admiral Keppel had not judiciously bore down to them, and the shattered state of Sir Hugh's, which disabled him from taking his place in the line, rendered it impossible to renew the attack on the evening of the 27th. I have often hold you that two fleets of equal force never can produce decisive events, unless they are equally determined to fight it out, or the commander-in-chief of one of them misconducts his line. I perceive it is the fashion for people to puff themselves, and no doubt you have seen, or will see, some of these accounts. For my part, I forbade the officers to write by the frigate that carried the dispatches.[23]

21 James, *The British Navy in Adversity*, p.138.

22 Barnes and Owen (eds), *Private Papers of John, Earl of Sandwich*, Vol.II, p.128.

23 H.W. Hodges and E.A. Hughes (eds), *Select Naval Documents* (Cambridge: Cambridge University Press,1922), p.157.

The leading French naval historian of the period, Georges Lacour-Gayet, reviewed the outcome of the battle:

> D'Orvilliers had forced his enemy to retreat, but Keppel had entirely preserved his fleet. Who was the victor? In fact, nobody was, as can be shown. It is not necessary to debate the result of the battles of Praya or Trafalgar. For Suffren and for Nelson, the end of a battle meant the destruction of the enemy, achieving this by an attack based on the concentration of force. D'Orvilliers, with the tactical science which he had involved, with a concept of naval warfare which consisted above all in preserving the fleet and frustrating the intentions of the enemy, represented the erroneous thinking that still reigned in the French navy about the conduct of fleet actions.[24]

24 G. Lacour-Gayet, *La marine militaire de France sous la régne de Louis XVI* (Paris: Honoré Champion, 1905), p.133.

13

Aftermath

Palliser wrote to Sandwich as soon as the fleet reached Plymouth. He sent him a short account of the battle of 27 July, telling the First Lord that they were only able to skirmish with the French 'for it can't be called a battle as we could not bring them to a general engagement to lie by each other'. However, he conceded that a good deal of damage had been done on both sides. He recorded the fleet's surprise at the disappearance of the French fleet during the night of 27/28 July, since 'they were forming a line to leeward of us and extending themselves parallel to us, so that we made sure of engaging them in the morning'.[1]

The government's fears about the risk to incoming convoys were much allayed when the East India convoy safely arrived in the Channel on 5 August, and still further when the expected convoy from the Leeward Islands arrived on 14 August. Sandwich had told Keppel that he could not advise him to send a detachment to meet the latter convoy 'till some decisive blow is given to the Brest fleet':

> In my opinion the principal object is watching and defeating the Brest fleet: if they detach, we may do so with safety, but it does not seem to me that that is their present [intention]; on the contrary my idea is that they mean to make their home fleet as strong as possible in order to overpower you with numbers when you next meet. However, if you get out expeditiously to sea, I hope you may meet them before they have recovered the blow you have lately given; and a decisive affair between the two fleets would have most amazing consequences to this country.[2]

At Plymouth, the returning fleet had been met with a hostile demonstration, so great was the disappointment of the public with the outcome of the battle. Work got under way at once to repair the damaged ships. The extent to which they had

1 Barnes and Owen (eds), *Private Papers of John, Earl of Sandwich*, Vol.II, pp.131-132.
2 Barnes and Owen (eds), *Private Papers of John, Earl of Sandwich*, Vol.II, p.139.

suffered was greater than had been supposed, as Palliser reported to Sandwich on 10 August:

> We find a great deal more to be done to make us fit for sea than we were aware of both in our masts, rigging, and (what is very surprising) an unusual number of shot holes deep under water, so that the *Robust, Egmont, Vengeance*, and *Courageux* are obliged to go within the island to give large heels to get at them (the *Egmont* is docked). This ship had above 70 shot holes in her side and 5 underwater: it is wonderful we lost so few men. No time will be lost in getting the whole ready. I am still firmly of the opinion, as I told your Lordship in my first letter (which I perceive you have not received), that the French will come out again to meet us, although I cannot persuade many here to think so. These contemptible opinions of our enemy are attended with many bad consequences; I do all I can to correct them.[3]

Although he did not say so, there can be little doubt that among those in his mind as holding such 'contemptible opinions' was his commander-in-chief. Palliser remained concerned about what the French could do; and 'if the Spanish join them,' he wrote, 'God knows what will happen'.

Sandwich had written to Keppel on 2 August with a suitably laudatory letter not only intended to boost the commander-in-chief's morale, but also to emphasise the need to get to sea again:

> I am very sorry you had not a more spirited enemy to deal with, but I am satisfied it was impossible for you to have done more than you did to bring on a decisive action. I cannot, however, omit joining my fullest congratulations to what I am persuaded will be the unanimous voice of the public relative to this transaction. Our great object now must be to get out your fleet again with as little delay as possible, otherwise the French will send out detachments to intercept our trade, and the Toulon squadron will join the fleet at Brest as it is reported to be already at sea.[4]

Sandwich, for the moment at any rate, was taking Keppel's claims of victory at face value, and concentrating on the need to get the fleet battleworthy as soon as possible, and he reassured him that nothing would be omitted to achieve this. The immediate problem at Plymouth was a serious shortage of great masts and yards; Keppel asked Sandwich to ensure that the Navy Board got sufficient completed for every port, to enable the fleet's needs to be promptly met. He was making do for

3 Barnes and Owen (eds), *Private Papers of John, Earl of Sandwich*, Vol.II, pp142-143.

4 Barnes and Owen (eds), *Private Papers of John, Earl of Sandwich*, Vol.II, p.132.

the present where he could; the *Victory*'s main mast should have been taken out, but he hoped 'to make a shift with it' until winter came.

The Cabinet continued to be impatient to see the Channel Fleet at sea; Germain suggested that 'whoever is first at sea may fairly claim the advantage in the late engagement'.[5] Keppel was unhappy about being charged with the duty of covering incoming trade convoys. He was convinced that a station off Brest would not achieve this, and he suggested that the Cabinet should consider 'for the safety of the trade, having the fleet twenty or thirty leagues to the westward of Scilly crossing two degrees of latitude'. He ended his letter of 2 August with a plaintive warning about his own state of health: 'I don't imagine your Lordship can possibly suppose the fatigue of mind I undergo; if it continues I must be knocked up, but I will endeavour to act as long as I am able'.[6]

The Admiralty was doing all it could to hasten the repairs to the fleet. Edward Hunt, one of the joint Surveyors of the Navy, was sent down to Plymouth to ensure that the work was completed as soon as possible, and he sent an encouraging report to Sandwich on 16 August, praising 'the great exertion and zeal of the officers and workmen'. Defective ships, however, were not the only problem Keppel faced; sickness had caused many officers and men to be sent on shore. The problem was particularly severe among warrant officers, many of whom were 'in real bad health and many others good for nothing'. Keppel told Sandwich that he feared that 'many very bad warrant officers have found their way into the fleet'.[7]

Meanwhile in London, the opposition, led by the Rockinghams, sought to gain some political advantage by suggesting that Keppel was denied the chance of a decisive victory on 27 July by the shortage of masts and yards. This, of course, had no foundation in fact; nor did Keppel even hint at it, contradicting it in private but allowing his party to profit from it.[8]

The Channel Fleet finally put to sea on 23 August; d'Orvilliers had beaten Keppel to it, having sailed from Brest on 17 August. He had with him his whole fleet, except the *Ville de Paris*, which had suffered particularly serious damage during the battle. D'Orvilliers's first objective was to protect the coasting trade of St Malo, and to clear the coast of British privateers, before attacking British trade. After an unsuccessful attempt on an incoming convoy in the mouth of the Channel, he sailed southwards as far as Cape Finisterre, before returning to Brest on 18 September. All he could show for this cruise was a total of three prizes; one of these was the frigate *Fox*, Captain Windsor, captured by the *Junon* off Ushant a week before the fleet returned to harbour. His failure to encounter the Channel

5 Syrett, *European Waters*, p.46.

6 Barnes and Owen (eds), *Private Papers of John, Earl of Sandwich*, Vol.II, pp.131-135.

7 Barnes and Owen (eds), *Private Papers of John, Earl of Sandwich*, Vol.II, p.155.

8 Rodger, *Command of the Ocean*, p.337.

Fleet led d'Orvilliers to reach the conclusion that Keppel was deliberately avoiding him. Writing to Sartine after his return to Brest, he observed:

> I cannot believe that the English have any serious intentions of meeting us. The French fleet has continually made their presence known by frequent gun signals and fireworks at night. At last, in returning to Brest, we made our landfall at Ushant, where the English fleet would have made certain of meeting us and where we saw no sign of them.[9]

Thereafter, d'Orvilliers began sending out small squadrons of two or three ships of the line accompanied by frigates. This was found to be a much more effective way of dealing with British privateers. He also increased the number of regular patrols by frigates and corvettes.[10]

Once at sea, Keppel had headed for Ushant, where he hoped to encounter the French fleet; he told Sandwich that he would be 'well pleased if they are brave enough to quit the idea of running towards Brest till the battle has its decision'. So far as he could tell from his intelligence, d'Orvilliers had some 32 ships of the line with him. Meanwhile he was particularly annoyed to learn that in France the battle of Ushant was being hailed as a victory; he wrote to Sandwich indignantly on 8 September:

> The vain boasting of the French court perhaps has obliged them to send their fleet to sea; but although the name of Monsieur d'Orvilliers has been lent to spread to Europe a most infamous lie upon the pretended success of their fleet, they are not themselves I believe so much in earnest in looking for the English fleet as I am in my endeavours to find them. The French King's honours and rewards to Monsieur d'Orvilliers seem political, to confirm the truth of his victory.[11]

The frustration of not being able to find the French was beginning to get to Keppel; next day, to Shuldham, he wrote: 'My patience is worn out, and I despair except by chance seeing the French fleet. I am as yet a stranger to the object of their going to sea; to look for the English fleet certainly has not been their business'.[12]

Intelligence was received by the government from various quarters indicating that d'Orvilliers had made for Cape Finisterre, his object being, it was supposed, to facilitate a junction between his fleet and the squadron from Toulon. Subsequently, it appeared that d'Orvilliers had long since left that quarter; the King told

9 James, *The British Navy in Adversity*, pp.137-138.
10 Dull, *French Navy and American Independence*, p.122.
11 Barnes and Owen (eds), *Private Papers of John, Earl of Sandwich*, Vol.II, p.159.
12 Barnes and Owen (eds), *Private Papers of John, Earl of Sandwich*, Vol.II, p.160.

'Les Héros Françoises. Monseig. le Duc de Chartres, & le Comte d'Orvilliers'. Satirical engraving by William Humphrey, mocking the French claims of victory at Ushant. (Anne S.K. Brown Collection)

Sandwich that it would be best not to send any instructions to go there which might only perplex Keppel. The latter had however already heard this news. He went some way southward in the Bay of Biscay, but in his opinion, for the French to go to Cape Finisterre would be 'an extraordinary station to find the English fleet'.[13] Sensibly, he resisted the temptation to go further until he knew how long the French intended to remain at sea:

> What can Monsieur d'Orvilliers be to do off Cape Finisterre? Is it in expectation of their East India ships coming in that track? Or is it a rendezvous to join the Toulon squadron? It surely cannot be with any hopes that d'Estaing could be upon that coast before they must return. I hope they never will be so strong as the junction of those two squadrons would make them; they would be upwards of fifty ships of the line.[14]

The third cruise of the Channel Fleet continued to be unproductive of result. The effect on the fleet was considerable; in practically all of the ships sickness was becoming a very serious problem. The commanders were also far from well; Keppel became quite seriously ill on 16 September, and reported this in a letter to Sandwich five days later:

> I now come unpleasantly to my own personal situation. For these five last days I have found my health promising unfavourably, and yesterday I was so thoroughly crippled with the spasms that I know not what I should have been able to have done if the moment had called upon me to direct the fleet properly in sight of the enemy.[15]

Palliser, too, was suffering badly from the old wound in his foot; the pain from this was such that he was rarely able to get more than an hour's sleep at a time.

By now, the autumn gales were severely hampering operations, damaging masts and rigging, in some ships so severely that they were obliged to return to port. What Keppel proposed to do was a matter of concern at home, not least to the King, who thought that for the fleet to return to Torbay without having met the French would be 'a most untoward event'. This concern, however, was unwarranted; in spite of all his problems Keppel continued to keep the sea. He considered it prudent occasionally, when the wind permitted, to take his fleet to the entrance to the Channel, just in case d'Orvilliers should get behind him and make his way up Channel, though he thought this unlikely. The condition of the fleet was such that it would soon be necessary for it to come in, but in the meantime the reality

13 Syrett, *European Waters*, p.47.

14 Barnes and Owen (eds), *Private Papers of John, Earl of Sandwich*, Vol.II, p.165.

15 Barnes and Owen (eds), *Private Papers of John, Earl of Sandwich*, Vol.II, p.169.

of the situation was, as the First Lord had observed on 3 October, that decisions to be made as to the disposition of the Channel Fleet depended entirely on the operations of the French, 'and the Western squadron must be at sea if the French leave their ports either in large or small force'.[16]

The fleet's ordeal continued until 26 October, when it finally dropped anchor at Spithead; Keppel had previously intended to make for Torbay, but changed his mind, to Sandwich's relief. Nevertheless, the task of refitting the fleet was likely to be too great for one port, and it was likely to be necessary to send part of the fleet back to Plymouth for repairs. There was, by now, no likelihood that d'Orvilliers would emerge again from Brest until after the winter. This was just as well, since the Channel Fleet was in no state to undertake a further cruise.

While awaiting the fleet's return, Sandwich was pondering the overall situation. The campaigning season was drawing to a close, but in a paper written for Lord North he considered that Britain's position was 'critical and alarming'. Although the Spanish ambassador had been making pacific noises, neither Sandwich nor anyone else put much trust in them. The First Lord reckoned that Spain meant to go to war without much delay, unless they were bought off; the price of doing that would be unacceptably high, including Gibraltar, Minorca and perhaps even Jamaica. So, the prospect of facing the combined force of France and Spain was becoming a reality; together they would be superior in naval strength to Britain, at least for some time. Jamaica, and probably also Minorca were, he considered, at the mercy of Spain unless reinforced. He reckoned that, for the moment, Britain must continue to temporise as long as possible; discussions with the Spanish might buy at least two months. Sandwich calculated that the navy had currently 95 ships of the line, a number that included 14 that should be ready by Christmas and another 14 during 1779, and five old vessels acting as guard ships. These figures, he noted, were not greatly different from the situation in 1759, four years after the start of the Seven Years War.

Their unavailing search for the French fleet had left both Keppel and Palliser tired and depressed, and in poor health, as their respective letters written to the First Lord on their return made plain. Keppel wrote that the fleet had been seriously damaged by the autumnal storms and that 1,400 sick men had been sent ashore. He was, he said, 'much fatigued in body and mind'.[17] He also expressed his sympathy for Palliser, who had, 'poor man, suffered most exceedingly in his old complaints during our cruise'. Palliser himself also wrote gloomily to Sandwich:

> Not having had the luck to meet the French fleet, everything else has been unpleasing. The first part was extraordinary fine weather, the middle and latter very boisterous and bad, by which many of the ships have suffered

16 Barnes and Owen (eds), *Private Papers of John, Earl of Sandwich*, Vol.II, p.176.

17 Syrett, *European Waters*, p.48.

> much in their masts and sails and the fleet has been dispersed. Some of them are very foul, and others leaky, particularly the *Ocean*, who has been so to a dangerous degree, owing chiefly to her sheathing having been kept on too long; it is so rotten it washes off in bad weather.[18]

Keppel, he said, had 'been very much afflicted with his disorder, and appears to be much chagrined at his bad luck'.

Exhausted and dispirited though both men were, there was no hint of the crisis that was about to erupt. On the surface, at any rate, the relationship between Keppel and Palliser seemed perfectly amicable, though there seems to have been a dispute between them while the fleet had been undergoing repairs at Plymouth. Samuel Hood alluded to this in a letter to George Jackson of 4 August: 'The master of a Plymouth Trader, that came here yesterday, talks very strangely of reports at Plymouth of an unpleasant disagreement between the chief and one of the Vice Admirals. Has any such account been brought to you? I don't like it'.[19] If there had been such a disagreement it had evidently soon been smoothed over, although a fortnight later the Duke of Richmond, in a letter to Keppel, referred to reports at Portsmouth of a misunderstanding between the two men.[20]

Once the fleet had dropped anchor, Keppel for the moment remained aboard his flagship, but Palliser went ashore 'for the sake of a little rest and quiet'. However, as he wrote to Sandwich on 28 October, this was 'very much interrupted by a paper put into my hands at landing'. This was a newspaper which contained a paragraph justifying Keppel's failure to continue the battle on 27 July and laying the blame for this on Palliser and his division:

> After such a publication I think the nation has a right to know, and I am determined shall be rightly informed, whether I or anyone else is blameable for what passed that day; nevertheless I shall not do anything rashly, although I think on the absurd assertion with the highest indignation.[21]

A fuse had been lit, which was ultimately to lead to an explosion of such personal bitterness as to seriously damage the morale and effectiveness of the entire Royal navy. Palliser had promised to do nothing rashly, but his fury knew no bounds and he told Sandwich that as soon as Keppel came on shore he would speak to him in very serious terms.

The anonymous article had been published in the *General Advertiser and Morning Intelligencer*, a London newspaper that supported the Parliamentary

18 Barnes and Owen (eds), *Private Papers of John, Earl of Sandwich*, Vol.II, p.184.
19 David Hannay (ed.), *Letters of Sir Samuel Hood* (London: Navy Records Society, 1895), p.2.
20 James, *The British Navy in Adversity*, p.138.
21 Barnes and Owen (eds), *Private Papers of John, Earl of Sandwich*, Vol.II, p.206.

opposition. The identity of the author has been considered by a number of historians, the general view being that the writer was Lieutenant George Berkeley, a relative of Keppel, who was serving aboard the *Victory*. Whoever it was, Palliser had no doubt that Keppel was the inspiration for the article, and he intended to have it out with him as soon as he could.

14

Recriminations

From now on one thing was to lead inexorably to another. Palliser set off at once for London. Furious though he was about the anonymous article, he had not at this stage abandoned all reason, writing a thoughtful letter to Sandwich on 31 October to confess that in his present situation he could not think about anything but what he should do. He told the First Lord that he had concluded that he had two alternatives in seeking satisfaction (without which, he said, he could neither serve nor live): 'The one an easy quiet way without disturbing the quiet of anyone else, the other a more direct way of coming at the point and matters of fact, but which may be productive of many things disagreeable to others which had better be avoided if possible'.[1] He said that he was taking time to reflect on which course to pursue, 'wishing to avoid anything that may be deemed rash'. All of which was very sensible; but much would turn on the interview with Keppel that he now sought.

Keppel returned to London on 3 November, and as soon as he learned of this Palliser sent him a letter asking Keppel to contradict the offending article by signing an account of the battle which Palliser would produce, and which then could be published. If Keppel did not agree to this, Palliser suggested as an alternative that they might jointly prepare an account for publication. Keppel did not reply, so next day Palliser went to see him, to seek his signature to the account which he had prepared. Keppel refused to sign it. Palliser then repeated that he would be content with a jointly agreed statement clearing his name. Keppel still refused to deny, or to confirm the truth of the article. The discussion became heated.

Bearing in mind the catastrophic course that events then followed, the question arises as to whether this could in any way have been avoided. We cannot know exactly what passed between them nor, more importantly, the tone in which Palliser asked Keppel to disavow the contents of the offending article. He may, as some have suggested, have 'demanded' that Keppel do so, in which case it is easy to understand Keppel getting on his high horse and refusing. Or he may have put

1 Barnes and Owen (eds), *Private Papers of John, Earl of Sandwich*, Vol.II, pp.206-207.

a perfectly moderate and reasonable case to Keppel, seeking his help in clearing his name from the dishonour which he believed himself to have suffered. In that case, Keppel's refusal might well have been actuated by the feeling that here was a chance to strike a blow at a political opponent, and through him at Sandwich and the government. Bearing in mind the sense of outrage which Palliser felt about the article, it is entirely possible that he was sufficiently assertive to annoy his erstwhile colleague, and that in the course of the interview he lost sight of the need to avoid doing anything rash. Nor, since Keppel would have seen at once the opportunity to embarrass a political opponent, and hence the government, can we know whether he hesitated for an instant to make use of it or gave consideration to where the dispute might lead. It is, of course, entirely probable that he had had some contact with his political colleagues about the matter. In considering Keppel's reaction, it must be borne in mind that he was extremely sensitive to any suggestion that he had not won a victory on 27 July. An opportunity to distract from any doubts that might exist in the public mind with regard to this, by transferring any implied criticism to Palliser, was in any case perhaps difficult to resist. At all events, Keppel subsequently told Jervis that he had been 'quite rude' to Palliser, and wished to have no more to do with him.[2]

Either way, Keppel's refusal led Palliser to raise the stakes by publishing a letter dated 4 November in half a dozen London newspapers. Reading this, the King felt that Palliser was obliged to take this step:

> Sir Hugh Palliser's account of the action, published in the newspapers of this morning, is a clear proof he did all that could be expected of him, and that the dispersing his division made the French fleet escape. This must make an eternal breach between the two admirals, and occasion much ill humour among those concerned in that day; but Palliser could not avoid the step he has been drove to without the greatest blame.[3]

The King's view that Palliser had no alternative was, looked at from the point of view of one seeking justice from public opinion, not unreasonable but it inevitably provoked a counter-attack. Sometimes George III saw things more clearly than his ministers, but on this occasion neither he nor they foresaw the violence of the storm that would break following the publication of Palliser's letter.

It is worth considering at this stage the nature of the underlying hostility between Keppel and Palliser. On the face of it, their conduct while both served in the Channel Fleet was entirely correct; the correspondence of each man displays sympathy for the other, and Palliser was actively supportive of Keppel in an effort to ensure that the long-standing enmity between the admiral and the First Lord

2 Syrett, *European Waters*, p.49.

3 Barnes and Owen (eds), *Private Papers of John, Earl of Sandwich*, pp.207-208.

was overcome, and in this way preventing their mutual cooperation being affected by the historical feeling. However, as the editors of Sandwich's papers point out, there was a wide social gulf separating Palliser and Keppel, which accounted in part for their being political opponents:

> Keppel was an aristocrat. He had had quick promotion and had seen the most interesting service in the last war. Engaging in his manners, fluent in speech, and popular with everyone, he was well fitted to become the national hero, although the indecisive engagement of Ushant certainly did not prove him a great commander-in-chief. Palliser, on the other hand, was a practical seamen and a person of high professional intelligence. Possessing no influence, he had had to fight his way up step by step, and although three years older than Keppel he got his flag thirteen years later. Compared with Keppel, he was a self-made man and therefore particularly sensitive to public criticism; and if he had once been a Roman Catholic, as was stated, he was particularly subject to it.[4]

Many years after the dust had settled, the distinguished Admiral of the Fleet Sir Thomas Byam Martin looked back at the dispute and took a similar view. His father had served under Keppel, and was greatly attached to him, and Keppel's acquittal was accordingly well received in the family. Byam Martin himself, in his memoirs, reviewed the relative merits of Keppel and Palliser:

> Admiral Keppel's popularity in all classes of society, even to those opposed to him in politics, gave him a great advantage over the less accomplished and less engaging manners of his Vice Admiral, Sir Hugh Palliser. But from all I have collected in conversation with old and intelligent officers, well acquainted with both, I cannot doubt that as a practical seaman Palliser stood far above his chief ... I have moreover of late years had occasion to read some papers written by Sir Hugh when he was Comptroller of the Navy, and they show, in every part, that he was a person of high professional intelligence – in short he was a perfect master of his business.[5]

With the dispute now out in the open, individuals at once began to take sides. One of the first to do so was John Jervis, who published a letter in which he asked why Palliser had not shifted his flag when he realised that his flagship was no longer capable of manoeuvring in accordance with Keppel's signals. Thereafter

4 Barnes and Owen (eds), *Private Papers of John, Earl of Sandwich*, p.191.

5 Admiral Sir R. Vesey Hamilton (ed.), *Letters and Papers of Admiral of the Fleet Sir Thomas Byam Martin 1773-1854* (London: Navy Records Society, 1901), pp.290-291.

Jervis began to act as a self-appointed campaign manager to Keppel; he was to be a passionate supporter of the admiral during the course of his court martial, and, as will be seen, active in persecuting Palliser thereafter.

Among others ready to express a view of the issue at the time was Captain Robert Walsingham, who regularly corresponded with Sandwich, and who wrote to the First Lord from Portsmouth on 11 November to suggest that Keppel was not to blame for the escalation of the dispute:

> Everybody laments it, and I can assure you that no one more than Mr Keppel did, or strove to suppress it. Whenever it is mentioned amongst us it is talked of as a most unhappy affair which rose from nothing and may end unpleasantly; but there is no party in the case, indeed there is no grounds for it. I believe I have traced the author of the letter. I have great reason to believe that he is a foolish boy, and from his own production confessedly a fool and a lubber. I hope to God it will drop. I shall be happy to contribute to it, wishing all parties well.[6]

The suggestion that Keppel 'strove to suppress' the issue does not seem very convincing, when set against his blunt refusal to accommodate Palliser in any way. Nor was it long before the opposition leaders resolved to take it up as a stick with which to beat the government.

In November, Sandwich drew up a list of the captains of the Channel Fleet which recorded the attitude of each to the protagonists in the ongoing dispute. Among those listed were the following:

> Captain Digby – a most excellent officer, sensible, prudent and discreet, laments the unhappy divisions in the fleet which he attributes principally to the insinuations of patriots to whom Admiral Keppel has listened too much.
>
> Captain Ross – one of the most violent men in the fleet, dissatisfied in everything: favours Admiral Keppel.
>
> Captain Jervis – a good officer, but turbulent and busy, and violent as a politician attached to Mr Keppel.
>
> Captain Duncan – a quiet man but a follower and dependent upon Mr Keppel.
>
> Lord Mulgrave – no better officer [exists], has industriously avoided showing his sentiments in the present business, seems to lean to Sir Hugh Palliser.[7]

6 Barnes and Owen (eds), *Private Papers of John, Earl of Sandwich*, Vol.II, pp.209-210.

7 Patterson, *The Other Armada*, p.88.

With the opening of the new Parliamentary session on 26 November, the scene accordingly shifted to the House of Commons. There, a huge row was anticipated, and this expectation was duly fulfilled. In looking at the unfolding course of events, it may be said that it was in the House of Commons that matters irreversibly took a turn for the worse. On 2 December, during the debate on the Navy Estimates, emotions ran high as the two men clashed angrily on the floor of the house. It was Keppel who opened hostilities:

> Keppel told the members of his surprise at the appearance of the newspaper statement, for he had many times been attacked in the press, he said, and had never appealed to the public. Until the matter was properly explained, he could not sail again with Palliser. "The oldest and most experienced officers in his Majesty's Navy, in every engagement, saw something which they were before unacquainted with," he continued, "and that day presented something new. He impeached no man of neglect of duty, because he was satisfied that the officer alluded to had manifested no want of what was most essential in a British seamen – courage".[8]

Palliser now demanded to know why, if there was any real ground of accusation, it was not made fairly and openly. He charged Keppel with seeming 'to speak with a kind of reserve, as if there was something behind; he heartily wished him to speak out ... With regard to the report of not obeying signals, it was a false report'.[9]

Keppel asserted that he was so shocked that he resolved never to set foot aboard ship again, because he thought 'there was an end to all obedience and command'. To this, Palliser replied that his letter had been published only after Keppel had declined to repudiate the anonymous article. He was, he said, guilty neither of neglect of duty nor of inactivity; and was 'by no means instrumental in preventing a renewed action with the fleet of Monsieur d'Orvilliers'.[10] Keppel replied to this in terms which brought matters to a boiling point:

> The Vice Admiral had alluded to signals, and said that it was no fault of his, that the fleet of France was not re-attacked. As to that, he could only say, that he presumed every inferior officer was to obey the signals of his commander; and now, when called upon to speak out, he would inform the House and the public, that the signal for coming into the Victory's wake, was flying from 3 o'clock in the afternoon till eight in the evening unobeyed.[11]

8 J.H. Broomfield, 'The Keppel-Palliser Affair, 1778-1779' in *The Mariner's Mirror* (August 1961), p.201.
9 Broomfield, 'The Keppel-Palliser Affair', p.202.
10 Syrett, *European Waters*, p.52.
11 Broomfield, 'The Keppel-Palliser Affair', p.202.

The dispute had now reached so violent a pitch that Palliser's judgment gave way completely. A week after the debate in the Commons, without apparently having consulted anyone, he wrote to Sandwich calling for Keppel to face a court martial for misconduct and breach of duty during the Battle of Ushant. It was an astonishingly foolish step to take and took the dispute to an even higher plane of controversy, and ultimately to Palliser's ruin.

It also created an extremely difficult situation for Sandwich. Matters had gone so far that if he refused Palliser's demand, he would be charged with using his position as First Lord to suppress the matter in an attempt to shelter Palliser; but if he ordered a court martial, he would be seen as using the issue to attack Keppel. It must have been immediately obvious to him, as it should have been to Palliser, that the proper course was for Palliser to have asked for a court martial on himself; that he did not take this course may have been due to the fact that in Parliament this was what the opposition were demanding. Perhaps, if Sandwich had been prepared to become more deeply involved, he might have attempted to persuade Palliser to abandon his demand for Keppel's court martial and to ask for his own to clear his name. But Sandwich appears to have thought that matters had gone too far for this, and he chose to order Keppel's court martial.

The consequences of this decision were entirely predictable. There was a violent storm of public disapproval, while the navy at once split into two factions, each of which expressed their views with extreme bitterness. In the House of Commons, the decision to order a court martial was denounced by the opposition as a plot to ruin Keppel. The Admiralty's response was that the Board had no discretion when charges of this kind were preferred, a suggestion that was roundly denied by the opposition, which cited precedents to show that this was not so.

On 11 December was a further angry exchange in the Commons between Keppel and Palliser. Keppel concluded his speech amid cheers from the opposition, being reported as saying:

> Thank God, he was not the accuser, but the accused! He was called out to serve his country at a very critical period; he performed his duty to the best of his abilities; and whatever the issue might be, he had one consolation, that he had acted strictly to the best of his judgment. He should decline to say a syllable to the question, as he could not think of voting, and should quit the House.[12]

The King was, naturally, extremely disturbed at the conflagration that was engulfing his navy; he wrote to North on 12 December with a suggested solution:

12 Syrett, *European Waters*, p.53.

> I am sorry to find the strange-managed dispute between the two admirals is to be canvassed in the House of Commons, but I think it may at the same time forward what seems much for the advantage of my service – the bringing Lord Howe to the head of the Board of Admiralty; for Administration will somehow or other be too much mixed in this affair, unless a change is made in that department.[13]

It was an understandable move, and was not without political merit, but it would have taken some extremely complicated negotiations to bring it off. It would have avoided a Parliamentary enquiry into the conduct of the war in North America by Howe and his brother, and might have had the effect of damping down the internal dispute within the navy; but if as a result Sandwich were to become a Secretary of State, Germain would probably resign. North considered that the price would be too high, and that in any case the government should be able to survive the crisis.[14] Nonetheless, he felt obliged in the face of continuing pressure from the King to conduct a discussion with Howe, though putting it off until the beginning of February. It soon became clear that North's belief that Howe's price was going to be much too high. In spite of the King's hope that he was going to be reasonable, Howe laid down four conditions; a military governorship for his brother, a peerage or suitable sinecure for himself, a public declaration of the ministry's satisfaction with his and his brother's performance in America; and the removal of Sandwich and Germain from the government. The discussions accordingly collapsed after three days. Although North, under pressure, made another attempt later that month to renew the negotiations with Howe, they got nowhere. Nor did the suggestion that he should replace Keppel in command of the Channel Fleet result in any reduction of the terms which Howe demanded. North resolved to stand firm, and Howe duly passed firmly into the opposition's camp.[15]

On 14 December the opposition pulled off a further success when one of their supporters, Vice Admiral Hugh Pigot, introduced a bill to provide that Keppel's court martial should be held on shore, rather than aboard ship as the law required, on the grounds of the admiral's health. At first the government resisted the proposal, but in the end allowed the bill to pass. The consequence, though, would be that the court martial would be conducted in the presence of a large number of Keppel's supporters. Meanwhile, anxious to ensure that Jervis, his most vigorous supporter among the captains of the Channel Fleet, would be available to give evidence at the court martial, Keppel wrote to the Admiralty asking that Jervis

13 W. Rodham Donne (ed.), *The Correspondence of King George the Third and Lord North* (London: W Clowes & Sons, n.d.), Vol.II, p.218.

14 Syrett, *European Waters*, p.54.

15 Ira D. Gruber, *The Howe Brothers and the American Revolution* (Williamsburg, VA: Atheneum, 1972), pp.332-335.

should be kept at home. The latter's ship the *Foudroyant* was due to go to the West Indies, and the Admiralty complied with the request and appointed an acting captain.[16]

Towards the end of December there was an intervention by 12 of the most senior admirals in the navy, who signed a Memorial to the King. This was inspired by Lord Bristol, always at the forefront of attempts to embarrass the ministry, and the Duke of Bolton. The Memorial contended that the court martial would be destructive of discipline and that it would not be easy for men of honour to serve, particularly as commanders in chief.[17] Bristol sent it down to Portsmouth, already bearing the signature of Lord Hawke who had been persuaded to head the list. It was also finally signed, among others, by Bristol, Bolton, Geary, Pigot, Samuel Graves (who at first refused to sign and later apologised to Sandwich) and Harland. Reporting on this to Sandwich, Samuel Hood told him that although he had not read it, he understood that the document 'bears very hard and conveys strong censure upon the Admiralty'. Bristol appears to have accompanied it by a circular letter to the proposed signatories, expressing confidence that it would bring down not only the Board of Admiralty but also the ministry.[18] When the Memorial was presented to the King on 30 December, however, he took no action with regard to it.

Meanwhile preparations continued for the opening of the court martial at Portsmouth. Hood, in his capacity as Commissioner there, had made careful provision for the members of the court martial to be well fed at the public expense; Middleton objected to this, suggesting to Sandwich that 'it would give a handle for abuse to those who are seeking the means of finding fault with your Lordship's administration'.[19]

16 Barnes and Owen (eds), *Private Papers of John, Earl of Sandwich*, Vol.II, p.212n.

17 Mackesy, *War for America*, p.241.

18 Barnes and Owen (eds), *Private Papers of John, Earl of Sandwich*, Vol.II, p.213.

19 Barnes and Owen (eds), *Private Papers of John, Earl of Sandwich*, Vol.II, p.194.

15

The Courts Martial

Palliser, having had no discussions with Sandwich before he called for Keppel's court martial, at least had the sense to consult with his lawyers as to the drafting of the charges. When it came down to it, the material on which to base these was not very substantial, but they did their best, and came up with five separate charges, worded to reflect those which Byng had faced in 1756. The first was that Keppel had failed to make the necessary preparations for battle and had attacked in disorder. Secondly, that after the van and centre divisions of the British fleet had passed the enemy's rear, he failed to double the enemy's line and left Palliser's division engaged with the enemy, and exposed to being cut off. Thirdly, that he hauled down the signal for battle too early. Fourthly, that he 'wore and made sail directly from the enemy', which was disgraceful to the British flag since it appeared to be a retreat which gave the enemy a chance to claim a victory. Finally, that on the morning of 28 July he failed 'to pursue the flying enemy'.[1]

The order for the trial embodying these charges was issued on 31 December, and the Court assembled aboard the *Britannia* on 7 January, before at once adjourning to the house of the governor of the Portsmouth garrison. The President of the Court was Admiral Sir Thomas Pye, the commander-in-chief at Portsmouth, who had tried unsuccessfully to get out of the assignment. The remaining members were Vice Admirals Matthew Buckle (who withdrew after six days on health grounds) and John Montague, Rear Admirals Mariot Arbuthnot and Robert Roddam, and Captains Milbanke, Penny, Bennett, Butler, Drake, Moutray, Duncan and Cranston.

It was always likely that the presence of so many of Keppel's supporters would turn the court martial into something of a circus, and so it proved. George Jackson, sent down to Portsmouth to serve as Judge Advocate General, reported the arrival of a large number of prominent members of the opposition: 'The Dukes of Cumberland, Richmond, and Bolton are here, the Marquesses of Rockingham

1 Blandemor (ed.), *Court Martial*, pp.2-4.

and Granby; Lord Effingham; Lieutenant General Keppel and Mr Burke; I do not know if Dunning is; I could see Mr Lee'.[2]

Palliser should not have been, and may well not have been, surprised that the court martial proceedings were a travesty:

> The president and members of the court acted with flagrant partiality, brow-beating witnesses, denying Palliser a hearing and manipulating the evidence. The court, ashore in Portsmouth, was crowded with Keppel's aristocratic friends, cheering points in his favour and hissing those few brave enough to testify for Palliser.[3]

The effect of this of course was to substantially increase the chances of a reply favourable to Keppel to the key question which was at the heart of his defence. Witness after witness would be asked if they had seen anything in the handling of the fleet to suggest that Keppel had negligently performed his duty during the course of the battle. Another aspect of Keppel's defence strategy was repeatedly to remind witnesses and the Court that he was on trial for his life.

Nevertheless, in spite of the ceaseless pressure of the vociferous audience of Keppel's admirers, some captains stood up for themselves. It took a lot of doing, since the Court, or at any rate some of its more vocal members, did not conceal their partiality. Of the latter, Montague was much the most outspoken. Sir William Burnaby, the captain of the frigate *Milford*, was strongly pressed by Montague: 'I must therefore ask you whether during the day of the action Admiral Keppel negligently performed the duty imposed on him'. To this, Burnaby replied: 'It is a question of the greatest importance, and far above me to determine. This Court are to judge of facts by evidence. Admiral Keppel is a brave and gallant officer, and it ill becomes me to give my opinion. I exceedingly respect the character of that worthy gentleman. I say it from my heart'. Montague then snapped that if the officers who were present refused to give their opinion, 'who is the Court to get information from?' This led to a dispute as to whether witnesses could be compelled to answer questions of opinion; Palliser submitted that the Court had no power to ask such questions. The Court retired to consider this; after an hour, its members returned, their ruling being 'that the Court has a right to put what questions they pleased'. In spite of this, and the question again being put to Burnaby, he refused to give an opinion. Montague continued to badger him: 'Can you say yes, or no?' Burnaby bravely refused to do so.[4]

A huge controversy erupted on the seventh day of the hearing over the question of whether Captain Alexander Hood, Samuel Hood's brother, had altered

2 Broomfield, 'The Keppel-Palliser Affair', p.203.
3 Rodger, *Insatiable Earl*, p.248.
4 Blandemor (ed.), *Court Martial*, p.32.

the logbooks of the *Robust*. The suggestion, repeatedly pressed by Keppel, was that Hood had done this after the court martial had been ordered in an attempt to support the allegations made against the admiral. Hood strenuously denied this, saying that when the alterations and additions were made to the log, he was unaware of the charges laid against Keppel; and that although he had corresponded with Palliser, he had not done so on the subject of Keppel's trial. Hood emphatically resisted Keppel's questions; the admiral then said that as the alteration in the logbook tended to affect his life, he would ask Hood no further questions. This led to a further altercation between Palliser and the Court; Montague said that 'the prisoner has a right to ask such questions, where his life was at stake'. Keppel then staged an emotional scene which was reported in these terms:

> Admiral Keppel then, with a most feeling sensibility, the tear starting from his eye, exclaimed, that his astonishment could not be expressed, when he first heard that his conduct on the 27th and 28th days of last July was accused, he knew of no one that could prove the charges laid against him, and was so unprepared that he had almost determined to set up a paper to the public, intreating all those that could, to come and clear his innocence, and from that moment prepared what evidence he could attain; and he hoped that his honour would come out unsullied.[5]

Thereafter Hood was pressed by Montague to answer the standard question as to whether Keppel on 27 and 28 July had 'by his conduct on either of those days tarnished the honour of the British flag'. Hood had held his ground, saying that he had given his evidence and that the Court must therefore decide and judge that question. Montague persisted; but Hood remained obdurate, saying that he had given his evidence and that it was the truth.

The incident over the logbook substantially enhanced Keppel's case, though the actual alterations were not of great significance. The King was following reports of the court martial very closely, and he commented that until this issue was cleared up, 'it certainly is a most favourable event for Keppel'. Jackson, reporting to Stephens, emphasised the point: 'You cannot conceive the impression the alteration in the *Robust's* logbook has made. A loud hiss took place below the bar, which was not rebuked by the Court.[6]

Alexander Hood, who as Lord Bridport would himself command the Channel Fleet at the end of the century, found that his career was seriously compromised by the row over the altered logbook. He felt profoundly bitter towards Keppel, whose rancour towards him at the court martial he saw as affecting the Admiralty's view of him. He wrote in an undated draft:

5 Blandemor (ed.), *Court Martial*, p.81.

6 Barnes and Owen (eds), *Private Papers of John, Earl of Sandwich*, p.216n.

> Should an officer dare for his own justification to say a word, or to alter a word in the logbook, those words are to be construed, by the admiral, into atrocious crimes. They must be meant to affect his life, and what on evidence is delivered under the oath he takes, is deemed falsehood, if that evidence does not come up to the admiral's feelings and those of his *party*.[7]

For Hood, matters came to a head when despite his seniority he was ordered in the *Robust* to North America, not as a commodore, which he took to be his right, but merely as a private captain, and he refused to go. It was the appointment of Kempenfelt, junior to him, as Captain of the Fleet, giving him a status effectively equivalent to that of rear admiral, which caused Hood's fury. Samuel Hood did all he could for his brother in impassioned letters to Sandwich, but the Admiralty insisted that he either go as ordered or be left on shore. Sandwich told Samuel Hood that in ordering the *Robust* to America, he had thought it 'the most friendly act' he could do. Alexander Hood maintained his refusal to go, and it was not until 1782, when he was appointed to command a division of the Channel Fleet, that he was able to resume his career; his wife recorded, in a letter to Lady Chatham, that Keppel, by then himself First Lord, 'received him at his bedside early on Monday morning, and was pleased to wish that what had passed might be forgot, which I think was a tacit acknowledgement of the injustice done to Mr Hood'.[8]

Another witness who earned the extreme disapproval of the members of the Court was Palliser's flag captain John Bazeley, whose evidence has been previously referred to. He was in the witness box over a period of three days, and in spite of aggressive questioning by Montague, Bazeley stuck to his guns. Asked whether the ships which had been ordered to chase the enemy on 27 July could have got into their station in the line of battle, he asked that his previous evidence be read over to him. Keppel objected to this; the Court pronounced in Keppel's favour, and Palliser furiously protested. The Court withdrew; on returning, it was announced 'that the words made use of by the prosecutor, seemed to convey an idea, that this Court acts upon interested and partial motives; they shall not therefore be admitted as part of the minutes of the Court, nor shall they be inserted in the evidence'.[9]

After this, Bazeley's ordeal continued, but he stoutly resisted Montague's continued pressure, and stood up courageously to Keppel's cross examination. The repeated insistence that captains should give their own opinion prompted an irritable letter from Samuel Hood to Sandwich on 18 January:

7 Barnes and Owen (eds), *Private Papers of John, Earl of Sandwich*, Vol.II, p.198.

8 Barnes and Owen (eds), *Private Papers of John, Earl of Sandwich*, Vol.II, p.199.

9 Blandemor (ed.), *Court Martial*, p.137.

> As the Court aim at making every evidence to give judgment upon his own testimony instead of judging upon the facts that are produced, the shortest way of coming to a conclusion would be for each captain to be called to declare once whether the commander-in-chief did right or not, and let most voices carry it.[10]

By the time that Keppel came to call his own witnesses it had become abundantly clear that the trial was going extremely well for him. Palliser had been keeping Sandwich closely informed of the progress of the hearing, and he was under no in illusion about the state of play:

> The business here goes on very heavily and disagreeably. The consequence of granting a court martial to be held on shore is felt very severely: besides the ill effect of the court's being filled with the great leaders of party, every good purpose is defeated that was intended by the regulations for courts martial.[11]

In the same letter, which Sandwich endorsed as having been received on 25 January, Palliser disclosed that although he had been shocked to read the article which had triggered such destructive chain of events, he had not been entirely taken by surprise. He said that he had expected that Keppel would seek to blame him for the outcome of the battle of Ushant: 'Therefore he had kept in his bureau a paper addressed to his Lordship, containing some particulars for his information to the purport of the present charge, that in case he should be killed in the expected engagement on the following cruise, his Lordship might be enabled to contradict any reflections on his memory'.[12]

Among Keppel's witnesses, two in particular were significant. One of these was Rear Admiral John Campbell, the Captain of the Fleet. It had been his signal to the faster ships of Palliser's division to crowd on sail to close the French fleet on the morning of 27 July which had been largely responsible for the relatively disordered way in which the rear came into action. Naturally, his evidence was strongly in Keppel's favour. One of the admiral's supporters wrote effusively:

> Never was there an exhibition of any scene more truly affecting, more noble, or more manly in the examination of the good old Admiral Campbell. United to one another by the strictest ties of the dearest friendship, the noble prisoner and he formed a picture the most sympathetic and expressive. Labouring with that variety of passions that the occasion

10 Barnes and Owen (eds), *Private Papers of John, Earl of Sandwich*, Vol.II, p.217n.

11 Barnes and Owen (eds), *Private Papers of John, Earl of Sandwich*, Vol.II, p.219.

12 Barnes and Owen (eds), *Private Papers of John, Earl of Sandwich*, Vol.II, p.218.

> of their meeting at the bar naturally created, they became too powerful for restraint. While the Rear Admiral answered his friend's question, respecting his having negligently performed his duty, he wiped away the tears from his cheek and could hardly articulate his words.[13]

Keppel's other key witness was Jervis, who had been active in assisting Keppel in the preparation of his case. He told the Court that Keppel had used his most unremitting endeavours to bring the French to action. Asked by Keppel his standard question as to whether the witness saw or knew of any instance in which he had negligently performed his duty on 27 or 28 July, Jervis made a point of asking that the question be put to him by the Court. When this was done, he replied in florid terms:

> I cannot boast of a long acquaintance with Admiral Keppel, I never served under him before; but am happy in this opportunity to declare to this Court, and to all the world, that during the whole time the English fleet were in sight of the French fleet, he displayed the greatest naval skill and ability, and the boldest enterprise on 27th July, which, with the promptitude and obedience of Vice Admiral Sir Robert Harland, will be subjects of my admiration and imitation as long as I live.[14]

Understandably, Palliser conducted a vigorous cross examination of Jervis; at one point he was evasive in replying to a question about wind and courses, saying that he had no minutes, and had brought with him nothing but the charges, and nothing else to guide him. Palliser told him to look at his logbook. This was too much for Montague, who interrupted to say that Jervis had said that he did not want his logbook: 'Why it should be crammed down his throat I cannot think!' Jervis said that he would not be bound by anything in the logbook, but he was then obliged to admit that he was in error about the shift of wind. Montague again intervened: 'Shut the logbook up, and let us hear no more of the logbook for God's sake, let us come to matters of fact, from your own knowledge'.[15] Palliser's cross examination continued, leading to further lively exchanges with Jervis, who was very tenderly treated throughout by the Court.

By 4 February, Sandwich was writing to Palliser to say that it was 'not difficult to judge what will be the issue of it,' and that in consequence he thought it inevitable that Palliser must also undergo a trial, and that it would be better for the Admiralty to order it than appear later to be compelled to do so by political pressure. Palliser accepted at once that this was so, writing to Sandwich next day:

13 James, *The British Navy in Adversity*, p.140.

14 Blandemor (ed.), *Court Martial*, p.351.

15 Blandemor (ed.), *Court Martial*, p.353.

'It is a very disadvantageous time for me, as the public prejudice and the stream is so strong against me; its being ordered to come on at a little distance of time will give me a chance for the prejudices produced by the violence of party subsiding a little'.[16]

As the trial neared its end, Jackson promised to send Sandwich a summary of the evidence no later than the time he received the sentence. He excused possible inaccuracies due to 'noise, hurry, interruption and excessive labour' but reassured the First Lord that there would be nothing deficient in point of fact. The evidence, he estimated, would amount to 1,200 pages. Palliser told Sandwich that he would seek leave to reply to Keppel's defence, once this was completed; if the Court did not permit it, he thought that it would be 'the most extravagant partiality'. As he had expected, in due course he was refused this right of reply and on 8 February the Court adjourned to consider its decision. This came on Thursday, 11 February. In 'fully and honourably' acquitting Keppel, the sentence recorded that the charge against him was malicious and ill founded, and that Keppel had 'behaved as became a judicious, brave, and experienced officer'.[17]

The intensity of public feeling throughout the trial had been so great that Palliser had told Sandwich that he considered that when the verdict should be announced, his life would be in danger. Events quickly showed that he had been entirely justified in his concern. As soon as the Court's sentence was delivered, a large crowd gathered to escort Keppel triumphantly through the streets of Portsmouth, led by a band playing 'See the Conquering Hero comes'. A not altogether dispassionate observer described the scene: 'The whole concourse and ladies from the windows supplied the vocal part, and the crowd closed each period of the harmony with a choral cheer … It is impossible to paint the joy that possessed every face. Holiday was expressed in every look, and the hearts of the people were in their eyes'.[18]

In London, the news of the outcome of the court martial was also greeted with an outburst of excitement. A mob formed, which tore off the gates of the Admiralty, and roamed through the streets breaking the windows of ministers' houses; Germain had all his doors and windows battered in, while 10 Downing Street was spared only by the turning out of the Guards and the reading of the Riot Act. Palliser's house was looted and his furniture burnt in St James's Square, and it was necessary for the military to patrol the streets for several days to restore order. In Parliament, resolutions were carried thanking Keppel for defending the kingdom, and the admiral was presented with the Freedom of the City of London.

Back in Portsmouth, Jervis was tireless in his continued campaign against Palliser, preparing and circulating a memorial for signature by the captains calling for his removal. Samuel Hood reported to Sandwich on 10 February that he had

16 Barnes and Owen (eds), *Private Papers of John, Earl of Sandwich*, Vol.II, p.222.
17 Blandemor (ed.), *Court Martial*, pp.378-379.
18 Barnes and Owen (eds), *Private Papers of John, Earl of Sandwich*, Vol.II, p.195.

been told by Jervis that 18 had already signed it, with six more promising to do so. Among those that had signed it were Harland, Campbell, Ross, Walsingham, Laforey and Marshall: 'What a glaring proof is this, my lord, of the malevolence and rancour of party; and what presumption to attempt to prescribe to his Majesty who he shall or shall not employ. Let Sir Hugh's fate be what it may, the King never had a more brave and able officer, or a more zealous and faithful servant'.[19] A number of captains, to their credit, refused to sign, including Robinson, Digby and Peyton.

Palliser, as he had promised, duly applied for his own court martial as soon as Keppel's trial was completed. There followed a disagreeable episode in the course of which Palliser was induced by what the King called a 'mean subterfuge' to resign his commission as Lieutenant General of Marines and the governorship of Scarborough Castle, as well as his membership of the Board of Admiralty, where his place was taken in due course by Vice Admiral Robert Man.

Palliser's court martial commenced on 12 April aboard the *Sandwich* in Portsmouth harbour. The President of the Court was Vice Admiral George Darby; the remaining members were Rear Admiral Robert Digby and Captains Ogle, Peyton, Robinson, Goodall, Linzee, Walters, Kempenfelt, Bayne, Duncan, Cranston (who retired on health grounds after three days) and Colpoys. Keppel had refused to act as prosecutor, and the order to the Court was that it should 'enquire into the conduct of the said Vice Admiral'. George Jackson again served as Judge Advocate General.

Palliser conducted his defence skilfully and with great dignity. He told the Court that 'all of those sufferings which now afflict me have been brought on by the pursuit of a candid and fair hearing, to defend my character against the unprovoked attacks of the most inveterate and unrelenting enemies'.[20] Although a dispassionate consideration of the matter should have told Palliser that there was little chance of his court martial going against him, he remained anxious throughout the hearing, writing to Sandwich on 22 April to appeal to him and his friends 'not to condemn me before I have made my defence'. He had already, he said, been condemned by one court without being heard, which had served the purpose of his enemies; he looked to his friends for their countenance and protection.[21]

Palliser put forward a comprehensive defence, dealing in detail with the allegations made against him by Keppel and the other witnesses at the latter's court martial, which formed the basis of the case against him. In particular, he disposed of the complaint that he had failed to send a frigate to Keppel by pointing out that he had no frigate to send until 8.00 p.m., because Burnaby's *Milford* had been called up by Keppel. Palliser added, though, that in any case he could not see why

19 Barnes and Owen (eds), *Private Papers of John, Earl of Sandwich*, Vol.II, p.228.

20 Anon., *Defence of Vice Admiral Sir Hugh Palliser*, pp.1-2.

21 Barnes and Owen (eds), *Private Papers of John, Earl of Sandwich*, Vol.II, p.250.

it would be necessary to send her, since 'the condition of the *Formidable* was so apparent as to make a message unnecessary'. The Court delivered its sentence on 5 May; it found that 'his conduct and behaviour on those days were in many respects highly exemplary and meritorious,' though the sentence did add that the Court thought it was incumbent on him to have made known to Keppel the condition of the *Formidable*. Apart from that, the Court considered that he was not in any other respect chargeable with misconduct or misbehaviour and accordingly acquitted him.[22]

Although he had been deservedly acquitted, Palliser's ruin was complete. He applied, unsuccessfully, to North to have his Lieutenant-Generalcy of Marines restored to him, and in the following year he asked Sandwich for a seat at the Admiralty. This appeal also failed; but in May 1780 he was made governor of Greenwich Hospital, an appointment which provoked a further storm in Parliament. Palliser was able to make a spirited defence of his conduct in a speech to a Committee of the House of Commons on 4 December, 1780, largely based on the defence which he had put forward at his own court martial, and this had a beneficial effect on public opinion. But he never served again. The Royal Navy had lost the services of one of its ablest officers, at a time when it could least afford to do so, and it was a tragic end to a career that had shown such promise.

Keppel never went to sea again. In March he was asked by the Admiralty whether he proposed to continue as commander-in-chief of the Channel Fleet. In his reply, he said that he was willing to risk his life in the service of his country, if at the same time he could be 'secure of his honour,' but he went on to say:

> It is next to impossible for me to render creditable and beneficial service to the King and the nation by my continuing in the command of the Western squadron, under the direction and authority of those whose approbation in the execution of my duty and support afterwards, experience has taught me, I cannot depend upon.[23]

Understandably, Sandwich could have little confidence in Keppel after all that transpired. The admiral had also set out his grievances about the way in which he had been treated in a letter to the King. The terms of his correspondence effectively put paid to any remaining hope of an amicable working relationship. After an exchange between Sandwich and Lord Thurlow, the Lord Chancellor, the question was settled; the use by Keppel of the words 'next to impossible' was to be taken as amounting to a resignation, and he was accordingly, with the King's approval, ordered to strike his flag.

22 Anon., *Defence of Vice Admiral Sir Hugh Palliser*, pp.69-70.
23 Barnes and Owen (eds), *Private Papers of John, Earl of Sandwich*, Vol.II, p.195.

The Royal Navy had thus lost another senior sea officer who at least brought badly needed experience to the Channel Fleet. Yet Keppel had shown himself to be no more than a second-rate naval commander, and really was no great loss. His exploitation of his popularity to bring down Palliser not only destroyed a political opponent, but also inflicted lasting damage on the navy. Nicholas Rodger thought that it looked very much as though Keppel himself had become little more than a glove puppet for the extremists of the Rockingham party. Broomfield considered that in the long run they might have gained little from the affair:

> Certainly it gained them some recruits from among the naval officers, but at the same time it may well have weakened their influence with the independents. The country gentlemen, arbiters of the fate of any eighteenth century administration, disliked the participation of army and navy officers in politics and, at a time when the nation was threatened from abroad, they were particularly suspicious of any who encouraged it.[24]

24 Broomfield, 'The Keppel-Palliser Affair', pp.206-207.

16

The Convention of Aranjuez

The long-drawn-out delay on the part of Spain in entering the war was part of a conscious strategy on the part of Floridablanca, who in negotiating the basis of an agreement with France was in no doubt of the advantages of playing hard to get. The proposal that Spain should embark on a mediation process was an important part of this. The historian Edward Corwin wrote:

> There were several reasons why it seemed good to Floridablanca to dress his monarch up as the champion of peace and capable in its interest of dispensing an even justice between France and her ally on the one hand and Great Britain on the other. For one thing, the proposal gave His Catholic Majesty that independent role which his affronted dignity demanded. Again, it furnished a new reason for delay. Lastly, in the form it finally assumed, it promised Spain an opportunity to curtail American independence.[1]

In August, Floridablanca told Montmorin that Spain would take no action until she knew the outcome of her attempts at mediation. At the same time, he confirmed that military and naval preparations were continuing, and he offered the French ambassador his thoughts on the way a joint campaign might be conducted, suggesting that a combined Franco-Spanish fleet of 60 ships of the line might conduct an invasion of southern England.[2] Floridablanca's suggestion did not make much appeal to Vergennes, whose response on 17 August to Montmorin realistically drew attention to the hazards involved. Such an invasion would require extremely elaborate preparation, and it would certainly not be possible in the current campaigning season:

1 Corwin, *French Policy and the American Alliance*, pp.180-181.
2 Dull, *French Navy and American Independence*, p.128.

> It could not be attempted before next year. A fleet of sixty French and Spanish ships could not easily be concentrated, and it would have to fight in the Channel against an English fleet of forty five of the line ...the issue of a naval battle is always uncertain; ... a storm or violent gale might disperse the combined fleets; France has no port in the Channel; in fact, innumerable mischances might ruin the enterprise.[3]

In passing on these considerations to Floridablanca, Montmorin told Vergennes that he went about this very cautiously: 'I tread very warily when it is a matter of pointing out the difficulties in the way of any enterprise proposed by M. de Floridablanca; I fear that if I showed them as they really are I would ... give him occasion to reproach us ... for wanting to wage only a cold and lifeless war'.[4]

The Spanish mediation stood very little chance of success, in spite of various proposals that were put forward that appeared to suggest flexibility. A hint had been dropped, for instance, by Lord Barrington, the Secretary at War, to the Spanish ambassador in London to the effect that Britain might be prepared to give up Gibraltar and Minorca. A Spanish suggestion of a lengthy truce between Britain and the Americans was not entirely ruled out by Franklin when Vergennes put it to him, provided that France and Spain accorded to the United States 'their goodwill and protection'.[5] However, when Spain formally invited the parties to state the terms which they would seek, it soon became clear that there were essential sticking points that could not easily be overcome. Britain was unwilling to make the sort of concessions that would be necessary and, in particular, was unwilling to contemplate ceding any territory.

After Floridablanca had reported this to Vergennes, two themes came to dominate Montmorin's reports of his discussions with the Spanish minister. They left Vergennes in no doubt about what Floridablanca was looking for. First, he sought to pin down France to a firm commitment to Spanish war aims; Vergennes perfectly understood the reasons for Spanish unease about this. Secondly, Floridablanca intended that these should be achieved by employing a military and naval strategy that was likely to be rapidly effective; by this, the Spanish minister meant an invasion of the British Isles which, if successful, would compel the British government to accept the terms demanded by the Bourbon allies.

The events of 1778 had confirmed Vergennes in his view of France's actual strategic situation. In spite of the massive strengthening of the French navy, and the fact that the diplomatic situation in Europe as it stood meant that the French army was free from any obligation to prepare for a continental war, Vergennes did not

3 Patterson, *The Other Armada*, p.41.

4 Patterson, *The Other Armada*, p.42.

5 Corwin, *French Policy and the American Alliance*, p.186; Dull, *French Navy and American Independence*, p.130.

suppose that France could achieve a decisive victory on her own. In America, the colonists could not be counted on to overwhelm the British armed forces there. Only if Spain fully honoured the Family Compact could his policy succeed. He must have Spain, as he had freely acknowledged to Louis XVI, which meant not only pledging unreservedly to support Spanish war aims; it also meant allowing Spain to dictate the strategic narrative for the conduct of the war.

As time went on Vergennes was becoming increasingly anxious that with the Spanish attempt at mediation still continuing, she would not be ready for joint action in the spring of 1779. He wrote to Louis XVI on 5 December to record his concerns:

> If it is a fact that His Majesty cannot struggle long on equal terms with the English and that a prolonged war, which would not be exempt from disadvantages, could entertain the ruin of his navy and even his finances, and finally that His Majesty, reduced to his own means, would be less able to make his enemies feel the need of peace than if he were acting in concert with a strong ally, then the most natural consequence is that everything invites him to take some risks in order to activate such a desirable alliance. I will not dissimulate, Sire, that the views and pretensions of Spain are gigantic, but it is necessary to consider that the time one uses to countervail against them will be lost for the establishment of combined operations which one cannot hasten too much to prepare.[6]

The Franco-Spanish discussions still had a considerable way to go. Louis XVI promptly accepted the principles that Vergennes had put before him, and the French minister, on 24 December, sent to Montmorin a plan of projected joint operations. In one of his covering letters he warned his ambassador not to trust Floridablanca, bearing in mind how he had been let down by him earlier in the year. He made it clear to Montmorin that his fallback position would be to require the minimum support provided for by the Family Compact of 12 ships of the line and five frigates. The plan which he put forward, which he said he had not discussed with professionals in order to maintain secrecy, was conservative. It substituted for Floridablanca's preferences for an attack on England, which would call for the deployment of 70,000 infantry and 5,000 cavalry, a descent upon Ireland by 27,000 infantry and 3,000 cavalry, made up as to half from France and half from Spain. He expected that a landing would encourage the Irish to rise against the English. He dismissed suggestions of attacks on Minorca and Jamaica as impracticable, and stated that France, having taken Dominica, desired no further conquests in the Caribbean.[7]

6 Dull, *French Navy and American Independence*, p.133.
7 Dull, *French Navy and American Independence*, p.134.

Floridablanca's reaction was still shifty. Montmorin reported on 12 January his first response to the proposals which Vergennes had made: 'His Catholic Majesty wished to show his nephew the same measure of confidence that the latter had shown him. He accordingly desired that His Most Christian Majesty should be the one to specify the conditions without which he would promise not to consent to peace'.[8] The Spanish minister did, however, let fall to Montmorin some hints as to what he was looking for; it seemed that he would accept a convention that assured Spain of Pensacola and Mobile, the ejection of English settlers from Honduras, and the restoration of Gibraltar. Reporting this, Montmorin added that the Spanish desire that France should put forward the terms of a deal was based on the belief that in this way France would feel more bound to respect them. Floridablanca still believed that Gibraltar could not be taken by direct assault, and could be recovered only as part of a general settlement after the outcome of a successful war.

While Spain and France were thus edging towards an agreement on war aims, the Spanish attempt at mediation was proceeding. A compromise proposal was put forward to the parties, by which Britain was to withdraw her troops from America, and a long term truce was to be concluded. The British reaction to this was initially to temporise, but in March the proposal was firmly rejected.

Meanwhile, on 12 February, Vergennes sent to Montmorin a draft of the convention which he proposed, and gave the ambassador full powers to negotiate 'any modifications or additions that might seem needful'. The draft provided that neither party should make peace without the consent of the other; that both parties agreed not to make peace until Britain conceded American independence; that France's right to fortify Dunkirk should be restored and that Britain should be excluded from Newfoundland, and that Spain should have fishing rights there; and it embodied the Spanish aims that Montmorin had reported.[9] Since this was more or less what Floridablanca seemed to have in mind, Vergennes might reasonably have hoped that it would be acceptable, and at first this seemed to be the case, but then the Spanish minister began to raise difficulties, to Montmorin's great frustration. Vergennes was not altogether surprised, commenting that 'from Spain nothing is to be got for nothing; we have from her directly that she wishes some advantages from the Americans as well as from us, and we will not oppose her'. Floridablanca was particularly discontented with the term that provided that peace should not be made without American independence; Vergennes, who was mindful of the terms of the secret treaty with the Americans, said that he would settle for anything provided that 'by the general tenor of the act we have not neglected the interests of this republic'.[10]

8 Corwin, *French Policy and the American Alliance*, pp.189-190.

9 Corwin, *French Policy and the American Alliance*, pp.190-191.

10 Corwin, *French Policy and the American Alliance*, p.192.

With this draft convention, Vergennes included the outline of a plan of operations. Since the Spanish had indicated that they would be able to contribute no troops for an invasion of Ireland, he withdrew that proposal, not least because if the operation was to be entirely mounted from French ports of embarkation the element of surprise would be lost, as he explained:

> It could succeed only by dint of secrecy, and how could that be guaranteed when all the preparations would point obviously to one objective? This drawback would have been much diminished if France and Spain had acted together. Their plans would not have been known, and the enemy's uncertainty as to the point threatened by each of the two powers would have given more possibility of success. But our intentions will be plain enough if we are seen to be mustering a force of 30,000 men in the Rochefort area.[11]

Instead of this, Vergennes now proposed a campaign to disrupt British trade and, if possible to destroy the Channel Fleet; this would be achieved by concentrating a fleet at the entrance to the Channel which would cover the landing of an expeditionary force on the Isle of Wight. From there, operations would be conducted against the Channel Fleet, which it was assumed would be in Portsmouth. He estimated that the Franco-Spanish combined fleet must consist of at least 45 ships of the line.[12]

Although in general terms approving the outline of the plan put forward, Floridablanca still did not intend to go to war until detailed operational plans were available which could be put into immediate effect. He insisted that he must have these before approving the draft of the convention which Vergennes had put forward. Montmorin protested that the work of preparing this would be hampered by the need to preserve secrecy. Floridablanca was displeased:

> We do not wish to commit Spain to entering the war merely in order to frighten England into a peace from which nothing but the independence of the Americans would be obtained … The moment of our declaration of war now depends on your Court. We are perfectly ready … But you must make up your minds, and convince us that you do not want us to declare war simply in order to terrify the English into making peace by a naval promenade in the Channel.[13]

11 Patterson, *The Other Armada*, p.44.
12 Dull, *French Navy and American Independence*, p.138.
13 Patterson, *The Other Armada*, p.45.

In order to assist the preparation of such plans, Floridablanca confirmed the scale of Spanish naval forces which would be available. He was prepared to contribute 20 ships of the line to act jointly with 30 French vessels, and to add further ships to ensure the maintenance of a ratio of 4:3 in favour of the allies. He thought that only 18,000 to 20,000 troops would be needed to take the Isle of Wight. He saw an invasion of England as the only way to achieve a quick victory.[14] On 10 March Vergennes met with the King, Sartine, Maurepas, and Montbarrey to initiate the planning process.

Meanwhile the final terms of the secret convention were being hammered out. Floridablanca wished it to come into effect upon the expected rejection by the British of a final ultimatum which Spain would now put forward, which proposed a truce in North America; after this, Spain would have the justification she needed for a declaration of war. The Convention of Aranjuez was finally signed by Montmorin and Floridablanca on 12 April but even now no date was set for the Spanish entry into the war. In the Convention the minimum war aims of the allies were set out; the war would not end until Spain achieved the restitution of Gibraltar and France obtained the abrogation of the 1763 restrictions on fortifying Dunkirk. Floridablanca had wished also to add Minorca and Florida to the list of Spanish war aims; instead, these were included in a separate list of other gains which each country hoped to be able to make.

Neither Vergennes nor Floridablanca was particularly keen on the idea of a large-scale joint operation against southern England, but Floridablanca remained convinced that it was the only way in which a rapid and decisive result might be obtained. It was now down to the professionals to work out the detailed plans for the operation, which would be extremely complex. There were plenty of precedents to which they could refer. Over the years many different schemes had been put forward for the invasion of England; but since the Norman Conquest none of them, with the exception of William III's bloodless invasion of 1688, had produced the desired result.

14 Dull, *French Navy and American Independence*, p.130.

17

Invasion Plans

The concept of winning a war by an invasion of the English coast had been explored by French strategists for more than a century and a half; indeed, as early as 1377 a French fleet had burnt Portsmouth and landed on the Isle of Wight, while in 1545 another fleet under d'Annibault launched an attack in the course of which the *Mary Rose* famously sank in the Solent. In 1692, after the Battle of Beachy Head, the French for the moment had the command of the sea, but de Tourville, the French commander, considered that a landing was too risky. After this, the idea of an invasion of England continued to be the subject of a number of projects submitted to the French government, but during the first half of the eighteenth century most attention was given to the plan for supporting a Stuart restoration. For this, landings in Scotland or Ireland appeared to offer the best chance of successfully provoking risings against the Hanoverian monarchy.

Admiral Richmond, in his analysis of the history of plans for the invasion of England, summarised the ways in which this might be undertaken:

> Broadly speaking, three courses of action are open to the would-be invader. He may convoy his transports with his fighting ships in one great body; he may leave his transports at home, and precede their movement by attempting to destroy the enemy fleet or to divert its attention from the desired line of passage; or he may use, and depend entirely upon, the weapon of surprise, preparing his movement in secrecy, and making the attempt without warning, and so deprive his enemy both of the time and the opportunity to obstruct his movements.[1]

The first of these options would always depend on obtaining a sufficient superiority at sea; historically, this has rarely been possible, and in any event a battle fleet which was encumbered with a large convoy of transports was at a serious disadvantage. The alternative option, of first disposing of the Royal Navy before

1 Admiral Sir Herbert Richmond, *The Invasion of Britain* (London: Methuen & Co, 1941), p.2.

launching the invasion, was equally risky. To do so directly, by winning a decisive battle, was always going to be difficult, while to do so indirectly by endeavouring to draw off the British fleet depended effectively on the British Admiralty making a major strategic error in its response to the French movements. That left only the third option, of launching a surprise attack, which would require the greatest care to be taken if secrecy was to be maintained. Concealing the preparations from the watchful eyes of British frigates would necessarily take a lot of doing.

During the eighteenth century a number of schemes for the invasion of southern England had been prepared. The first to be adopted as a serious attempt at a large-scale invasion was drafted in the autumn of 1743, at a time when Britain and France were not yet at war. It was then estimated that the largest defence force that could be assembled in Britain at short notice in any one place would be no more than 5,000 men strong, so it was calculated that an invasion force of 10,000, landed suddenly in the Blackwater, would be sufficient to brush aside opposition and take London. Accordingly, such an army was secretly assembled at Dunkirk, and the necessary fleet of transports was only very gradually built up. The original scheme was for the invasion convoy to be escorted only by frigates, to avoid arousing suspicion by the fitting out of a battle fleet at Brest. However, as planning proceeded the decision was taken that this would be too risky, and four ships of the line were earmarked to be sent from Brest to escort the convoy. Meanwhile, the rest of the battle fleet would launch an attack on the British fleet, which it was assumed would be found at Spithead. In spite of the maintenance of a high level of secrecy while the preparations were being made, intelligence that something was up reached Britain, and the Channel Fleet was mobilised at Portsmouth. The news that their design had been penetrated did not reach de Roquefeuil, the commander of the French fleet at Brest, until after he had put to sea. When he received this news, he concluded that he must now take the whole fleet to Dunkirk to cover the operation. The embarkation began, but when it was approximately two thirds complete, the British fleet under Sir John Norris appeared. It was unable to launch an attack at once due to the calm conditions and a west setting tide. In the night, the French fleet cut its cables, and drifted silently and unseen down Channel on the ebb tide. A fierce easterly gale then sprang up, but the fleet safely reached Brest ahead of the Channel Fleet. However, the transports at Dunkirk that had already put to sea were scattered in the storm, and many were wrecked.[2]

At the start of the Seven Years War, in July 1756, an army of 50,000 troops was assembled in northern France. The plan now was to launch an invasion of the south coast of England, an advanced guard being landed to seize a port, to be followed by the main body. At the same time a diversionary attack on Minorca was planned. The invasion of England never materialised, because command of the Channel could not be won, but Minorca was captured after the battle which ultimately cost Admiral Byng his life. In 1759 the French tried again. At this time

2 Richmond, *Invasion of Britain*, pp.24-25.

a much more complex scheme was planned. 20,000 men, sailing from Ostend, would be landed in the Blackwater, and another 20,000, from Brittany, would sail for the Clyde, escorted by the whole French fleet from both Brest and Toulon. This, after covering the landing, would sail northabout around Scotland to cover the convoy from Ostend as it carried out the landing in the Blackwater. At the same time, a raid on Ireland was also planned. The scheme failed; Boscawen defeated the Toulon fleet off Lagos in Portugal and in November Sir Edward Hawke caught the Brest fleet under Conflans and destroyed it in Quiberon Bay, in a battle in which both Keppel and Howe distinguished themselves.[3]

This disaster did not mark the end of French invasion planning. When, following the conclusion of the Bourbon Family Compact, Spain joined the war, the French chief minister Choiseul prepared a very different and much less ambitious plan. This scheme was to be undertaken in absolute secrecy. A small force assembled between Calais and Dunkirk would cross the Channel to seize a beachhead, after which the bulk of an army of about 50,000 men, which to avoid causing suspicion had been assembled inland, would march to the coast to be embarked. This plan depended on achieving command of the Channel for at least five weeks, which Choiseul optimistically believed was possible. The war ended, however, before this scheme could be attempted.[4]

The most ambitious of the invasion plans prepared in France after the end of the Seven Years War was the work of Comte Charles-François de Broglie, the younger brother of the commander of the army in Normandy. In 1765 he submitted an elaborate scheme, based on a principal attack by French and Spanish forces on the south coast of England, supported by six diversionary operations. These included attacks on Gibraltar, Jamaica and Ireland, in which Spain was to participate, and three more, which the French would undertake, against Scotland, Minorca and in the Indian Ocean. The invasion force was to consist of 60,000 men in four divisions, landing at Rye, Winchelsea, Hastings and Pevensey. Once ashore, it was to march on London.[5]

De Broglie summed up the essential basis on which he had prepared his plan:

> The principal object should always be the landing in England … All other projected expeditions must have the essential object of puzzling the enemy, of occupying his attention, and dividing his forces, so that he shall be unable to prevent the passage of the army and its disembarkation on the English coast.[6]

3 Norman Longmate, *Island Fortress: The Defence of Great Britain 1603-1945* (London: Grafton, 1991), pp.179-180; Richmond, *Invasion of Britain*, pp.26-27.

4 Longmate, *Island Fortress*, p.187.

5 Patterson, *The Other Armada*, p.7.

6 Richmond, *Invasion of Britain*, p.28.

De Broglie proposed to concentrate, as far as was possible, the French naval forces to achieve local superiority in the Channel; the diversionary attacks for the purpose of compelling the British navy to detach ships would as far as possible be carried out by Spanish forces. He was concerned to ensure that the French navy would not be scattered on minor operations: 'No little squadrons, no convoys, no distant expeditions; great fleets, all our forces in one sea, a naval battle at the outset, a lively and short war'.[7] De Broglie calculated that in this way the British would have no more than 45 ships of the line available to meet the French fleet of 40 ships of the line; he believed that individually the French ships would be superior in fighting power, and would be capable of beating the British. Patterson cites the French historian René Castex, who considered that this was the best of the many invasion plans that had been put forward over the years, but that de Broglie had been at fault initially in not grasping how essential it was that there must first be a decisive victory over the British fleet.[8] Subsequently, however, he revised his scheme to take account of this.

After a lengthy period during which de Broglie had to overcome the reluctance of Louis XV, he was finally authorised to proceed with his planning in conjunction with Choiseul. In due course this led to a plan which was submitted to Spain for approval at the time of the Falklands crisis of 1770, and which provided for a fleet of 30 French and 20 Spanish ships of the line to conduct the operation. The peaceful resolution of the crisis meant that no further work was done on this scheme.

Meanwhile, however, invasion plans continued to be discussed, and these began to focus on the idea of treating Portsmouth and the Isle of Wight, rather than London, as the primary objective, and this was to lead in due course to the scheme submitted by Vergennes to Floridablanca in 1779. In 1768 *Colonel* de Béville had been sent by Choiseul to reconnoitre the south of England. He produced a plan for the landing of an army between Littlehampton and Chichester Harbour, which would then divide, one part marching on Dorking and Guildford, and the other westwards to attack Portsmouth from the landward side, while the fleet attacked the Portsea Lines and landed additional troops to take Gosport. After a successful siege of Portsmouth, the Isle of Wight would then be occupied, while the rest of the army joined the force occupying Dorking and Guildford for an advance on London.[9] Another proposal, fairly similar to that put forward by de Béville, came from the Comte de Guines, the French ambassador in London from 1770 to 1776. In his paper, which he submitted in 1773, he expressed the view that one decisive naval victory would have the effect of ruining Britain's finances. Thereafter, he proposed, there should be an invasion of the south coast, an attack on Portsmouth and a subsequent march on London.

7 Richmond, *Invasion of Britain*, p.29.
8 Patterson, *The Other Armada*, pp.8-9.
9 Patterson, *The Other Armada*, pp.9-10.

While the French were thus contemplating a variety of schemes for a possible invasion, there was naturally considerable thought being given in Britain as to what might be expected. Major General Sir Guy Carleton produced a memorandum in 1771, which warned of the extreme danger if the French actually succeeded in making a landing: 'The only difficulty France has to fear, in carrying a plan of invasion to execution, arises from our superior fleet; could her transports pass the sea unmolested, our land forces, were they much more numerous than at present, could not guard our extensive coast, nor prevent an enemy's getting ashore'.[10] Carleton concluded that notwithstanding the difficulty of successfully transporting an army across the Channel, it was likely that France would indeed attempt an invasion at the opening of the next war, since 'the most judicious way of carrying on war with Great Britain is to establish the seat of war in England'. He speculated that it was possible that the British fleet might be driven into harbour by winter storms, and prevented from getting out by the same wind from the southeast that carried the French invasion force across the Channel. He suggested that the French might assemble one army 40,000 strong, and put it ashore in five divisions at Hythe, Rye, Brighton, Shoreham, and Arundel. The division at Hythe would march on Maidstone, Chatham and Sheerness, and that at Arundel on Portsmouth, while the remainder headed for London. Once ashore, the army would face little serious opposition, since there were no more than 10,000 regular troops scattered about the British Isles, and the 31,000 militia were of doubtful quality.

The plan which Vergennes had submitted to Floridablanca was based on a scheme put forward by a renegade Scottish naval officer named Robert Mitchell Hamilton, who had become a captain in the French navy. He was employed in reviewing the various points on the English coast at which an invasion might be aimed. Of these, he strongly recommended an assault on Portsmouth and the Isle of Wight. This coincided with the views of the 39-year-old *Colonel* Charles François Dumouriez, the future victor of Valmy, who had since January 1778 been commander of the garrison of Cherbourg. He had also been investigating the possibilities of an assault on the Isle of Wight, and in March 1779 he produced a project for a sudden landing there by 12,000 troops, assembled at Cherbourg on the pretext of working on the new fortifications there, which would be transported to the southwestern coast of the island. After the Isle of Wight was taken, the entrance to Portsmouth harbour would be blocked by transports loaded with stones which would be sunk at Spithead. In his scheme, Dumouriez opted for a sudden overnight dash rather than for a more extended operation covered by the French fleet.[11]

Many years later, in his autobiography, Dumouriez reflected on the possibilities which his scheme had offered:

10 Richmond, *Invasion of Britain*, p.30.

11 Patterson, *The Other Armada*, pp.17-18.

> Seeing the shortness of the crossing, the frequency of fog in the Channel, the length of the October and November nights, and the species of calm that characterises this narrow sea for more than six weeks of December and January, I deemed the obstacles by no means insuperable, especially for partial 'diversions' and in the winter of 1777-8 I laid before the ministry the plans of an expedition against the Isle of Wight which were but the preliminary of a great project of descent ... In 1778 England had 50,000 men in America and not 10,000 regulars at home that could be collected at any one given spot. The militia were not embodied ... There were in Portsmouth only one battalion of foot, 600 pensioners, a few Marines doing duty in the port, or ready for drafting on to the ships of frigates then fitting out ... The Isle of Wight contained a large number of sick men in Newport hospital, the corn and foodstuffs for the Portsmouth squadrons at Brading and St Helens, and stacked timber and shipyards in full work for the frigates, corvettes, and cutters of the Portsmouth division at Cowes. All the defence of the island consisted of a little artillery in Shanklin fort, with 150 pensioners.[12]

Dumouriez considered that the Isle of Wight would be an excellent stronghold, capable of resisting a lengthy siege if the British attempted to retake it.

Although Vergennes had on 8 March assured Montmorin that plans could be provided that would be 'sufficiently to the taste of M de Floridablanca', it was still his aim to restrict the scope of the operation to be undertaken against southern England, for fear that if it was too successful it might alarm the other European powers. A. Temple Patterson argued:

> For this purpose the project of an attack on Portsmouth seemed much more suitable than de Broglie's rival plan, with its objectives of the capture of London and the overrunning of all of the south of England. From de Broglie, however, Vergennes borrowed that absolute insistence on a decisive naval victory and complete command of the Channel which bulked so large in his proposals.[13]

Patterson notes the striking fact that, at the meeting of 10 March which was convened to agree the outline of the scheme, no consultation took place with either d'Orvilliers or any of the military commanders.

Vergennes was accordingly determined that the plans to be prepared should not be overambitious; the objectives should not be to overrun England or to aim at

12 Longmate, *Island Fortress*, pp.186-187.

13 Patterson, *The Other Armada*, p.46.

the capture of London, but should have as their targets Portsmouth and the Isle of Wight. Such an attack,

> … even if only half successful, would spread consternation in England and weaken her resources, which would certainly be inadequate to repair the damage in the course of the same campaign. Besides, since her trade would suffer greatly once France was in control of the Channel, she would lack the means to continue the struggle and would have to accept peace on our terms or suffer a general bankruptcy that would totally deprive her of the possibility of making war.[14]

As finalised, the plan was for a fleet including 30 French ships of the line to be fitted out at Brest by the beginning of May, which would then join a fleet of 20 Spanish ships of the line at Corunna by 15 May. The Spanish were to reach that port first, so that if adverse winds prevented the French fleet when it arrived from entering the harbour there, the Spanish would be ready to come out to join their allies. If the Spanish chose to provide an equal or greater number of ships of the line, there would be no objection to a Spanish commander-in-chief; otherwise, d'Orvilliers would be in command. The troops to form the invasion force would be 20,000 strong, all infantry save for a few hundred dragoons, under the command of *Lieutenant-Général* de Vaux; *Maréchal* de Broglie had fallen out of favour. Other substantial forces would be assembled in Brittany and Dunkirk to distract the British. The plan was for an attack to be made on the Isle of Wight, and then on Gosport; from there Portsmouth and its dockyard could be bombarded. There was to be no attempt to land elsewhere, for instance with a view to taking Portsmouth from the landward side. There would, however, be a number of diversionary attacks. In case the main assault failed, consideration could be given to attacks on the Channel Islands or Plymouth.[15]

This plan was sent to Floridablanca at the end of March, and he professed himself entirely satisfied with it. He told Montmorin that the Spanish fleet was almost ready, though this was certainly an over optimistic assessment. He now proposed to embark on the closing stages of the Spanish mediation, which would culminate in the ultimatum to Britain which would justify the Spanish declaration of war, and it would therefore still be some time before this occurred. The ultimatum proposed an indefinite truce in America, during which Britain would be allowed to remain in possession of the territory she still held there. When these terms were reported to Vergennes on 12 April, he was dismayed, and wrote to Montmorin:

14 Patterson, *The Other Armada*, p.40.
15 Patterson, *The Other Armada*, pp.48-49.

> The more we examine them and weigh them, the less we see any way of reconciling them with what the King owes himself or his new allies … Endeavour, I pray you, to prevent any further condescensions of the sort, for they can only be fatal to the dignity of the King, and the humiliation resulting from them the King his uncle will necessarily share.[16]

Vergennes's great anxiety was that the terms of the ultimatum might have provided the British government with an opportunity to take advantage of disrupting both the Franco- American alliance and the Family Compact, and over the next month he sent repeated complaints to Montmorin about the Spanish proposals. Fortunately for him however the British response missed the chance that caused Vergennes such anxiety, and in due course the Spanish ultimatum was rejected. At last, therefore, preparations for the joint operation could go forward.

16 Corwin, *French Policy and the American Alliance*, pp.214-215.

18

Hardy

If it had been possible to induce Howe to become First Lord of the Admiralty, Sandwich would have been appointed as Secretary of State in succession to Lord Suffolk. As it was, Sandwich remained at the Admiralty, with the King's entire approval; he wrote to North on 6 April: 'I cannot have the smallest doubt of the propriety of keeping Lord Sandwich in his present employment, and even saying that at this hour no person is so well qualified for holding it'.[1] The departure from the scene of both Keppel and Palliser meant, though, that important decisions must be taken as to their replacement. Palliser's place on the board of Admiralty was offered by North to the 63-year-old Admiral Sir Charles Hardy, but he declined to accept the post unless he was also appointed as Lieutenant General of Marines, since he would have to give up his lucrative governorship of Greenwich Hospital. The King shared with Sandwich and North the view that this was unreasonable, and the position on the board went instead to Vice Admiral Robert Man, who had hitherto been a member of the opposition in Parliament. Consideration appears to have been given to appointing Captain George Johnstone to the post, evidently on the strength of his coming over from the opposition to support the government; but Mulgrave insisted that there must be at least one admiral on the Board. The Lieutenant Generalcy of Marines remained vacant for the time being; an application for this appointment was made by the unctuous Rear Admiral James Gambier on 14 May, which Sandwich had no difficulty in refusing. Ultimately, Admiral Sir Thomas Pye was appointed to the post in September 1780.

The obvious choice to lead the Channel Fleet would have been Howe, but his terms for accepting the appointment were no different from those that he had insisted on for his possible appointment as First Lord, and these were still regarded as unacceptable. It was obviously desirable that the next commander-in-chief should be someone not only of sufficient seniority and ability, but also with a personality that might go some way to repairing the damage to the navy's morale caused by the disastrous feud between Keppel and Palliser. Sandwich now turned

1 Donne (ed.), *The Correspondence of King George the Third*, Vol.II, p.243.

'Sir Charles Hardy'. Mezzotint by Philip Dawe, after Thomas Hudson. (Yale Center for British Art, Gift of Mr. and Mrs. J. Richardson Dilworth, B1973.3.2)

to Hardy, whose character certainly rendered him suitable, and he had a long record of distinguished service. Joining the navy in 1731, he became lieutenant in 1737 and post captain in 1741. He served as governor of New York in 1755, and in the following year was promoted to rear admiral. He served as second in command under Boscawen and Hawke, and was made vice admiral in 1762. He reached the rank of admiral in 1770. He was not a controversial figure, having never been active in politics. In his biography of Sandwich, Nicholas Rodger wrote of Hardy that 'his seniority put him beyond the reach of jealousy, and his popularity and relaxed manner were well calculated to calm the heats of faction'.[2] However, Hardy was not in good health, and although he had gained a wide experience during his career, he had not commanded at sea for 20 years.

The position of Captain of the Fleet had been held by Rear Admiral Campbell under Keppel. The duties of the post had never been formally defined, but progressively they became, effectively, that of a chief of staff. Given Hardy's lack of experience as commander-in-chief, the appointment was particularly important. The King suggested Richard Kempenfelt; several other candidates were also considered, or put themselves forward. One such was Sir Samuel Hood, whom Sandwich probably discounted as his work as Commissioner at Portsmouth dockyard was so crucial; another was Captain John Elliott, who declined, saying that Kempenfelt was the 'fittest officer' for the post. This reflected the good opinion in which Kempenfelt was held throughout the Navy; he had been ashore since the end of the Seven Years War, but he enjoyed a considerable reputation, and he was duly appointed. History has been provided with a comprehensive record of Kempenfelt's views of his time as Captain of the Fleet in the extensive correspondence which he carried on with Middleton.

Kempenfelt himself had been diffident about accepting the appointment; he was only two years younger than Hardy, and he was concerned that the burden of the post would be too much for his health. Nevertheless, he served for two and a half years, throughout which he endured the constant strain of facing an enemy that was always in much greater strength.[3] His letters to Middleton were not so much newsletters as a continuous and wide-ranging series of comments on the tactics and strategy of the Channel Fleet, and on the navy as a whole, as well as containing candid observations about the commanders-in-chief whom he served. The clarity and conviction with which he expressed his opinions have led Rodger to describe him as 'a historians' admiral'; as a result they have found him, he says, 'plausible and agreeable, and have allowed too little for the bias inherent in his position'.[4] This is a view with which it is possible to disagree; Kempenfelt was a man of unquestionable ability, and showed himself capable of making dispassionate judgments that were based on undoubted facts.

After he had been in post for about a year, Kempenfelt wrote to Middleton regarding the lack of precision of the scope of the duties of Captain of the Fleet:

> I don't suppose that there is an office in the whole state that is considered to be of any consequence, whose duty is so vague and undetermined as that of an admiral's first captain. If it ever had a prescribed duty, it has been lost and forgot with the disuse of the office. Some think that the

2 Rodger, *Insatiable Earl*, p.257.

3 Barnes and Owen (eds), *Private Papers of John, Earl of Sandwich*, Vol.III, p.3.

4 Rodger, *Insatiable Earl*, p.261.

> origin of admiral's first captain was to have the particular charge of his squadron or division of the fleet, as the commander-in-chief's care and concern for the whole occupied too much of his time to attend to the detail of his own squadron or division.[5]

In the first letter which he wrote to the Comptroller after his appointment, Kempenfelt reflected on what he had learned from the courts martial of Keppel and Palliser; he had served as a member of the court which tried Palliser. On 28 April he wrote to Middleton to say that he now had a clearer idea of the action on 27 July:

> The different state the two fleets were in after the action confirms most strongly what I have always thought; that is, that the disabling of your enemy in his masts and rigging should have no small share of your attention and your fire. In this skirmish between the two fleets there was at least as many shot sent from us to them as they sent to us; I should think many more, as several of their ships could not open their lower ports and most of ours could. Now let us take a view of the conditions of the two fleets after action, owing to the different directions of their fire; ours, except the red division, so totally shattered in masts, rigging, and sails that for the whole evening of that day they could not all form into a line. The French ships, on the contrary, were so little injured in these particulars that they had the perfect command of their yards and sails, and immediately after action ceased formed a regular line on the starboard tack, pointing towards our fleet, and placing those ships in their van which were the van on the other tack, as being fresh ships.[6]

The conclusion, he thought, was obvious; the French, 'having the command of motion and direction,' had a decisive superiority. Without this, there was no strength and force: 'Deprive a giant of one of his legs and a stripling shall master him'. He thought that the British should make use of langridge, which was much more destructive of rigging and sails than grapeshot.

It was not to be hoped that passions in the fleet would quickly cool, and Sandwich was obliged to face the possibility that some captains, and even admirals, might decline to serve. He was, therefore, very pleased to receive a letter from Harland dated 31 March, who wrote that he was ready to continue in the fleet under Hardy, although he had not 'the like opinion of the abilities of that gentleman I had of Admiral Keppel'. The King was pleased, too, writing to Sandwich that it was 'impossible to pen a more becoming letter. It is very fair and shows he deserves the

5 Laughton (ed.), *Barham Papers*, Vol.I, p.320.

6 Laughton (ed.), *Barham Papers*, Vol.I, pp.290-291.

character universally given of him'. Regrettably, Harland was not long to remain on the side of the angels, angrily writing on 10 May to Stephens declining to serve. This, the King sadly commented, seemed to have been dictated by passion rather than by reflection.[7]

At Portsmouth, meanwhile, feelings were running strongly among the seaman. Pye had to take steps to ensure that the *Formidable* and *Victory* were moored separately, since he feared that if their companies met 'it would be fatal to many of them as there is such an inveteracy towards each other'.[8]

It was on 7 April that Sandwich suffered the appalling personal tragedy of the murder of Martha Ray, his long-time mistress and the mother of two of his sons. It was a devastating blow, as a result of which he wrote that he had been 'robbed of all comfort in the world'. In deference to his loss, Lord Bristol, in a deeply sympathetic letter, willingly agreed to defer the debate in the House of Lords, on his motion for Sandwich's removal as First Lord, until 23 April. Sandwich had been defended strongly by Lord North, who had published on 3 March a formal statement of the responsibility of the whole Cabinet for Admiralty measures, to the effect that a vote of censure against one member of the Cabinet involved the whole:

> Every expedition, in regard to its destination, object, force and number of ships, is planned by the Cabinet, and is the result of the collective wisdom of all his Majesty's confidential ministers. The First Lord of the Admiralty is only the executive servant of these measures; and if he is not personally a Cabinet Minister he is not responsible for the wisdom, the policy, and the propriety of any naval expedition. But if he is in the Cabinet, then he must share in common with the other ministers that proportional division of censure which is attached to him as an individual. In no situation is he more or less responsible to his country than his colleagues from any misconduct which flows from a Cabinet measure.[9]

When the opposition motion in the House of Lords came to be debated it was soundly defeated, by 78 votes to 39. Sandwich vigorously defended his tenure of office, pointing out that when he was appointed to the post of First Lord in 1771, the fleet was 'in a most deplorable state, the ships decaying and unfit for service, the storehouses empty, and a general despondency running through the whole naval department'. He did not despair, he said, but set his hand and heart to the work, and was now able to prove that the fleet was in as good a condition as it had ever been. The effort that had been made to reequip the fleet had increased its strength in ships of the line from a starting figure of 36 in commission in 1777;

7 Barnes and Owen (eds), *Private Papers of John, Earl of Sandwich*, Vol.II, p.242.
8 Barnes and Owen (eds), *Private Papers of John, Earl of Sandwich*, Vol.II, p.243.
9 Barnes and Owen (eds), *Private Papers of John, Earl of Sandwich*, Vol.II, p.255.

this compared with the figure of 61 with which the fleet had begun the Seven Years War. There were now 90 ships of the line in commission. When he came to office there were only 18 ships, large and small, building; now there were 77. Sandwich took the motion very seriously, meeting the criticisms with detailed statements of the navy's strength that answered not only the complaints made in the House of Lords, but also those raised earlier in the House of Commons.[10]

No one was under any illusion about the scale of the task faced by the Channel Fleet. It had only been with great difficulty that approximate parity with the French fleet had been achieved in 1778; now, with the Spanish fleet to contend with as well, it was certain that numerically the odds would be heavily against the British. Nor was it only a question of ships; the navy faced grave difficulties in manning the fleet. Finding the necessary manpower required an enormous administrative effort and depended heavily on a general press, which was ordered on 14 April. It had been estimated in March that the ships of the line in commission in home waters were short of 5,668 seaman and marines out of a full complement of 24,800. At this time desertions from the navy, averaged over the last four years, were running at the rate of nearly 10,000 a year.[11]

Sickness was also an extremely serious factor. The total strength of the navy voted by Parliament was 70,000 sailors and marines. The Channel Fleet had sent a total of 21,940 sick men ashore from its ships at Portsmouth and Plymouth, not all of whom had been fit to return to duty; the problem was created by the practice of press gangs in seizing already sick men for service in the fleet, with the result that it was repeatedly swept by infectious diseases.[12] As the year went on the press was intensified, removing exemptions from most categories of seamen.

The quality of some of the men gathered in by the press can be seen from the letter written by Walsingham, captain of the *Thunderer*, on 4 June:

> Most of the men on [the enclosed] list entered on board the *Culloden* since she came home; and added to their want of knowledge, they are the poorest, dirty vermin that ever came on board a man-of-war. What men I had last cruise that were good it was my misfortune to bury, so that exclusive of 40 seaman I got from the *Sandwich* I do not believe I have 10 on board.[13]

Everything possible was being done to maximise the effectiveness of the press; John Robinson, the Secretary to the Treasury, wrote to Sandwich in the middle of June to report a discussion with North, in which the Prime Minister expressed

10 Barnes and Owen (eds), *Private Papers of John, Earl of Sandwich*, Vol.II, pp.258-279.

11 Barnes and Owen (eds), *Private Papers of John, Earl of Sandwich*, Vol.III, p.4.

12 Syrett, *European Waters*, p.66.

13 Barnes and Owen (eds), *Private Papers of John, Earl of Sandwich*, Vol.III, p.4.

the view 'that you must immediately press for everything and take every man that can be got'. North also thought that the army should take a hand in supporting the activities of the press gangs.[14] Middleton, too, had a number of ideas to put forward, suggesting that the standing gangs should be taken from all the tenders, and that application should be made to the mayors of seaport towns for two thirds of their protected fishermen, who would be asked to serve for one year. He too thought that the army should be asked to help, by taking up smugglers, together with one landsman from each parish. He recognised that to avoid excessive desertion it was desirable that such classes of recruits should be required to serve only for a limited period.

By the end of May considerable inroads had been made into the shortfall of seamen in the Channel Fleet. Mulgrave was able to report to Sandwich that the total deficit had been reduced to 1,416 men, the shortage falling on 12 ships of the fleet. He suggested to Sandwich the way in which the deficits should be made good:

> I think it will be necessary to complete the ships in equal proportions from those left in the harbour after 1 June, which will be the most effectual hint and best example to officers of spirit not to trifle their time away. The departure of this fleet is in my opinion so very essential that all other considerations should be overlooked.[15]

Meanwhile there had been an unexpected distraction from the task of preparing the Channel Fleet for sea. On 1 May the French launched an assault on the island of Jersey, with a force of some 5,000 men commanded by the Prince of Nassau. The attack failed completely; but when news of it next day reached Vice Admiral Arbuthnot as he set off down Channel with a large military convoy bound for New York, he decided that he should sail at once with the convoy's escort and some troops to the Channel Islands to support their defence. By the time that he arrived, the danger had passed, so Arbuthnot returned to his convoy, which had by now reached Torbay. There he was held up for several days by adverse winds. Meanwhile the Admiralty received news of considerable French naval activity at Brest and Rochefort, and it was decided that Arbuthnot should have additional cover until he was safely out of the zone in which attack by elements of the French fleet was to be feared. Accordingly, Vice Admiral George Darby was ordered on 13 May to sail from St Helens with 12 ships of the line to join the convoy and its escort. Due to continuing westerly winds, he did not leave until 24 May, which meant a considerable delay in the convoy setting off for its destination. Darby did not return until 10 June.[16]

14 Barnes and Owen (eds), *Private Papers of John, Earl of Sandwich*, Vol.III, p.24.
15 Barnes and Owen (eds), *Private Papers of John, Earl of Sandwich*, Vol.III, p.15.
16 James, *The British Navy in Adversity*, p.171; Syrett, *European Waters*, pp.67-68.

Aware of the delay that had been experienced in getting Darby away, Sandwich wrote to Hardy on 21 May to urge him to hasten his own preparations to sail: 'If there is any circumstance in which you think my interposition can be of use, I conclude you will let me know it and that you will depend upon every degree of assistance that it is in my power to give; for all mankind begin to be extremely anxious about getting you to sea'.[17] He added that if the adverse winds continued for another ten days, he took for granted that Darby would be able to sail with the rest of the Channel Fleet when it was ready, since there would be no need to reinforce Arbuthnot once the whole fleet was at sea.

Next day the Cabinet met to approve the draft of the orders to be sent to Hardy, which were duly endorsed by the King, and which went to the commander-in-chief on 29 May. They directed him to cruise near Ushant and off Brest, taking care not to be driven too far to the west, in order to blockade the port. If he found that he was stronger than the French fleet, he was to detach cruisers to prevent any additional French ships from Lorient, Rochefort or Toulon from joining d'Orvilliers. If the French fleet was already at sea, or came out and slipped past him, Hardy was to:

> [P]roceed in pursuit of it, if … you judge there may be any probability of your being able to come up with it without leaving Great Britain and Ireland exposed, the protection of which must always be the principal object of your care and attention; but if … you do not judge, from the intelligence you may receive, that there is a probability of your coming up with the enemy's fleet or if you should not be able to obtain any well-founded information of the route it may have taken, you are … to proceed off the Lizard, giving us notice thereof by the most expeditious means and waiting for orders.[18]

Hardy was directed to stay out as long as he could, before returning to reprovision the fleet at Torbay. As for Spanish ships, he was to seize them if they were acting in conjunction with the French or were headed for French ports; otherwise he was still to treat them as belonging to a friendly power.

On 12 June news reached London that d'Orvilliers had put to sea, and Hardy was ordered to sail without 'a moment's loss of time'. This he did on 16 June, with 30 ships of the line; Darby's return to re-join the fleet on 10 June, following his detachment to escort Arbuthnot, meant that little time had been lost in getting away. Hardy flew his flag in the *Victory*; Darby led the van division, aboard the *Britannia*, and Digby the rear, aboard the *Prince George*. Ross, the fourth in command, was aboard the *Royal George*, sailing as part of the centre division.

17 Barnes and Owen (eds), *Private Papers of John, Earl of Sandwich*, p.13.

18 Barnes and Owen (eds), *Private Papers of John, Earl of Sandwich*, Vol.III, pp.4-5.

Mulgrave, in the *Courageux*, was also in the centre division, as were Jervis in the *Foudroyant* and Duncan in the *Monarch*. Mulgrave, reporting to Sandwich on 10 June, was encouraging about the impression which the new commander-in-chief had made on the fleet:

> He is constantly on board, very diligent, and hitherto much liked from the great good humour with which he conducts himself... As to the ships, the weekly accounts will show you how far they are short; in every other sense they are well manned and in fine order, except the *Namur*, which is I believe much in want of seamen and should be looked to particularly in the arrangement of manning ...I never saw more universal good humour in a fleet or a fair prospect of everything being carried on with the most cordial zeal.[19]

However, the news from Hardy himself was less encouraging. On 13 June he told Sandwich that 'several men that have been brought here in tenders are very poor; indeed I may say very bad men'. He went on to say that some that had come from Cork two days previously were so bad that he could not receive them on board and others brought from Plymouth had been condemned as unfit for service 'not only as bad men, but in such a state of health that it was not safe to take them on board'.[20]

Back in London, it was on the day that Hardy finally put to sea that Duque de Almodóvar finally presented the Spanish ultimatum, and on the following day fresh orders went to Hardy that he should now 'seize and destroy all ships and vessels belonging to Spain or Spanish subjects which he may meet with'. His new orders went on to say that if he should learn that the French and Spanish fleets had combined, and concluded that their superiority would be so great as to 'make it improper to risk the event of a battle,' he was to return home, either to Torbay or Spithead, and await further orders.[21]

Mulgrave, when he subsequently saw the orders that Hardy had received, was horrified, as he wrote to Sandwich on 2 July, at which time the fleet was off the Lizard:

> I own I was much concerned to see any orders for retreating without a battle, in any circumstances, as I think our fleet in its present situation equal to meeting anything, both from the strength of the ships, for their number, and the great superiority of our discipline to that of the Spaniards

19 Barnes and Owen (eds), *Private Papers of John, Earl of Sandwich*, Vol.III, p.17.

20 Barnes and Owen (eds), *Private Papers of John, Earl of Sandwich*, Vol.III, p.18.

21 Barnes and Owen (eds), *Private Papers of John, Earl of Sandwich*, Vol.III, p.5.

> till they have been a considerable time at sea. The last is an advantage I should be sorry we lost, particularly as it must lessen every day.[22]

It was Mulgrave's view, which was also held by both Kempenfelt and Pye, that a fleet of more than 30 ships of the line was virtually unmanageable, and that the Channel Fleet at its present strength was 'sufficient at least to fight any force of the enemy's they may meet,' and he saw no advantage that could be gained by retreat; it would be safer, he thought, at sea rather than in Torbay. When the King read Mulgrave's letter, he thought that it was 'very sensible'.[23]

The news that Hardy had sailed had lifted the King's spirits, and he wrote to Sandwich on 17 June to say that he expected great efforts from the fleet, and that he would not be satisfied if persons simply counted the number of ships brought against it:

> It was the vigour of mind shown by Queen Elizabeth and her subjects, added to the assistance of Divine Providence, that saved this island when attacked by the Spaniards. It is necessary to be active on the present occasion, and to bring the enemy as soon as possible to decisive action.[24]

It was the King's hope that the sailing of the fleet would similarly encourage the members of his Cabinet, among whom he detected a lack of constancy. North, who frequently made known his wish to retire, was not the only one whose morale had been damaged by the lack of military success and the consequent unrelenting pressure of the opposition. On 21 June George summoned the members of his Cabinet to his presence, and sat down with them in his library to discuss the position. During the course of his talk, he reviewed the course of the ongoing crisis, reproaching himself only for changing his ministry in 1765 and for permitting the repeal of the Stamp Act. If his ministers felt they lacked strength, he said, he was willing to bring in new blood. He thanked Sandwich for the respectable state of the navy, and the Treasury for ensuring the constant flow of supplies to America, whither he had sent his best generals. It was his duty to God and his people to preserve his dominions, and he would part with his life rather than relinquish any of them. From his ministers, he expected firmness and support for his policies.[25] That night he wrote to North to restate his call for courage and resolution: 'I hope, after having so fully stated my sentiments this day to the efficient Cabinet, that I trust everyone felt how I am interested in the present moment, and consequently

22 Barnes and Owen (eds), *Private Papers of John, Earl of Sandwich*, Vol.III, p.33.
23 Barnes and Owen (eds), *Private Papers of John, Earl of Sandwich*, Vol.III, p.33.
24 Barnes and Owen (eds), *Private Papers of John, Earl of Sandwich*, Vol.III, p.20.
25 Mackesy, *War for America*, p.264.

will feel that they can alone hope for my support by showing zeal, assiduity, and activity'.[26]

As further ships became available, they were to be added to the Channel Fleet. On 20 June Hardy arrived off the Lizard, having covered the movement of several outward bound convoys, and he then sailed to a position off Ushant, which was where he received his new orders. Hardy was also collecting intelligence from captured French and American vessels indicating that both the French and Spanish fleets were at sea, but without any firm information as to their movements. He decided to return to the Lizard, which he reached on 2 July. He resolved that, if the wind turned westerly, he should go to Torbay, and this in fact happened; he arrived at the roadstead there in a brisk gale on 5 July. At this point Hardy had with him 31 ships of the line with three more expected to join shortly; he had eight frigates, and five fireships, with two sloops and four cutters. The ships of the line included no less than nine three deckers, and mounted in all 2,452 guns, with a total complement of 20,300 men.[27]

It had not taken Kempenfelt long to assess the quality of the fleet's new commander. He wrote a brief note to Middleton when off the Lizard on 2 July, to tell him of a report, from a Genoese ship, that it had sighted a fleet of more than 40 French ships of the line on 10 June. He went on to express his extreme concern about the leadership of the fleet:

> My situation is extremely disagreeable; I would give all the little I am worth to be out of it. Does the people at home think the nation in no danger? Where is Lord Howe at this alarming period? I can't say more; you will divine the rest. I can foresee no prospect at present. All seems to depend upon the abilities which this fleet is conducted – let that be well considered.[28]

26 Donne (ed.), *The Correspondence of King George the Third*, Vol.II, pp.260-261.
27 Barnes and Owen (eds), *Private Papers of John, Earl of Sandwich*, Vol.III, p.36.
28 Laughton (ed.), *Barham Papers*, Vol.I, p.292.

19

The Combined Fleet

In planning for the invasion of Britain, one essential was the gathering of up-to-date intelligence. Over the years, the French government had collected a good deal of information about Portsmouth and the surrounding area; now, in the spring of 1779, Vergennes sent an engineer officer, *Major* Berthois de la Rousseliére, with one companion, to conduct a detailed survey of the area of the landing sites. They paid a number of visits to the fortifications, to Gosport, and to the Isle of Wight, and visited the anchorages of Spithead and St Helens. They also examined the Portsea Lines, which they described as 'an entrenched camp with its wings resting on the creeks, composed of a double earthwork with a fosse in the middle'.[1] Gosport they found to be poorly defended; its capture would make it possible to enter the harbour and attack and destroy the town of Portsmouth. The Isle of Wight had only a weak and scattered garrison. La Rousseliére returned to France on 7 May, delivering his report with a detailed plan of attack. He noted that the first essential must be to get the British fleet out of the way, before a landing of some 4,000 troops was effected on the Isle of Wight at Cowes, and a simultaneous assault made on Gosport by 6 to 8,000 men.

La Rousseliére also put forward a detailed proposal for the subsequent occupation and retention of Portsmouth. This, it was estimated, would require 30,000 troops. It would be a hazardous operation, involving a landing on Portsea Island from the east, and a night attack across the harbour from the troops occupying Gosport. At first, only the more limited operation was to be the objective of the expedition; but as hopes rose for an early junction between the French and Spanish fleets, consideration was given to adopting the much more ambitious plan. On 11 June Aranda, the Spanish ambassador, presented Vergennes with a paper calling on the French to increase the strength of the expeditionary force by 50 percent, which would involve a commitment in excess of 30,000 men. Jonathan Dull regards this decision as a serious mistake: 'This was virtually the only occasion during the war in which the council permitted enthusiasm, overconfidence,

1 Patterson, *The Other Armada*, p.55.

and inflated ambition to overcome realism, prudence, and commonsense. (It was also one of the few times the council ignored the advice of Sartine and Fleurieu.)'[2] On the following day a conference attended by the King, Maurepas, Vergennes, Sartine, Montbarrey and de Vaux agreed to attempt the larger scheme. A number of amendments were made to La Rousseliére's plan, however; the attacks on Gosport and Portsea Island were now to be made simultaneously, while only part of the division under Rochambeau which was to attack Portsea Island would do so, the remainder landing on Southsea and Eastney Beaches.[3] It was a very bold plan indeed; but it depended entirely on the Combined Fleet meeting with success at sea, and this was a very large ask.

The logistical task facing the French and Spanish navies of assembling the Combined Fleet and the invasion convoy was enormous. There were a number of particular difficulties to be overcome. So far as the French were concerned, one of the most serious was the lack of manpower. It has been calculated that during the course of 1779 some 76,912 sailors were employed by the French navy, and the number called upon would continue to grow thereafter, putting a huge strain on the French system of conscription of seamen, so much so that it has been suggested that once war had been declared the system broke down almost completely. Sartine was obliged to hire large numbers of foreign sailors, to cut back on crew sizes and the proportion of trained seamen, to employ untrained volunteers and soldiers, and to increase the level of conscription in maritime areas.[4]

The French dockyards, which had performed so well in the years before the war in building up the fleet, soon began to experience serious problems as a result of the added pressure now put upon them, which was exacerbated by a run of bad luck. In the early months of 1779 the ship of the line *Roland* and the frigate *Zéphyr* were destroyed in a dockyard fire, and the process of overhauling the *Ville de Paris* and equipping her to carry 104 guns was seriously delayed; the attempt on the Channel Islands which had completely failed meant the loss of the squadron involved; and the fleet at Brest was short of nine ships of the line which had been planned to join it, four from Toulon, three from Rochefort, and two more which were escorting a convoy bound for India. Thus, when d'Orvilliers arrived at Versailles on 21 April with du Pavillon he was obliged to report that the fleet was not yet ready, and would not be before the end of May. This meant that Vergennes had to let Floridablanca know that the date for the rendezvous of the two fleets could not be met.

Explaining this to Montmorin on 29 April, the French minister warned that it would be safest to work on the basis that the French fleet would not sail before the first week in June. The delay brought with it a real anxiety that the plans of

2 Dull, *French Navy and American Independence*, p.151.

3 Patterson, *The Other Armada*, p.58.

4 Dull, *French Navy and American Independence*, p.144.

the allies might be completely upset if in the meantime the British mounted a blockade of Brest. Not only would this mean that d'Orvilliers might have to fight a battle in order to get to sea; it also meant that if the Spanish fleet arrived there with the British fleet already on station, it too might have to face a premature encounter.

Vergennes, however, brushed this pessimistic view aside; his information about the strength of the British fleet suggested that it was not strong enough to mount a blockade and at the same time to send a squadron of any strength to intercept the Spanish fleet. In his opinion the squadrons at Cadiz and Ferrol should not wait for news that d'Orvilliers had put to sea, but should themselves leave port as soon as possible and head northward. The suggestion was that westerly winds would soon blow any fleet blockading Brest off station and into the Channel, and when the wind changed the French could come out before the British were able to return.[5] Vergennes accordingly told Montmorin that he should urge on the Spaniards the importance of their sailing first, the Ferrol squadron on 20 May and the Cadiz fleet between 25 and 30 May. However, he no longer considered the cramped port of Corunna as being suitable for a rendezvous, not least because the northerly winds made it a lee shore. D'Orvilliers had advised that a rendezvous some 25 or 30 leagues off Cape Finisterre would be better, with an alternative of Cape La Roque in the event of fog. Passing this on to the Spanish, Vergennes also expressed concern that their fleet was apparently to carry only four months' worth of provisions, which would leave barely enough time for an adequate campaign, even if the movements of the two fleets were up to schedule.

It was soon apparent that this was not so. Floridablanca had been suggesting that the Cadiz fleet would be ready to sail in the second or third week of May, but the reality was that it was not in a satisfactory state to do so, as Montmorin's military attaché had advised in a report which was forwarded to Vergennes on 30 March. Grave doubts were expressed in this report about the competence of the 73-year-old commander Don Luis de Córdova and his leading admirals. In addition, there were other and even more serious shortcomings:

> The number and quality of the ships were "more impressive than the crews who manned them or, above all the officers who commanded them". The general level of the officers was wretchedly low, because wholesale and often arbitrary promotions had been made recently in order to increase their numbers rapidly. Hence youths without either ability or industry had been rushed through a very brief cadetship and commissioned as sub lieutenants.[6]

5 Patterson, *The Other Armada*, p.60.
6 Patterson, *The Other Armada*, p.63.

This report was an ominous indicator of the difficulties that d'Orvilliers would face in trying to weld the Combined Fleet into an effective fighting force; but there was not much that could be done about these deficiencies at this stage, nor about the quality of the armament of the Spanish ships, which was noted as being very defective. Nor was the fleet well provisioned, even before it sailed. The Ferrol squadron was commanded by Don Antonio d'Arce, who was said to be 'experienced and intelligent but timid and irresolute':[7] though better stocked than the Cadiz fleet, its magazines were probably inadequate for an extensive campaign.

In the light of this, it was apparent to Vergennes that Floridablanca was being overoptimistic, just as he had himself been. His meeting with d'Orvilliers and du Pavillon had shown that the French fleet was also well behind schedule. However, in an effort to keep up the pressure on the Spanish, he wrote to Montmorin on 3 May expressing the hope that the Brest fleet might be ready by 20 May.

While this correspondence was continuing, though, the whole process had been subject to the delays caused by the working out of the Spanish mediation process. On 17 May Floridablanca announced that the Ferrol squadron would sail at once and that the Cadiz fleet would sail as soon as it had familiarised itself with the French signalling system, which would be by the first week of June. He agreed to change the point of rendezvous, now proposing a point some eight to ten leagues off the Sisargas Islands. These three small islands were about 20 miles west of Corunna. The Spanish minister also accepted the sensible suggestion which Vergennes had made as to the intermingling of the two fleets by organising it in ten divisions of five ships each with a light division comprising the rest. As to the invasion force, it was decided to divide it into two parts, half at Saint Malo and half at Le Havre:

> There were insufficient escorts to protect the transfer of all the ships to one port. Saint Malo and Le Havre cleared with the same wind (from the east) so the two parts could sail simultaneously. The force at Saint Malo was to consist of 20 battalions of infantry, one of Lauzun's legions, and 46 pieces of artillery. That of Le Havre was to contain 14 battalions of infantry, four battalions of artillery, 400 heavy cavalry (dragoons), and 50 pieces of artillery.[8]

A further 10 infantry battalions, 16 squadrons of heavy cavalry and a regiment of hussars would be held back in reserve. The invasion force would proceed to sea under the escort of the light division of the Combined Fleet once the British fleet had been defeated or driven into port.

7 Patterson, *Other Armada*, p.64.
8 Dull, *French Navy and American Independence*, p.148n.

At Brest, the dockyard was working flat out to prepare the fleet for sea. By 25 May most of the fleet was lying at anchor in Brest roads, and four days later d'Orvilliers was sent his sailing orders. He was to put to sea as soon as he had 28 ships of the line ready, and he was to leave sealed orders to join him for any smaller ships that had been left behind. En route to the Sisargas, he was to watch out for Arbuthnot's convoy, but his priority was to be the junction with Córdova. If the British fleet was out, he was to avoid an engagement if he could. Once he met the Spanish he was to coordinate their understanding of the signalling system, and practice joint fleet evolutions. Beyond these initial instructions, his orders went on to set out the objectives for his fleet, which were to head for and enter the Channel, and if he met the British fleet to engage it. His principal task was to gain command of the sea and in particular to get between the Channel Fleet and the Isle of Wight so that the invasion could be launched, when he would cooperate with the army in its attack on Portsmouth.[9]

The rush to get the fleet to sea before a British blockading fleet appeared was to lead to the most serious consequences. D'Orvilliers would leave port with his ships seriously short of trained seamen. It had been intended for the Régiment de la Reine to provide some 2,000 soldiers to serve aboard the fleet as seamen, but it failed to arrive at Brest in time, and d'Orvilliers was obliged to obtain last minute drafts from regiments based near to Brest. Their colonels apparently took the opportunity to send him their worst men. The fleet left without sorrel or lemons and thus would be unable to prevent the incidence of scurvy. The fleet accordingly went to sea inadequately manned and without sufficient supplies. Even more importantly, it left without sufficient medical stores or doctors.[10]

D'Orvilliers finally sailed on 3 June; once he had passed through the Goulet at the entrance to Brest Roads, he paused overnight in Bertheaume Bay to await three ships of the line which had delayed their departure to take on board further soldiers that had arrived at Brest. Next day the fleet sailed southwards in perfect weather, and a courier rode off for Spain with the news that they were on their way. There was no sign of the British; the need for Darby's squadron to be detached to escort Arbuthnot and his convoy safely out of harm's way meant that while awaiting his return the Channel Fleet had missed whatever chance it might have had to disrupt the operations of the Combined Fleet by instituting a blockade of Brest.

Although the weather changed, and the French fleet was held up for three days by contrary winds, d'Orvilliers reached the Sisargas on 10 June, sending a frigate into Corunna to announce to d'Arce his arrival at the rendezvous. The latter, however, inexplicably delayed his departure from port for no less than three weeks. D'Arce was said to have an intense dislike for the French, and Patterson suggests that it was this that accounted for his failure to put to sea, rather than the various

9 Patterson, *The Other Armada*, pp.68-69.

10 Patterson, *The Other Armada*, p.68.

unconvincing excuses which he put forward. It took peremptory orders and the threat of his removal from command before he finally sailed on 2 July. Meanwhile Córdova, with the Cadiz fleet, did not sail until 23 June, and, when the fleet did sail, it was held up by northerly winds, so that nothing was heard from it until it finally appeared at the rendezvous a month later.

For Vergennes, these weeks of inaction were a time of intense anxiety. One fear in particular haunted him, and that was that Hardy, whose movement to the western entrance of the Channel had been reported, was intent on sailing south to attack d'Orvilliers before the Spanish finally arrived; he wrote to Montmorin on 28 June: 'If I were Minister of England I would insist on his seeking out d'Orvilliers and attacking him, in order at least to cripple him'.[11] Nearly a month later, having still received no news of any effective activity, Vergennes's morale was at a particularly low ebb:

> I do not know what the weather is like at sea, but it is terrible here – gale after gale with violent rainstorms ... even if the fleets have joined, I doubt if they would dare to operate in the Channel. Yet if we cannot establish ourselves in England before the end of August there will be no time left for an operation of any importance ... What a wonderful opportunity is slipping from our grasp ... England, without resources or allies, was on the point of being taught a lesson ... But the elements are arming themselves against us and staying the stroke of our vengeance.[12]

Given the limitations on time imposed by the provisions carried by the Combined Fleet, and the importance of taking advantage of as much of the campaigning season as possible, the delays on the part of the Spanish were as inexcusable as they were incomprehensible. Yet Vergennes's anxiety that Hardy might launch a pre-emptive attack on d'Orvilliers was without foundation; as has been seen, once he had put to sea, he cruised off the entrance to the Channel before returning and anchoring in Torbay on 2 July.

By now there was very grave concern about the vulnerability of southern England. The possibility that the French might launch an invasion had been obvious for a long time, but it was only when more concrete information about the French military preparations began to reach Britain that really serious activity for the island's defence began to be put in hand. It was calculated that in June there were a total of 52,602 troops, of which 28,998 were militia, in Britain and a further 10,529 in Ireland. Necessarily these were widely scattered, but defensive steps began to be taken to strengthen the obvious danger points. A bill to increase the strength of the militia was passed in Parliament; a battalion of infantry was

11 Patterson, *The Other Armada*, p.161.

12 Longmate, *Island Fortress*, p.205.

sent to Plymouth; all horses in coastal areas were to be removed further inland, and navigation aids were removed from the Thames estuary.[13] However, a substantial army sufficient to resist a determined invasion could not be created overnight, and it was abundantly clear that it was only at sea that a French invasion could be successfully resisted.

Amherst had been giving particular thought to the defences of Plymouth, and went down to the city on 4 July. He wrote to the governor, Sir David Lindsay, on 6 July with his recommendations:

> From a view of this place and its environs and the situation of the troops in the barracks and those in camp, with the probable attacks which may be made by an enemy to destroy the dockyard, I think the ground near Cawsand Bay and the landing place should be immediately taken possession of, and that a battery should be made on the right of the proposed camp to obstruct the approach of any vessel, armed boats, or craft with troops; that the landing places in the Bay (on the appearance of an enemy) should be entirely obstructed by having trees ready prepared for putting *en horison*, which will effectually prevent boats from coming on shore, and as the two landing places are very narrow, this work may be easily effected.[14]

He also recommended that two battalions should be posted at Cawsand Bay, and that the other available troops should move nearer the coast.

It soon became apparent that there was a good deal of bad blood between the dockyard administration and the army. Captain Paul Ourry, the dockyard Commissioner, would not allow naval gunners working there to serve as artillery men, nor would he allow other dockyard workers to have time off for military training. The Navy's attitude was that its needs must come first. Notwithstanding this, a lot was done to strengthen the defences of the port, and by early July the garrison had reached a total strength of 4,800 men.[15]

The military Governor of Portsmouth, Lieutenant General Robert Monckton, was rather more distinguished than his Plymouth counterpart; he had been second in command to Wolfe at Quebec. It was evident to him that the Isle of Wight was extremely vulnerable, and that steps must be taken to repair and improve such fortifications as existed there. Gosport was also, he could see, open to assault, and if it was taken, the dockyard would become untenable. He reported to Amherst that a serious shortage of artillery men was 'a very material defect in our situation'. Monckton put in hand works to strengthen the fortifications on Southsea

13 Syrett, *European Waters*, p.76.

14 Barnes and Owen (eds), *Private Papers of John, Earl of Sandwich*, Vol.III, p.38.

15 Longmate, *Island Fortress*, p.203.

Common and Portsea Island, and recommended that arms be issued to the male population of the Isle of Wight between the ages of 17 and 50; supported by army engineers, he reckoned that they should provide an effective defence force.[16] Whether they would have been able to stand up to elite French infantry if these got ashore seems rather doubtful.

The news that Hardy had returned to Torbay was met with serious disapproval in Whitehall. The King was particularly concerned to ensure that Hardy should put to sea again as soon as possible, writing to Sandwich on 8 July:

> I hope, in addition to the orders transmitted to him to take the first opportunity to get far enough from the Lizard not to be driven in by westerly wind, that Lord Sandwich will write a private letter to the admiral, acquainting him how anxious I am personally that he should not lose the first minute that may offer to get out again, and not wait for the ships now sending to reinforce him.[17]

The First Lord needed no urging, writing that same day to Hardy:

> I am very glad to find that the gale that has driven you into Torbay has not damaged any of your ships, so that I hope you will be able to return to sea again without delay. There is every reason imaginable to expect that the combined fleets will attempt something against England or Ireland, and the more time is given to them the greater their strength will be; therefore the sooner things come to decision the better it will be. I well know our Royal Master's sentiments, and that he has such reliance on the valour and good intentions as well as the ability and experience of his officers and seamen that he has little apprehension of the event, if the fleets come to action.[18]

It had also been Mulgrave's view that as soon as there was some firm intelligence of the movements of the Combined Fleet, the Channel Fleet should be sent out at once; on the other hand, he wondered whether the enemy objective might actually be the incoming convoys from the West Indies. In any case, he favoured frequent returns to Torbay to ensure sufficient provisions which hopefully might help to reduce the risk of sickness.

Middleton, on the other hand, took a different view. In a letter to Sandwich of 9 July he suggested that to send Hardy to sea when the odds against him were so great would be to run needless risks, when in the meantime the Channel Fleet's numbers

16 Longmate, *Island Fortress*, p.202.

17 Barnes and Owen (eds), *Private Papers of John, Earl of Sandwich*, Vol.III, p.40.

18 Barnes and Owen (eds), *Private Papers of John, Earl of Sandwich*, Vol.III, pp.40-41.

could be rapidly built up. He also reminded the First Lord of Kempenfelt's advice about the use of langridge, urging that the fleet be issued with supplies of both this and case shot. In this letter, however, Middleton was even more concerned to get Kempenfelt transferred to join him at the Navy Board as soon as possible:

> In the meantime, my Lord, let me have the assistance of Captain Kempenfelt when he can be spared from the use of the fleet. I really want more assistance in my own line, and do not like determining so many things of moment, as am obliged to do at present, on my own judgment only. Captain Kempenfelt is not merely a sea officer, but a man of deep knowledge in most professions. He will be a great acquisition to his Majesty's service as well as of much assistance to me when he comes to the Navy Board; and if your Lordship could see the multiplicity of Board business which every day I am obliged to go through, you would allow that the Comptroller of the Navy ought to have a sea officer next in authority to himself at the Navy Board.[19]

There was, of course, no question of Kempenfelt being released from the Channel Fleet in the immediate future.

The view that Hardy must sail as soon as possible, not surprisingly, prevailed. On 10 July Hardy assured Sandwich that he would not lose a moment's time in putting to sea, and this he achieved four days later, heading for Ushant. For some time he had no news of the Combined Fleet, but then on 21 July, when he was some 40 miles south of Ushant, he learned from two ships that the Cadiz fleet was now at sea. Since it could be assumed that by now it had joined d'Orvilliers, Hardy retreated to a position off the Lizard. Strong westerly winds, however, drove him eastwards, and by 24 July he found himself off Plymouth, from where he wrote to Sandwich to seek further orders. Since he was short of supplies, he suggested that he should put into Plymouth, or even Portsmouth if the winds forced him further eastwards, in order to reprovision the fleet. His report of 25 July to Sandwich caused the First Lord considerable unease, and the latter replied on 28 July:

> I have received your private letter of the 25th instant and am truly concerned at finding it dated from so small a distance from home; your returning into port at this time will occasion very extraordinary sensations in this country, and I earnestly pray that the wind may not drive you either into Torbay or any other port. As to the particular destination of the enemy's combined fleets, we have no more certainty than you can have upon that subject; my conjecture, and that I believe of the greatest part of mankind, is that their design is to invade either England or Ireland

19 Barnes and Owen (eds), *Private Papers of John, Earl of Sandwich*, Vol.III, pp.42-43.

> or both, and to intercept the great West and East India fleets which are shortly expected, and which nothing but the interposition of your force can prevent.[20]

Hardy was, the First Lord added, the best judge of what to do: 'Every eye is upon you; and I have that confidence in your ability and zeal for the service of your country that I am persuaded you will do what is right at this very important crisis'.

Kempenfelt was still extremely unhappy about the situation of the Channel Fleet, writing to Middleton on 27 July to record his view as to the way in which the oncoming Combined Fleet should be met:

> Much, I may say almost all, depends upon this fleet; 'tis an inferior against a superior fleet; therefore the greatest skill and address is requisite to counteract the designs of the enemy, to watch and seize the favourable opportunity for action, and to catch the advantage of making the effort at some or other feeble part of the enemy's line; or, if such opportunities don't offer, to hover near the enemy, keep him at bay, and prevent his attempting to execute anything but at risk and hazard; to command their attention, and oblige them to think of nothing but being on their guard against your attack. Have the ministry sought for a head capable of such management and dexterity, or, do they think that ships are sufficient of themselves, without wisdom to direct and order their operations? So much indifference at so dangerous a crisis is astonishing and alarming.[21]

Kempenfelt's was not the only voice expressing concern. Benjamin Thompson was an American loyalist. Born in 1753, he had served as a lieutenant colonel in the King's American Dragoons in the early stages of the American war before coming to Britain. From a boy he had been fascinated by science. During the fighting he began to conduct experiments to measure the force of gunpowder. His work with the British forces led to his house being sacked and he left America, coming to England to become an adviser to Germain. He sailed with the Channel Fleet in order to make a study of ballistics, serving as one of three volunteers aboard the flagship, the others being *Kontreadmiral* Graf Moltke and his nephew Graf Wedell, both of the Danish navy. This enabled him to make a series of private reports to Germain. Nicholas Rodger has no time at all for him, sarcastically noting that one of the themes of these reports 'is the extraordinary brilliance of Benjamin Thompson, superior in knowledge and talent to everybody with whom he came into contact, infinitely better qualified than any sea officer to handle a fleet'.[22] He

20 Barnes and Owen (eds), *Private Papers of John, Earl of Sandwich*, Vol.III, pp.49-50.
21 Laughton (ed.), *Barham Papers*, Vol.I, pp.292-293.
22 Rodger, *Insatiable Earl*, p.261.

finds it surprising that historians should have used what Thompson wrote as a source of fact. Typical of Thompson's letters to Germain was the first in the series, dated 20 July:

> I can stand it no longer. Those who are interested in the disgrace of our commander may laugh at our blunders, but I who do not feel those prejudices which are but too common in the profession am hurt beyond measure to find how little dependence is to be put in our skill in manoeuvring this great and respectable fleet.[23]

Rodger is obviously correct in his assessment of Thompson as a conceited and self-important individual whose observations must be taken with a pinch of salt. He certainly lacked the qualification to make the sweeping judgments to be found in his letters, such as his observation on 26 July that Hardy was 'not a fit person to command this great fleet at this time'. In the same letter he went on to comment :

> Every step he takes clearly proves to me that he does not mean to quit his hold of English ground, and that nothing but the most positive orders will ever carry him fairly off Brest. He means to procrastinate as long as he can and when he is obliged to act he will make ministers responsible for the consequence if he fails.[24]

In later reports he was to be much less critical of Hardy, for whom he seems to have formed a genuine affection, writing of the admiral that 'he is a worthy good man, and I respect and love him from my heart'. For some of Hardy's staff, Thompson had a very low opinion, but on the other hand he recorded that Kempenfelt was 'a brave, good, sensible officer' whom he greatly respected. Thompson was however not just a puffed up nobody; he subsequently became a very distinguished scientist, and later entered the service of the Bavarian government where he was ennobled as Count von Rumford.

For the King, 'suspense was the most shocking of all situations'. He was anxious that the instructions given to Hardy should not encourage a retreat from the Combined Fleet. Having considered the instructions that had been given to Hardy, he wrote to Sandwich on 28 July to say that he should not be ordered to risk an engagement in all events:

> But he should be informed that, having received a very large reinforcement since the date of those instructions, it is his duty to take such steps as the valour and discipline of the squadron under his command may

23 W.G. Perrin (ed.), *The Naval Miscellany* (London: Navy Records Society 1928), Vol.III, p.127.

24 Perrin (ed.), *Naval Miscellany*, Vol.III, p.139.

> naturally encourage, and should the joined fleets of the enemies be too strong for him with any probability of success to risk a general action, he should at least so watch them as to avail himself of every favourable contingency.[25]

A retreat without having done everything that could be done would, he thought, be of 'such infinitely serious consequence that the whole nation must be so intimidated or so disgusted as to produce universal confusion'.

Hardy was accordingly sent fresh instructions:

> You are ... to proceed as far to the westward as you may judge necessary, and use all possible means, with the Force under your command, to prevent the enemy from carrying their designs into execution; and not to leave your station while your provisions and water will allow you to keep the sea, unless driven off by stress of Weather, or that some other event should happen which from your professional knowledge and experience may lead you to think it absolutely necessary to return into Port.[26]

In reply, Hardy wrote that if the winds allowed he would cruise from ten to twenty leagues west-southwest of the Scillies, where he could best protect the important incoming East Indies and West Indies convoys, as well as be best placed to intercept the Combined Fleet. Sandwich thought it advisable on 3 August to re-emphasise his concern that Hardy should do all he could to get into a westerly position:

> I cannot avoid troubling you with another letter to point out to you the necessity of your using every means on your part to get well to the westward. I dread the thoughts of your coming into port; for believe me the public will not be satisfied, if you return for want of provisions or even if you are driven in by contrary winds. Your enemies and mine are watching to take every advantage against us, and nothing can give them fairer ground than your coming home without having seen the enemy's fleet.[27]

This extremely pointed letter produced from Hardy what has been described as 'a self exculpatory, reasonable but totally uninspired and inspiring reply, in which his thoughts seemed to dwell more upon the opposition at home than the enemy at sea'.[28]

25 Barnes and Owen (eds), *Private Papers of John, Earl of Sandwich*, Vol.III, p.51.

26 Patterson, *The Other Armada*, p.176.

27 Barnes and Owen (eds), *Private Papers of John, Earl of Sandwich*, Vol.III, p.55.

28 Patterson, *The Other Armada*, p.177.

Meanwhile Kempenfelt was becoming increasingly frustrated with Hardy, and his dismay burst out in an emotional letter to Middleton of 6 August:

> In confidence, I must inform you the confused conduct here is such that I tremble for the event. There is no forethought, therefore no events provided against; we are every day, from morning till night, plagued and puzzled in minutiae, while essentials are totally neglected. An odd obstinacy and way of negativing everything proposed, makes all advice useless. There is a fund of good nature in the man, but not one grain of the commander-in-chief. I hear it often said the salvation of Britain depends upon this fleet. I never hear the expression but I turn pale and sink. My God, what have your great people done by such an appointment![29]

He followed this with a more measured analysis of Hardy's performance as commander-in-chief, but which was damning in that he disclosed his anxiety that the command had been placed in hands 'extremely unequal to the charge. How you can now remedy the evil of this injudicious appointment I can't say':

> A man who never thinks beforehand, and therefore is always under the confusion of a surprise when anything happens; always in such a hurry when he takes in hand to do anything that he never does it; puzzling himself and all about him in little detail minutiae, whilst essentials are never thought of; not the least idea of what the officer should be, so that he destroys his own authority and those in command next under him; uses directions to the captain of the ship [or] to the lieutenants, without their ever passing through me. It is with the greatest difficulty I can ever prevail upon him to manoeuvre the fleet.[30]

He had written, he told Middleton, to show that 'the person you have chose is not in any degree equal to it. Find a man if possible capable of it; and don't, in so careless a manner, destroy all our hopes'. Whether Middleton conveyed the sense of Kempenfelt's correspondence to Sandwich we cannot know, but even if he did, the First Lord would have found it extremely difficult to act on Kempenfelt's opinion and remove Hardy.

At the same time, Sandwich was receiving a very different view of the admiral's competence. Mulgrave wrote to him on 12 August:

> I must do Sir Charles the justice to say that no endeavours have been wanting on his part; so very large a fleet is very unmanageable and cannot

29 Laughton (ed.), *Barham Papers*, Vol.I, p.293.

30 Laughton (ed.), *Barham Papers*, Vol.I, pp.293-295.

> be reckoned upon from what may be done with a smaller force and under more favourable circumstances. I think the judgment he has shown in conducting the fleet highly meritorious. Allow me to observe to you that people at a distance are more apt to form their judgment of a conduct from their own hopes and wishes than from circumstances which must affect it, and which those only who are on the spot and feel the effects of them can be aware of. The westerly winds that brought in the convoys prevented our getting out and will always operate as the best protection.[31]

Mulgrave concluded his letter with an urgent appeal to Sandwich not to let Hardy be badmouthed in any way: 'Let me recommend it to you particularly not to suffer our commander to be run down either publicly or privately … I think you may depend upon his zeal and diligence; and I have not the smallest doubt, should the enemy venture this way, but that the conduct of the fleet will be such as will do credit to those who have equipped as well as to those who command it'.

The likelihood of battle, for which so many longed, was increasing daily. Although there was no firm intelligence as to the progress of the Combined Fleet, there was no doubt that it was now approaching. Should the fleets engage, not only would Hardy's capacity in battle be tested, but also it would become apparent whether a force of some thirty ships of the line was adequate to deal with one which, on paper at least, was roughly twice as large.

31 Barnes and Owen (eds), *Private Papers of John, Earl of Sandwich*, Vol.III, pp.57-60.

20

Plymouth

D'Orvilliers, reporting to Sartine after his arrival at the Sisargas on 10 June, was at first in buoyant mood. The health of his crews at this time seemed excellent, as he explained:

> The change of air has entirely delivered us from the epidemic from which we suffered so badly at Brest. This deliverance by Divine Providence lifts my confidence and I hope that notwithstanding the inexperience demonstrated by some of my captains, all will go well if our allies are active in their cooperation.[1]

A few days later, however, reporting on a meeting with his subordinate commanders and his captains, d'Orvilliers told Sartine that he had found it necessary to draw attention to their poor station keeping. He went on:

> The number of mediocre captains is greater in this campaign than in the last. This is troubling. But as we will be stronger, if the junction with the Spanish goes well, these faults will be of little consequence. Moreover, I have seen for myself, today, when I manoeuvred the fleet, that my rebuke had had an effect, and the errors were not as bad as had previously been the case.[2]

By 29 June, though, d'Orvilliers's optimism was beginning to wane. He had spent nearly three weeks at the rendezvous without news of the Spanish. He was coming round to the view that d'Arce, with the Ferrol squadron at Corunna, about 20 miles away, was prepared to resort to any pretext to avoid joining him. Without any news at all of the Cadiz fleet having put to sea, he feared that the planned campaign might after all prove abortive. Although d'Arce did finally appear on

1 Lacour-Gayet, *La marine Militaire*, p.256.
2 Lacour-Gayet, *La marine Militaire*, p.256.

2 July, bringing with him news that Córdova had put to sea with the Cadiz fleet on 23 June, a serious potential threat had materialised. Sickness had begun to reappear in the ships of the French fleet. By mid-July an epidemic of smallpox and putrid fever was beginning to spread throughout the fleet. The grave consequences of the hurried departure from Brest without adequate medical staffing or resources would soon be all too apparent. Two ships of the line, the *Couronne* and *Saint Esprit*, had already been obliged to put into Corunna to land the sick.

At first, the reports which d'Orvilliers made were hopeful, saying that the number of men so far falling sick was not excessive:

> We are in a good state to attack the enemy, and to begin our operations. But every moment becomes more precious as the season advances, and the fleet may not be able to maintain itself for more than a month or six weeks, and it is to be feared that sickness may spread through our vessels, where we have putrid fever and smallpox … I am persuaded of the valour and goodwill of our allies, but what I see of their manoeuvres confirms my view that they are a long way from becoming good sea officers.[3]

Córdova finally arrived on 20 July, prompting d'Orvilliers to report to Sartine that he hoped in a very few days to set off for the Channel. This, however, was not immediately possible. To his amazement, he found that nothing had been done by the Spanish fleet to familiarise itself with the French signalling system. It was a huge task for du Pavillon and the Spanish chief of staff Don Jose de Mazarredo to make good this crucial deficiency, and to coordinate not only the signalling arrangements but also the standing orders for the fleet's movements. By 29 July, however, this exercise had been completed.[4]

All the while, however, the sickness was spreading, and it brought to d'Orvilliers a tragic personal loss when his only son, serving as a lieutenant aboard the flagship *Bretagne*, became a victim of the epidemic. For several days the grief-stricken father was incapable of putting pen to paper, and it was left to du Pavillon to report to Sartine the departure of the Combined Fleet when it finally sailed on 30 July. By now there were some 1,500 sick throughout the fleet.

As it set off, it was now organised in five divisions, each composed of both French and Spanish vessels, together with a reserve division under Córdova.[5] This prudent arrangement had previously been suggested by Vergennes, but it tended to accentuate the effect of the poorer sailing qualities of the Spanish ships, which soon became apparent, so that each of the divisions was held back by the speed of the slower vessels. The centre of the fleet consisted of 45 ships

3 Lacour-Gayet, *La marine Militaire*, p.258.
4 Lacour-Gayet, *La marine Militaire*, p.260.
5 Patterson, *The Other Armada*, p.167.

'D. Luis Córdova y Córdova'. Plate from Historia de la Marina Real Española. (Public Domain)

of the line, of which 27 were French and 18 Spanish; d'Orvilliers led the white squadron, aboard the *Bretagne*. In the van, the blue squadron was led by de Guichen, with his flag flying in the *Ville de Paris*. De Ternay, aboard the *Saint Esprit*, commanded the third squadron which was designated by a blue flag with a white cross. Córdova's reserve division consisted of 16 ships of the line and two frigates, all Spanish; his flag was flying aboard the *Santissima Trinidad*, of 114 guns, the most powerful vessel in the entire fleet.[6] To the right of the main body

6 Lacour-Gayet, *La marine Militaire*, p.264.

of the fleet sailed a light division consisting of five ships of the line, three French and two Spanish, under the command of Latouche-Treville, in the *Couronne*. The ships of the line were followed by the frigates and corvettes, together with the supply ships and hospital ships.

By 2 August d'Orvilliers felt able to resume his correspondence with Sartine, writing from a position some 51 leagues south-west of Ushant:

> The Lord has taken from me all that I have in the world, but he has left me the strength to carry on this campaign and the greatest desire that it will be to your satisfaction. The afflictions that we have suffered have lost us time; but there remains sufficient to carry out our operations successfully, if Providence protects them.[7]

He was hopeful that if the winds continued to be favourable he would reach the Channel within two or three days, and within a week could get as far as St Helens as he searched for the enemy. On the following day, however, he suffered a serious setback when the winds turned against him, and he was unable for the moment to make further progress.

As he approached his destination d'Orvilliers was badly let down by the Ministry of Marine. He had reported to Sartine the extent to which his extended stay at the Sisargas had depleted his resources, and had been promised that a convoy would join him off Ushant bringing provisions. On 6 August he asked also for 'hospital ships, galleys, anchors, cables, hawsers and other gear,' but all he got was a small supply of timber.[8] Nor was d'Orvilliers helped by the attitude of Córdova, who was at odds with him over his intentions, and which led du Pavillon to say despairingly that it was useless to resist for much longer against opinions so incorrect but firmly embedded for nearly 80 years in the head of a reputable officer. D'Orvilliers, in spite of what he had told Sartine about his strength and determination, may, as Lacour-Gayet suggested, have lacked the moral energy to deal with his recalcitrant colleague. At all events, he wrote to Córdova on 4 August: 'With complete respect, esteem and confidence in your talents, I accept and approve all the dispositions with which during the course of our journey and the plans of attack and defence in which you have had the goodness to take part'.[9]

By 8 August a clear difference had emerged between what the ministry required of the Combined Fleet, and what d'Orvilliers intended. Sartine instructed him that he must first entirely clear the British fleet from Spithead before embarking on the operations to lead to the invasion. D'Orvilliers, on the other hand, having

7 Lacour-Gayet, *La marine Militaire*, p.266.
8 Patterson, *The Other Armada*, pp.167-168.
9 Lacour-Gayet, *La marine Militaire*, p.267.

finally reached a workable agreement with Córdova, wrote to Sartine to inform him of his plans:

> We shall search for the enemy along the coast as far as St Helens Roads, and then if I find the roads empty or am able to take possession of them I shall send word to Marshal de Vaux at Le Havre, in accordance with your instructions, and inform him what steps I should take to ensure the safety of his passage, which will depend on the main force of the English fleet; that is to say, I shall dispose on the one hand the Combined Fleet to contain the enemy, and I shall detach on the other hand a light squadron and a sufficient force of ships of the line and frigates, or I shall propose to M. de Cordoba to carry out that duty, in order that the army may have a clear and safe passage. I anticipate that then either by the battle I shall force on the enemy or by his retreat into harbour, I shall be certain of his situation and of the success of the operations.[10]

There were however, much more fundamental changes in the scheme of invasion in contemplation, as pessimism began to take hold not only of Vergennes, but also the army commanders in Normandy. With no news that the Combined Fleet had actually sailed, Vergennes was in a state of mounting agitation, writing on 30 July:

> This delay would exhaust the patience of a saint, and I am far from being one. I can hardly write. I do not know what to do or say. Our most experienced seamen regard the Channel as most dangerous even from the beginning of August. Moreover, an invasion is becoming more difficult every day, because every day the defences grow stronger.[11]

Meanwhile Dumouriez, noting that the invasion transports would be ready no later than 30 July, had written on 21 July:

> The concentration and embarkation of the army will take five or six days … But we are still without news of M. d'Orvilliers, and the slowness of the Spaniards will end by ruining everything. It makes me wonder if they have any intention of entering the Channel, of which they know nothing … And is it possible that even our own naval officers are hesitating to get themselves in that sea so near the end of the campaigning season? I foresee a fatal outcome … France and Spain, having neither affection nor esteem for each other, are going to ruin this business by mutual suspicion

10 James, *The British Navy in Adversity*, p.178.
11 Patterson, *The Other Armada*, p.165.

> and recriminations. My letter reflects the gloomy atmosphere of our headquarters.[12]

It was in this despondent environment that a radical change in the invasion plans had begun to take shape. Aranda, the Spanish ambassador, had previously floated the idea of a landing in Cornwall; now, at the beginning of August, he suggested that this should take the place of the proposed landing on the Isle of Wight. Given all the anxieties that had grown up around the original plan, Vergennes jumped at the idea, reporting it to Montmorin on 6 August and on the next day dispatching new orders to d'Orvilliers. The objective would now be a landing close to Falmouth, which did have quite a lot to commend it:

> Aranda's plan did present the advantages that Falmouth would require no long siege to capture, and that it was within striking distance of the major port of Plymouth. Most important, once ashore the expeditionary force would be relatively self-sufficient. Cornwall was a natural fortress once a defence line could be established around Bodmin or along the Tamar river.[13]

A landing in Cornwall would also meet Floridablanca's insistence that England must continue to be the main objective rather than, as Vergennes was beginning to think would be best, switching the principal forces of the allies away from Europe. It would of course also mean that it would no longer be necessary for the Combined Fleet to penetrate as far eastward as St Helens, though it would still obviously be necessary to seek out and neutralise the Channel Fleet.

The British intelligence network, meanwhile, had enabled some inkling of the Combined Fleet's sickness problems to reach the Admiralty. This prompted the sending of fresh orders to Hardy, which referred to 'the long delay of the appearance of the enemy' and to reports of sickness in the fleet, as well as of damage to ships in the bad weather. This gave reason to believe that the Combined Fleet meant to avoid action and go to Brest. If Hardy's information confirmed this, he was instructed 'not to confine yourself to any station which will hinder you from doing your utmost to give the enemy battle and prevent them from going into port'. These orders did not reach him until after he had already been made aware that d'Orvilliers had arrived in the Channel.[14] At the time that these orders were sent, the Channel Fleet was in fact some 30 or 40 miles further west than the station which Hardy had intended to take up.

12 Patterson, *The Other Armada*, p.166.

13 Dull, *French Navy and American Independence*, p.156.

14 Barnes and Owen (eds), *Private Papers of John, Earl of Sandwich*, Vol.III, p.7.

After several frustrating days the winds finally relented and the Combined Fleet was able to resume its journey northwards. Rounding Ushant, it made for the Lizard and by 15 August had reached a position 18 miles to the south of that point, but without any information as to the location of the Channel Fleet. Next day the Combined Fleet came in sight of Plymouth in clear weather and a calm sea, and d'Orvilliers sent off a report to Sartine:

> The Combined Fleet is at this moment becalmed and anchored within sight of the Tower of Plymouth. The weather is very unfavourable to my intention to proceed directly to St Helens in order to attempt to engage the enemy, which it is all the more important to achieve soon, because the situation of the French ships of which I have informed you is becoming worse every day, both because of the sickness which is prevalent and because of the small amount of water and provisions which they have left. These considerations do not permit me to carry out any other project. To become masters of the Channel, in accordance with the King's orders, so as to bring about the passage of the land army, and to receive the supplies of water and provisions which this army will require – these are the two objects which concern me at present.[15]

D'Orvilliers also renewed his request that the despatch of pilots familiar with these waters should be hastened; the lack of these he found extremely worrying. At this time he was convinced that the Channel Fleet had taken refuge in Plymouth harbour, having had no hard news of its movements for some time.

That evening, however, at 7.00 p.m., as the Combined Fleet lay at anchor off the port, the fresh orders issued by the ministry as to the objective of the invasion force reached d'Orvilliers. He learned for the first time of the abandonment of the plan to land on the Isle of Wight or anywhere else in that region; instead, de Vaux, with that part of the invasion army at St Malo, was to land on the south coast of Cornwall at Falmouth. D'Orvilliers was also told that in order to enable the Combined Fleet to keep the sea for as long as possible, even for several months, a supply convoy would be leaving Brest to join him.[16]

D'Orvilliers was appalled. Although reiterating his willingness to carry out the orders that he had now received, he pointed out the difficulties of executing them. To reprovision the fleet at sea would be a hazardous operation. Weather conditions in the Channel might be extremely unfavourable. Even if he found and beat Hardy, several of his ships would inevitably be badly damaged in the course of the encounter, and it would be necessary to protect them in a secure anchorage, and there were none such available to him. It appeared to him that it might be

15 Lacour-Gayet, *La marine Militaire*, pp.271-272.
16 Lacour-Gayet, *La marine Militaire*, p.272.

better to call off the attempt to invade and try again in the following year. As for Falmouth, it was the advice of the renegade Hamilton that the harbour there was bad, and could only contain six or eight ships, was exposed to strong winds and was surrounded with dangerous rocks. D'Orvilliers was also sceptical about the value of occupying a point so far from London.[17]

The arrival off the English coast of the Combined Fleet had been spotted on 15 August some fourteen leagues south-east of the Scillies by a group of ships making their way to join the Channel Fleet; these were the ships of the line *Marlborough*, 74, and *Ramillies*, 74, the 50-gun ship *Isis* and the sloop *Cormorant.* At first the British ships thought that they had met the Channel Fleet and only narrowly escaped being taken. Captain Penny, of the *Marlborough*, wrote a report of the sighting, which Sir Jacob Wheat, his first lieutenant, took aboard the *Cormorant*, in which he sailed for Plymouth while the other ships resumed their search for Hardy and the Channel Fleet. Wheat reached the port early on 16 August, and rode off to London using relays of horses that were on standby for such an emergency. Soon after midnight on 16/17 August he arrived at Sandwich's house at Blackheath with the momentous news that had so long been expected.[18]

The King, when Sandwich passed on the news to him, was delighted:

> I had rode out before Lord Sandwich's box arrived, or I should have sent it sooner back. Decision is the joy of my life; as such I cannot but feel happy that now the fleets cannot fail, within very few days, of coming to battle. I trust in Providence, and therefore have not the smallest uneasiness as to the issue of it.[19]

He did not, though, think it necessary to summon the members of the Cabinet, most of whom were out of town, to come to London, apart from Amherst.

When Middleton received the news, his immediate thought was that Hardy should not be needlessly committed to a premature engagement, as he wrote to Sandwich on 19 August:

> There seems to be the greatest necessity of informing Sir Charles Hardy of every measure you are taking here to reinforce him with ships and fire ships, so as to lead him to avoid an engagement till he can avail himself of their assistance. Every day's delay is in our favour while they continue in the Channel at this season of the year, and every additional ship of consequence in such a contest as this.[20]

17 Lacour-Gayet, *La marine Militaire*, pp.273-274.
18 Patterson, *The Other Armada*, pp.180-181.
19 Barnes and Owen (eds), *Private Papers of John, Earl of Sandwich*, Vol.III, p.61.
20 Barnes and Owen (eds), *Private Papers of John, Earl of Sandwich*, Vol.III, pp.62-63.

In his correspondence with Kempenfelt, the most recent letter which he had received had been dated 14 August, when the Channel Fleet was to the west of the Scillies. Kempenfelt had been musing unhappily about what he saw as the difference between the opposing fleets, and the need to impose a better tactical discipline on the British fleet:

> That we have no regular system of naval tactics you know; also that tactics are as necessary for fleets as armies, to give regularity, activity and force, and that that force may be directed in the best manner. Of two fleets, if one acts by a regular system of tactics, when the other has none, I needn't say where the advantage must lay. Our enemies have theory, we were superior in practice. They are in a way to remove the difference in the last, and how will the comparison then stand between us? Our fleet, under its present deficiency of discipline for regular manoeuvring and fighting, is to a fleet that acts by a well formed system, just the same as an army composed of raw militia would be to one formed of regulars under an experienced general. The expediency of having some person at the head of the fleet capable of introducing such a discipline is become absolutely necessary, and should be immediate.[21]

Sandwich was getting a good deal of advice at this time. Among his correspondents was Palliser, who had remained in touch with him and who wrote to suggest that with Hardy far to the west and d'Orvilliers off Plymouth, it would be wise to send detachments of frigates off Le Havre and other ports to prevent the invasion fleet from sailing. He followed this with a further letter 19 August reiterating this advice. He went on:

> For God's sake and for your own sake, call upon and take the opinion of as many sea officers on the spot as may be confided in upon this and other important points. This seems to me to be highly necessary, as well for the good of the service as for your Lordship's justification. These are the considerations that urge me to take this liberty.[22]

Sandwich remained entirely calm at this moment of crisis; there was not a lot he could do, since Hardy, who would by now have been made fully aware of the presence of the Combined Fleet off Plymouth, would naturally be doing all he could to get back from his present position. The insistence that he should take station so far to the west had meant that d'Orvilliers was able to arrive at a point between the Channel Fleet and its bases, and it would depend on a change in the direction

21 Laughton (ed.), *Barham Papers*, Vol.I, p.245.

22 Barnes and Owen (eds), *Private Papers of John, Earl of Sandwich*, Vol.III, pp.63-64.

of the wind if the position was to be recovered. The First Lord summed up the position as he saw it: 'Sir Charles Hardy is off Scilly, and while the wind is easterly cannot get back into the Channel, but the first shift of wind must bring him back, and a battle seems inevitable'.[23]

Hardy's first news of the arrival of the Combined Fleet came with the frigate *Southampton*, which joined him on 17 August. She and the *Marlborough*, which had been chased by ships of the Combined Fleet as far as Plymouth, had succeeded in stealing back westwards close inshore, and thus evading the enemy. At this point the Channel Fleet was some 20 leagues south-west of the Scilly Isles. Hardy now had with him 38 ships of the line, three 50-gun ships, and 17 frigates and smaller vessels. He had at once begun the task of working back to the eastward, in the face of almost continuously contrary winds, and it was not until 29 August that he was in sight of Land's End. That afternoon, at about 4.00 p.m., the *Cumberland*, 74, signalled that she had sighted enemy ships to the southward, and it was assumed that these were part of the Combined Fleet. The wind was now in the east-south-east, and Hardy signalled to his fleet to form line of battle and steer south. At midnight the wind came around to the south; by the morning of 30 August the enemy ships were no longer in sight, and fog had descended, seriously reducing visibility. For the moment the fleet stood on southwards.[24] The ships that had been seen were not, however, part of the Combined Fleet, but were from the convoy which had been sent out to resupply it.

The arrival of the Combined Fleet itself off Plymouth had caused immense alarm, which was deepened on the following day. The *Ardent*, 64, commanded by Captain Philip Boteler, had been lying in Torbay on its way to join the Channel Fleet. At midnight on 16/17 August she put to sea, heading westward; neither the *Cormorant*, nor a lugger carrying Captain Berkeley of the *Firebrand*, which were at sea on the lookout for the *Ardent* in order to warn her of the presence of the Combined Fleet, was able to make contact with her. At 4.00 a.m. on the morning of 17 August the *Ardent*'s first lieutenant, who had the morning watch, relieved the fourth lieutenant, and it was at this time that a number of sails were seen to the west. One of these might have been the *Cormorant*, but the *Ardent* sailed on, stopping to interrogate a Danish brig from which no useful information was obtained. As she resumed her journey, more sails were seen to the southward, and it was assumed that these must be part of the Channel Fleet. Unsuspecting, the *Ardent* continued westward; then, first the French frigate *Terpsichore* and then the *Gentille*, both from La Touche-Treville's flying squadron, came up with her. Those aboard the *Ardent* still did not realise their peril, even when the French ships failed to acknowledge the private signal. By now she was sailing into a huge crescent of enemy ships, and her fate was sealed when another frigate, the *Junon*, came up

23 Syrett, *European Waters*, p.76.
24 Syrett, *European Waters*, p.77.

with her. Beyond came the *Couronne*, 80, the *Saint Michel* and *Triton*, both 64s, and the Spanish *Septentrion*, 64, and *Miño*, 74. At 10:30 a.m. the *Junon* was within gunshot, and hoisted French colours. The ensuing engagement could have only one outcome, though the *Ardent*'s resistance was hampered by the fact that her colours were shot away, leaving it to be supposed by many aboard her that she had struck. In the following year the circumstances of her loss would be investigated by a court martial, which concluded that Boteler had not done his utmost and ordered that he be dismissed the service.[25]

The action had taken place close inshore, and many at Plymouth watched it anxiously, although the outcome was not understood by many of the spectators. Various reports quickly circulated; some suggested that the *Ardent* had been destroyed, others that she had been taken. Another report was to the effect that she had 'fought and crippled the two frigates that attacked her and had outsailed the line of battleships and got safe thro' the enemy's fleet,' while yet another claimed that, greatly damaged, she had made it into Plymouth Sound. Sandwich observed to the King that so contradictory were the reports it was difficult to know what to make of them.[26]

What was certain was that the action had provided a striking demonstration of the reality of the situation; an enormously powerful enemy fleet lay off Plymouth, and panic seized many of the inhabitants. Indeed, not only the inhabitants; Commissioner Ourry lost his head almost completely. He began feverishly to organise his dockyard workers into some kind of military formation, and was active in preparing a boom with which he planned to block the harbour, which would have had the effect of rendering it unusable by the British fleet. He reported somewhat incoherently to Sandwich on 20 August:

> I need not inform you of our situation last Monday, and particularly on Tuesday noon when I saw two grand divisions of the enemy's fleet leading into the Sound by two of their admirals. I did not think at that time and as the wind was that I should be Master of the Dockyard in ten hours longer ... For some days past I put the question to myself, shall I, Paul Ourry, or you, Jack Dorvilliers, set fire to the dockyard? I think for reasons which I may give at another time that I would not set fire to or destroy it. Your Lordship's on such like occasion opinion would relieve my mind very much, though I hope now that we shall not be drove to such determination, as I hope all we have sent out must be with Sir Charles Hardy.[27]

25 G. Rutherford, 'The Capture of the *Ardent*' in *The Mariner's Mirror* (February 1941), pp.106-131.

26 Rutherford, 'The Capture of the *Ardent*', p.127.

27 Barnes and Owen (eds), *Private Papers of John, Earl of Sandwich*, Vol.III, pp.64-67.

Sandwich replied to the effect that he thought that Ourry desponded too much, 'and that the consequence of being attacked will not be the loss of the place, especially as I perceive that both by sea and land you are using every exertion to put everything into a proper state of defence'. Middleton's reaction was rather less composed in expressing his opinion of Ourry's conduct, which he thought was that of a madman; he wrote to Sandwich on 22 August:

> I am very much concerned at the wild conduct of the Commissioner at Plymouth, and know of no way so effectual to stop it as by acquainting him that it is his Majesty's pleasure he should give up the defence of the harbour to the Admiral and confine himself to the civil duty of the yard. If this is not done, and he is permitted to continue the military system that seems to have seized his brain, there will be a stop to every work carrying on at that yard.[28]

The First Lord was relieved to discover that Shuldham, the commanding admiral at Plymouth, was taking an altogether more measured view of the situation, and he wrote to him on 23 August in an effort to get Ourry under control:

> I can't help troubling you with a word or two, merely confidentially to yourself, to ask whether you cannot give a little check to Mr Ourry's military spirit, in which his business as Commissioner of the Yard, which is a civil office, seems totally absorbed. I do not understand whether the boom that is preparing to be laid across the harbour will be fixed there immediately. If it is, it will in my opinion be a most fatal and useless measure, as it will hinder our own ships from getting in and out … The more the defence of the harbour is left to the Admiral in general, and the less to the Commissioner, the better my opinion will be of the resistance you will make in the day of attack.[29]

Sandwich was keen that the able Captain Edward Le Cras, one of Middleton's key staff at the Navy Board, should be sent down to sort things out. The Comptroller, on the other hand, was firmly opposed to this suggestion, protesting that it was with the utmost difficulty that he was able to keep the business of the office under:

> Send the whole of the pen and ink gentlemen except the Clerk of the Acts, and I shall never miss them, but I flatter myself your Lordship will give up the idea of Mr Le Cras, unless you should think the quieting of a madman

28 Barnes and Owen (eds), *Private Papers of John, Earl of Sandwich*, Vol.III, pp.69-70.
29 Barnes and Owen (eds), *Private Papers of John, Earl of Sandwich*, Vol.III, pp.71-72.

> of more importance to his Majesty's service than providing the several yards as well as the whole fleet with stores.[30]

Sandwich, however, was insistent, and paid a visit to Middleton to persuade him to release Le Cras, who went down to Plymouth on 24 August for a flying visit. He put paid to the idea of the boom, and was able to reassure Shuldham, who later told Sandwich that he had been himself 'unable to restrain the impetuosity and the freedom of speech as well as correspondence' of Ourry. Le Cras was also able to ensure the return to their proper duties of the dockyard workers whom Ourry had enrolled in his version of the Home Guard. This seriously upset Lindsay, who wrote to Amherst to reiterate his desire to resign as Military Governor, which he had previously made known. Amherst recommended that he be replaced by Lieutenant General William Haviland; pending the latter's arrival, Lieutenant General Sir William Draper would take over the command. Le Cras, meanwhile, reported back to Sandwich on 25 August that the boom would not be laid until he had had an opportunity of seeing the First Lord, and also that the shipwrights were all at work.

While all this was going on, the immediate threat to Plymouth evaporated. The easterly wind which had faded to a near calm while d'Orvilliers was off the port sprang up again, and by 20 August it had carried the Combined Fleet beyond the Lizard. At the same time Hardy was continuing his efforts to work his own way eastwards and regain a position beyond the enemy. It was while he was engaged in this that the abortive encounter with the French supply convoy had taken place on 29 August. After he had lost sight of them overnight, and fog had descended on the following morning, at about 11.00 a.m. a light north westerly breeze sprang up. At this point the *Shrewsbury* signalled that 11 vessels were in sight to leeward. This was in fact a further sighting of the supply convoy, which appeared to be ignoring the ships of the Channel Fleet. In the event the convoy failed to locate the Combined Fleet and made its way back to Brest.

Hardy apparently sent an upbeat report to the Admiralty on 29 August, or so at least Benjamin Thompson asserted, claiming in a letter of 4 September to Germain to have drafted it for the admiral:

> What do you think of my dispatch to the Admiralty, my dear Lord? You see it was sent after all, just as I prepared it. I think it will prove to you one of two things, that is that the Admiral felt bolder on Sunday [the 29th] than he afterwards did on Tuesday [the 31st] or that he signed it merely to please me, without considering the consequences of giving you so much reason to expect a spirited conduct on his part. I wish he would let me

30 Barnes and Owen (eds), *Private Papers of John, Earl of Sandwich*, Vol.III, pp.69-70.

> write all his dispatches, please God I would dip him in so deep that it should be impossible for him to be off from beating the French.[31]

No trace of such a dispatch, however, could be found by W.G. Perrin, the Secretary of the Admiralty, editor of the *Naval Miscellany.*

Inevitably, it was the wind that was determining the movements of the opposing fleets. The easterly wind that had forced d'Orvilliers away from Plymouth continued to blow:

> The east wind continued to chase d'Orvilliers out of the Channel; on August 22, he was twenty two leagues north west of Ushant, that is to say fully into the Atlantic. However, he still spoke of returning to Plymouth and of detaching two divisions for St Malo and Le Havre. As for giving himself heart, he said that all had not been lost in this sad cruise: "Certainly, we have been held up by the delay in our junctions and by the epidemic which afflicts us so cruelly. Nevertheless, it has already resulted in movements of the fleet which have astonished and perhaps frightened the English, forcing them to take refuge in Plymouth and to witness the taking of a ship of the line".[32]

In the dispatch quoted, d'Orvilliers asserted that he was now 'mistress of the Channel'; this, Lacour-Gayet considered a remarkable claim, since the Combined Fleet was able neither to enter it or to disembark troops there.

On 25 August, to d'Orvilliers' surprise, since he still believed the Channel Fleet to be in Plymouth, he received news from a passing vessel that Hardy was some hundred miles to leeward of the Scilly Islands.[33] Accordingly, he at once convened a Council of War aboard the *Bretagne*, attended by seven French and five Spanish admirals (but not, oddly, by Córdova). It was obvious to all those present that they had only a limited time left if they were to strike a blow at the Channel Fleet. It was their unanimous decision that they should now head for the Scilly Isles in the hope of finding Hardy there, but that this must be their final attempt, and if they had not made contact by 8 September they should in any case return to Brest. D'Orvilliers reported the meeting to Sartine: 'So there it is, Monseigneur, that is my task and I will manoeuvre accordingly, unless I receive contrary orders'.[34] It was this decision which almost brought about the engagement which was so keenly sought by the governments on both sides.

31 Perrin (ed.), *Naval Miscellany*, Vol.III, pp.145-146.

32 Lacour-Gayet, *La marine Militaire*, pp.282-283.

33 James, *The British Navy in Adversity*, p.182.

34 Lacour-Gayet, *La marine Militaire*, p.284.

Soon after daybreak on 31 August, when the Channel Fleet was about 25 miles south west of Land's End, Hardy received a signal that strange ships had been sighted astern. It was soon apparent that this must be the Combined Fleet, since a total of 56 sail was signalled stretching from the southwest to the northwest. D'Orvilliers, for his part, when the enemy were reported in sight, ordered de Guichen to close the land in order to prevent Hardy from seeking refuge in harbour; it took time to execute this manoeuvre as it was necessary to transfer men from the frigates into de Guichen's ships of the line. At this time the wind was in the northwest.

Sir Richard Bickerton, the captain of the *Terrible*, sent Sandwich an account of what followed:

> Tuesday morning soon after break of day, saw the Land's End in the NE quarter eight or nine leagues off. And at the same time some ships made signals for strange sails to the westward, and soon after for a fleet; a frigate was observed three or four leagues off to be making signals; and we then discovered from the decks some, but from the masthead many, ships astern extending from the SW to the NW. We were now satisfied it was the enemy's fleet, seemingly forming a line with a variety of signals at their mastheads. The Admiral made a signal for a closer order of sailing and signals for different ships to take the fire ships in tow, standing for the Lizard with a smart breeze of wind from the NW quarter, proportioning his sail to that of the heaviest going ships of the fleet. Some of the enemy's light frigates came within three or four miles of the sternmost ship of the fleet, the *Romney*, who tacking upon them and chasing, obliged them to tack towards their own fleet. The gross of the enemy's fleet did not appear to come up with us by the time we had got the length of the Lizard. About 4 o'clock fifty six sail were seen from our masthead. Towards night, the wind coming to the eastward, we stood to the offing with little wind.[35]

Hardy had thus been able to take advantage of the wind to edge away to the eastward, so that when, as evening fell, he had got into a windward position. By 6.00 p.m. only six enemy ships could be seen from the masthead of the *Terrible*. Thanks to the wind, to the occasional incidence of fog, and to darkness, Hardy had achieved his object of getting to the east of the Combined Fleet, and his intention now was to lure it up the Channel after him, where he would progressively be able to fight at an increasing advantage.[36]

Aware that Hardy had now got to the east of him, it was d'Orvilliers's intention that the Combined Fleet should pursue. This pursuit, such as it was, was

35 Barnes and Owen (eds), *Private Papers of John, Earl of Sandwich*, Vol.III, pp.89-91.

36 Patterson, *The Other Armada*, p.195; Barnes and Owen (eds), *Private Papers of John, Earl of Sandwich*, Vol.III, pp.7-8; Syrett, *European Waters*, p.77.

interrupted by the sighting of another fleet to the southward, but upon investigation it proved to be a convoy of Dutch East Indiamen. Meanwhile Hardy, who in any case could outsail his opponent, reached a point five miles south of the Eddystone at 11.00 a.m. on 1 September, where he briefly anchored to avoid being driven back to the west by the wind and the making tide.

In London, Middleton had been continuing to offer advice to Sandwich, writing to him on 1 September to urge that Hardy should be supplied 'with every frigate, sloop and cutter that can possibly be spared' which in case of a defeat might be the means of saving every disabled ship. He also suggested that Sandwich should put to Hardy the idea of organising his fire ships 'under the direction of a discreet experienced captain'. Middleton was entirely aware that one of the difficulties which from time to time arose was that of persuading Hardy actually to accept advice, so he wrote to Kempenfelt to put this suggestion to him, in order that he might then lay it before the admiral, albeit very carefully. It would, he told the First Lord, give credit to Hardy as well as to Sandwich: 'I have hinted it to Kempenfelt, but not to come from himself lest jealousy should prevent it being adopted'.[37]

While he was briefly anchored off Plymouth, Hardy sent a report of his movements to Sandwich, telling him of his intention of continuing to head up Channel, and saying that he planned to make for St Helens or Spithead to obtain reinforcements, take on fresh water, and land his sick, of which he said there were a substantial number. Before he received this report, Sandwich had written to the admiral on 2 September:

> I am made very happy by finding that you are got within the enemy's fleet; for, as I think a battle is inevitable, it will certainly be much to your advantage to fight them in the Channel with our own ports under your lee. We will strain every nerve to give you reinforcement; but I hope you will not be necessitated to come into port … I need not tell you that the eyes of all the world are upon you, and that no man in this kingdom ever had such an opportunity as yourself of serving his country, his connections, and himself.[38]

The text of this letter rather suggests that Sandwich was still not entirely confident that Hardy would do all he could to force an engagement on the Combined Fleet. He added a postscript to his letter in the terms suggested by Middleton as to the employment of the fire ships.

The Channel Fleet caught no further sight of its opponent, and it continued to make its way eastward. Its arrival at Spithead surprised Mulgrave, who wrote from there to Sandwich on 3 September:

37 Barnes and Owen (eds), *Private Papers of John, Earl of Sandwich*, Vol.III, pp.83-86.
38 Barnes and Owen (eds), *Private Papers of John, Earl of Sandwich*, Vol.III, pp.88-89.

> We are to my astonishment arrived at Spithead. I was in hopes we should not have gone further than St Helens. The Admiral told me today his reason was to complete the ships more expeditiously. Should the French push up to St Helens we shall be blocked up, or go out at the greatest disadvantage. I think the spirit of our people, the honour of our fleet, and perhaps safety of our country depend upon our not remaining here more than is inevitably necessary. I wish to God that you would come down, as I think your presence here would be of the utmost service.[39]

The King also thought that it was an excellent idea that Sandwich should himself go down to Portsmouth, 'and seeing no time is lost in putting on board the several ships what may be absolutely necessary for enabling Sir Charles Hardy to go and meet the Combined Fleet of France and Spain now within the Channel'. He was, he said, certain that Hardy 'must be eager to meet these faithless people'.[40] He made no secret of his concern that Sandwich should go down to Portsmouth, writing no less than three times to the First Lord during the course of 4 September.

Kempenfelt wrote on 5 September to Middleton from Spithead. He had been reflecting on the best way in which to meet a force of the size of the Combined Fleet:

> We don't seem to have considered sufficiently a certain fact, that the comparative force of two fleets depends much upon their sailing. The fleet that sails faster has much the advantage, as they can engage or not as they please, and so have always in their power to choose the favourable opportunity to attack. I think I may safely hazard an opinion that twenty five sail of the line, coppered, would be sufficient to hazard and tease this great, unwieldy, combined armada, so as to prevent their effecting anything; hanging continually upon them, ready to catch at any opportunity of a separation from night, gale or fog; to dart upon the separated, to cut off any convoys of provisions coming to them; and if they attempted an invasion, to oblige their whole fleet to escort the transports, and even then it would be impossible to protect them entirely from so nimble and active a fleet.[41]

Kempenfelt had not, however, changed his mind about the leadership of the Channel Fleet, going on to reiterate his 'great astonishment so little care was taken in the choice of the conductor':

39 Barnes and Owen (eds), *Private Papers of John, Earl of Sandwich*, Vol.III, pp.91-92.

40 Barnes and Owen (eds), *Private Papers of John, Earl of Sandwich*, Vol.III, pp.92-94.

41 Laughton (ed.), *Barham Papers*, Vol.I, pp.296-297.

> As a private man he is worthy of esteem, but as an officer, I am afraid the fleet has neither esteem for or confidence in him; a serious thing at so critical a juncture. The fleet wants a sensible, active and strict officer at the head of it, to brace up relaxed discipline, to give alertness and activity to it, in which consist great part of its force. There is none of that ardour remains now that upon extraordinary occasions urged everyone to try and have his ship the first ready; but there is a supine languor and indifference reigns now: it is the epidemic disorder of the nation and affects all.[42]

It was a damning, if sweeping judgement from someone with the ability to see the wood from the trees.

Kempenfelt was not alone in thinking that the Channel Fleet could be better led. Walsingham, still an opposition sympathiser, wrote to Sandwich on 3 September: 'All Party now I hope is laid aside: give us a man to command us that we have confidence in (you have more than one), and we will ensure your success. We must be equal either in force or ability; give us the latter, the other will follow'.[43]

Sandwich reached Portsmouth on the morning of 5 September, and at once met with Mulgrave. From him he got a much more favourable view of Hardy's performance; Mulgrave was, though, still very much aware of the political dimension, reckoning that Hardy should be supported against those of Keppel's adherents who remained with the fleet, a group which included Jervis and MacBride, and possibly Ross as well. Of Darby, Mulgrave spoke particularly favourably, telling Sandwich that he was 'quite adored in the fleet'. He also thought that the general demeanour of the officers and men of the fleet was as good as could be expected. His overall assessment, therefore, differed considerably from that of Kempenfelt.[44]

When Sandwich met with Hardy, he accepted the admiral's view that the return to port had been essential. On the other hand, he considered that the sickness level, to which Hardy had attached considerable importance, was not something about which to be concerned. At a later meeting with Kempenfelt, he found the Captain of the Fleet, whatever he may have privately felt, to be entirely supportive of Hardy and of the decision to go to Spithead, considering that the fleet could load there five times as fast as it could do at St Helens. Among others to whom Sandwich spoke, he found Captain George Johnstone to be particularly hostile to the suggestion of either Howe or Keppel taking command. The First Lord also paid two visits to the Victualling Board to ensure that everything was being done to resupply the fleet. When he reported this to the King, the latter was very pleased, reckoning that it was the most efficacious manner in which the sailing of the fleet might be hastened.

42 Laughton (ed.), *Barham Papers*, Vol.I, pp.297-298.

43 Barnes and Owen (eds), *Private Papers of John, Earl of Sandwich*, Vol.III, p.92.

44 Patterson, *The Other Armada*, pp.202-203.

By the time that Sandwich returned to London from Portsmouth, the threat from the Combined Fleet was beginning to recede, as further intelligence was received that conveyed the extent of the epidemic from which it was suffering. There was a sudden alarm when it appeared that the French were preparing for an attack on the Channel Islands, and Ross was sent to sea with three ships of the line, a dozen frigates and some fire ships, but this threat did not materialise, and Ross was back in Spithead by 25 September, the Channel Fleet having been ordered to stand fast in the meantime.[45]

In fact, the threat of invasion in 1779 had finally evaporated. In Normandy, there had been mounting dissatisfaction in the army about the way in which the ministry had dealt with the matter. The Duc de Chatelet wrote to the Duc d'Harcourt, the commander of that part of the invasion force concentrated at Le Havre, to express his disgust at the apparent decision to leave it to d'Orvilliers to decide whether to land in the Isle of Wight or at Falmouth:

> Therefore which of these will happen will depend on his operations and judgment; and between ourselves I do not know of any thing more absurd, but we shall see plenty of others, although we have experienced some already. Our fate is therefore, as you will see, in the hands of M. d'Orvilliers. Our ministers have acted like weak minded people who never know what they want to do until the moment comes to do it, and who are never happy except when giving conditional and confused orders.[46]

This was not entirely fair; the change of plan reflected the determination of Vergennes to get a result for the campaign in the Channel in 1779 notwithstanding the less favourable circumstances, though Chatelet was certainly right when he concluded that a large part of the problem lay in the unconditional commitment to do whatever the Spanish wanted.

As it was, Hardy's retreat out of reach of the Combined Fleet meant that the campaign was effectively at an end. D'Orvilliers made an unconvincing claim of success, writing to Sartine on 3 September that the result had been 'to put to flight the pretended masters of the sea in a manner which had been so precipitate that it was difficult to comprehend'.[47] D'Orvilliers now took the fleet to a point off Ushant; in the meantime Sartine had, following the report of the Council of War's decision, accepted that no more could usefully be done, and on 3 September issued an order that the Combined Fleet return to Brest. On 11 September, the fleet anchored in the Iroise; the process of passing approximately 100 vessels through the Goulet and anchoring in Brest roads took five days. D'Orvilliers, his spirit

45 Syrett, *European Waters*, p.79.

46 Lacour-Gayet, *La marine Militaire*, pp.277-278.

47 Lacour-Gayet, *La marine Militaire*, p.286.

entirely broken, submitted his resignation, which was duly accepted. The failure of the campaign could not fairly be laid at his door, but French public opinion squarely blamed him; and perhaps the ministry was content to allow this view to prevail, but he was not, however made the subject of any official reproach. D'Orvilliers retired to his home at Moulins, where he died in 1792 at the age of 82. In looking to assign responsibility for the failure of the campaign, one historian of the French navy has suggested that perhaps d'Orvilliers might have made a firmer attempt to seize the initiative, which is perhaps true, but there was really not much more he could do in the face of the dilatory conduct of the Spaniards.[48] It is in this that is to be found the principal reason for the disastrous outcome of the project. As recorded in Chapter 16, Vergennes had in August 1778 clearly spelled out to Floridablanca the 'innumerable mischances' which could ruin an attempt to invade Britain. French military and naval planners failed to take adequate account of such risks, of which delay was potentially the most serious. Having overcome all the difficulties in getting the huge Combined Fleet to sea, it was regrettable that it was not adequately supported with the necessary supplies once it reached the battle area. Despite all this, the venture might still have succeeded but for the catastrophic outbreak of sickness that swept the French fleet. Taking into account the scale of the operation which he was required to undertake, and the difficulties which he encountered, d'Orvilliers can be seen as a tragic figure, but nevertheless a competent and thoughtful commander, even if his tactical approach was based on the traditional defensive doctrine of the French navy.

French historian Georges Lacour-Gayet mournfully summarised the crushing disillusionment of the campaign which had promised so much:

> One may ask if there have been in the history of the French navy sadder pages than those which recount the naval campaign in the Channel during the summer of 1779. It is not that our navy suffered disasters such as those which had destroyed, twenty years earlier, the fleets of La Clue and Conflans, or those which would destroy, one day, those of Brueys and Villeneuve. No: in 1779 d'Orvilliers's fleet sortied from Brest without difficulty, held the sea for three months, and returned without difficulty: and never, during this time void of engagements, could it be compared with Lagos or Quiberon, still less with Aboukir or Trafalgar. Then why do such patriotic griefs envelop one's soul, when one reads the despatches where are found day by day all the incidents in this campaign of three months? It is because of the bitter disappointment with which one sees a gigantic effort reduced precisely to nothing.[49]

48 Jenkins, *History of the French Navy*, p.161.
49 Lacour-Gayet, *La marine Militaire*, p.231.

21

Post Mortems

For a month after the return of the Combined Fleet to Brest, the intention to invade England was kept alive. The command was entrusted to the dependable Comte Louis-Charles du Chaffault, and a number of possible schemes were examined. Vergennes had written to Montmorin after the fleet had been recalled to confirm that the policy to be adopted would continue to be that of compelling Britain to concentrate forces in Europe.[1] To this, Floridablanca replied that he had not abandoned hope of renewing an invasion attempt before the end of the year. On 3 October, though, a council of land and sea officers was convened to discuss the matter; this finally put paid to the project, and the allies began to consider the strategy to be adopted in 1780. This was, however, by no means plain sailing. Vergennes told Floridablanca that France would not have enough ships available to implement an invasion plan in the following year. The Spanish minister was not at all inclined to accept that this was in fact the case, and for the moment there was deadlock between the Bourbon allies on the issue. Córdova left Brest on 9 November with 15 ships of the line, leaving Don Miguel Gaston there with the rest of the Spanish fleet for the moment.

In Britain, it was not immediately clear that the threat of invasion had been lifted. The King had accepted, though with some reluctance, that Hardy's withdrawal to Spithead had been justified, but he was still eager to confront the Combined Fleet, writing to Sandwich on 7 September to suggest that Hardy should 'have pretty clear orders to pursue the enemy if retiring out of the Channel … The wind blows here very strong this day, which must cripple some of the combined fleet'.[2] Hardy, reflecting on 14 September that it was still not known if the Combined Fleet was at sea, was anxious that he should not be sent out until the detachment sent with Ross to the Channel Islands had returned. He had been left in no doubt of the government's desire that he should put to sea as soon as possible.

1 Dull, *French Navy and American Independence*, p.163.

2 Barnes and Owen (eds), *Private Papers of John, Earl of Sandwich*, Vol.III, p.96.

Middleton, on the other hand, was much opposed to any idea of a late autumn campaign. It would greatly hinder his plan to copper every ship of the fleet, and he was anxious to get as many ships of the Channel Fleet refitted as soon as possible. The question of whether, if the Combined Fleet was in port, it would come out again was widely debated in the fleet, though Hardy claimed not to have heard any of his officers in conversation suggest that the campaign was over. This was surprising, since Kempenfelt was confident that it would not come out again, as he told Middleton on 19 September. In that letter he once again repeated his opinion of Hardy as a commander: 'When I considered that all depended on the wise conduct of the fleet, I trembled for the event; I suffered the severest anxiety; I opened myself to you, and to you only'.[3] The opinion in the fleet that the campaign was over was soon widely held; Osborne, Hardy's own secretary, reported to Sandwich on 9 October that this was the case.

Kempenfelt's letter was, however, important because it addressed one of the key aspects of the Navy which he considered must be a subject for immediate reform. The Admiralty, he wrote, should have as a 'grand object' the restoration of a strict, orderly discipline in the fleet:

> Captains should not be absent from their ships, nor lay onshore when at Spithead. The relaxation of last winter was of great prejudice to the fleet; no admiral particular to attend to their conduct, captains mostly absent, and the greatest part of the lieutenants likewise; the men, left in a great measure to themselves, became riotous and licentious, and such opportunities given for desertion that the numbers lost was shameful. Men must be constantly employed to keep them orderly. When ships are not fitting for sea, they should be at sea ... I don't think the Admiralty support their authority with sufficient vigour and spirit. They should make themselves feared and respected, to make a whole under them more orderly. There is a languor and inertia hangs upon us which must be shaken off before we can act with vigour.[4]

On 7 October the Admiralty sent Hardy his orders to put to sea. He was to cruise between the Lizard and Ushant 'or on any such station as from any intelligence you may receive of the emotions of the enemy's fleets,' with the object of protecting the British and Irish coasts and the incoming trade convoys. He was to remain out for as long as its provisions and water allowed. In fact, the same day, Hardy received firm intelligence that the French fleet had entered the inner roads at Brest.[5] The wind was now in the west, however, and it was not until 22 October

3 Laughton (ed.), *Barham Papers*, Vol.I, p.298.
4 Laughton (ed.), *Barham Papers*, Vol.I, p.299.
5 James, *The British Navy in Adversity*, p.184; Syrett, *European Waters*, p.80.

that Hardy was able to sail from Spithead, putting to sea with 37 ships of the line. He was not out for long; the weather forced him into Torbay, where he remained until 16 November, when he again set off to take up his station at the western end of the Channel. His autumn cruise finally ended on 22 November when he was ordered to return to port in order to avoid damage to his ships due to the worsening weather.

Ever since his original return to Spithead, Hardy had been jealously guarding his fleet from any suggestion that detachments might be made from it. This gave rise to a long-running dispute with Johnstone, who wrote angrily to Sandwich from Torbay on 3 November to complain that the admiral was refusing to release the ships that were to be placed under his command: 'Upon repeated conversation with Sir Charles I find there is not the least probability that he will ever deliver to me my orders from the Admiralty, or detach any part of the force under his command while the matter is left discretional with him'.[6] In the face of this obduracy, Johnstone turned to Kempenfelt, who strongly supported him in his request to be allowed to take five frigates and smaller vessels to cruise off Brest; but Hardy would have none of it.

Kempenfelt was in no doubt as to the winter strategy that should be adopted by the Channel Fleet, writing to Middleton on 16 November to restate his view of the improbability of the Combined Fleet coming out again during the winter; long nights and heavy gales, he said, were formidable enemies to large fleets:

> But suppose the enemy should put to sea with their fleet – a thing much to be wished for by us. Let us act wiser, and keep ours in port; leave them to the mercy of long nights and hard gales. They'll do more in favour of you than your fleet can. A large fleet never tacks or wears when it blows hard in a dark night without risking damage. We have had occasion to do it three times since we have been out, and each time with narrow escapes. If the wind comes to the eastward we shall proceed westward to our station, and if it should continue a stiff and long winded wind, we may be drove 100 or 150 leagues to the westward and perhaps not be able to recover the Channel for six weeks or two months; a pretty situation for the fleet to be in to protect this island![7]

And he expressed the same view as Middleton with regard to the effect that this would have on the preparation of the fleet for a spring campaign.

Meanwhile the debate between Vergennes and Floridablanca as to the proper strategy for 1780 continued. While there was no agreement between them on the operations to be undertaken in Europe, each proposed to strengthen their forces

6 Barnes and Owen (eds), *Private Papers of John, Earl of Sandwich*, Vol.III, pp.103-106.
7 Laughton (ed.), *Barham Papers*, Vol.I, pp.303-304.

further afield. The theatres of war of most concern to Spain were the Caribbean, where it was proposed to reinforce Havana, and Gibraltar, which was above all other targets the one to which particular importance was attached. For her part, France intended to send a further 4,000 troops to the West Indies.[8] In his negotiations with Floridablanca, Vergennes had one high card to play, and that was to insist that before an invasion of England or Ireland was undertaken, Spain must agree in writing to share the cost, which had not been the case in 1779. Montmorin, when he received instructions to put forward this disagreeable proposition, predicted that this would effectively cool Floridablanca's enthusiasm for an invasion, and it soon became clear that this was the case. Montmorin also reported that Spain planned to strengthen the squadron at Gibraltar to 16–18 ships of the line, and also to launch a major attack on Pensacola.[9]

At the French Navy Ministry, Fleurieu had been working on the strategy for 1780, and in November produced a report. In this, he calculated on having 65 ships of the line, 60 frigates and 90 corvettes available. He reviewed the possible areas in which action might be undertaken. He rejected for the moment the idea of large-scale operations in the West Indies, and in the Indian Ocean, because the campaigning season in these regions was too far advanced; a major offensive in the United States raised difficult questions as to the expense and likely duration of the operations there; and he doubted whether a war on trade would produce a decisive result. For these reasons he still regarded an invasion of the British Isles as the best bet. At the same time, though, he was prepared to support the idea of operations against Gibraltar and Minorca.[10] French naval planning for 1780 was hampered, however, for some considerable time, by the lack of sufficient funds, and by the delayed return of d'Estaing's ships from America, as well as by the agreement to support a Spanish attack on Florida. In addition, a lengthy period of bad weather held up preparation of the fleet for the West Indies, and there was above all a severe shortage of crew men.[11]

It was clear in Britain that urgent action must be taken to relieve Gibraltar, where the garrison of 5,000 men faced a growing Spanish army. This had by 26 July taken up a position two miles from the outer works of the fortress. A Spanish squadron under Don Antonio Barcelo had established a blockade of the Bay, supported by a squadron of ships of the line in Algeciras, as well as by Córdova's fleet at Cadiz. There was no doubt at all that the Spanish meant business, and that something must be done if the fortress was not to be taken. On 16 September, while still uncertain about the movements of the Combined Fleet, the Cabinet resolved to send four ships of the line to escort a convoy to Gibraltar; this force was thereafter

8 Dull, *French Navy and American Independence*, p.166.
9 Dull, *French Navy and American Independence*, p.167.
10 James, *The British Navy in Adversity*, p.188.
11 Dull, *French Navy and American Independence*, pp.168-169.

to proceed to the West Indies. Middleton wrote a paper summarising the way in which the relief should be undertaken:

> Sending supplies of provisions and ammunition to Gibraltar seems practicable under a proper escort and good management. The transports that carry this supply ought to be of size, some force, and good sailers … The number of ships of war ought to equal those of the convoy; and each ship will in that case be able to take one in tow, and which seems a necessary measure for getting in. Two precautions will be proper in conducting this business: the first is that Admiral Duff should have information of their intention and a single date fixed for them, and that the convoy keep at a distance from the Spanish shore and enter the Gut on the African side. To prevent disappointment in case of capture or separation, the ships of war should carry as much provisions as possible and some of the ordnance stores and recruits.[12]

The only British ships presently in the Mediterranean under Vice Admiral Robert Duff were the *Panther*, 60, three frigates and a sloop. It was clear that if the relief convoy was to arrive safely at Gibraltar the escort must be backed by further units from the Channel Fleet. On 27 October the Cabinet directed Sandwich to bring forward a proposal for the operation, which should be carried out as quickly as possible, precautions being taken to ensure secrecy while preparations were made. The crucial, and somewhat controversial, decision was taken that the expedition should be commanded by Sir George Rodney.

Judged only on his professional merits, and his successful record as an accomplished and aggressive commander, Rodney's appointment to an important command was long overdue. Unfortunately, however, his record as a greedy and unscrupulous individual capable of abusing his position to help himself to public monies had made it difficult to employ him. Sandwich was obliged to write to Lady Rodney in reply to her letter seeking employment for her husband, to tell her that 'there are reasons that make it impossible for me to prevail on his Majesty to appoint him to the command of a foreign squadron … As a man in office, your husband has deprived me of the power of being useful to him'.[13] Added to this, Rodney's poor health and his unfortunate relationship with subordinates made him in any case a risky choice. However, he was a strong supporter of the government's American policy, and in the autumn of 1779 it was resolved to bite the bullet and send him out to the Leeward Islands command, conducting the relief of Gibraltar en route. Sandwich took the precaution, however, of appointing a sound man as his flag captain; Lieutenant Walter Young, a senior and valued member of

12 Barnes and Owen (eds), *Private Papers of John, Earl of Sandwich*, Vol.III, pp.172-173.
13 Barnes and Owen (eds), *Private Papers of John, Earl of Sandwich*, Vol.III, p.155.

Middleton's staff at the Navy Board, was promoted to post captain and entrusted with the task of keeping his mercurial commander on the rails.

The Admiralty's formal proposal for the expedition was approved by the Cabinet on 4 November. Rodney was to sail from Spithead with five ships of the line, four frigates and a sloop, escorting an outward-bound convoy heading for the West Indies. He was to be joined off Plymouth by the rest of the convoy intended for the relief of Gibraltar. Two of his frigates and the sloop were to be detached to escort the West Indies convoy, while he went on to Gibraltar. The Admiralty proposal had allowed for a detachment of ships of the line to be made from the Channel Fleet to accompany Rodney to Gibraltar; this, the Cabinet for the moment did not adopt, but it was subsequently agreed that a large detachment should in fact be made, under the command of the capable Rear Admiral Robert Digby, which brought Rodney's fleet to a total of 22 ships of the line. The work of assembling the convoy began at once, but to Sandwich's intense frustration it was not until late December that the wind came round and enabled it to get away. The expedition finally sailed at Christmas, but not before Rodney had endured very considerable administrative difficulties. As he put to sea, he wrote to Germain: 'The delays that have been at this port and the almost total loss of naval discipline is almost beyond comprehension. It shall be mine to restore it'.[14] He also wrote a characteristically unctuous letter to Sandwich: 'Accept once more my most sincere thanks for the command you have given me. That you may overcome all your enemies is the most ardent wish of your old faithful friend, and one your Lordship may depend upon will do his duty towards your obtaining a victory over them'.[15]

Before Rodney finally sailed, however, Sandwich had a battle of his own to fight in Parliament, the winter session of which opened on 25 November. The attack on the government in the House of Lords during the debate on the Address of Thanks was led by the Duke of Richmond. For him and the rest of the opposition, Hardy's retreat up Channel to Spithead had been a humiliating and disgraceful flight in the sight of the British coast before an 'insulting and triumphing enemy'. Hardy, he claimed, had exhibited:

> [A] spectacle never before recorded to have happened in the English annals; he fled before a pursuing enemy, by gradual progresses, from the very mouth of the Channel to Falmouth, Plymouth, Portland, to St Helens; and as if a universal panic had seized the whole fleet, he did not look upon himself as safe, till by the aid of the next tide he found himself safely moored at Spithead.[16]

14 James, *The British Navy in Adversity*, p.190.

15 Barnes and Owen (eds), *Private Papers of John, Earl of Sandwich*, Vol.III, p.191.

16 Patterson, *The Other Armada*, pp.218-219.

Richmond went on to denounce the lack of adequate preparations to resist an enemy landing notwithstanding the frequent and strong warnings of the importance of Plymouth, which must certainly have fallen if the enemy had chosen to attack it. His criticism of this failure, he said, was squarely directed at Amherst. When the commander-in-chief rose to reply he made only an ineffective response to the charges laid against him.

Sandwich, on the other hand, put up a strong defence. The notes which he made of the points made by each of his critics during the debate, who predictably included Lord Bristol and Lord Shelburne, appear as an appendix to Volume III of his edited private papers, and show that he was able to made an effective reply to each of the points made. Most persuasively, he produced a paper headed 'state of ships' which compared the navy's strength in November 1779 with that of November 1759. Although in the former year there were 97 ships of the line compared to 88 at the present time, 29 of them had been only of 60 guns, whereas in 1779 only six were of the size. There were now 14 ships of 50 guns compared with 21 in 1759 but the number of frigates had risen from 187 to 258. The total complement of men had risen from 86,732 to 89,243.[17] As for Hardy's retreat up Channel, he argued that it had been prudent not to seek an engagement. The admiral had retired to a part of the Channel where his fleet would have been able to fight with the greatest advantage, and where, if he was successful, 'the enemy would be more exposed to destruction, as being further from their main sea, and that part of their own coasts where they could take shelter'. Both his King and his country should be highly indebted to an admiral who had caused the Combined Fleet to cut such a 'paltry figure'.

In the House of Commons Lord North faced a series of attacks on broadly similar grounds. Lord John Cavendish referred to 'the shameful and ignominious sight of a British fleet flying from the enemy and abandoning a naked coast to their insults'. Temple Luttrell, a regular critic of the Admiralty, had some fun with the way in which, according to government speakers, Providence had played a part in the nation's deliverance; in future, he suggested, it would be acting as 'our general, our admiral, secretary of state and president of our councils … likewise… our foreign ally, the only ally we have a chance of'.[18]

The unfortunate Lord North had been enduring a difficult time in the days before the debate in the Commons. The King was by no means satisfied with his response to the overall situation faced by the country. It had become the Royal practice to write private letters to John Robinson, the Secretary of the Treasury, and on 21 November he sent him a letter in which he observed: 'I am willing to take my share of labour or personal hazard to save my country … But Lord North must rowze his mind and must treat his colleagues with confidence and civility

17 Barnes and Owen (eds), *Private Papers of John, Earl of Sandwich*, Vol.III, pp.313-316.

18 Patterson, *The Other Armada*, p.222.

the want of which has caused much of the mischief'.[19] Unfortunately, this letter arrived for Robinson at a time when Lord North was with him, and he felt obliged to show it to him. The Prime Minister was understandably much put out. He wrote to the King a long letter to convey his sense of grievance: 'I have been miserable ten years in obedience to your Majesty's commands … Really it is impossible to bear misery and guilt at the same time … I must look upon it as a degree of guilt to continue in office, while the Publick suffers'.[20]

North's state of mind continued to deteriorate, so much so that he briefly decided on 24 November to resign, before later that day changing his mind. He was, though, profoundly depressed, and it was certainly regrettable that at this point he was required to put the government's case in answer to the opposition's amendment calling on the King to change his ministers. Nevertheless, he did his best, claiming that if Hardy had known of the state of the Combined Fleet 'he would have wished and sought an engagement,' adding that he personally would have had no anxiety about the outcome. He asserted that reinforcements were not sent to Plymouth because the government was satisfied that d'Orvilliers did not intend a landing there, a statement which was hardly in accordance with the case then being put in the Lords by Amherst. North also claimed that the Channel Fleet had been successful in protecting incoming convoys, which prompted an intervention by Keppel who was reported as saying: 'The language of the noble Lord was not the language of a seaman, nor of any person who conversed with seamen. The reasonings and assertions of the noble Lord in the Blue Ribbon were those of a landsman, and that landsman, he did not scruple to say, was the Earl of Sandwich'.[21]

In both the Lords and the Commons, the opposition speeches were shot through with a bitter personal contempt for the ministers in general, and Sandwich in particular; but in the end the government had a comfortable majority in both Houses of Parliament, defeating the amendments in the Lords by 82 to 41 and in the Commons by 233 to 134, and the Cabinet could now get on with the task of planning the strategy for 1780. At the Navy Board, Middleton had very strong views about the policy to be adopted in respect of the Channel Fleet and, indeed, the rest of the Navy. What was essential, he considered, was an immediate and orderly programme of coppering as many ships as possible. Beyond this, his great fear was that it would be totally impracticable to refit the Channel Fleet if it were kept at sea, and then later returned to port for refitting all at once:

> My request therefore is that the ships intended to be refitted shall be considered in time – that they may be ordered in succession and not in

19 H. Butterfield, *George III, Lord North and the People* (London: G. Bell & Sons, 1949), p.131.
20 Butterfield, *George III, Lord North and the People*, p.131.
21 Donne (ed.), *The Correspondence of King George the Third*, Vol.II, p.289n.

> a lump – that the frigates and smaller vessels may never be paid off nor refitted at the western ports without consulting the Navy Board, and that the Ordnance [Board] may have early information of such as require the first supply of guns and carronades. Unless they cooperate, we propose in vain; and the ships are furnished with a weight of metal we never intended them to carry.[22]

Middleton had been in receipt of a steady stream of confidential information about the Channel Fleet from Kempenfelt which he found extremely disturbing. He saw much of the problem as being in the Admiralty itself, and he conveyed his opinions to Sandwich in outspoken terms on more than one occasion. Typical of the views he expressed were those in a rough draft of a letter written probably in 1779:

> The office I am in is of that nature as to see every branch of the service and how it is conducted. My zeal for its success often carries me out of my own line. If I was free to declare my opinion, the fleet is terribly managed, it is in a terrible condition, and cannot be otherways while the present system continues. The cause of every disaster, my lord, is in the Admiralty, and till a reformation is begun there, no good can be expected from any other quarter. For want of proper men to conduct the business of the ports, no expedition is used in refitting the ships. The officers are not kept to their duty. The men are daily deserting in scores, and those who remain are inclined to mutiny.[23]

There is a strong flavour of Kempenfelt about this document, and it is evident that Middleton was taking very seriously the need to pass on the advice which he was getting from his friend.

22 Barnes and Owen (eds), *Private Papers of John, Earl of Sandwich*, Vol.III, pp.177-181.

23 Laughton (ed.), *Barham Papers*, Vol.III, p.7.

22

The Moonlight Battle

Rodney finally sailed from Plymouth on 29 December after he had collected the rest of his convoy. He had with him 22 ships of the line, with 14 frigates and smaller vessels, escorting an enormous fleet of store ships, victuallers, ordnance vessels, troopships and the West Indies convoy of merchantmen. By 4 January, having reached a position some 300 miles west of Cape Finisterre, far enough out in the Atlantic to be reasonably safe, Rodney was able to detach the West Indies convoy. It was escorted by the *Hector*, 74, and three frigates, under the command of Captain Hyde Parker, Junior.

At dawn on 8 January, 22 sails were sighted in the north-east; the British fleet had evidently passed them during the night. Ordering the convoy to lie to under the escort of the *Pearl*, 32, Rodney set off in general chase of the strangers with the rest of his fleet. It was the kind of windfall to gladden his heart. It was a convoy sailing from San Sebastian to Cadiz under the command of Don Juan Augustin de Yardi, consisting of 15 merchantmen, of which 12 were provision ships, escorted by the ship of the line *Guipuzcoana*, 64, with the *San Carlos*, 32, *San Raphael*, 30, *Santa Teresa*, 28, *San Bruno*, 26, *San Firmin*, 16, and *San Vicente*, 10, belonging to the Royal Company of Caracas. Rodney's ships were soon up with the convoy; the *Guipuzcoana* put up a token resistance before striking her colours to the *Bienfaisant*, and was soon followed by the rest. By 2.00 p.m. all were in British hands. Rodney at once decided to take the *Guipuzcoana* into British service, renaming her *Prince William*, in honour of the King's son who was serving in the fleet. She was a brand new and well-built ship, and he also added the *San Firmin* and *San Vicente* to his fleet. He decided to take the provision ships with him as part of the relief convoy for Gibraltar, and sent all the rest of the prizes back to Britain escorted by the *America*, 64, and the *Pearl*.[1]

Thereafter, the fleet resumed its passage towards Gibraltar down the coast of Spain and Portugal, lying to every night. On 13 January the fleet was reduced by two, when the *Dublin*, 74, lost her fore top mast, broke her fore yard, and had to be

1 David Spinney, *Rodney* (London: Allen & Unwin 1969), p.305.

'George Lord Rodney'. Engraving by H. Robinson after Joshua Reynolds. (Anne S.K. Brown Collection)

escorted into Lisbon by the *Shrewsbury*, 74. As the fleet made its way southward, intelligence was received from time to time from passing ships to the effect that there was a Spanish squadron cruising off Cape St Vincent, said by some to consist of as many as 14 ships of the line. Rodney accordingly issued orders to his captains to be prepared for a fleet action.

On the night of 15/16 January the fleet laid to as usual to allow the heavy sailers and stragglers to come up. At dawn, land was in sight. According to Walter Young, it had been his suggestion that Rodney should 'run into the latitude of the Cape before we bore up to make it, by which blunder we were very near being embayed to the northward of it'.[2] At all events, the ships began to round Cape St Vincent,

2 Laughton (ed.), *Barham Papers*, Vol.II, p.65.

some 10 to 15 miles offshore. At this time the wind was blowing from the west; the sky was overcast, and visibility was very poor. There was a heavy swell.

By noon, most of the British ships had passed the Cape. At 1.00 p.m., the leading ship, the *Bedford*, 74, reported a fleet of 15 sail to the south-east, and soon after this 11 of them could be seen from Rodney's flagship, the *Sandwich*. Rodney himself was at this time so ill with gout that he was confined to his bed. Accordingly, the admiral's orders to his fleet had to be conveyed by Walter Young. The latter's account of what followed came in a letter which he wrote to Middleton on 24 July, but this has not generally been accepted as wholly accurate by most historians. David Spinney put it thus:

> Young, in describing the business later, was not above raising his own credit with a picture (too partial to be wholly convincing), of an alert and purposeful captain guiding the decisions of an inept and vacillating commander-in-chief. But as this is the only picture we have, it cannot be ignored.[3]

Throughout his correspondence with Middleton, Young makes it plain that he had a very high opinion of his own abilities, and most of the time a low opinion of those of his admiral.

Sir John Knox Laughton, editing the first volume of Middleton's papers, was likewise dubious about the emphasis in Young's letter, but since the fact of Rodney's being in bed could hardly have been invented, 'we must believe that the orders were really given by Young in the way he describes, though whether he did so on his own initiative may be doubtful':

> The unhesitating dash at the enemy has often been referred to as an illustration of Rodney's character, the engaging to leeward as a stroke of Rodney's genius. Young implies that these were all his own; that Rodney had nothing to do with. Confined to his bed, Rodney could evidently only see with Young's eyes, and must have been, to a great extent, guided by Young's opinion.[4]

He left it to the reader to judge the matter, while noting that Young, though middle-aged, had only held the rank of post captain for less than four months.

Since night was coming on, Young argued for a general chase in line abreast, but at first Rodney preferred to order line ahead; soon after, the order was given for a line abreast at two cables' distance. By 2.30 p.m. the signal for general chase was made; according to Young, this was after he had perceived that the enemy were

3 Spinney, *Rodney*, p.306.
4 Laughton (ed.), *Barham Papers*, Vol.I, pp.xlii-xliii.

making sail to escape, 'when our ships got up the signal to engage to leeward and in succession and the signal for close action at the same time'.[5] Almost at once, the fleet began to string out as the fastest ships drew ahead. The signal to engage to leeward was one which had been specially added by Rodney to the Additional Fighting Instructions, since he strongly favoured this mode of attack in certain situations, of which the present was one, since the heavy swell prevented the Spanish from opening their leeward lower deck gun ports.

The Spanish squadron, commanded by Don Juan de Langara, with his flag in the *Fénix*, 80, consisted of 11 ships of the line and two frigates. It had not been expected that the relief convoy for Gibraltar which he was waiting to intercept would have a substantial escort, and, in any case, it was supposed that any ships of the line intended for the West Indies would by now have parted company. The main Spanish fleet under Córdova, with 20 ships of the line, lay in Cadiz, and had it been at sea with Langara would have presented an altogether more serious opponent.

As it was, it soon became apparent to Langara that he was heavily outnumbered. As his squadron headed in flight southwards in considerable disorder, the British copper-bottomed ships quickly began to overhaul him. There was no escape for the Spanish, as one by one the British ships came up with Langara's Squadron. The first to be in range was the 74-gun *Edgar*, which opened fire on the sternmost Spanish ship, the *Santo Domingo*, 70, as she swept past her at about 4.00 p.m. Next to arrive was the *Marlborough*, 74, which also gave the *Santo Domingo* a broadside, followed by the *Ajax*, 74. At about 5.00 p.m., just as the *Bienfaisant* closed on the stern of the Spanish ship, she blew up. Only one of her complement was saved. Meanwhile the *Princesa*, 70, the next Spanish ship, was raked by the *Montagu*, 74 and by the *Marlborough* and *Ajax* before, after a lengthy engagement with the *Bedford*, she struck her colours and was taken by a boarding party from the *Resolution*. By 7.30 p.m. the *Defence*, 74, was in action against the *Fénix*. Daylight had faded and it was by the light of the moon that the two ships exchanged broadsides; then, after an hour and a half the *Montagu* joined in, carrying away the bowsprit of the *Fénix*. Next on the scene came the 100-gun *Royal George* which with her first broadside shot away the Spaniard's mizzen mast. In the course of these engagements, Langara was wounded. His flagship was now helpless, and when the *Bienfaisant* ranged up she was obliged to strike.

Captain MacBride of the *Bienfaisant* wrote a report to Rodney of the destruction of the *Santo Domingo*:

> At a quarter before five, being then about half a cable distant from one of them and just going to engage, she fired some of her quarter guns, by some means took fire, and instantly blew up. Had this awful event taken

5 Laughton (ed.), *Barham Papers*, Vol.I, p.65.

'The defeat of the Spanish fleet under Don Juan de Langara, by Sir George Brydges Rodney, Decr. 16th 1779, off Cape St. Vincent – most humbly inscribed to Prince William Henry'. (Library of Congress)

> place a few minutes later we most probably would have shared her fate; it was impossible to avoid the wreck, great part of it falling athwart us, many small pieces thrown on board, by which three men were slightly wounded.[6]

MacBride also reported the taking of the *Fénix*, and the problems which, on the morning after the battle, he faced in trying to save her: 'When day broke, the condition of so large a ship, a perfect wreck, a gale of wind and a leeshore, I found myself in a very interesting situation with infinite risk'. He went on to tell Rodney of the arrangements he had made with the injured Langara. The *Bienfaisant* was at this time badly affected by an outbreak of smallpox, and in a chivalrous gesture towards the Spanish admiral, his officers and men, he agreed that they should not be removed from the *Fénix* into his ship. For his part, Langara gave his word that they would not interfere subsequently if any Spanish attempt was made to retake the flagship. Very good relations had been established from the outset between the Spanish officers and their captors.[7]

6 Barnes and Owen (eds), *Private Papers of John, Earl of Sandwich*, Vol.III, p.196.
7 Barnes and Owen (eds), *Private Papers of John, Earl of Sandwich*, Vol.III, p.198.

The British ships hurried on towards the head of the Spanish line. The *Montagu* chased the *Diligente*, 70, for three quarters of an hour; when, at 9.15 she closed within musket shot and gave her a broadside, the *Diligente* struck. The remaining five Spanish ships of the line pressed on, but could not escape their pursuers. The *San Eugenio*, 70, fought hard against the *Cumberland*, 74, and shot away her main top mast, but at 11.00 p.m. all three of the Spaniard's masts came down, and she struck. Meanwhile the *Culloden*, 74, and Digby's flagship the *Prince George*, 98, moved on towards the head of the Spanish line. The *San Julian*, 70, was putting up a good fight against the *Culloden*, but by the time Digby's three decker closed with her at 12:30 am she had been badly damaged and she struck her colours.

Meanwhile the *Sandwich*, some way adrift, pressed on to try to join in the fight. Rodney is said to have called her master to him, and said: 'Master, this ship is not to pay any attention to the merchantmen or small ships of war. Lay me alongside the biggest ship you can, or the admiral, if there be one'.[8] Up ahead of the flagship could be seen the *Monarca*, 70, which at 1.00 a.m. had brought down the *Alcide*'s main top mast, and might have escaped but for the vigorous action against her waged by the frigate *Apollo*, commanded by Captain Pownall. By now the *Sandwich* was closing on the *Monarca*, and she struck; Pownall claimed that she surrendered to the frigate, but if she did, it was probably because the *Sandwich* was in range and had just fired her port broadside into her.

In the end four of the Spanish ships of the line managed to escape; these were the 70-gun ships *San Augustin*, *San Gennaro*, *San Justo*, and *San Lorenzo*. The last two of these had been badly damaged. The two frigates *Santa Gertrudis* and *Santa Rosalia* also got away. When dawn broke, the British fleet was deployed around the prizes. The gale was still blowing, as the log of the *Royal George* recorded: 'strong gales and thick weather. No sight of the Sun'.[9] During the day the prize crew aboard the *Monarca* managed to get her clear of the rapidly shoaling water, but the *San Julian* was not so fortunate, driving ashore later that night. Later she was salved by the Spanish. The *San Eugenio* suffered the same fate but once ashore she broke up. The remaining three prizes, *Diligente*, *Princesa* and *Fénix* managed to work offshore and together with the *Monarca* their prize crews were able to bring them safely to Gibraltar. During 17 January the convoy caught up with the battle fleet and the whole expedition resumed its course for Gibraltar.

In the letter which he wrote to Middleton giving an account of the battle, Young was severely critical of Rodney and the part which the admiral played:

> The admiral's ill state of health and his natural irresolution occasioned our shortening sail frequently, which prevented me from bringing the *Sandwich* so early into battle as I could have wished; and it was with

8 Spinney, *Rodney*, p.310.
9 Spinney, *Rodney*, p.311.

> difficulty that I succeeded at last, as he attempted several times to have the ships called off from chase; but on representing to him that they were too far ahead to either see or hear our signals, and that it was our business to be at the head or near to them, that we went on and stopped one of the enemy who had prepared to evade us.[10]

Even if this self-satisfied account was entirely true, the fact remains that it was Rodney as commander-in-chief upon whom fell the responsibility for the battle, and it was not wholly unjust that he should receive praise, amounting almost to adulation, for the victory. Britain badly needed success at sea at this moment, and the capture of the convoy and the destruction of Langara's squadron provided the required tonic. Rodney himself wrote a glowing public despatch to the Admiralty: 'The gallant behaviour of the admirals, captains, officers and men, I had the honour to command, was remarkably conspicuous. They seemed actuated with the same spirit and anxiously eager to exert themselves with the utmost zeal to serve his Majesty and humble the pride of his enemies'.[11] This was for public consumption, and was, however, by no means the whole story as far as Rodney was concerned. In a private letter to George Jackson he wrote outspokenly and rather incoherently of the breakdown in discipline in the fleet:

> Providence has allowed me to be the happy instrument of restoring in some measure the honour of the British flag, to restore the old, good, necessary discipline, of the British navy will be of much more consequence, it is lost, it shall, it must be restored. I avoid all complaints, many, many, I had the greatest reason to make, and if the fleet I am going to command, should be as negligent and disobedient as part of that which sailed from England with me, you will hear of dismission, upon dismission, I must, I shall be obeyed. I will not tell you particular men, many brave excellent, active good offices. Others negligent, slow, inactive, disobedient, and fit for nothing.[12]

To Sandwich he wrote the kind of letter that the First Lord must have come to expect from Rodney:

> I most sincerely congratulate you on the great success that has attended his Majesty's arms. I hope your enemies will now be confounded and that you may long continue at the head of that Board you so ably direct, happy if by doing my duty I can again possess that complete confidence which

10 Laughton (ed.), *Barham Papers*, Vol.I, pp.65-66.
11 Syrett, *European Waters*, p.89.
12 Syrett, *European Waters*, p 90.

> was my boast, and the loss of which I have most sincerely felt. I am truly sensible that the artful insinuations of designing men robbed me of that friendship I am sure your Lordship unwillingly withdrew.[13]

In fairness to Rodney, it should also be noted that he was unstinting in his praise for Walter Young, who was 'the very man I could have wished, excellent, diligent, brave, good officer endued with every quality necessary to assist a commander-in-chief. I think myself much indebted to him for the late action, and am not ashamed to acknowledge it'.[14]

The garrison of Gibraltar was holding its breath; then, one by one, several brigs arrived, the third of which, arriving on 18 January, was one of the Caracas provision ships bringing news of an engagement off Cape St Vincent. Soon, the ships of the expedition could be seen arriving off Europa Point; the Spanish squadron that had been blockading the fortress hurriedly made its way to the safety of the batteries of Algeciras. However, the weather, which was dull and threatening, did not permit the expedition's prompt arrival:

> The wind puffed fitfully and died away altogether. Against the sombre background of sea and sky the distant ships wallowed impotently. Vivid flashes of lightning picked them out, their sails hanging limp from the yards. Under the eyes of the enthralled but powerless watchers they drifted helplessly past.[15]

The flagship and a large part of the fleet were taken to a point some 50 miles eastward of Marbella, before they could begin to beat back to Gibraltar, a process which took many of the ships up to a week. The first to arrive was the *Fénix*, escorted by the *Edgar*, which entered the Bay on 19 January, followed later by the *Defence*, *Invincible* and *Prince George* with a dozen ships of the convoy. The *Sandwich* finally dropped anchor in Gibraltar Bay on 25 January.

A number of urgent decisions had to be taken, and a Council of War was convened aboard the *Sandwich*. It was agreed that the Spanish sick and wounded should be repatriated as soon as possible. As for the rest, Rodney was determined to recover the prize crews that had been captured when the two Spanish ships which had been taken were driven ashore in the gale. He proposed a man-for-man exchange for these, and also for British subjects detained in Spain. When the Spanish government dragged its heels over this, Rodney threatened to send Langara, with whom he was personally on very good terms, together with his men

13 Barnes and Owen (eds), *Private Papers of John, Earl of Sandwich*, Vol.III, p.193.

14 Barnes and Owen (eds), *Private Papers of John, Earl of Sandwich*, Vol.III, p.195.

15 Spinney, *Rodney*, p.313.

back to England as prisoners of war. This did the trick, and the exchange was duly carried out.

It was also necessary to make arrangements to send on that part of the convoy intended for Minorca. Rodney selected three of his fastest-sailing ships of the line to escort this, the intention being that they should return in time to re-join Digby's squadron of the Channel Fleet when it set off for England. The second battalion of the 73rd Highland Regiment was to have gone to reinforce the garrison of Minorca, but at the last minute General George Eliott the Governor, refused to allow this, insisting that these troops were required for the defence of Gibraltar. At Minorca, Lieutenant General Murray was so angry when his reinforcements failed to arrive that he refused to release 400 British sailors who were in Port Mahon.[16]

One matter with which Rodney was particularly concerned during his stay in Gibraltar was the refitting of the captured Spanish ships of the line. He wrote to the First Lord to tell him of the high opinion which he held of them:

> I have the sincere satisfaction to assure your Lordship that the five Spanish men of war are as fine ships as ever swam and far superior to our 74 gun ships. They are now completely refitted, manned, and put in the line of battle; and I will answer for them will do their duty as English men of war should the enemy give them an opportunity.[17]

Having previously given the name *Prince William* to the *Guipuzcoana*, he now gave the name *Gibraltar* to the *Fénix*; the *Diligente*, *Monarca* and *Princesa* retained their Spanish names.

When the news reached England of the Moonlight Battle and the relief of Gibraltar, there were widespread feelings of relief, and the general gloom occasioned by the frustrations of 1779 was for the moment dispelled. At Portsmouth, Samuel Hood wrote to a friend on 29 February:

> What a glorious business! I dare say the Spaniards will secede from France altogether very soon. I am persuaded they will never make a junction with the French fleet again. The arrival of Sir George Rodney was very providential, as the garrison had but a few days provisions left. 30,000 troops encamped at St Roche [San Roque] immediately made off, with great precipitation, upon the appearance of our fleet.[18]

16 Spinney, *Rodney*, p.314.

17 Barnes and Owen (eds), *Private Papers of John, Earl of Sandwich*, Vol.III, p.199.

18 Roy and Lesley Adkins, *Gibraltar: The Greatest Siege in British History* (London: Little Brown 2017), p.114.

The report about the departure of the Spanish troops was, though, entirely false. Among the Spanish prisoners, however, there did appear to be a marked resentment in their feelings towards the French.

Sandwich's letter of 8 March, congratulating Rodney on his victory, was flattering in the extreme:

> I scarcely know how to find words to congratulate you enough upon your late glorious successes, and upon the eminent services you have done your country. The worst of my enemies now allow that I have pitched upon a man who knows his duty, and is a brave, honest and able officer. I will not tire you with panegyric, but I am not the less eager in dealing out to all around me the praises due to your merit. I have obtained you the thanks of both Houses of Parliament; in the House of Lords I made the motion myself, and mentioned what perhaps you yourself was not aware of, that you had captured more line of battleships than had been taken in any one action in either of the two last preceding wars.[19]

The First Lord went on to warn Rodney about the content of letters which he might write to members of the opposition, which he told him was being perverted and put to uses that the admiral had not intended; he cited reports that the *Sandwich* was not fit for service and that this information came from Rodney. He also responded to Rodney's comments about discipline in the fleet:

> I fear the picture you give of the faction in your fleet is too well drawn; it is still very prevalent here, but not what it was a year ago. Time and moderation in those who are high in the naval department will by degrees get the better of this bane of our discipline and of everything that is valuable and comfortable in the Service. I trust in your perseverance in discouraging it as I do, and by pursuing a steady plan here and within your command, which is now almost equal to our force at home, I doubt not but that we shall lay this many headed hydra at last asleep.[20]

Bearing in mind the strong views which he had expressed on the same subject, it is doubtful whether Kempenfelt would have regarded this as a sufficiently assertive response on the part of the Admiralty.

Notwithstanding his extravagant praise of the admiral, Sandwich was far from pleased with a decision taken by Rodney which was directly in breach of his instructions. Duff had told Rodney that he wanted to return to England on the grounds of his health; he may also have had in mind that the tiny force in the

19 Barnes and Owen (eds), *Private Papers of John, Earl of Sandwich*, Vol.III, pp.205-206.
20 Barnes and Owen (eds), *Private Papers of John, Earl of Sandwich*, Vol.III, pp.206-207.

Mediterranean which he commanded was scarcely appropriate for a vice admiral. Agreeing to his departure, Rodney authorised Captain John Elliot of the *Edgar* to hoist his broad pennant as a Commodore and to remain behind at Gibraltar when the fleet departed. It was Elliot who was said to have declined the post of Captain of the Fleet and recommended instead that Kempenfelt be appointed. Sandwich, writing to Elliot, spelled out the position emphatically; while telling him that no man was more fit to be entrusted with an important command, he said that 'so valuable an officer as yourself, and so fine a ship as the *Edgar*, cannot with propriety at this time be locked up from services from which they cannot be spared'. Elliot could, he said, if he chose, remain at Gibraltar; but the *Edgar* must unquestionably be sent home.[21]

Sandwich also took Rodney to task:

> I am very sorry that you left the *Edgar* in the Mediterranean. It has given us the trouble and risk of sending a frigate on purpose to order her home immediately; and if you will look into your original instructions, you will find there was no point more strongly guarded against than that of your leaving any line of battle ship behind you.[22]

Once the ships sent to escort the convoy to Minorca had returned, Rodney was finally able to sail from Gibraltar on 13 February. He had with him the ships of the line *Sandwich, Ajax, Montagu* and *Terrible*, the frigate *Pegasus*, 32, and the sloop *San Vicente*. He took the *Terrible* because the *Shrewsbury* had sprung a mast, and the *Pegasus* and *San Vicente* because the two sloops promised him had not arrived. With him sailed Digby's squadron returning to the Channel Fleet. Rodney wrote to Sandwich to tell him of his departure:

> I have the pleasure to inform your Lordship that on the 13th we had the good fortune to get out of the Straits, all the ships detached with the convoy having joined me the same day, after having seen the convoy safe into Port Mahon. Not a French or Spanish ship was to be seen, although his Majesty's ships beat it back again with a westerly wind and made both the European and African shores.[23]

In this letter, Rodney was still exercised about the factions in his fleet:

> It is with concern that I must tell your Lordship that my brother officers still continue their absurd and illiberal custom of arraigning each other's

21 Barnes and Owen (eds), *Private Papers of John, Earl of Sandwich*, Vol.III, p.208.
22 Barnes and Owen (eds), *Private Papers of John, Earl of Sandwich*, Vol.III, p.210.
23 Barnes and Owen (eds), *Private Papers of John, Earl of Sandwich*, Vol.III, p.200.

> conduct. My ears have been attempted to listen to the scandal; I have treated it with the contempt it deserved ... The unhappy difference between Mr Keppel and Sir H Palliser has almost ruined the navy. Discipline in a great measure is lost, and that eager willingness of executing the orders given by the Board of Admiralty, or by those acting under their authority, is turned into neglect; and officers presume to find fault and think, when their duty is implicit obedience.[24]

Digby, meanwhile, separated from Rodney on 18 February and proceeded on his way to England, having with him 15 ships of the line and a convoy of empty store ships, transports and victuallers. He had reached a point to the west of Brittany when on 23 February he sighted a French convoy of thirteen merchant vessels bound for Mauritius escorted by the *Protée*, 64, and *Ajax*, 64, and the frigate *Charmante*. Digby at once ordered a general chase, but the commander of the escort, the Comte de Chilleau, resolved to sacrifice his own ship, the *Protée*, in an effort to save the convoy, which he ordered to scatter. The *Resolution* and *Bedford* engaged the *Protée*, which was in due course obliged to strike to them, but Chilleau's sacrifice had not been in vain. Only three French snows were taken; the rest of the convoy, with the *Ajax* and *Charmante,* were able to escape.[25] Digby sent a report of the action to Sandwich on 2 March, telling him that he had sent the *Protée,* with the prizes and with the *Royal George* and *Bienfaisant* into Plymouth. Sir John Ross, when he arrived at Plymouth aboard the *Royal George*, gave the First Lord the good news that the *Protée* was 'sheathed and fitted and in every prospect fit for immediate service,' and that she carried specie to the value of £70,000.[26]

24 Barnes and Owen (eds), *Private Papers of John, Earl of Sandwich*, Vol.III, p.201.

25 Syrett, *European Waters*, p.93.

26 Barnes and Owen (eds), *Private Papers of John, Earl of Sandwich*, Vol.III, p.204.

23

Kempenfelt's Reforms

Aboard the *Victory* during the winter of 1779–1780, as the return of Digby's squadron was awaited, and while the refitting of the rest of the Channel Fleet was put in hand, Kempenfelt had plenty of time to continue his reflections on tactical principles and the reform of the signal code. There was something of the absent-minded professor about the Captain of the Fleet. Hilary Rubinstein has quoted the account given by the Scottish poet Hector Macneill, who had come aboard to serve as an assistant secretary to the commander-in-chief, of his first encounter with Kempenfelt:

> I perceived issuing from under the deck an elderly grave man who on advancing eyed me with a keen scrutinising look. The appearance of this personage instantly indicated little of superior station on board. He was dressed in an old shabby uniform coat with waistcoat and breeches richly ornamented with Scotch or Spanish snuff, which had nearly obscured the original colour, an old weatherbeaten hat of an extremely small size together with a tie periwig so scanty as barely sufficed to cover his ears. In his right hand he held a handkerchief, the colour of which beggars all description, and with his left he ever and anon applied his finger and thumb to his waistcoat pocket, where unconfined by aught but a chamois lining an ample provision of the above-mentioned ornament remained for the gratification of his nostrils. Notwithstanding these plain externals there was however something not only in his aspect but in his deportment that indicated authority and station.[1]

Macneill was told by Turnbull, another assistant secretary, just who this 'grave and elderly personage' was, and that he was engaged in considering naval tactics and the revision of the signal code.

1 Hilary Rubinstein, *Catastrophe at Spithead* (Barnsley: Seaforth Publishing 2020), pp.64-65.

Kempenfelt was making good use of his time. The substantial body of work that he produced was the subject of extensive correspondence with Middleton. Brian Tunstall wrote of this: 'Never in the history of any navy, at any period before or since, have so many signal books and fighting instructions been issued by one man in the space of only twenty seven months, during at least ten of which the main body of the fleet was laid up for the winter'.[2]

The systems which Kempenfelt inherited when he became Captain of the Fleet have been described in Chapter 5. His study of signals and their necessary reform was reported to Sandwich when Middleton wrote to him on 9 July 1779 to tell him of the work that Kempenfelt had been doing:

> As your Lordship mentioned his Majesty's inclination to have the subject of signals considered for the use of the fleet, I must inform you that I have had a great deal of correspondence and conversation with Captain Kempenfelt on that head; and it was agreed before he left London to introduce the French system, if practicable, into Sir Charles Hardy's fleet. That gentleman has well considered the subject, but at this juncture it would be dangerous to exchange even a bad set of signals that are generally known for a better which the greatest part of the officers are unacquainted with. Whenever it is his Majesty's pleasure that that this subject should be considered and your Lordship can spare Captain Kempenfelt from the service of the fleet, I will engage with the assistance of that gentleman and of some other senior officers which I can name to simplify this very complex business and to reduce it within the practice of the most ordinary understanding.[3]

Kempenfelt, by reason of his frequent travels in France, which had given him a considerable understanding of the French navy and its systems, would in due course translate for Middleton the chapter on signals in Bourde de Villehuit's work of 1769 on naval manoeuvring.[4] For the moment, Middleton was obviously right when he referred to the danger of introducing a new system without ensuring that it was fully understood by those who would use it; but Kempenfelt was in no doubt that reform was urgently necessary. Another view of this came from Benjamin Thompson, who wrote in his letter of 20 July to Germain about the problems arising from the use of the current signal code in the Channel Fleet:

> It has always been more than two hours before the ships ahead have got into their stations in the order of sailing. This has arisen sometimes from

2 Tunstall, *Naval Warfare in the Age of Sail*, p.146.

3 Barnes and Owen (eds), *Private Papers of John, Earl of Sandwich*, Vol.III, p.42.

4 Rubinstein, *Catastrophe at Spithead*, p.59.

> one cause, and sometimes from another, but I don't remember a single instance in which we have attempted to manoeuvre when we did not make at least one evidently wrong and contradictory signal.[5]

When Kempenfelt took up his post as Captain of the Fleet, he inherited the instructions for the Channel Fleet that had been issued by Keppel. He soon began to revise the Fighting Instructions and Additional Instructions and the signals associated with them. Brian Tunstall made a detailed examination of the changes introduced by Kempenfelt during the course of the 1779 campaign, noting that the general purpose of articles 6 to 17 of the day signals 'was first, to give the admiral better control of the fleet, and second, to standardise methods for carrying out various evolutions'. The new instructions would in due course be embodied three years later in Howe's 1782 'Instructions for the Conduct of the Ships of War, explanatory of, and relative to the signals contained in the signal book herewith delivered'. The question then arises of whose was the directing mind that originated the innovations; Tunstall observes that 'it is tempting to make Kempenfelt the inspirer of Howe's innovations; it may however, equally have been Howe who was supplying Kempenfelt with ideas'. The two men were evidently in close touch; Howe wrote to Kempenfelt on 10 September, 1779 enquiring what had been done to introduce the new system of signals in the Channel Fleet:

> I should be glad to know what part of our signals have been adopted; I should thence be able to form an opinion of the principle upon which that great machine (the Grand Fleet) is to be put in motion. Our signals were adopted rather for a single squadron; and, though most of the articles might be applied to a larger force, (fleets being composed of squadrons collectively arranged), the necessary continuation of the signals being different, the propriety of their use under different circumstances will vary also. In the disposition of them I had those objects in view. But the choice to be made of the expedients which any set of signals has provided for, will constitute, as we know, the ability of the flag officers'.[6]

Howe had returned to England on 25 October 1778 and since then had been at leisure while onshore to review the progress of tactical and signals reform, and it was entirely to be expected that he would keep in touch with Kempenfelt on a subject of such importance and of mutual interest. Nevertheless, it was Kempenfelt who was responsible for devising and introducing the new systems.

5 Perrin (ed.), *Naval Miscellany*, Vol.III, p.123.
6 Tunstall, *Naval Warfare in the Age of Sail*, pp.147-148.

The essence of Kempenfelt's reforms lay in a completely different approach to the way in which signals were to be used to give a fleet commander greater freedom of action. As Julian Corbett summarised it:

> His idea was not to add to the established list of technical devices, but to provide a simple system of signals and evolutions whereby an admiral could order and perform securely any manoeuvre which his tactical abilities might see the moment called for. Under his system, as under both the earlier and later systems of Howe, the Fighting Instructions entirely disappear. Their place is taken by 'Instructions Explanatory to the Signal Book'. The idea is not to provide the admiral with ready-made tactics, but to insure that any movement he orders will be clearly understood by his subordinates and carried out in a prompt and uniform manner. That he studied deeply the French system is certain; but with the clear eye of a real master of war he was able to see what was good in it and what was bad, and the outcome of it all was that he sought and found not a system of tactics but a system of evolutions. In his eyes this was the secret by which precision and uniformity could be attained without formality and without loss of mobility and freedom.[7]

One of the issues which most concerned Kempenfelt was the difficulty of managing a very large fleet of ships of the line. He recognised that to direct a fleet of some 40 of these effectively, the traditional division of the fleet into van, centre and rear would not do. His solution was to create an 'Order of Sailing' which organised the fleet into five divisions. The Centre Division, under Hardy, would be followed by a Fourth Division and the Rear Division, and these would together make up the First Squadron. Ahead of them, the Van Division followed by the Fifth Division would now constitute the Second Squadron, also designated the Advanced Flying Squadron.[8] Kempenfelt also favoured the French concept of sailing in columns in line abreast which with the signals he now introduced would vastly improve the ability of the fleet commander to deploy his force for action. His scheme was to abolish the previous clumsy system in favour of the simple formation of the divisions sailing abreast, each in single line ahead, with the ships in their battle stations, which thenceforward became the rule.[9]

During the autumn and winter that followed the Channel Fleet's return to Spithead, Kempenfelt continued his work of tactical reform and prepared his signal book and explanatory instructions. In his letter to Middleton of 17 October,

7 Julian S. Corbett (ed.), *Signals and Instructions 1776-1794* (London: Navy Records Society, 1908), pp.33-34.

8 Tunstall, *Naval Warfare in the Age of Sail*, p.148.

9 Corbett (ed.), *Signals and Instructions*, p.47.

he had advocated the introduction of a numerary system, which did not require many flags:

> However there must be three of each sort, or you can't express a number which consists of three figures of the same rank, as 222 or 333, etc, and for expedition in making the signals there should be the whole nine flags ready for each masthead. This way of pointing out the signal is very convenient for those to whom they are addressed, for the ready finding out their meaning, and a very great ease to the compiler of the signals.[10]

Kempenfelt noted that the were a number of objections to the system, but reckoned that these could be overcome. He favoured the system of numerary signalling which had been used by d'Orvilliers, and he told Middleton that in less than a week, if he was allowed to work without interruption, he could arrange the British signalling system accordingly. For the moment, Kempenfelt's immediate concern was to get the Fighting Instructions and Additional Instructions reissued to the fleet embodying his first thoughts for reform, and this was done in September 1779. Again, Corbett provides a summary:

> The old General Fighting Instructions he retained as in duty bound, but the Additional Instructions he appears to have remodelled by breaking them up into separate sections, each section having its own numbering. The grouping is difficult to reconstruct with any degree of certainty. All that we can tell is that the arrangement was entirely different from the old-established Instructions which Rodney took out to the West Indies, or from those which Howe had been using in America, and that it appears to have been founded on that drawn up by Morogues in his *Tactique Navale*.[11]

The signals that he now introduced incorporated those which Howe had drafted in 1777, but he added a number of innovations of his own:

> For those which are not in Howe's book his obligation to the French authorities appears throughout, and especially in his reintroduction of the order of retreat, of doubling, of Torrington's method of engaging a superior fleet, which Hoste on Tourville's authority so highly approved, of a sailing order in three columns, and finally of the manoeuvre of breaking the line in line ahead. This last is of course their most striking feature. Nothing indeed could more thoroughly upset current impressions of

10 Laughton (ed.), *Barham Papers*, Vol.I, p.301.
11 Corbett (ed.), *Signals and Instructions*, p.118.

> tactical history than to know that such a signal existed in the Channel Fleet two years before Rodney made or was persuaded to make the manoeuvre.[12]

Kempenfelt had also been giving consideration to the size and design of the signal flags. In his letter to Middleton of 20 March 1780, he suggested dimensions of nine yards in length by five-and-a-half yards deep, revising this on the following day to nine yards by five to accord with existing practice. Mindful of the difficulty of distinguishing the flags at any distance, and particularly in battle, he suggested that when a flag was formed of two colours, in order to make the contrast stronger the white should be joined with the red and the yellow with the blue. He sent Middleton his designs, including triangular flags for the different squadrons and distinguishing pennants for each division.[13] Later in the year, he further revised the dimensions, suggesting seven yards by five for ships of the line, and six yards by four for frigates.

Kempenfelt continued to work for the reform of tactics based on the French systems, and by 6 April he was able to give Middleton a draft of the system which he proposed:

> Those movements and evolutions which I put into your hands this morning are so frequently practised in a fleet, that some rule, which is proved to be the best, should be laid down for the execution, that all captains may be acquainted with the manner, and cooperate suitably; otherwise irregularity and confusion must attend the movement. The rules laid down for the movements must be comprehended by any that know the first rudiments of geometry. There may perhaps some obscurity arise from the manner of expression. I should be glad you would mention such as you meet with. It is rough wrote; I intend to correct it.[14]

Kempenfelt prepared a summary for Hardy of his scheme for the organisation of the fleet in divisions:

> When a fleet consists of fifteen or more ships of the line, they should be divided into three squadrons. From fifteen to twenty sail, both numbers included, there will be no occasion for divisions in the squadrons. From twenty seven to forty five sail, each squadron should have two divisions. From forty five sail (included) and upwards, each squadron should have three divisions. In such a fleet, where it is necessary that each of the

12 Corbett (ed.), *Signals and Instructions*, p.120.

13 Laughton (ed.), *Barham Papers*, Vol.I, pp.314-315

14 Laughton (ed.), *Barham Papers*, Vol.I, p.322.

> squadrons should have three divisions, whatever rank the admirals may be of, they should, notwithstanding, bear the proper flags for a complete fleet.

When he went through these proposals with Hardy he did not obtain a very satisfactory response:

> He said that we did very well last summer in the manner the fleet was then divided, and he did not therefore see any occasion for alteration. I replied by just mentioning the conveniences of a regular division by thirds, and the inconveniences that attended any other mode; and said no more, as I knew by experience reasoning would make no impression upon him.[15]

This sort of reaction was not encouraging to a man of perceptive and enquiring mind, and it did little to encourage Kempenfelt in his view of the status of the position of Captain of the Fleet. He had remarked to Middleton on 5 April:

> I don't suppose that there is an office in the whole state that is considered to be of any consequence, whose duty is so vague and undetermined as that of an admiral's first captain. If it ever had a prescribed duty, it has been lost and forgot with the disuse of the office. Some think that the origin of admiral's first captain was to have the particular charge of his squadron or division of the fleet, as the commander-in-chief's care and concern for the whole occupied too much of his time to attend to the detail of his own squadron or division.[16]

He argued that the position should be more clearly defined and a number of principles laid down. Above all, he insisted that all orders from the admiral should be issued through the Captain of the Fleet, who should also be regarded as the first captain of the ship, so that nothing was done without his direction and consent; otherwise there would be a clash of authority.[17]

Kempenfelt acknowledged that this would have the effect of greatly reducing the authority of the ship's captain; but as things stood, if an admiral delivered his orders to the ship's captain instead of passing them through the Captain of the Fleet, 'what a ridiculous situation is this last reduced to!' Next day he wrote again to Middleton to suggest that the admiral should choose the Captain of the Fleet, and that the latter should then choose the captain of the ship.

15 Laughton (ed.), *Barham Papers*, Vol.I, p.323.
16 Laughton (ed.), *Barham Papers*, Vol.I, p.320.
17 Laughton (ed.), *Barham Papers*, Vol.I, p.321.

Kempenfelt, for whom the speed of sailing of ships of the line was of crucial importance, was wholly convinced of the necessity of coppering the fleet, as he had made clear in his correspondence with Middleton. For his part, the latter missed no opportunity to emphasise to Sandwich the importance of this; in a letter to the First Lord of 15 September outlining the plans for the refitting of each of the ships of the Channel Fleet after the end of the 1779 campaign, he observed: 'If taken in hand according to their dates and as soon as you can spare them, we shall produce a useful coppered fleet early in the spring; and which I flatter myself will bring credit to your Lordship and do material service to his Majesty's service. I would propose coppering every ship, and we are laying in accordingly'.[18]

The process of coppering the fleet went on as well as Middleton had hoped, and by the spring of 1780 it had been effectively completed. It represented an enormous effort on the part of the dockyards at Portsmouth and Plymouth; during the 1779 campaign only a few of the Channel Fleet's ships of the line had been coppered, so a great deal of work had to be done to complete the task. In the autumn of 1779 Middleton, who had an unswerving belief that copper sheathing would be decisive, had written to Sandwich a paper outlining the plans that he suggested for the immediate future:

> I must not however conclude without explaining that all my confidence in the practicability of this plan, as well as every other success, is founded on a supposition that the whole fleet of England is coppered with all possible dispatch. This first of all naval improvements seems at this critical period the means which Providence has put into our power to extricate us from present danger, and it will be the height of imprudence not to make use of them. Such ships are ready at twelve hours' notice for the most distant services. It is actually more than doubling our number of ships; and in point of activity there is no calculating the advantages arising from it. I say nothing at this time of the economic part of the improvement, as that will in time prove itself; but I am now considering the subject the great line of service, and applying it to the present situation of this country.[19]

Middleton was never one to avoid hyperbole; but there was a growing realisation in the navy that the operational advantages of coppering were very considerable indeed. The serious doubts about the protection of the iron bolts from the corrosive effects of the copper had not yet begun to be generally raised.

On 7 March 1780 the Cabinet ordered that the Channel Fleet, comprising 30 ships of the line, should be ready to put to sea by 1 May. Hardy hoisted his flag aboard the *Victory* at Spithead on 17 May, but it was soon apparent that he was

18 Barnes and Owen (eds), *Private Papers of John, Earl of Sandwich*, Vol.III, p.102.

19 Barnes and Owen (eds), *Private Papers of John, Earl of Sandwich*, Vol.III, pp.175-176.

seriously ill, and he was taken ashore suffering either from what was called 'gout in the stomach' or 'inflammation in the bowels'. He died at the Fountains Inn at Portsmouth in the early hours of the following morning. According to one account, Kempenfelt was with him until he died.[20]

The news was sent at once to Sandwich, who wasted no time and wrote immediately to Vice Admiral Samuel Barrington, asking him to come to town to discuss his proposed appointment to command the Channel Fleet, assuring him that the King considered that 'this important charge, upon which the fate of this kingdom very possibly depends, cannot be better entrusted than to your management'.[21] Sandwich ended his letter to Barrington with a promise that nothing would be wanting on his part 'to make this arduous task as easy and agreeable to you as the nature of it will allow'. He was in no doubt, however, that persuading the admiral to accept the command was going to be extremely difficult.

20 Rubinstein, *Catastrophe at Spithead*, p.63.

21 Barnes and Owen (eds), *Private Papers of John, Earl of Sandwich*, Vol.III, p.279.

24

Geary

Sandwich's meeting with Barrington did not go well. The admiral's mood was not improved when the First Lord kept him waiting for an hour. Barrington had neither forgotten nor forgiven the slight which he believed himself to have suffered at Sandwich's hands in respect of his command in the Leeward Islands. He made clear from the outset of the meeting that he would not accept the command of the Channel Fleet. He wrote a memorandum of their conversation, from which it appears that he put his refusal on the grounds of his health; he recorded telling the First Lord: 'I was by no means equal to such an arduous task; that I was of such an anxious disposition that it would kill me in a fortnight; that what I had already seen, had I been Commander-in-Chief, would have made me run mad'.[1] Sandwich did his best, using a number of arguments in an endeavour to persuade Barrington to change his mind, but to no avail.

Before they parted, the Admiral offered some comments on the subject of the current state of the Channel Fleet:

> I then begged leave to lay before him the condition of the fleet, which had been ruined by dragging men, contrary to their inclinations, from one ship to another and was the occasion of infinite discontent and desertion; that there were certainly many excellent captains, many that had been so, but worn out, and many entire blanks.[2]

At the conclusion of their meeting, Barrington told Sandwich that he should call on Keppel to lead the Channel Fleet, as the man who could serve his country best, adding that 'his decisions on the most important occasions were clear quick and determined'.

1 Bonner-Smith (ed.), *Barrington Papers*, Vol.II, pp.339-340.
2 Bonner-Smith (ed.), *Barrington Papers*, Vol.II, p.340.

'The Honourable Samuel Barrington, Vice Admiral of the Blue, and Commander in Chief of His Majesty's ships at the reduction of St. Lucia'. Mezzotint by Richard Earlom after Joshua Reynolds. (Anne S.K. Brown Collection)

Barrington was anxious that his position should not be misunderstood, and he wrote to Middleton on 22 May to explain to him personally his reasons for declining the command:

> A man must see with my eyes, and have my feelings before he can account for my refusing the command. If our superiors had those feelings, and only their King and country's interest at heart, we might in time be ourselves again. Had I been in command, what I have seen since I have been here would have made me run mad. A total relaxation of discipline,

> and the rule laid down by a great man that we are all alike, must in the end be productive of bad consequences.[3]

Sandwich was not surprised by Barrington's reaction; he had evidently told the King of the alternative candidate he had in mind, since when the latter acknowledged the news of the admiral's response, he expressed the hope that 'no time will be lost in calling out Admiral Geary, who I trust will instantly accept'. Middleton, kept informed by Sandwich of the situation, was also optimistic: 'I hope you will find everything settled to your satisfaction and Admiral Geary of a disposition to carry on the service to your mind. It will be necessary however to send immediately for Captain Kempenfelt to induce him to continue in the *Victory*, and I write to the same purpose.[4]

Admiral Francis Geary was 70 years of age. He has been rather unfairly portrayed as a naval nonentity; Admiral James, for instance, dismissed him as not having 'any special claim for selection'.[5] In fact, he had a solid record of achievement in the navy, which he had joined in 1727. He held a number of commands in the early part of the War of Austrian Succession, in the course of which he acquired the Duke of Bedford, then First Lord, as a patron. The end of that war saw him in command of the *Culloden*, 74, and he briefly hoisted his broad pennant as a commodore. When peace came, he retired to his estate, but returned to service in 1755 as captain of the *Somerset*, 70.

Geary served on the court martial of Admiral Byng, and commanded two more ships of the line before being promoted to rear admiral in 1759. He was appointed as third in command of the Channel Fleet under Hawke, but missed the battle of Quiberon Bay because the *Sandwich*, 90, his flagship, had lost her mainmast. He continued to serve with the Channel Fleet, and before the end of the war was promoted to vice admiral. He served briefly as commander-in-chief at the Nore, and in 1769 became commander-in-chief at Portsmouth. His promotion to Admiral of the Blue came on 31 March 1775. Professor Rodger has written of him: 'A fine seaman and gallant officer, Geary could be trusted to carry out unambiguous orders with the minimum of fuss'.[6] All things considered, therefore, the decision to appoint him was not unreasonable.

Mulgrave was pleased with the selection of Geary, writing to Sandwich on 22 May:

> I think the appointment of Geary very proper. I know him to be a very worthy, honourable and gallant man. He has much experience, is greatly respected, and most universally beloved as a man in the service. I like

3 Laughton (ed.), *Barham Papers*, Vol.I, p.366.

4 Barnes and Owen (eds), *Private Papers of John, Earl of Sandwich*, Vol.III, pp.279-280.

5 James, *The British Navy in Adversity*, pp.243-244.

6 Rodger, *Insatiable Earl*, p.281.

> this much better than if your first application had succeeded. I agree with you entirely as to the inexpediency of employing in great trust a declared enemy; but if there is any person still more exceptionable, it is one of the character of the person you mention.[7]

When, therefore, Geary was invited to accept the command of the Channel Fleet, he had not been to sea from more than 20 years, and had never held an independent seagoing command. On the other hand, he had not been involved in politics, and he was extremely popular in the fleet, both of which factors were in the present situation very important. The breakdown in discipline which Kempenfelt had reported, and to which Barrington had referred, was a matter of grave concern to many of the more thoughtful senior officers; Samuel Hood had written to his brother of the spirit of discontent in almost every ship: 'Such a want of discipline and order throughout the Navy was never before known, or such a want of regard and attention to the good of the king's service. The negligence of officers in general is really astonishing, and God only knows to what extent the mischief will go!'[8]

When the offer was made to him, Geary accepted at once, and no time indeed was lost in putting the new command structure in place. He arrived at Spithead on 23 May and hoisted his flag aboard the *Victory* on the following day. Barrington agreed to serve as second-in-command, with Darby as third, and rear admirals Digby and Ross also continued with the fleet. Importantly, Kempenfelt remained as Captain of the Fleet.

Nor was time wasted in drawing up Geary's orders. Intelligence had been received that a squadron of seven ships of the line fitting out at Toulon under d'Estaing was intended for Cadiz, where it would join the five French ships of the line already there. The fear was that then, with the Spanish squadron, it would proceed to Brest. Geary was instructed that as soon as he had 24 of the line ready for sea he was to 'cruise upon such station as he shall judge most proper for intercepting the said squadrons, and use his utmost endeavours to take or destroy them, making it his chief purpose if possible to engage them separately'.[9] He was to remain at sea as long as his provisions and water allowed, before returning to Torbay or Spithead for further orders. In addition, of course, he was so far as he was able to provide protection for trade convoys.

Geary had always been close to Hawke, his old commander, who had a good opinion of him, having chosen him as his third in command. He had written to Anson privately after Geary had been promoted to rear admiral to say that he was 'an honest man and a good plain officer'.[10] When Geary was appointed as

7 Barnes and Owen (eds), *Private Papers of John, Earl of Sandwich*, Vol.III, pp.280-281.

8 Barnes and Owen (eds), *Private Papers of John, Earl of Sandwich*, Vol.III, p.275.

9 Barnes and Owen (eds), *Private Papers of John, Earl of Sandwich*, Vol.III, p.276.

10 Ruddock F. Mackay, *Admiral Hawke* (Oxford: Oxford University Press 1965), p.228.

commander-in-chief, he wrote to Hawke to tell him that he would be made happy by having so many of his old sea friends with him. On 6 June the 75-year-old Hawke wrote to him affectionately with some sage advice:

> This is principally to thank you for the favour of your letter of the 3rd instant, and for all the kind acts you have been able to do. I find by the papers that you are getting ready for sea with all the despatch that is possible and that you will sail the instant that it is in your power; and, though I could wish this could get to your hands first, yet the times are so very pressing, from many unfortunate events, that I think the sooner you get to my old station off Brest, the better it will be for my country. When you are there, watch those fellows as close as a cat watches a mouse; and, if once you have the good fortune to get up to them, make much of them, and don't part with them easily! Forgive my being so free! I love you. We have served long together, and I have your interest and happiness sincerely at heart. My dear friend, may God Almighty bless you, and may that all-powerful hand guide and protect you in the day of battle![11]

Geary put to sea with 22 ships of the line and seven frigates, having issued to each of his captains Kempenfelt's new book of signals and supporting documents. On 16 June he picked up the *Cumberland* and *Alfred* from Plymouth and set out to carry out his instructions. In respect of these, his problem was one that was familiar to most commanders in chief of the Channel Fleet, since they effectively required him to be in more than one place at the same time. So far as the Toulon squadron was concerned, Geary's chance of intercepting it depended on prompt and accurate intelligence of its movements, since otherwise d'Estaing would have little difficulty in reaching Cadiz before the Channel Fleet could put in an appearance.

Meanwhile, French and Spanish naval planning for the 1780 campaign had substantially lost its focus, due in large part to the setback that Spain had suffered at the hands of Rodney. When information had reached the Bourbon allies that a relief of Gibraltar was planned, together with the despatch of reinforcements to the West Indies, it had been firmly believed that Rodney, with his ships of the line, would escort the Gibraltar convoy for only part of the way. Vergennes assumed, therefore, that the 16 to 18 Spanish ships of the line off Gibraltar should be sufficient to intercept the convoy.[12] When news reached France that Rodney had sailed with 24 of the line, Vergennes suggested that Gaston's squadron of 20 Spanish ships of the line, reinforced by four French ships of the line under *Chef d'Escadre* Antoine Hilarion de Beausset, should sail from Brest to Gibraltar in the hope that it could get there before Rodney's convoy. Gaston, however, only sailed on 14

11 Geoffrey Callender, 'With the Grand Fleet in 1780' in *The Mariner's Mirror* (September 1923), pp.202-203.

12 Dull, *French Navy and American Independence*, p.171.

January, far too late to affect the situation. Langara had thus been left unsupported to face Rodney, and went down to inevitable defeat. Even if the assumption that Rodney would not go as far as Gibraltar was still made, the failure of Córdova to put to sea remains extremely surprising.

The departure of Gaston's squadron from Brest finally put paid to any thought of reviving the Combined Fleet for another invasion attempt. As it was, Langara's defeat had left Spain's planning for the year at sixes and sevens. At the end of February, Montmorin reported to Vergennes on a Spanish plan to send some eight or 10 thousand troops with 12 to 14 ships of the line to strengthen the position in the West Indies, adding that a French offer of two thousand troops and three or four ships of the line would be accepted. Meanwhile, in support of the siege operations at Gibraltar, 28 sail of the line would be based at Cadiz and Algeciras. Montmorin also told Vergennes that there was now a strong disposition in Spain to hold Floridablanca responsible for the setbacks.[13] Overall, Montmorin made clear his pessimism about Spain's ability to achieve anything very much.

Vergennes's response was to propose the reinforcement of Córdova at Cadiz by increasing the French squadron there to nine or 10 ships of the line, these to come from Toulon. His plan was that the squadron should cruise in the Atlantic, with a reasonable chance of intercepting British convoys, while still remaining close to Gibraltar. Then, at the end of the summer, the opportunity would be taken of replacing some 15 worn out ships of the line in the West Indies with battleworthy ships available in Europe. Floridablanca accepted this proposal, but urged that still more French ships should be concentrated at Cadiz, or at least at Ferrol. The French Ministry of Marine saw the building up of the combined fleet at Cadiz in this way as a means of creating a fleet in being, of which the British would be obliged to take notice.[14]

Thus there was no coherent integrated strategy for the Allies to pursue in 1780. The setback suffered by Spain at the start of the year had been more damaging than a mere calculation of the losses would indicate, and Jonathan Dull has suggested that this had given Britain its supreme opportunity of the war to seize and hold the initiative. The allies, like Britain, were devoting a large part of their naval resources to the protection of trade, but their convoys were necessarily still vulnerable. The particular chance which he contends that Britain missed was the huge convoy of 146 merchantmen and transports sent by Spain to the West Indies, which left Cadiz on 28 April escorted by a squadron of 12 ships of the line under *Teniente General* Jose Solano. If, when it reached its destination, Rodney had been able to capture it, Dull reckoned that 'the psychological blow of another defeat would almost certainly have knocked Spain out of the war'. As it was, when it

13 Dull, *French Navy and American Independence*, pp.179-181.

14 Dull, *French Navy and American Independence*, p.182.

got there, de Guichen was able to meet the convoy in the passage between Santo Domingo and Guadalupe and safely escort it into port.[15]

Mindful of his instructions to prevent the junction of the French and Spanish fleets, Geary first took the Channel Fleet to a position off Ushant, remaining there until 27 June. He then concluded that it was better to move further southward into the middle of the Bay of Biscay, and he reported next day to the Admiralty his decision to cruise there as long as he thought necessary, and thereafter to return northward to cover incoming trade convoys from the East and West Indies.[16] The move south towards Cape Finisterre reaped no reward, however; there was no sign of either the French or Spanish fleet being at sea.

Meanwhile, however, the Admiralty had received information which resulted in a change in Geary's orders. Commodore George Johnstone had, since the previous November, been in command of a small squadron operating off the coast of Portugal, and on 8 June he received intelligence that two enemy squadrons were being prepared at Cadiz and Ferrol to attack convoys outward bound for the East and West Indies. The larger of these was said to consist of five French and four Spanish ships of the line and two frigates; the other, of seven Spanish ships of the line with three frigates and two smaller vessels. This news led to the issue of an order to Geary, sent on 25 June and received four days later, by which he was

> [R]equired and directed forthwith to detach from the fleet under your command one or more admirals with a squadron of ten sail of the line and a proper number of frigates to look out for the above-mentioned squadrons of the enemy and to use their utmost endeavours to take or destroy them.[17]

Geary was, however, given an option; if he thought such a detachment inadvisable, he could 'suspend the execution of these orders, acquainting us as soon as possible with your reasons for the same'.

Geary at once convened a council of his flag officers, attended also by Kempenfelt. Apart from Johnstone's report, they also had before them some intelligence of their own from Captain Byron of 28 June, which suggested that the French squadron had sailed from Brest. The council decided unanimously not to split the fleet as ordered, 'but proceed together first of Ferrol, and not meeting with the ships as mentioned in Captain Byron's intelligence of the 28th instant to proceed according to their Lordships' directions in quest of the ships mentioned in Commodore Johnstone's intelligence'.[18]

15 Dull, *French Navy and American Independence*, pp.187-189.

16 Callender, 'With the Grand Fleet in 1780', p.264.

17 Bonner-Smith (ed.), *Barrington Papers*, Vol.II, pp.342-343.

18 Bonner-Smith (ed.), *Barrington Papers*, Vol.II, p.345.

Although he had signed the unanimous opinion of the council of flag officers, Kempenfelt disagreed with the decision that was taken, telling Middleton:

> Our frigates are now reduced to 3. We are here cruising between the latitudes of 40° 30' and 39° 20', from twenty to seventy leagues from the shore, in quest of a squadron of the enemy sail said to be in this station, looking out for our homeward and outward-bound trade. But this is not the track of either East or West India ships, and I therefore conceive no station for the enemy to cruise in. It appears to me by placing ourselves here we leave the enemy at liberty to join their different squadrons, and have put ourselves out of the way of receiving intelligence or directions from the Admiralty, or of preventing any designs the enemy may have upon us at home. I therefore wish we were in your neighbourhood again ... Our chief is much perplexed; he wants to square his conduct to the approbation of Admiral Barrington and Lord Mulgrave. But that is impossible, as these gentlemen think differently. However, he pays much attention to the advice of the former, and indeed don't take any step without it. But a man who has no opinion of his own, but acts from those of others, can never act regular and consistent.[19]

In this judgment, Kempenfelt was undoubtedly correct, as Admiral James pointed out: 'Whilst in the south, the fleet had cruised between 60 and 200 miles off the coast of Portugal. It was an area of no strategical importance and Kempenfelt's criticism was fully justified'.[20]

As the Channel Fleet headed south in accordance with the council's decision, it encountered on 3 July a French convoy inward bound from Santo Domingo. Although hampered by fog, 12 merchant ships were taken, as Geary was able to report with undisguised satisfaction to the Admiralty. The convoy had consisted of between 25 and 30 sail, escorted by two warships: 'and, had it not been for the sudden coming on of the fog at the hour I have mentioned, it is my opinion that every ship of them would have been taken'.[21]

It was the prolonged chase of this convoy that gave rise to the account given by Sir John Barrow, in his biography of Howe, of an incident which illustrated not only the difficulties faced by a fleet in mastering a new signal system, but also perhaps the agreeable personality of the commander-in-chief:

> One day a fleet of ships, supposed to be that of the enemy, hove in sight; the signals were resorted to, but, in the hurry and confusion of preparing

19 Laughton (ed.), *Barham Papers*, Vol.I, pp.326-327.
20 James, *The British Navy in Adversity*, p.245.
21 Callender, 'With the Grand Fleet in 1780', p.265.

> for battle, they somehow or other were not managed so well as when made at more leisure. Geary at last grew impatient, and going up to Kempenfelt, and laying his hand gently on his shoulder, exclaimed with a good-natured earnestness, 'Now, my dear Kempy, do, for God's sake, do, my dear Kempy, oblige me by throwing your signals overboard, and make that which we all understand – "Bring the enemy to close action!"[22]

This was, however, the only action which the Channel Fleet saw. Soon after taking the convoy Geary received intelligence that some 20 enemy ships of the line had been sighted off Cape Ortegal. In bad weather, which did the ships no good, he beat towards the cape and then continued as far south as Cape St Vincent, without any sight of the enemy.[23] He then turned back northwards to take up again his station off Ushant. At the Admiralty, the threat that the Cadiz fleet would come out to join the fleet in Brest was still taken very seriously; Sandwich wrote to Johnstone on 17 July to express the hope that Geary would be 'so fortunate as to meet them if they put to sea; he has a fine fleet, the number of which (if the enemy allows us time) will be considerably increased'.[24]

On 2 August the Channel Fleet met a large British convoy of 63 ships, most of which were bound for Jamaica, but including a number of East Indiamen. In addition to victuallers and military store ships there were a number of transports carrying the 90th Regiment. It was escorted by the *Ramillies*, 74, commanded by Captain John Moutray, and two frigates, *Southampton* and *Thetis*, together with the *Inflexible*, 64, and *Buffalo*, 60. The two latter ships had orders to accompany the convoy until it was clear of the Channel. Geary kept company with the convoy until that point and then saw it on its way, ordering the *Inflexible* and *Buffalo* to join the Channel Fleet. Proceeding on his way with the reduced escort, Moutray next encountered a northbound convoy the escort of which was commanded by Captain George Johnstone in the *Romney*. It appears that the latter warned Moutray of significant enemy activity in the area. On 8 August, hearing from neutrals of enemy vessels in the vicinity, Moutray apparently dismissed them as 'nothing but Dutchmen'. On the following day the convoy was intercepted by a large part of the Combined Fleet under Córdova to the west of Cape St Vincent.

The Spanish admiral had with him 32 French and Spanish ships of the line, and the convoy stood no chance whatever. It seems that when Moutray discovered his peril, and signalled for the convoy to tack and stand to the northward, few of the merchant ships saw or obeyed the order, due to a hazy dawn and light winds. Only the *Ramillies* and the two frigates, with five of the merchantmen, got away, after having been pursued by Beausset with his squadron of seven French

22 Sir John Barrow, *The Life of Richard Earl Howe* (London: John Murray 1838), p.141.

23 Callender, 'With the Grand Fleet in 1780', p.268.

24 Barnes and Owen (eds), *Private Papers of John, Earl of Sandwich*, Vol.III, p.287.

ships.[25] The Admiralty had only learned that Córdova had put to sea on 4 August, and there was no time to warn either Geary or Moutray of the danger. It was a colossal disaster; apart from the ships taken, 3,144 men and goods to the value of £1.5 million had been lost. Moutray was court martialled and dismissed his ship. On one view, this was a decision that was wholly unjust. Sending a crucially important convoy with so feeble an escort into waters which might easily contain substantial enemy forces was the fault of the Admiralty, not Moutray. Another opinion, though, has been expressed by Richard Woodman, who commented that the escorts 'abandoned their charges and ran for safety, escaping capture along with a mere five West Indiamen'.[26] Admiral Mahan observed:

> It was the greatest single blow that British commerce had received in war during the memory of men living, and a general inclination prevailed to lay the blame on some individual, who might be punished according to the magnitude of the object, rather than in proportion to his demerit.[27]

Not only did this stunning defeat outweigh Rodney's success in the Moonlight Battle; it also effectively put paid to the secret negotiations which were being conducted by a British envoy, Richard Cumberland, with the Spanish government, which were intended to take Spain out of the war.

On 8 August, when the Channel Fleet was some 47 leagues west of Ushant, Geary took the decision to return home, and reported to the Admiralty that he intended to proceed to Spithead. The squadron was badly afflicted with scurvy, and had been some nine weeks at sea without fresh provisions. He gave his reasons for choosing Spithead: 'There is no hospital at Torbay for the sick and it will be attended with great inconvenience to get top masts, yards, stores, beer, water and other provisions there'.[28]

The decision to go to Spithead rather than Torbay was taken in the teeth of the advice of the Captain of the Fleet. Kempenfelt wrote on the same day to Middleton to protest:

> Torbay, which has many advantages to recommend it, it is judged will not answer upon this occasion. How dispose of the sick? And how receive provisions and beer with any despatch there. For despatch, and the better accommodation of the sick, it would be best for part of the fleet to go to Plymouth, and the rest to Spithead; but would not a separation be dangerous? Spithead seems in the opinion of most to be the proper place;

25 Lacour-Gayet, *La marine Militaire*, p.318.
26 Richard Woodman, *Britannia's Realm* (Stroud: History Press 2009), p.80.
27 Mahan, *Major Operations*, p.158.
28 Callender, 'With the Grand Fleet in 1780', p.268.

> and yet, the fleets going there will be attended by many inconveniences, which would be avoided at Torbay.[29]

Ten days later, the Channel Fleet dropped anchor at Spithead, and on the following day Kempenfelt wrote again to Middleton, not only to reiterate his disapproval of the decision that the whole fleet should go to Spithead, but also to repeat his opinion of Geary as commander-in-chief:

> In fine, if the Admiralty will not appoint a suitable person to command the fleet, you must expect nothing but bad conduct, and, in consequence, bad success; the present person is brave, generous and may perhaps have been a good officer; but he is wholly debilitated in his faculties, his memory and judgment lost, wavering and indetermined in everything.[30]

Callender, in his account of this cruise of the Channel Fleet, accepted that in the debate over its homeward destination it was Kempenfelt's view that was correct, but noted that Geary's will had prevailed, and saw this as a corrective to 'the modern tendency to attribute to Kempenfelt the entire control of the fleet during this trying and neglected period'.[31] The Captain of the Fleet, however, would certainly not have agreed that he had 'the entire control'; his not unreasonable complaint was that Geary paid too little attention to his advice.

The news that part at least of the Cadiz fleet was at sea, and of the loss of Moutray's convoy, disturbed the government extremely, and on 25 August Sandwich wrote to Geary to say that another such blow 'would occasion such distress in this country that no one can tell the consequences it might have'. Accordingly Geary would receive orders on the following day to put to sea with his whole fleet. If it could not be completely made ready to sail at once he could send a separate squadron. Sandwich's letter conveyed the grave anxiety which was felt in London: 'I hope to God that the assistance we have given you towards manning your fleet will enable you to carry the whole with you'.[32] Geary replied promptly. He asked for directions as to where he should order Digby, with 10 or 12 ships of the line, to cruise to protect the incoming trade. Apart from manning problems, he hoped to be ready to leave within days.

Perhaps Hawke, who had been in correspondence with Geary since his return to port, had some inkling that his protégé's morale needed bolstering. At all events, on 26 August he wrote to Geary another lengthy, affectionate and encouraging letter, wishing him 'all imaginable good fortune when you go out again'. Hawke went on:

29 Laughton (ed.), *Barham Papers*, Vol.I, p.327.

30 Laughton (ed.), *Barham Papers*, Vol.I, p.329.

31 Callender, 'With the Grand Fleet in 1780', p.270.

32 Barnes and Owen (eds), *Private Papers of John, Earl of Sandwich*, Vol.III, pp.290-291.

> I trust in God your next cruize will be a happy and glorious one, both for your country and yourself. My good friend, I have always wished you well, and have ever talked freely and openly to you upon every subject relative to the service. Recollect some of these passages; and for God's sake, if you should be so lucky as to get sight of the enemy, get as close to them as possible. Do not let them shuffle with you by engaging at a distance, but get within musket shot if you can … May the hand of Providence go with you and protect you in the day of battle, and grant you victory over your perfidious enemies; and may you return with honour to your country and family again![33]

That same day Barrington was writing to Hawke, telling him that Geary was so good as to place confidence in him, and that he should never want for 'an honest, disinterested opinion'. He went on to observe that Geary had 'not lived much in the wicked world; and has so little art himself as not to suspect others. He has done well hitherto, and yet should anything happen they mean to lay all on him'.[34]

Kempenfelt was much cast down by the news of the loss of Moutray's convoy, remarking on 25 August: 'That our fleet instead of them had not fallen in with the French and Spaniards chagrins and mortifies extremely. To reflect how near to the most favourable event that could possibly happen for this country – that is, falling in with the Cadiz fleet – is distracting'. He thought that he was getting too old, and that he should retire before he was told so.[35] Two days later, he was sending a grave warning to Middleton that another command crisis was almost at hand:

> The fatigue is too much for Mr Geary. I have just left him in bed, ashore, much indisposed. This increases our embarrassment and must produce delay. In my opinion, he'll not go to sea with the fleet. It was wrong to pitch upon him, and still more so in him to accept the command of the fleet – a more arduous task now than ever since our time. What you'll do I don't know; but if the fleet is not put into able hands, you are not to expect success.[36]

Kempenfelt's assessment was correct. That same day Geary wrote to the Admiralty to announce that he was too ill to leave his bed, and applying for leave until his health recovered. This was granted, and he went home to Polesden Lacey in Surrey, and the government had once more to face the need that Barrington should be asked to exercise the command. It was not unexpected that he should decline to do so; when he did, he told Stephens that it was for the reasons he had given to

33 Laughton (ed.), *Barham Papers*, Vol.I p.330.

34 Mackay, *Admiral Hawke*, p.352.

35 Laughton (ed.), *Barham Papers*, Vol.I, p.331.

36 Laughton (ed.), *Barham Papers*, Vol.I, p.331.

Sandwich when he was previously offered the command. His letter was dated 29 August; on 1 September he wrote to Stephens to say that as, in Geary's absence, he could not possibly take charge of the fleet, he had asked Admiral Pye to take direction of it for the time being.[37]

Sandwich was extremely angry. He wrote to North to tell him that he imagined that there was 'a plan to get the command of the fleet into Admiral Keppel's hands'. Geary, he thought, was a weak man governed entirely by Barrington:

> If these gentlemen think we are to be intimidated, there is an end to all discipline in the Navy, at least while I am at the head of that department. Therefore my advice is that Admiral Barrington should have leave to quit, and Admiral Darby immediately go out with the fleet, unless Mr Geary gets back time enough to command it himself.[38]

Sandwich was entitled to be enraged; there could now be no question of leaving Barrington with the fleet, and on 4 September he was ordered to strike his flag and come on shore. The King shared Sandwich's fury, remarking that 'it is impossible for any man to have more thoroughly thrown off the mask than Vice Admiral Barrington'.[39] His conduct, he considered, was so very improper that he should certainly be ordered to strike his flag.

Geary's formal resignation arrived some days later, emphasising that it was solely on the grounds of his ill-health. He felt, he said, that it was his duty to the King, his country and to Sandwich to resign when it appeared to him that his health would not permit him to resume his command. In fact, his health did recover; Geary lived for another 16 years. His reputation had not been enhanced by his term in command of the Channel Fleet, though Nicholas Rodger has done his best to rehabilitate it:

> Geary was in many ways another Hardy, and he has been condemned on the same grounds, with the complaints of the same commentators, especially Kempenfelt. Once again the root of the complaint was Geary's refusal to be managed by his subordinates … As it was he did all that he reasonably could have done.[40]

A refusal to take advice, though, is not necessarily a matter for commendation, unless of course the advice was unsound; but perhaps Rodger, not for the first time, was being deliberately provocative.

37 Bonner-Smith (ed.), *Barrington Papers*, Vol.II, pp.350-351.

38 Barnes and Owen (eds), *Private Papers of John, Earl of Sandwich*, Vol.III, pp.294-295.

39 Barnes and Owen (eds), *Private Papers of John, Earl of Sandwich*, Vol.III, p.299.

40 Rodger, *Insatiable Earl*, p.281.

25

Darby

As had been the case on the occasion of Hardy's sudden death in May, Geary's abrupt departure presented Sandwich with a command problem that must be solved at once, if the fleet was to get to sea to counter the perceived threat from Brest. The First Lord did not hesitate; in the current situation the appointment of Vice Admiral George Darby was practically inevitable, and orders went to him at once to take command of the fleet. It was supposed at first that Kempenfelt would not be serving as Captain of the Fleet. One reason for this was his own reluctance to continue in the post; but Middleton took a hand, as he reported to Sandwich on 7 September: 'I have therefore wrote to Kempenfelt in the most pressing terms to accommodate himself to the necessity of the present juncture, however contrary to his feelings, and to suspend any other inclination till the campaign is ended'.[1] Kempenfelt relented; but it seems that his promotion to rear admiral was already under consideration, and the question was raised as to whether that would make him ineligible; but in the event it was concluded that it did not, and Jackson, who seems to have been dealing with most of the important correspondence at this time, confirmed to Kempenfelt his appointment as Captain of the Fleet on 8 September.[2]

The departure of both Geary and Barrington left two vacancies for flag officers in the Channel Fleet; in addition to appointing Darby, Sandwich at once filled the other by transferring Rear Admiral Francis William Drake from his command in the Downs. Drake, who was promoted to vice admiral on 26 September, hoisted his flag in the *Victory*, Darby having chosen to remain aboard the *Britannia*, where he was joined by Kempenfelt. The Captain of the Fleet was still concerned about his health, and repeated to Middleton his conviction that he was unequal to the task. However, he was properly appreciative of hearing from Middleton on 16 September of the proposal that he be promoted, though on the following day he felt obliged to tell the Comptroller that he did not think that he was fit for active

1 Barnes and Owen (eds), *Private Papers of John, Earl of Sandwich*, Vol.III, p.302.
2 Barnes and Owen (eds), *Private Papers of John, Earl of Sandwich*, Vol.III, p.303.

service, and that he ought to retire. Fortunately for the Navy, he did not persist in this.

The new commander-in-chief was 60 years of age. He had had a sound record of achievement, becoming a lieutenant in 1742 and post captain in 1747. When war broke out in 1756, he was appointed to the *Seahorse*, 24, and then in the following year to the command of the *Norwich*, 50. He served first in the West Indies and then, under Rodney's command, at the bombardment of Le Havre. In 1760, commanding the *Devonshire,* 66, he took out a convoy to North America, and subsequently served in the Leeward Islands, taking part in Rodney's capture of Martinique in 1762. To mark his success in that operation, he was sent home with the despatches announcing the victory. After a lengthy period ashore, he returned to service in 1778 and was promoted to rear admiral; he became vice admiral in the following year. His service in the Channel Fleet as third in command was generally regarded as exemplary, and he was a man of whom few had a bad word to say. His appointment was well received in the fleet; Sandwich's confidence in him was such that a few days after taking up his command he was appointed to the Board of Admiralty in succession to Vice Admiral Robert Man. Importantly, he had not been involved in any political faction, though he was elected as a member of Parliament for Plymouth during 1780.

Darby was relieved that Kempenfelt was to continue as Captain of the Fleet, and wrote to Sandwich on 10 September to thank him. On the same day Mulgrave wrote to the First Lord with some suggestions for the orders to be given to Darby: 'It occurs to me for your consideration that it might be right to direct him, should the wind continue easterly, to proceed immediately off Brest to reconnoitre the enemy's force, and either to stay with or leave as he shall judge most proper sufficient force to watch them'.[3]

The principal concern of the Admiralty at this time was the protection of incoming convoys, and Mulgrave suggested that the Channel Fleet should take up a position 300 miles into the Atlantic, where it would be well placed to meet the first of those expected.

Darby sailed from Spithead on 12 September, and joined Digby in Torbay, where the latter had taken a division of ships of the line in August. On 21 September he reported to Sandwich that the winds were causing him some anxiety; at one point the *Foudroyant* was in danger of being driven ashore. He had sent five ships to cruise off the Lizard for the protection of trade, and was thinking of taking the rest of his force there by divisions, which would be more straightforward than trying to get the whole fleet away together in adverse winds. Darby had evidently been taking notice of Kempenfelt's advice as to the organisation of the fleet into divisions, of which he arranged six, under the command respectively of himself, Drake, Digby, Ross and Captains Innes and Wallis. Each division was composed

3 Barnes and Owen (eds), *Private Papers of John, Earl of Sandwich*, Vol.III, p.105.

of four or five ships of the line and a frigate or fire ship. It was Drake's division that had been sent to cruise off the Lizard.[4]

As it turned out, the bulk of the fleet was trapped by adverse winds in Torbay for practically six weeks, to Darby's great frustration. Kempenfelt used the time there to continue his reflections on the desirability of choosing younger commanders. He wrote from Torbay on 3 October:

> It is a misfortune to this country that persons are not called to places of consequence, especially in our line, until their abilities are on the decline. The evil of this struck me when I was young, and experience has more confirmed it. If you wish success in your armies or fleets, look out for persons of middle-age – I mean about forty – to conduct them. You can't be too nice in the choice of a commander-in-chief for your fleet; order, discipline, ability, everything that gives force and consequence to the fleet depends on him.[5]

The winds continued foul, and in the autumn gales a number of ships suffered serious damage. While the fleet was thus imprisoned, the Admiralty withdrew a number of ships of the line in order to reinforce Rodney in the Leeward Islands, so that it was reduced to 22 in number when Ross was ordered to Portsmouth on 15 October with the *Royal George* and three old 90-gun ships, *Namur*, *Ocean* and *Union*, each of which had been 'disabled in their rudders'. Notwithstanding a report which had been received, Darby did not himself believe that the Combined Fleet was at sea, reckoning that if it was, the gale that was blowing would put an end to its campaign.

This was on 10 October. A few days later Darby had high hopes of being himself able to put to sea, but the weather again deceived him: 'It this time blew if possible beyond any other. Some sails and topmasts have suffered, with cables parting on bringing the ships up, for which we have wrote to Lord Shuldham, who will soon remedy them with a supply'.[6] There was, however, some news of the enemy; apparently an outward bound convoy was due to sail from Brest, while de Guichen was said to be escorting a homeward bound convoy, and a fleet of French and Spanish ships were cruising off Cape St Vincent. Kempenfelt, meanwhile, was drawing some conclusions about the remarkable number of ships that had suffered damage to their rudders. This, he reckoned, was mainly due to their tillers breaking and there not being time with chocks and a spare tiller to stop the violent motion of the rudder which resulted. His advice was that ships should be prepared for this by having their chocks and spare tiller in the wardroom ready for use. Even in a

4 Barnes and Owen (eds), *Private Papers of John, Earl of Sandwich*, Vol.III, p.306n.

5 Laughton (ed.), *Barham Papers*, Vol.I, pp.333-334.

6 Barnes and Owen (eds), *Private Papers of John, Earl of Sandwich*, Vol.III, p.308.

relatively sheltered anchorage like Torbay, the attritional damage to a fleet could be considerable.[7]

Darby finally managed to put to sea on 26 October. His immediate objective was de Guichen's convoy, but in fact this had already made port in Cadiz, arriving there on 23 October. From 31 October until 6 December the Channel Fleet cruised between 100 and 200 miles off Cape Finisterre. On 30 November, and again on the following day there were sightings of what was believed to be an enemy fleet, and the *Victory* at any rate cleared for battle, but no contact was made. It is entirely possible that it was indeed the enemy; the 38 French ships of the line that had over the past months built up into an impressive fleet had put to sea under d'Estaing on 6 November, cruising several times in the region of Cape St Vincent, but made no sighting of the Channel Fleet. After having been at sea 58 days, d'Estaing took the fleet northward to Brest to refit, where he arrived on 3 January 1781.[8]

Deeply disappointed, and coming to the end of his provisions, Darby had no choice but to abandon his cruise, and he turned back northwards, dropping anchor at St Helens on 21 December. En route he sent a disconsolate letter to the First Lord expressing his greatest regret and concern that the fleet in been so long at sea without achieving anything. He believed that the sightings which had been made were indeed of the enemy fleet; but if they had been, there was not much he could have done against such a force, having that time only 17 ships of the line with him, although later re-joined by three others that had briefly become detached: 'Had I seen the smallest prospect of doing any one piece of service, would have still persevered by staying out some days longer, though our provisions would but ill have allowed it'.[9]

Darby had understandably been disappointed by his lack of success, but he had at least evidently convinced his critical Captain of the Fleet of his competence. In Kempenfelt's correspondence with Middleton there was no complaint about Darby, and this, having regard to his outspokenness on the subject of the admiral's two predecessors, amounted to a favourable appraisal. Hilary Rubinstein has, however, quoted one press reference to Kempenfelt and his admiral; this appeared in the *London Courant* of 13 February 1781, and portrayed Kempenfelt as remarking, as he walked down Piccadilly, taking snuff: 'Copper-bottoms, damn me, what are these copper-bottoms good for, if they won't help us take a look at the enemy at least? Why, as we made no use of them, we might as well have had foul ships! Darby, Darby, copper-bottoms – Pshaw![10] Whether or not the story is true, it certainly correctly expressed Kempenfelt's view of what could be done with coppered ships.

7 Laughton (ed.), *Barham Papers*, Vol.I, p.334.

8 Lacour-Gayet, *La marine Militaire*, p.323.

9 Barnes and Owen (eds), *Private Papers of John, Earl of Sandwich*, Vol.III, p.309.

10 Rubinstein, *Catastrophe at Spithead*, p.71.

Mulgrave, who had written so favourably of both Hardy and Geary, was equally enthusiastic in his opinion of their successor. On 19 February he wrote to Sandwich to dispel rumours that he was discontented about serving under Darby:

> I never saw an officer who took such proper pains to make himself agreeable to those under his command, without sacrificing the discipline of the service. I have seen many instances of steadiness and temper in his behaviour that showed his fitness for employment, and nothing to make me doubt of his acquitting himself in every situation of service with honour to himself and advantage to his country. I say this the more freely, as I have never been consulted in his measures, which, I believe, are generally taken as they ought to be from his own judgment, which is very sound, or when that is proper, by the advice of the flag officers serving with him.[11]

The first weeks of 1781 were characterised by a particularly sharp dispute between Middleton and Sandwich. The former never hesitated to offer extremely critical comments on the conduct of the Admiralty and even from time to time of the First Lord personally, and the tone of some of his correspondence since the previous autumn had been particularly hostile. On 22 October, for instance, Middleton had written of his own conduct that it had been 'uniformly open and faithful,' but that he felt the necessity from time to time of making remonstrances of 'notorious remissness in office'. He ended that letter: 'That the Admiralty cannot stand upon its present foundation I am morally certain because its own weight must necessarily pull it down'.[12] This followed a previous letter to the First Lord in which Middleton allowed himself to make a number of especially personal and insulting remarks which were astonishing in their belligerence. Rodger, in his biography of Sandwich, noted that Middleton never apologised for letters of this kind: 'But Sandwich never altered his calm and reasonable tone. Under provocation which would certainly have aroused almost any other Cabinet minister or peer of the day to dismiss Middleton, Sandwich remained firm but friendly'.[13] It was a stance which did the First Lord great credit, but the row which broke out in January 1781 was a particularly severe test of his patience.

Middleton began the campaign with a letter of 4 January addressed to Philip Stephens. The problem as it appeared to him was the lack of influence of the Navy Board over dockyard promotions of yard officers and officers of the Ordinary, which lay in the Admiralty's hands. Nor did the Navy Board have any power over the appointment of workmen, which belonged to the officers of the yards,

11 Barnes and Owen (eds), *Private Papers of John, Earl of Sandwich*, Vol.IV, p.31.

12 Laughton (ed.), *Barham Papers*, Vol.II, pp.8-10.

13 Rodger, *Insatiable Earl*, p.164.

a situation that had obtained since as far back as 1662.[14] The only area in which the Navy Board was able directly to control promotion was in respect of those men below the rank of master. It has been noted that the 'particular point at issue concerned the promotion of shipwright officers, since there was no one who could reliably assess an individual's competence in a trade that was more an art than a science'. Shipwrights learned their trade as apprentices and rose to the top of their service as craftsmen rather than theoreticians.[15] It was an issue that Kempenfelt regarded as important, as he wrote to Middleton on 9 April, 1780:

> The want of a good foundation laid of mathematical knowledge prevents our builders from rising to eminence; for want of this light, they are often obliged to grope in the dark; they guess, because they have not mathematics to calculate certainty; when they give their bottom any particular form, they guess at the effect. More acquaintance with mathematics would give them certainty.[16]

The war of words between Comptroller and First Lord raged on throughout January, with Middleton becoming increasingly outspoken. On 21 January he claimed that if Sandwich had followed 'the disinterested advice' which he had given him, he would have had no 'party opposition to contend with in the fleet'. This prompted Sandwich in his reply to remark that his long experience was that when friends differed, discussions in writing always tended to widen the breach. He remained, however, firm in his refusal to accept the claims of the Navy Board with regard to dockyard appointments. After further exchanges on the same lines, Middleton gave up, wisely choosing not to send a letter which he had drafted which would have made matters very much worse.[17] So the dispute came to an end; the episode illustrated once again just how chaotic and inefficient was the structure responsible for managing the navy – but which was nevertheless able to deliver astonishingly successful results.

One cloud on the diplomatic horizon with which the Cabinet had to contend during 1780 was the emergence of Russia as a potential threat. This arose out of the British desire to restrict the trade of neutral states with the enemy. A list of goods regarded as contraband had been published, and British patrols had been searching and detaining neutral ships, a practice which caused increasing resentment. In February 1780 Catherine the Great sent a declaration to the British, French and Spanish governments protesting about the interference with Russian trade, and threatening to back her demand that neutral ships should enjoy free navigation by

14 R.J.B. Knight, 'Sandwich, Middleton and Dockyard Appointments' in *The Mariner's Mirror* (1971), p.176.
15 Knight, 'Sandwich, Middleton and Dockyard Appointments', p.179.
16 Laughton (ed.), *Barham Papers*, Vol.I, p.325.
17 Laughton (ed.), *Barham Papers*, Vol.II, pp.17-30.

force if necessary. On 10 March the Russian government published a 'Declaration of the Empress of Russia regarding the Principles of Armed Neutrality'. This called for the right for neutrals to navigate freely along the coasts of the belligerent nations, and that the property of such nations should be free on board, with the exception of contraband. The definition of contraband should be that contained in the Russo-British trade treaty of 1734; a port, the Declaration contended, should only be regarded as validly blockaded when the ships of the attacking power were located in a position to make access dangerous; and the principles set out should determine the legality of prizes. On 3 April the governments of the Netherlands, Denmark, Prussia, Sweden and Portugal were invited to join a League of Armed Neutrality which would use its combined naval forces to enforce compliance with the Declaration.

France and Spain speedily accepted the principles of the Declaration. However, it affected Britain much more adversely, which was accordingly placed in a difficult position. It was not clear how far the threat of armed force was merely a bluff or whether, if it was not, Russia could be bought off in some way. A particular problem concerned the Dutch, whose merchant ships carried most of the naval stores to France and Spain which Britain wished to interdict. That the Russian government wished to be taken seriously was shown by its order to put 20 ships of the line into commission. Throughout the year, therefore, the British government remained in a quandary; in July the League of Armed Neutrality could count on 84 warships in commission. But the government for the moment stood firm, warning that if Russia applied the principles of the Declaration to the Dutch it would be 'a measure little short of direct hostility and as pernicious in its consequences as actual war'.[18]

So far as the Dutch were concerned, Britain could not afford to allow them the freedom of navigation called for by the Declaration, and it seemed likely that Russia was bluffing. There was an inherent improbability in the threat that Russia would go to war when so few of her own ships had been affected by the British stop and search policy, and indeed one of the most serious complaints which the Russians made concerned a Spanish interception of one of her ships. However, with the commitments that the British Navy already had, to ignore Russia entirely was risky. With this in mind, orders went to all British warships to confine the seizure of Russian ships to those actually carrying munitions, rather than general naval stores and provisions. At the same time, a significant part of the threat from the League evaporated when Denmark and Sweden signed conventions that allowed naval stores to be defined as contraband, thus effectively allowing the British navy to interdict Danish and Swedish vessels carrying such goods.[19] Thus the only really

18 Syrett, *European Waters*, p.122.

19 Syrett, *European Waters*, p.133.

serious diplomatic issue remaining was what should be done about the Dutch, who had by far the largest share of the trade in question.

The Netherlands had accepted the Russian principles of neutrality in April, but hesitated to join the League, in part in the hope of obtaining a Russian guarantee of the Dutch possessions in the East and West Indies, but this never materialised. On the other hand, the French had succeeded in developing their canal system to such an extent that by the autumn of 1780 naval stores could be transported by inland routes from the Netherlands all the way to the port of Nantes. At sea, there were no legal grounds for the British to seize Dutch merchant ships carrying goods which were Dutch property from a neutral Baltic port to the Netherlands. This meant that naval stores which arrived there in this way could then be transported safely to a French destination, and thus circumvent the British blockade. On 24 November the States General of the Netherlands, under pressure from Russia, finally voted to join the League. The immediate consequence of this decision was that the British ambassador at The Hague was withdrawn.

War with the Dutch had been seen in Britain as offering considerable opportunities. The Dutch were quite unprepared to go to war, and it was not only that their lucrative trade in naval stores could now be largely cut off, but also that their considerable overseas possessions lay open to attack. The formal ground for the British declaration of war, which came on 20 December, arose from the seizure of a ship carrying Henry Laurens, an American envoy to the Netherlands. Among his papers was a draft treaty between Congress and the city of Amsterdam; although it was unsigned, the British government chose to regard it as 'to all intents and purposes, equivalent to actual aggression'.[20]

The British took the position that their declaration of war against the Netherlands was not a ground for war with the rest of the League, since they contended that the Dutch had not entered it as a genuine neutral. In addition to this, however, the British government took advantage of a Russian suggestion of a possible mediation, and announced that it would accept mediation not only by Russia, but also by Austria. This put both Vergennes and Floridablanca in a difficult position; and for the moment it left Britain free to carry on the war against the Dutch while complex diplomatic negotiations continued.[21]

The British Cabinet now began to look eagerly at what items might be snapped up from the Dutch overseas empire. At the same time, it was recognised that it was still necessary to take account of the Dutch navy, which although unready was still not inconsiderable. It possessed 12 ships of the line and 15 frigates in home waters, with five of the line and 10 frigates in the West Indies, and four of the line in the East Indies, with some seven ships of the line in reserve.[22] Although the Royal

20 Syrett, *European Waters*, p.128.

21 Dull, *French Navy and American Independence*, pp.211-213.

22 James, *The British Navy in Adversity*, p.250.

Navy was considerably overstretched already, it did have sufficient resources to mount a blockade of the Dutch coast, and if it became apparent that the Dutch fleet was preparing to make an attempt to break the blockade, it ought to be possible to transfer ships temporarily to reinforce the British units in the North Sea in time to prevent it.

However, even having faced down the threat from Russia during 1780, and with the Dutch situation having been simplified by the actual outbreak of war, the British government still remained anxious. Somewhat surprisingly, therefore, the Cabinet thought it would be desirable to buy off the Russians, and the prospect was mooted of offering Minorca as a bribe to ensure her passivity. It was not something that King George approved of; as always, he objected to any voluntary cession of territory, but the Cabinet instructed the British ambassador in St Petersburg to float the idea. Sandwich favoured this, speaking at length in support of the proposition at a Cabinet meeting of 19 January 1781, setting out the benefits that he contended would flow from such a deal. His analysis of these now appears somewhat far-fetched:

> If we agree to cede Minorca to Russia, it is expected that she shall previously engage to secure us such a peace as we can with honour and safety accept. Our colonies will return to their obedience, and this country, as before, enjoy an exclusive trade with them. We shall recover our possessions in the West Indies, and those on the continent of America that are now in the hands of Spain; and our fishery at Newfoundland will remain in the same state that was settled for it at the Peace of Paris.[23]

In the event, though, the proposal went nowhere, not least because Russia had no real interest in acquiring an island in the western Mediterranean.

23 Barnes and Owen (eds), *Private Papers of John, Earl of Sandwich*, Vol.IV, pp.23-26.

26

The Second Relief of Gibraltar

Operationally, it had become clear by the beginning of 1781 that the naval priority must be to undertake a further relief of Gibraltar, and on 1 January the Cabinet resolved on this. The expedition was to be escorted by the whole of the Channel Fleet, a plan that was acknowledged to carry with it a serious risk, since it would leave behind nothing for the protection of the coastline of England. The orders which went to Darby were based on a letter from the Secretary of State to the Admiralty recording the Cabinet's decision:

> Your lordships will require and direct [Darby] not to wait the unloading of any of the store ships or victuallers at Gibraltar, but leaving them to return to England or Ireland as opportunity may offer, avail himself of the first favourable moment to come out of the Straits of Gibraltar (taking care not to leave any of the line of battleships behind him on any account whatsoever) and to make the rest of his way into the English Channel.[1]

The risks were obvious; apart from the possibility that the French, operating from Brest, might attempt something in the Channel, or take advantage of the opportunity to send reinforcements overseas, intelligence was received on 18 January of the presence of French ships supporting some 25 Spanish ships of the line at Cadiz. The relief convoy and the Channel Fleet must pass both enemy bases to reach Gibraltar. It has, however, been suggested by Jonathan Dull that the project to relieve Gibraltar was both unwise and unnecessary:

> For such strategic ineptitude the British Cabinet could have no excuse. The blockade of Gibraltar was so loose that with a willingness to accept occasional losses it could have been replenished by unescorted merchantmen. The West Indies could have been rendered safe for an entire campaign by merely forcing de Grasse's squadron to wait until the whole Brest fleet

1 Barnes and Owen (eds), *Private Papers of John, Earl of Sandwich*, Vol.IV, p.5.

> was ready to cover his departure (for Darby hardly needed to fear the Spaniards coming so far north alone) … Even against all the ships in Brest the British could have fought in June at no worse a disadvantage than 35 ships of the line to 45.[2]

Dull's proposition is questionable; in any case the government could scarcely properly have gambled the safety of the fortress on so haphazard a means of support. In addition, it was also necessary to resupply Minorca, while the Channel Fleet could on its way southward also shield outward bound trade convoys as they travelled past the key enemy bases.

In February and March, while waiting for the Channel Fleet to set off for Gibraltar, Kempenfelt wrote a lengthy series of letters to Middleton, setting out in considerable detail his signalling system and the flags required for it. On 9 March he laid out the case for introducing a new system:

> It has been a common saying that it is an advantage to go by signals that we have been used to, and when a new set comes out, to say we have our trade to learn again. This style was very proper with respect to the different signals used by different admirals formerly, when the signals were jumbled together without form or order, and when a long acquaintance with them was necessary to find out the meaning of any signal that was made in the chaotic state in which they were. But when signals are formed upon a proper plan they require no study to comprehend them, and when a signal is made you can immediately turn to the article or order alluded to. If the greatest novice can't do this, the plan is faulty … What is good must be clear and simple.[3]

Kempenfelt went on in this letter to reflect that if he had been able to remain on shore, he would have been able to improve his system, taking into account the suggestions he had received, and his own observations. Getting approval for a new system, however, had not been a straightforward matter: 'The plan I followed in the signals I made was not that which I most approved of. That which I would have adopted – though most evidently the best – I could not get any of the admirals or officers of note to approve and countenance. I therefore followed in a great measure Lord Howe's mode, he being a popular character'.

Introducing innovation to a conservative profession was never going to be easy.

Completing the fitting out of the ships of the Channel Fleet, and assembling the convoy, took a considerable time, and it was 13 March before Darby was able to put to sea. He had with him 28 ships of the line, 10 frigates and four fire ships with

2 Dull, *French Navy and American Independence*, p.225.
3 Laughton (ed.), *Barham Papers*, Vol.I, pp.340-341.

which to escort the Gibraltar and Minorca convoy. He was obliged to call at Cork to pick up the victuallers; he arrived there on 17 March, but it was 10 days before they were able to leave port due to contrary winds. In addition to the trade convoys, he was taking with him a total of 97 merchant ships for the Mediterranean.

While Darby was held up at Cork, the French fleet under de Grasse was able to depart from Brest unmolested together with the squadron for the East Indies under Suffren. This was an event which led to considerable criticism of the Admiralty, but Admiral James notes that intelligence of the intended departure of the French fleet was probably not available.[4]

When it was finally able to get to sea, the Channel Fleet made good progress, and by 31 March was off Cape Finisterre, from where Sir John Ross, in the *Royal George*, sent a letter ahead to Eliott at Gibraltar: 'What is to become of the fleet [I] cannot at present say… We are to meet 82 sail of the Spanish fleet off Cape St Vincent'.[5] As the fleet neared its destination, it was located by three Spanish frigates, which retreated to the safety of Cadiz when approached by the *Alexander*, *Foudroyant* and *Minerva*. Pursuing them, the British ships looked into Cadiz, where the Spanish fleet was seen. Back home, the King was delighted to receive news of a possible engagement off Cape Saint Vincent, writing to Sandwich on 14 April: 'I know the justice of our cause; I know the excellence of our fleet; therefore have reason to expect success. Perhaps no country ever had, except near home, an event on which so much depends'.[6]

Yet there was to be no battle. Córdova, with 32 ships of the line at Cadiz, failed to appear. Morale in the Spanish fleet appears to have been at a low ebb. A junior officer recorded the situation as it appeared to him:

> It is six months since the King has given me as much as a quarto, and he does not think of doing it …Every evening I am ordered to take information to the Admiral as regards the daily happenings, and thus I am deprived of the sole means at my disposal to reduce my expenses, which is to remain on board ship… 22 millions have arrived and nevertheless there is not a real in the Naval Treasury nor any hope of receiving anything for a long while past. Orders have just been given to use the money in the convoy, which has lately been captured, to pay for the provisions of several captains.[7]

Quite apart from this, there seems to have been a serious doubt among those at the head of the Spanish Navy about the wisdom of attempting to engage the

4 James, *The British Navy in Adversity*, p.303.

5 Adkins and Adkins, *Gibraltar*, p.186. The quotation is reproduced as given, but the reference to 82 Spanish sail seems unlikely; the original citation is the the Gibraltar National Archive.

6 Barnes and Owen (eds), *Private Papers of John, Earl of Sandwich*, Vol.IV, p.34.

7 James, *The British Navy in Adversity*, p.304.

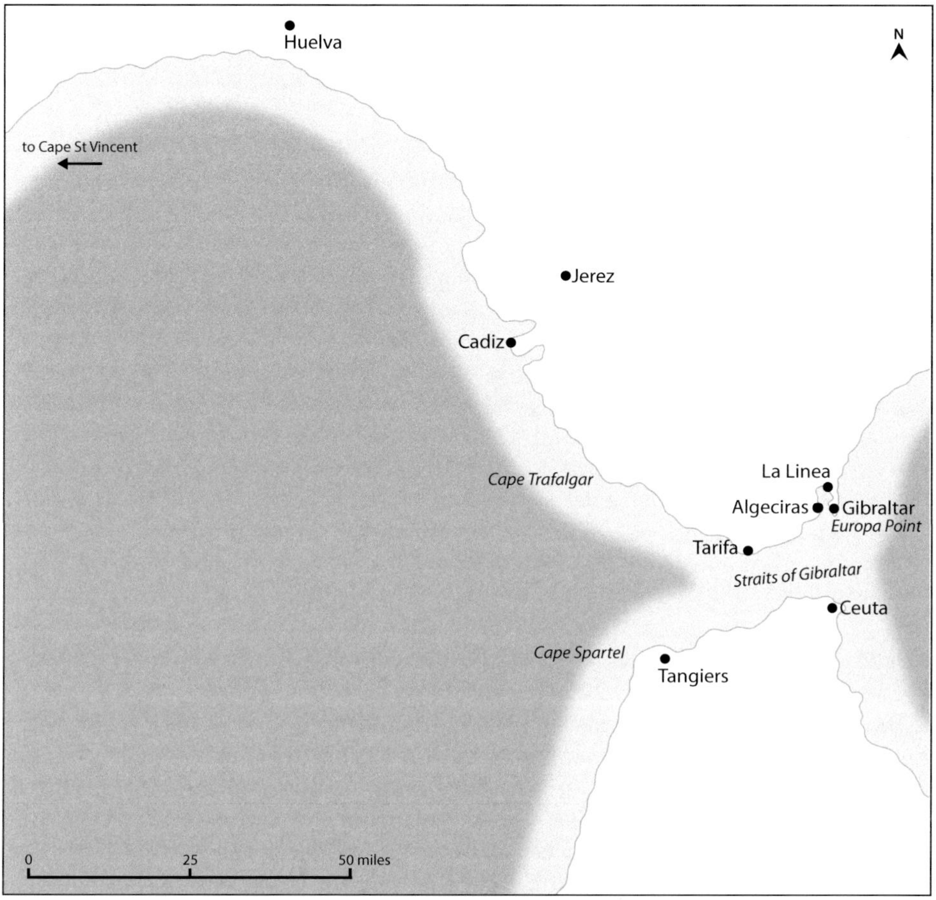

Approaches to Gibraltar.

British fleet. Admiral James quotes the opinion of one naval adviser that it would be advantageous to avoid attacking, 'for it is impossible to prevent the arrival of help to the besieged town'. Instead, the writer recommended that the fleet should be preserved so that when the British fleet left, other projects could be carried out.[8]

Darby arrived off Cape Spartel, at the entrance to the Straits of Gibraltar, on 11 April, reporting to Sandwich on that day that but for calms and fogs between Cape St Vincent and the Straits he would have made an extraordinary passage. He believed that Córdova had been at sea for two months in the immediate past,

8 James, *The British Navy in Adversity*, p.305.

which was indeed the case, the Spanish admiral having taken his fleet to sea for exercises before returning to Cadiz.

In obedience to his orders, Darby did not go inside Gibraltar Bay, but sent word ahead that he could not help much in unloading the convoy, for 'my stay will be no longer until the wind permits my re-passing the Straits'. In reply, Eliott pointed out the danger that the convoy would face from gunboats and fire ships, and urged Darby to reconsider. In his reply of 14 April, the Admiral insisted that he must take his great ships home with the first easterly wind, but agreed to leave two frigates and two cutters behind him until the transports were cleared. He reminded Eliott of the gravity of the position at home:

> You must be very sensible in what situation everyone is until the return of this squadron, and what a great risk it was, so late in the year of our sailing, to suffer us to go at all. Of course they must every day wish and expect to hear of our arrival. I am at the same time very sensible that the garrison of Gibraltar is a very grand object, or at the season we would not have been sent. But as the first is the greatest, I should not think myself by any means justifiable in breaking my instructions: therefore, cannot permit myself to leave one line of battle ship behind.[9]

As soon as he arrived at Gibraltar, Darby sent on the Minorca convoy, consisting of 13 supply ships escorted by the frigates *Flora* and *Crescent.*

In deference to Eliott's concern, Darby ordered Ross to shift his flag from the *Royal George* to a two decker, and with as many other two deckers as he thought necessary, to enter the bay to assist with the unloading and to meet the threat from the gunboats and fire ships. The rest of the fleet remained offshore; for the moment, the wind was in the west, preventing the fleet from setting off home. The Spanish not only launched attacks with a force of 15 gunboats; they had also commenced, on 12 April, a fierce bombardment of the fortress and the anchorage, which inflicted heavy damage and considerable casualties in Gibraltar town, which was set on fire in many places. In spite of this, however, the unloading went ahead. At Eliott's request, Darby also landed 2,000 barrels of gunpowder, a quantity of ships' biscuit, and all the pitch that his ships could spare.

The wind came around on 20 April, and Darby signalled to the fleet to put to sea at 9.00 a.m., although it was not finally able to get away until 5.00 p.m. It was accompanied by 40 empty victuallers, which parted company under the escort of two cutters two days later. Darby sent Jervis in the *Foudroyant* to look into Cadiz to see what he could of Córdova's fleet. Nothing was to be seen outside the port, and Darby concluded that the whole of the Spanish were certainly inside the harbour, and he continued on his way northward, reaching a point off the Scilly

9 Barnes and Owen (eds), *Private Papers of John, Earl of Sandwich*, Vol.IV, p.5.

Isles by 16 May. The relief of Gibraltar had been an efficiently conducted operation, completed as swiftly as possible; but a serious consequence of stripping the Channel completely now appeared.

In Brest, Toussaint-Guillaume La Motte-Piquet was extremely impatient to get back to sea. He had returned from America on 3 January 1781, after two years campaigning there. He wrote a number of times to the ministry urging that he be allowed to take a squadron to cruise in the Atlantic.[10] His frustration was shared by a large number of French officers, among whom it was widely believed that it would be better to send out squadrons of ships of the line to prey on British shipping, rather than frigates which experience had shown were easily picked off. La Motte-Picquet's pressure finally paid off in April, when he was successful in persuading the ministry to his view.

He sailed on 24 April with a squadron of six ships of the line: the new 100-gun *Invincible*, the *Bien-Aimé* and *Actif*, each of 74 guns, the 64-gun *Alexandre, Hardi* and *Lion*, with the frigates *Sibylle* and *Nereide* and the cutters *Chasseur* and *Levrette*. Officially, his destination was Ferrol, but he sailed out into the Atlantic in his search for British convoys. Considering that the Channel Fleet was known to be at sea, this venture was not without risk, but before long his initiative was rewarded. After cruising for a week in the Soundings, he sighted the convoy from St Eustatius carrying the booty which Admiral Rodney and Major General Vaughan had so energetically harvested there. It was escorted by Commodore William Hotham; when the French appeared, he stood little chance, having only the *Vengeance*, 74, a small frigate and two Dutch prizes encumbered with prisoners of war, to protect a convoy of 30 heavily laden merchant ships. Hotham ordered the convoy to scatter. The escorting warships, together with half a dozen merchant ships, managed to escape and reach Berehaven; the rest of the convoy, with a cargo that was estimated as worth £5 million, was taken. Lacour-Gayet wrote of La Motte-Picquet's brilliant success: 'Fortune favoured his audacity and vigilance with the greatest prize which the French had taken in the course of the war; and it brought him not only glory, but the chance to exact retribution for a gigantic act of piracy'.[11]

The British government had taken the risk of sending away the whole Channel Fleet with its eyes open. The news which reached London on 10 May that La Motte-Picquet had put to sea realised their worst fears, and an urgent message was sent to Darby to warn him. He was ordered to detach eight ships of the line to search for La Motte-Picquet and 'to cruise for the protection of the homeward bound trade'.[12] The frigates *Juno* and *Proserpine* were sent out in an effort to intercept the incoming convoy from St Eustatius and redirect it north about round Ireland and

10 Lacour-Gayet, *La marine Militaire*, p.371.

11 Lacour-Gayet, *La marine Militaire*, p.372.

12 Syrett, *European Waters*, p.142.

Scotland. It was too late, though the *Juno* later met a convoy from Jamaica and sent it north out of harm's way.

Darby had received the Admiralty's warning off the Scillies on 16 May, though by then he had already heard of the taking of Hotham's convoy. He obediently detached Digby with eight ships of the line, with orders to cruise for 14 days or until he met the incoming Jamaica convoy. When Darby arrived in the Soundings with the main body of the Channel Fleet he had missed the last of La Motte-Picquet's ships by a matter of hours. Two days earlier, the *Nonsuch*, 64, sailing ahead of the fleet, had encountered the *Actif*, chasing her all day before on the following morning engaging her for two hours. In the course of this fierce and ultimately inconclusive exchange, the *Nonsuch* suffered 90 casualties killed and wounded, and had five guns dismounted.[13]

By 15 May the Admiralty had learned that La Motte-Picquet might have as many as eight ships of the line with him, and further orders were sent to Darby: 'Their Lordships conclude that you will think it advisable to detach at least ten … Which may be done with the more safety as the force remaining with you will be greatly superior to any force the enemy may have at Brest, few of their ships, if any, being ready for the sea'.[14] When he received this message, Darby sent off two more ships of the line to join Digby, and took the rest of the Channel Fleet into port, some ships going to Plymouth and some to Spithead.

In the meantime, the threat that was apparently posed by La Motte-Picquet had caused particular alarm at Plymouth, where it was again proposed to construct a boom to prevent enemy vessels forcing their way into the Hamoaze. It was a suggestion which Middleton, once again, dismissed out of hand, writing to Sandwich on 18 May: 'The gentlemen at Plymouth seem to be out of their senses, and unless the Admiralty put an immediate stop to their proceedings, the works of the yard will be at a stand. It is ships and not booms that we are in want of at present'.[15] The First Lord agreed, and wrote a tactful letter to Shuldham at Plymouth to suggest that he was 'rather too hasty' in his apprehension of the danger from La Motte-Picquet; on the contrary, he said, it would be most fortunate if the French admiral did come into the Channel with Darby on his back, 'as he must fall into our hands with his whole squadron'. A boom, he said, was not necessary; and its construction would suggest both to the nation and the enemy that attempts on British ports were more practicable than they really were.

The Admiralty was in a decidedly nervous state. On 19 May it had a further alarm, with news that *Chef d'Escadre* the Marquis de Vaudreuil might have sailed from Brest with eight more ships of the line to join La Motte-Picquet. Orders went off to Darby that he was to stay out with as many of the ships of the Channel

13 Lacour-Gayet, *La marine Militaire*, p.372.

14 Barnes and Owen (eds), *Private Papers of John, Earl of Sandwich*, Vol.IV, p.8.

15 Barnes and Owen (eds), *Private Papers of John, Earl of Sandwich*, Vol.IV, p.37.

Fleet that were a fit state to do so, or to reinforce Digby sufficiently for him to outnumber La Motte-Picquet and Vaudreuil combined. By the time that this order actually reached Darby, he had gone ashore on leave, but he sent down an order for six ships of the line to put to sea to join Digby. This order was countermanded when the Admiralty realised that the news about Vaudreuil was a false alarm. Digby returned with his force to Spithead on 4 June.

Having by the relief expedition to Gibraltar exposed home waters to enemy operations, with the consequence that de Grasse and Suffren were able to depart from Brest without interference, and that the St Eustatius convoy was lost, the government was throughout the summer of 1781 on the back foot. The prospect of the separate parts of the Combined Fleet uniting and threatening British trade convoys haunted the Cabinet, and the Admiralty sent out a stream of orders in an effort to anticipate the threat that might at any time materialise.

On 2 June the Cabinet decided that Darby's fleet should consist of 26 ships of the line, and that as soon as 20 of them were fit for service he should go to sea. Sandwich hoped that Kempenfelt would continue as Captain of the Fleet, but this was not to be. Kempenfelt had gone ashore, very unwell, as he explained to Sandwich on 6 June:

> My declining to serve at present is not a matter of the will or choice. It is a matter of necessity arising from the very low and ill state of health I am in, which has been gradually increasing upon me for some months, and which at present totally disqualifies me from executing any charge. Country air and exercise is the only thing I know that promises to restore me, which if it effects, my services then shall be at your Lordship's command.[16]

Anxious as always to look after his friend's interests, Middleton on the same day wrote to Sandwich to suggest that when Kempenfelt's health permitted he should be given 'now and then the command of ships sent from the Western Squadron on detached services. The opportunity of exercising his own signals, and distinguishing himself otherwise, will naturally be agreeable to him'. Confining him to a post of drudgery, Middleton thought, would 'naturally cool the zeal of a less discerning man'. Middleton added that his desire was 'to secure the friendship of so able an officer to your Lordship's interest'.[17]

Darby put to sea on 9 June, his objective being the protection of trade. He told the Admiralty that he planned to take up a position 20 or 30 leagues west of the Scillies. The Jamaica convoy had already been intercepted and sent north about; on 17 June Darby met the Leeward Islands convoy, and escorted it safely into the Channel. He had not waited until he had the suggested 20 ships of the line, sailing

16 Barnes and Owen (eds), *Private Papers of John, Earl of Sandwich*, Vol.IV, p.43.

17 Barnes and Owen (eds), Private Papers of John, Earl of Sandwich, Vol.IV, p.44.

with only nine; three more subsequently joined him. There was a lot going on. Hotham, in Ireland, was ordered to make his way to England with the rump of his original convoy and another from the Carolinas, under the protection of Darby's frigates, while in addition to covering the other convoys already mentioned, outgoing convoys destined for the West Indies and North America were preparing to sail. Darby, though, was doubtful if he would be able to keep the sea for long, as the incidence of scurvy in the fleet was increasing. By 4 July, when he was off the Lizard, he reported that because many of his ships had spent so little time in port they would be 'useless for want of men'. On 7 July the Channel Fleet was forced into Torbay from whence it proceeded to Spithead.[18]

In the relationship between France and Spain, there was a good deal of mistrust, and agreement between them as to the naval operations to be conducted in 1781 had been hard to come by. French proposals for the campaign, both in European waters and overseas, were contained in a memoir prepared by the Ministry of Marine over the signature of a new minister. Sartine had been replaced in October 1780 by the Marquis de Castries; his fall was in part due to the machinations of Jacques Necker, the new finance minister, who disliked him and wished to reshape the composition of the *Conseil d'Etat,* and in part due to the fact that the Spanish unfairly regarded Sartine as blameworthy for the allied failures at sea. It has been suggested that he was regarded as expendable because the talented Fleurieu was still available at the ministry, and that Vergennes and Maurepas were well experienced in the conduct of the war.[19]

Castries was a military man, but he was an able and forceful administrator, and well regarded by the French naval officer corps. His proposals for 1781 were sent by Vergennes to Montmorin in mid-February. For the operations in European waters, they effectively gave Spain the choice between mounting a fresh invasion attempt or blockading the entrance to the Channel while a major expedition to the West Indies was mounted. At the beginning of March Floridablanca suggested an attack on Minorca; the capture of the island had always been high on the Spanish government's wish list. The Spanish went ahead at Cadiz with preparations for this, although without actually acknowledging to Montmorin what these were for. Meanwhile in order to reassemble the Combined Fleet, the French had agreed to send de Guichen from Brest to Cadiz.

De Guichen sailed with eighteen ships of the line on 22 June, arriving at Cadiz on 6 July. It was agreed that the Combined Fleet should put to sea to ensure the security of the convoy carrying the troops on Minorca, and it did so on 21 July with no less than 49 ships of the line, taking up a position in the Atlantic to prevent any British attempt to interfere. The Minorca expedition sailed two days later, carrying some 7,500 troops under the Duc de Crillon aboard 85 transports

18 Syrett, *European Waters*, p.143.

19 Dull, *French Navy and American Independence*, pp.200-201.

escorted by two ships of the line and six frigates.[20] Once it was safely through the Straits of Gibraltar, de Guichen and Córdova decided to take the Combined Fleet north to the western approaches of the Channel, where it would be well placed to intercept both inbound and outbound convoys.

None of this was known to the British Admiralty, or to Darby, who was engaged in replenishing his fleet. In reply to urgings from the Admiralty to go back to sea as soon as he could, Darby pointed out that the fleet had been in port barely a week, and that in any case it had been so hurried out previously that many ships had gone to sea with their reprovisioning incomplete. As it was, the wind had been against them, so that they could not have got to the westward. He finally sailed on 19 July, taking with him a small squadron under Digby which was to sail to North America, which he was ordered to escort to a position as far as 150 leagues west of the Lizard, after which he was to seek de Guichen's fleet, which was supposed to be covering the departure from France of a squadron of four ships of the line and 80 transports heading for the East Indies. Darby parted from Digby some 94 leagues west of the Lizard, and hurried south to take up his station off Cape Finisterre, which he reached on 2 August. He cruised there for two weeks, at times stretching some 30 leagues out into the Atlantic.[21]

For once, the Admiralty had been totally let down by its intelligence sources, no word of the sailing of the Combined Fleet having reached London. The first intimation of its movements came when one of Darby's frigates spoke with a Portuguese merchantman on the evening of 16 August. This reported seeing about 40 French and Spanish ships of the line two days earlier, about 200 miles to the north, apparently steering for the Channel. Darby discussed this news with Ross and Elliott, and sent off a sloop to notify the Admiralty while himself turning north. It was evident to him that if he encountered the enemy he would be heavily outnumbered, as he wrote to Sandwich on 17 August: 'From their strength you will likewise judge it highly necessary to reinforce the squadron greatly. The whole of us are at present altogether; and I do not doubt, if I find it necessary, that we shall be able to out sail all those who are not coppered'.[22]

On his way north Darby had no further news of the Combined Fleet, leading him to conjecture that it had put into port. Sandwich and the Admiralty, when they heard the news of the enemy, did not at first believe that the Combined Fleet was really in the approaches to the Channel, since the intelligence which they did have suggested that it was still somewhere near Gibraltar. Darby made for Torbay, where he arrived on 25 August. The first order sent by the Admiralty to Darby there was to the effect that he should put to sea again at once to cover the arrival of an extremely valuable convoy from Jamaica.

20 Dull, *French Navy and American Independence*, p.234.

21 Barnes and Owen (eds), *Private Papers of John, Earl of Sandwich*, Vol.IV, p.11.

22 Barnes and Owen (eds), *Private Papers of John, Earl of Sandwich*, Vol.IV, p.49.

Darby, however, did not comply with this order. When he arrived at Torbay, mindful of the enemy's great superiority in numbers, he took up a defensive position which he described in a letter to Sandwich on 4 September:

> In my last letter to your Lordship, mentioned in a light way our situation, which has been ever since the day after we arrived here in the form of a crescent in two lines, the three-decks in the outer one and two-deckers within to haul in between the intervals of the three-deck ships, which makes us such a line of fire that it would be a happy thing was the enemy to attack us here while the wind continued to the westward.[23]

Darby's disobedience was entirely prudent, although he conceded that if the Combined Fleet was to pass him sailing to the eastward and anchor at St Helens he would have to make the tricky passage to Spithead through the Needles.

It was a dangerous moment. A very large outbound convoy for North America was assembled in Cork, which was a poorly defended harbour; several valuable inbound convoys were expected daily; and the Combined Fleet was double the strength of the Channel Fleet. Darby wisely sent out frigates to seek out and warn the incoming trade even before the Admiralty issued him orders to do so, when it accepted his decision to remain in his defensive position at Torbay. It was not long before positive news of the Combined Fleet began to arrive; several neutral merchantmen reported sighting it west of the Scillies, and on 30 August the *Agamemnon*, 64, sighted the Combined Fleet 30 leagues west of the Lizard. Her captain had taken her close enough to count the enemy fleet, putting its strength at between 44 and 47 ships of the line, before hastening with the news to Plymouth. In London, meanwhile, fresh intelligence had now been received confirming the Combined Fleet's presence in the Channel with a force estimated at 49 ships of the line.[24]

From Torbay, Mulgrave wrote to Sandwich on 31 August. He was unhappy about the situation of the Channel Fleet. Although it was perfectly safe where it was, he thought that if the Combined Fleet sailed up Channel it would be 'a very mad attempt' to go through the Needles, 'as should the wind fail or shift the ships might go onshore, not being able to anchor'. He speculated that the enemy might be contemplating a detachment of ships to give them superiority in the North Sea. Alternatively, if their aim was to intercept the incoming convoys, the Channel Fleet could not prevent this while it was securely anchored at Torbay.[25]

At this time, Sandwich was not short of advice as to what should be done. The King, hearing a rumour that de Guichen might be detached with 14 ships of the

23 Barnes and Owen (eds), *Private Papers of John, Earl of Sandwich*, Vol.IV, p.60.

24 Syrett, *European Waters*, p.146.

25 Barnes and Owen (eds), *Private Papers of John, Earl of Sandwich*, Vol.IV, pp.50-51.

line to attack Cork, thought that in that case Darby would be strong enough to beat the rest of the Combined Fleet without waiting for reinforcements. Mulgrave, meanwhile, wrote again to Sandwich on 3 September; if the convoy was exposed to serious risk, he rather diffidently had a suggestion to make:

> If the enemy's fleet consists of forty three or forty seven sail of the line, nineteen of which at least I suppose to be coppered, I doubt much whether we could make head against them for such a defensive battle as would secure the convoy, as they would have sufficient force to fight us with superiority and detach a considerable number to attack the convoy. I have an idea that could this fleet be got between the enemy and the convoy, great use might be made of it and the convoy perhaps be secured, but this cannot be done and ought not to be attempted unless the commander has confidence in his own power of doing it.[26]

Mulgrave thought, though, that the suggestion of such a risky stroke should be put forward from the Admiralty, and that Darby should not know that it originated from him.

Middleton, too, had proposals to make, writing to Sandwich on 5 September to stress the advantage possessed by an inferior fleet of coppered ships:

> If coppered ships, meeting with squadrons or convoys of the enemy, will instead of attack wait for opportunities, they will from circumstances of negligence and weather be sure to meet with them and generally have it in their power to turn them to advantage. Such commanders as are afraid to adopt this Fabian plan are unfit to command a coppered squadron.[27]

This advice appeared to the Cabinet to be the best strategy to adopt, and at a meeting of 6 September it was agreed that Darby should put to sea at once, and seek out the enemy, looking for opportunities to pick off detachments or separated ships while making the most of the advantage that his copper bottomed ships gave him to avoid an engagement with a superior force. Darby, meanwhile, reported on 9 September that Kempenfelt was to hoist his flag in the *Victory* as third in command. He was, he said, 'happy in having him in any shape, but the nearer would have been most agreeable'. In the meantime he would give some thought, he said, to the question of appointing a new Captain of the Fleet. He told the First Lord that he was very conscious of the difficult task which he faced in putting to sea 'with half the force the enemy has, with that to protect and convoy two large fleets of trade, at the same time to prevent a descent upon Ireland'. He was

26 Barnes and Owen (eds), *Private Papers of John, Earl of Sandwich*, Vol.IV, pp.55-58.
27 Barnes and Owen (eds), *Private Papers of John, Earl of Sandwich*, Vol.IV, pp.61-62.

pessimistic about the likely outcome: 'From the circumstances of the difference between the two fleets I own that I am doubtful of being able to do any one thing'.[28]

Two days later, as the Channel Fleet was on the point of sailing, Mulgrave wrote to the First Lord a letter which was rather more reassuring. He told Sandwich that he might be perfectly satisfied with everything; there was 'a manliness and plain firm sense about Admiral Darby that will make him do everything for the best'. He was glad that in the event he had not taken Kempenfelt to be his Captain of the Fleet: 'It would have had an appearance of his being managed, which, if it really existed, would have been for the worse. Kempenfelt will command a division well'.[29]

The Channel Fleet did not get away from Torbay until 14 September, but by then in fact the threat from the Combined Fleet had ceased to exist. Córdova, who was nominally in command of the Combined Fleet as the senior officer, reckoned that once it had reached Ushant it had completed its mission, which he saw solely as being to ensure that there was no interference with the Minorca expedition. During the course of a council of war convened to discuss the possibility of attacking Darby as he lay in Torbay, de Guichen argued strongly in favour, but Córdova, remembering the past failure, was dead against it. The third in command of the Spanish fleet, Don Vincent Dos, supported de Guichen, but on the other hand de Beausset opposed it, pointing out the technical difficulties involved in an attack upon a line of anchored ships. Instead, he advocated a war on trade; but in the event, nothing at all was done. De Guichen had a continuing anxiety about the safety of a convoy departing for North America under Monteil, but on 5 September the fleets separated, Córdova heading south for Cadiz, and de Guichen returning to Brest; discouraged and ill, the French admiral gave up command of the fleet for the time being.[30]

Darby learned of the retreat of the Combined Fleet on 19 September, and this enabled him to send home a number of ships that badly needed dockyard attention. He remained at sea for the protection of trade until all the incoming convoys had passed safely up Channel, and then returned home, anchoring at Spithead on 5 November, after a cruise that had lasted 52 days.

28 Barnes and Owen (eds), *Private Papers of John, Earl of Sandwich*, Vol.IV, pp.63-64.

29 Barnes and Owen (eds), *Private Papers of John, Earl of Sandwich*, Vol.IV, p.65.

30 Lacour-Gayet, *La marine Militaire*, p.376.

27

The War in the North Sea

The need to maximise the strength of the Channel Fleet for operations against the French inevitably meant that there were few ships to spare with which to oppose the Dutch in the North Sea. Nevertheless, the Dutch trade in naval stores in particular remained a crucial target for the Royal Navy, and it was essential that an effective blockade of the Dutch coast be mounted. In addition, although the Dutch fleet was not powerful, it was still capable of threatening British trade convoys, which therefore required constant protection.

Before the outbreak of war, the views of Sir Joseph Yorke, the British ambassador to the Netherlands, were sought as to the best means of striking at the Dutch. Consideration had been given to launching an attack on the Dutch navy and its bases, but Yorke advised against this, due to the shallowness of the waters at the Texel which made it more or less secure: 'It would be much more effective to blockade the ports, seize as many as possible of the vessels of the Republic in the open sea and attack her especially in the West Indies, where immediate action should be taken because the West Indies possessions were her goldmine'.[1]

Immediately after war with the Dutch had been declared, Sandwich received a number of applications for the command of any squadron that might be assembled for service in the North Sea, including from Rear Admiral Sir John Ross and Captain the Hon. Keith Stewart. The First Lord preferred the latter; but for the moment he made no appointment, as he wrote to Stewart to explain on 10 January 1781: 'We have no ships at present disposable for that station, and as it is impossible to say as yet when we shall ... I must avoid for a little time longer the binding myself down to any engagement'. In addition, he noted that Ross would be gone to sea in a fortnight, and he thought it better not to decide the matter finally 'till he has left the land'.[2] Stewart was one of a considerable number of Scottish officers in the navy; an enduring feature of personal relationships within the service was

1 F. Edler, *The Dutch Republic and the American Revolution* (Baltimore, Md: Johns Hopkins Press, 1911), p.181.
2 Barnes and Owen (eds), *Private Papers of John, Earl of Sandwich*, Vol.IV, pp.83-84.

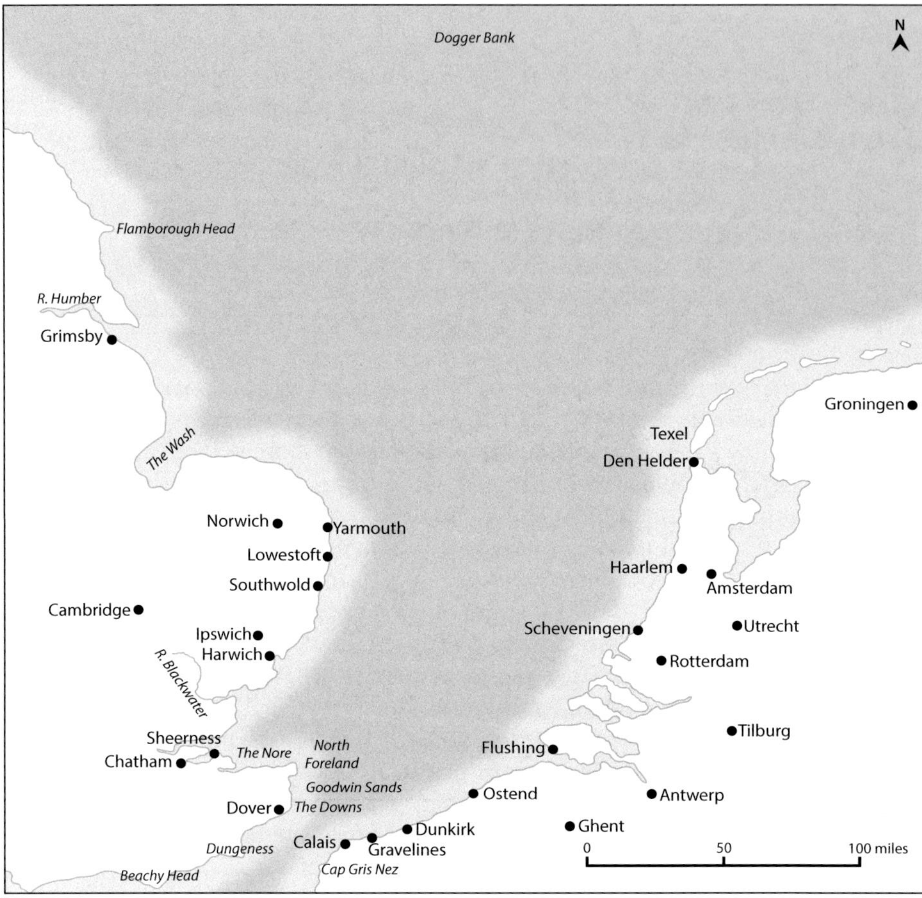

The North Sea.

that many of their English colleagues felt a considerable dislike for them. Stewart, in command of the *Berwick,* 74, had seen a good deal of action during the war. He had been present at the battle of Ushant, serving with the Channel Fleet during 1779, and in the West Indies in 1780.[3]

On 17 February the Cabinet decided to send a small force of troops and artillery to the Shetlands, noting that it would be expedient to have a naval force based there 'for annoying the enemy's trade and fisheries and defending our own'. Stewart was in due course appointed to command a small squadron, hoisting his pennant as a commodore. It consisted of the *Berwick*, 74, with seven frigates and

3 James, *The British Navy in Adversity*, pp.432-440.

four cutters. The *Berwick* and four of the frigates were initially deployed cruising off the Shetlands; one frigate and a cutter cruised to the north of the Firth of Forth and two frigates and a cutter covered the East Coast as far south as Yarmouth.

It was not long before the British blockade of the Netherlands began to have a severe effect on Dutch seaborne trade. It also inflicted increasing damage on the national economy. By August 1781 the effect had been so great that an intelligence report which reached the British Admiralty reported that 'the harbour of Amsterdam was like a desert, and nothing going forward either hostile or mercantile'.[4] Long before this, it had become apparent to the Dutch that their navy must be called on to make a major effort to try to break the British stranglehold.

In March, there were indications that the Dutch were now planning a substantial operation to protect their trade. Stewart wrote to the First Lord on 16 March 'There is great reason to believe that the Dutch mean to employ four or five two deck ships and a considerable number of frigates to cruise off Shetland for the protection of their India trade and their ships bound to Holland, coming north about'.[5] Stewart reckoned, though, that they probably would not be out until mid-May, so that there was plenty of time to arrange for the addition of the obviously necessary reinforcement. When the news came that the Dutch were indeed putting to sea, it caused the King some alarm, as he wrote to Sandwich on 15 May:

> I, you know, have ever since Vice Admiral Darby sailed, thought that Vice-Admiral [Hyde] Parker ought to be at Spithead ready to proceed with the ships there. Now the Dutch ships are out, if they have the smallest activity, they may do some mischief before he can, as he is only now setting out from Portsmouth to collect the ships for sea. The old proverb of shutting the stable door when the steed is stolen rather resembles this manoeuvre.[6]

Hyde Parker, who had only lately returned in a fury from the West Indies after what he considered his grossly unfair treatment by Rodney following the Battle of Martinique, was an admiral of whom Sandwich had a good opinion, and he was quickly appointed to command the squadron being assembled to deal with the Dutch. It was not, however, a very impressive force of which he took command, as Mahan observed:

> The British vessels, besides being of different rates, were chiefly very old ships, dragged out from Rotten Row to meet the pressing emergency caused by the greatly superior forces which were in coalition against Great Britain. Owing to the decayed condition of some of them, their batteries

4 Syrett, *European Waters*, pp.129-130.

5 Barnes and Owen (eds), *Private Papers of John, Earl of Sandwich*, Vol.IV, p.85.

6 Barnes and Owen (eds), *Private Papers of John, Earl of Sandwich*, Vol.IV, p.87.

'Sir Hyde Parker Bart. Vice Admiral of the Blue Squadron of His Majesty's Fleet; Commander in Chief of His Majesty's Ships at St. Lucia, the 25th of March 1780; And on the Dogger Bank, the 5th of August 1781'. Mezzotint by Charles Townley after George Romney. (Anne S.K. Brown Collection

> had been lightened, to the detriment of their fighting power. Two of them, however, were good and new seventy fours.[7]

The squadron consisted of the *Princess Amelia*, 80, *Fortitude*, 74 (flag), *Bienfaisant*, 64, *Buffalo*, 60, *Preston*, 50, *Dolphin*, 44 and the *Alert* sloop. Parker was subsequently joined by Stewart, in the *Berwick*, together with his frigates.

7 Mahan, *Major Operations*, pp.189-190.

When Hyde Parker was given his instructions, on 31 May, his first duty was stated to be the protection of an immense convoy bound for the Baltic, part of which was sailing from the Nore under the escort of the frigates *Latona*, 38 (commanded by the admiral's son Captain Sir Hyde Parker), *Cleopatra*, 32, and *Tartar*, 28. The remaining part was assembled at the Firth of Forth, and was to be convoyed by the *Artois*, 40, and the *Leith* armed ship. Once the convoy had passed Elsinore, Parker was to return to Scotland, covering the incoming convoy from the Baltic.

Parker was able to leave the Nore on 5 June with the convoy from that port, and escorted it northward, but was then obliged by bad weather to make for the Firth of Forth, which he reached on 10 June. He finally got away from there with the whole of the Baltic trade on 27 June, departing before a letter arrived from the Admiralty to warn him that the Dutch were expected to be at sea, and to tell him that Stewart had been instructed to join his force.

When he reached Elsinore on 3 July, Parker sent the *Latona*, *Artois*, *Leith* and a cutter through the Sound to escort the convoy into the Baltic, and then cruised with the rest of his squadron off the Skaw. Stewart joined him on 16 July with the *Berwick*, *Belle Poule* and *Tartar*. Stewart had spent most of June in looking out for the Jamaica and St Eustatius convoys, which the Admiralty had hoped had evaded the enemy and made their way around the north of Scotland to be out of harm's way. By 21 June, when he had hoped to send a frigate to cruise off the Norwegian coast, all Stewart's frigates were short of water, while the *Berwick*'s provisions were also very low. On 14 July he had heard of three Dutch East Indiamen having got into a Norwegian port, and eight more were expected to be in the vicinity, but in response to the direct order which he had received from the Admiralty he at once gave up what had looked like a very promising lead and set off to join Parker. When he reported to the First Lord on the activities of his squadron, Stewart was evidently uncomfortable about his lack of any positive achievement. He wrote, he said, 'lest the bad success which has attended the squadron put under my command should be attributed to any misconduct, negligence or want of activity'. He added that he hoped that he would soon be sent back to his northern station.[8]

The frigates that had been sent into the Baltic re-joined Parker's squadron on 28 July, bringing with them the homebound trade, consisting of around 120 sail. Next day Parker received hard intelligence from the Admiralty to the effect that a Dutch squadron had sailed from the Texel on 18 July escorting a convoy consisting of ships bound both for the East Indies and for North America, which it was to see safely clear of the Orkneys before returning. Parker was accordingly ordered, once he had passed the Texel, to send his convoy on, escorted by a frigate, and then to cruise with the rest of his squadron to intercept the Dutch squadron on its return to Holland. He was also informed that the *Sampson*, 64, *Apollo*, 32, and *Myrmidon*,

8 Barnes and Owen (eds), *Private Papers of John, Earl of Sandwich*, Vol.IV, pp.91-92.

22, were to join him from the Gunfleet. Parker sent there an order to Captain Dickson of the *Sampson* to join him at a prescribed rendezvous, but Dickson, who had reached the Gunfleet on 31 July, did not receive this until 7 August.

The Admiralty letter told Parker that the Dutch squadron consisted of one 74, one 64, one 60, three 50s, a 44, a 40, four 32s, a 28 and a cutter. This gave him some idea of the force which he was likely to meet, though in its details it was far from accurate. The Dutch squadron, which was commanded by *Schout-bij-nacht* (equating to rear admiral) Johan Arnold Zoutman, in fact consisted of six ships of the line and a heavy frigate together with 10 more frigates and sloops. The convoy which Zoutman was to escort consisted of 70 merchant ships some of which were destined for the Baltic, and the rest to go further afield by way of the northern passage out of the North Sea. Zoutman finally put to sea on 1 August.

The news that the Dutch were out led Parker to remain with his convoy for the moment. Early on the morning of 5 August he came in sight of Zoutman's squadron and his convoy, roughly halfway between the Texel and the Skaw, on the edge of the Dogger Bank. Parker immediately sent his convoy away under the escort of several of his frigates and smaller vessels, and formed line of battle. This was led by Stewart in the *Berwick*, followed by the *Dolphin* and *Buffalo*. Next came Parker with his flag in the *Fortitude*, and then the *Princess Amelia*, *Preston* and *Bienfaisant*. Zoutman, meanwhile, was also forming line of battle, keeping his convoy for the moment under his lee. The Dutch were led by the *Erfprins*, 54, followed by the *Admiraal Generaal*, 74, the *Argo*, 40, and the *Batavier*, 54. Zoutman's flag was aboard the *Admiraal de Ruijter*, 68, which came next and the line was then completed by the *Piet Hein*, 54 and *Holland*, 64. Thus each admiral had seven ships in his line. There was a fresh north-easterly breeze, but the sea was smooth. The Dutch calmly awaited the British attack as Parker's squadron bore down. Parker was in a combative mood; it is said that when told the strength of the opposing squadron, he replied, pulling up his breeches: 'It matters little what their force is; we must fight them if they are double the number'.[9] His first signal was to order a general chase with a view to bringing on the action as soon as possible. Each of his ships set as much sail as they could, the slowest sailers being obliged to set their studding sails in order to keep up. Mahan suggested that Parker's belligerence owed something to his resentment about Rodney's comments, and also to the Admiralty's previous criticism of him while he had been temporarily in command in the Leeward Islands for failing to attack French islands.

At 6:10 a.m., with the squadron running fast before the wind, Parker signalled the squadron to take up line abreast, in order to be able to bring his ships into more regular order, the leading ships taking in sail to allow the slower vessels to catch up. Neither squadron fired a shot as they closed. At 7.36 a.m. Parker hoisted the

9 Mahan, *Major Operations*, p.190.

signal for battle. Zoutman was quite as pugnacious and ready for a fight as Parker; a British observer described the Dutch squadron as they closed:

> They appeared to be in great order; and their hammocks, quartercloths etc were spread in as nice order as if for show in harbour. Their marines also were well drawn up, and stood with their muskets shouldered, with all the regularity and exactness of a review. Their politeness ought to be remembered by every man in our line; for, as if certain of what happened, we came down almost end on upon their broadsides; yet did not the Dutch admiral fire a gun, or make the signal to engage, till the red flag was at the *Fortitude*'s masthead, and her shot finding their way into his ship. This was a manoeuvre for which Admiral Zoutman should not be warmly thanked by their High Mightinesses; as he had it in his power to have done infinite mischief to our fleet, coming down in that unofficer-like manner. Having suffered Admiral Parker to place himself as he pleased, he calmly waited till the signal was hoisted on board the *Fortitude*, and at the same time we saw the signal going up on board Admiral Zoutman's ship.[10]

Aboard the *Berwick*, a pilot was told to assist in laying her close to the leading Dutch ship. 'By close, do you mean about a ship's breadth?' he asked, and, in fact, neither squadron fired until 'within half a musket shot'.[11] It was at this point that Parker fell into error. His flagship, the *Fortitude*, was fourth in the British line, but Zoutman's flagship was in fifth position. Parker, seeking according to tradition to engage his opponent's flagship, accordingly made for the *Admiraal de Ruijter*, which meant that the *Bienfaisant* at the end of the British line had for the moment no opponent, while the *Dolphin* and *Buffalo* were engaged by three of the Dutch ships.

Once firing became general, the British and Dutch ships engaged each other at point-blank range, inflicting considerable damage. Stewart, at the head of the line, gained the upper hand over the less powerful *Erfprins*, but could not take advantage of this, the *Berwick* being crippled aloft. Following him, the *Dolphin* and the *Buffalo* were also disabled, and forced out of action. The *Princess Amelia* meanwhile was fiercely supporting the *Fortitude* as she engaged Zoutman's flagship.[12] Having at 10.43 a.m. re-hoisted the signal for line ahead after some three hours' fighting, Parker at 11.00 a.m. made sail aboard the *Fortitude*, and followed by the three rearmost ships passed between the *Buffalo* and the enemy. As he did so, there was a heavy exchange of fire with the Dutch ships. Parker had been endeavouring

10 Mahan, *Major Operations*, p.191.

11 Mahan, *Major Operations*, p.191.

12 Barnes and Owen (eds), *Private Papers of John, Earl of Sandwich*, Vol.IV, p.20.

The British and Dutch lines at Dogger Bank; Parker's fleet coming into action from the left of the image. Engraving by J. Weuyster. (Rijksmuseum)

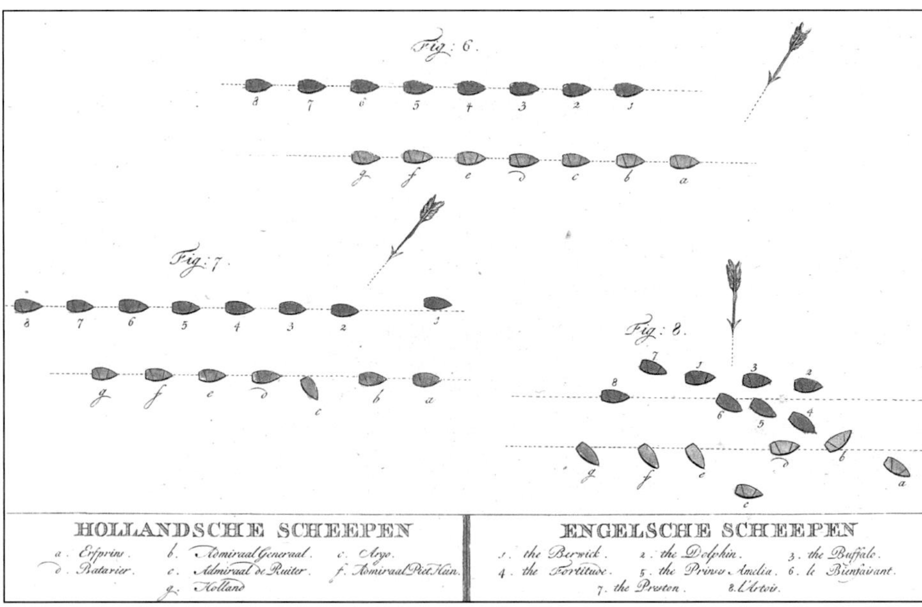

Positions of the Dutch and English Ships at the Battle of Dogger Bank. Contemporary engraved plan. (Rijksmuseum)

The end of the action at Dogger Bank. Engraving by J. Weuyster. (Rijksmuseum)

to re-form his line of battle, but as he wrote in his subsequent report: 'I made an effort to form the line, in order to renew the action, but found it impracticable'. Accordingly, he ordered his squadron to wear, and this then brought the action to an end.[13]

It was now about noon. Both sides had suffered severe damage in the hard fought engagement. In his report to the Admiralty, Parker wrote: 'The enemy appeared to be in as bad condition. Both squadrons lay to a considerable time near each other, when the Dutch, with their convoy, bore away for the Texel. We were not in a condition to follow them'.[14] Zoutman took his squadron and his convoy back home; he reported that 'on all vessels officers and men had shown great courage and had fought like lions'.[15] Parker's convoy meanwhile duly made a safe landfall at the Nore.

Sandwich, when he reported to the King on the outcome of the battle, identified one of its features from which a tactical lesson might be learned for fleet actions, particularly when a relatively small squadron was engaged, observing that the English frigates were not engaged, though some of the Dutch frigates had been. The small two-deckers *Dolphin* and *Preston* had been deployed in Parker's line of battle, but no British frigate took any part in the action notwithstanding that the *Latona*, which mounted 38 guns, and the *Artois*, with 40 guns, were the equal

13 Mahan, *Major Operations*, p.192.

14 Mahan, *Major Operations*, p.192.

15 Edler, *Dutch Republic and the American Revolution*, p.192.

of the Dutch *Argo*, which also carried 40 guns and which had been included by Zoutman in his battle line. On the other hand, the smaller frigates *Bellona* and *Dolfijn* did support the Dutch van when it was hard pressed. Reviewing this, the editors of Sandwich's papers commented:

> In similar circumstances, when the *Berwick* drove to leeward and the *Dolphin* and *Buffalo* had to haul up out of action, the British frigates outside the line would have proved invaluable had they been called upon for service. It must have galled Sir Hyde to lie by idly, watching his father fight two or three Dutchmen at once, and McBride of the *Artois*, and for that matter Philip Patton, whose *Belle Poule*[16] was fully equal to the *Bellona* and should have smothered the little *Dolfijn*.[17]

Tactically, it had been drawn battle. The British casualties amounted to 104 men killed and 339 wounded; the Dutch lost 142 killed and 403 wounded. On his way back to port, Zoutman lost the *Holland*, 64, which sank as a result of the damage she had sustained. Next day the *Belle Poule* found her lying in 22 fathoms, with her top masts still showing above the water, with a pennant still flying.[18] Mahan in his account of the action noted that the casualties suffered were nearly as great as at the Battle of Ushant, where 30 ships fought on each side, or at the Battle of Martinique, a few months earlier, when the British had 20 ships of the line; and greater than would prove to be the case at the Chesapeake later in 1781: 'This was a most satisfactory exhibition of valour, and a most unsatisfactory battle; magnificent, but not war'.[19]

Returning home, Parker met *Sampson* and her two frigates off Yarmouth, and sent them with four of the frigates from his own squadron to cruise off the Dutch coast under the command of his son in the *Latona*. With the rest of his squadron, the admiral proceeded to the Nore, where he was told that he would meet the King, who intended to visit the squadron to offer his congratulations. Parker told Sandwich that he was 'most truly sensible of this distinguished mark of his Majesty's royal approbation'. This did not, however, inhibit him when he met the King. Always outspoken, he did not mince his words, and had much to say about the quality of the ships with which he had been expected to fight the Dutch: 'I wish your Majesty better ships and younger officers. For myself, I am now too old for service'.[20] No rewards were given to the British squadron; but the States General in the Netherlands responded very differently: 'Zoutman was promoted

16 The *Belle Poule* had been captured by the ship of the line *Nonsuch* in July 1780 and was taken into the Royal Navy. As was usually the case, her original name was left unchanged.

17 Barnes and Owen (eds), *Private Papers of John, Earl of Sandwich*, Vol.IV, p.20.

18 Syrett, *European Waters*, p.131.

19 Mahan, *Major Operations*, p.193.

20 Mahan, *Major Operations*, p.193.

Johan Arnold Zoutman. Oil on canvas by Cornelis van Cuylenburgh. (Rijksmuseum)

and presented with a gold sword, and nearly all the junior officers received some mark of appreciation such as permission to wear gold epaulettes on one shoulder. Medals were struck and the men received two months' pay'.[21] Reporting to the United States Congress, John Adams told of the huge enthusiasm among the people of Amsterdam, where the battle was regarded as a 'glorious victory' for the Dutch.[22]

Notwithstanding his suggestion that he was too old to serve, Parker was offered and accepted the command in the East Indies. He sailed from England later in the

21 James, *The British Navy in Adversity*, p.312.

22 Edler, *Dutch Republic and the American Revolution*, p.192.

year aboard the *Cato*, 50, to take up his post, but never arrived; the vessel was lost at sea and nothing more was heard of her.

In the North Sea, where Stewart was now in command, there would be no more engagements with the Dutch fleet. Nor were any convoys sent out from Dutch ports for the rest of the year. Nevertheless, it was still considered necessary to maintain a respectable force in the North Sea to deal with what was seen as a continuing threat. Off the Texel on 11 September McBride, in the *Artois*, sailed close in to the Texel, and reported to Sandwich that he had seen seven ships of the line from 68 to 54 guns, one of 44 guns, five of 38 to 34 guns, a small frigate and a schooner, as well as armed East Indiamen, while inside the Texel he saw another ship of the line, four frigates and two smaller vessels. He commented: 'Your Lordship may depend upon it that no ships were ever closer viewed: a fine day and good glasses. They are in their present state of very respectable force'.[23]

The threat posed by this force led to the strengthening of Stewart's squadron, which maintained a constant watch off the Texel; he now had seven ships of the line with him, four smaller two-decked ships, the frigates *Latona* and *Artois* and half a dozen smaller vessels. Such a concentration of force could be ill spared from the Channel Fleet, but it was maintained until a violent gale at the end of October, which lasted several days, drove Stewart back to the Downs. He then took the decision to keep all his heavy ships there, leaving it to Captain Sir Hyde Parker to continue the watch on the Texel with the frigates and cutters.

Thereafter, from time to time the Admiralty received intelligence reports suggesting that a possible breakout was planned; but none came, though on two occasions during 1782 it was thought necessary temporarily to reinforce the North Sea squadron. Until the end of the war, the blockade of the Dutch coast was continued; neutral vessels were searched for contraband, and enemy cruisers were, when reported, hunted down. Stewart had suggested to Sandwich at the end of September that the greatest threat would come from Dutch vessels operating from the Norwegian coast, and he proposed that two frigates and two cutters should be stationed there. He also expected, however, that there would be considerable activity on the part of French and Dutch privateers, and argued that these would be best checked by stationing a frigate, a sloop and a cutter at Leith permanently ready to go to sea whenever the weather permitted, and similarly a frigate and cutter at Cromarty. The rest of the squadron should, he suggested, be based in Leith roads.[24]

In September, a large convoy from the Baltic, escorted by the *Africa*, 64, and several small frigates, arrived unmolested. The *Africa* then, on her own, went back to the Baltic to pick up another convoy, which also arrived home safely. On the debit side, however a Dutch convoy from the Mediterranean under *Vice Admiraal*

23 Barnes and Owen (eds), *Private Papers of John, Earl of Sandwich*, Vol.IV, p.97.

24 Barnes and Owen (eds), *Private Papers of John, Earl of Sandwich*, Vol.IV, pp.97-100.

van Byland succeeded at the end of the year in slipping past Stewart's squadron as it lay in the Downs, taking advantage of thick weather.[25]

The war against the Netherlands called for the employment of naval resources which were constantly needed elsewhere, but it did seriously reduce the quantity of naval stores reaching France and Spain. It was never going to be possible to cut off the enemy's Baltic trade completely, but it certainly required great effort, and great expenditure by the French and Spanish to procure what their navies required. As David Syrett observed, though, the real victim was the Netherlands; the economic damage which it suffered was huge, and it took the nation many years to recover.[26]

25 James, *The British Navy in Adversity*, p.312.
26 Syrett, *European Waters*, p.132.

28

Kempenfelt and de Guichen

Even before Darby returned from his cruise at the beginning of November, the British government had begun to receive reports of extensive French plans to reinforce both the East and West Indies with ships, troops, guns, and stores. The Cabinet considered the matter on 20 October, at which time the intelligence indicated that 'a large train of artillery, five regiments of infantry, and at least seven ships of the line' under Vaudreuil would be going to the West Indies. The Cabinet concluded 'that it would be of the greatest consequence to intercept or even to retard this squadron', which it was thought was destined for an attack on Jamaica, and Sandwich, who was not present, was asked to report to the next meeting as to the most effective action that could be taken. On 22 October, it was resolved that Darby should be ordered into port as soon as possible to revictual his fleet, and that a detachment should be made ready before the sailing of the French convoy from Brest in the hope of intercepting it. Despatches were sent to the West Indies warning of the expedition in preparation at Brest.[1]

Darby, when he came ashore on 5 November, was by no means well; he had been prone to attacks of scurvy, and on 12 November he wrote to Sandwich to ask that he be excused from commanding the squadron to be sent out to intercept the French convoy. He had some suggestions to make: 'If the French have 12 sail it would be proper to have 14 or else the convoy will escape should they be met with. At the same time some large frigates will be wanting. At this time of the year, if the squadron could be composed of two deck ships it would make them the more active'. He thought that Kempenfelt was the better for his cruise, and that he would readily go in command of the squadron to be sent.[2]

The suggestion that Kempenfelt should be appointed was at once taken up by the Admiralty, and he re-hoisted his flag aboard the *Victory* on 19 November. He was disturbed to find, however, that although his squadron was being given priority,

1 Barnes and Owen (eds), *Private Papers of John, Earl of Sandwich*, Vol.IV, pp.70-72.

2 Barnes and Owen (eds), *Private Papers of John, Earl of Sandwich*, Vol.IV, pp.74-75.

several of the ships assigned to him were still 'very backward in point of readiness for sea', and he wrote at once to Sandwich to express his concern:

> The long cruising the ships have had has occasioned large demands for new sails, and made it necessary for several ships to overhaul their standing rigging – others have required a good deal of caulking and carpenters' work. Several ships have been obliged from leaks or the powder having been a long time on board to send it onshore to be dried and sifted.[3]

It was intended that he should have 14 ships of the line, a 50 gun ship and six frigates, but when his orders dated 22 November arrived, they suggested that he might sail with a lesser force: '[You are] so soon as the ships under your comd, or such a number of them as you shall judge necessary shall be ready, hereby ordered to cruise on such station as you judge most likely for intercepting the said fleet'.[4] These orders reached Kempenfelt two days later, followed closely by a letter from Sandwich regretting that the *Namur*, 90, and *Hercules*, 74, would not be able to form part of his squadron.

Kempenfelt responded at once, writing to Sandwich to say firmly that by reason of the strength of the enemy he judged it necessary to take the whole of the ships that had been put under his command; and he wrote to Middleton in similar terms:

> I this morning by express received my orders to sail as soon as ready, with the object for which I am sent out, as you informed me before. It says: 'to sail with ships as soon as they are ready, or with such part of them as I may think necessary for the service'. To be sure I shall think the whole necessary, when they tell me the enemy's escort is eighteen sail of the line, four of which are armed *en flûte.5*

He was entitled to be alarmed by the tone of these instructions and he followed up his letters with another next day to Middleton to complain in the strongest terms:

> This will be a great reduction of the force the squadron was named at, and not adequate to ensure the success of what they so ardently wish for. If we should fall in with them, we should have a force sufficient to cope with their ships of war, while others at the same time fall upon the convoy. Frigates may not be sufficient for that purpose without they are numerous, as the enemy would probably have several of that class with them … As the enemy's squadron is of such force as fourteen of the line complete in

3 Barnes and Owen (eds), *Private Papers of John, Earl of Sandwich*, Vol.IV, p.76.

4 J.H. Owen, 'Operations of the Western Squadron 1781-1782'in *The Naval Review* (1927, XV:1), p.36.

5 Laughton (ed.), *Barham Papers*, Vol.I, pp.350-351.

> guns and four armed *en flûte*, does the Admiralty mean I should go to sea deficient of the number they appointed? If they would have me go to sea with what ships of my squadron are here, I wish they had ordered it; then I should clearly have known what to do.[6]

Kempenfelt feared in particular that he would have to go out with an inadequate number of frigates; only two of the six assigned to his command were with him at Spithead, two were at sea, and two at Plymouth. His understandable concern was that the Admiralty were passing to him the responsibility for deciding what was a sufficient force, so that if the operation failed because that proved to be insufficient, the blame must fall on him. This was obviously wrong and unfair, and Middleton, on reading Kempenfelt's first letter, had written at once to Sandwich to tell him so: 'No seaman would undertake this service with so inferior a force on their own opinion, but would readily sail if ordered to do so'.[7] As both Kempenfelt and Middleton well knew, there were other ships available, including those preparing to go to the West Indies with Rodney and others intended for the East Indies under Commodore Bickerton.

In spite of these protests, nothing was done to strengthen Kempenfelt's squadron. When he sailed from Spithead on 2 December, he had with him 11 ships of the line: *Victory*, 100, *Britannia*, 100, *Duke*, 98, *Queen*, 98, *Union*, 90, the 74-gun ships *Edgar*, *Valiant*, *Courageux*, and *Alexander*, the *Agamemnon*, 64, and the *Medway*, 60. He also had the 50-gun ship *Renown*, two frigates, *Prudente* and *Monsieur*, and the fireship *Tisiphone*. On 5 December he was joined halfway between the Lizard and Ushant by the frigates *Arethusa* and *Tartar* and two cutters, and then on 10 December by the *Ocean*, 90. Kempenfelt's second-in-command was Commodore John Elliot, with his broad pennant in the *Edgar*.

Kempenfelt spent the afternoon of 10 December exercising his squadron in tactics. At the end of the day, when the ships were back in sailing order, the *Edgar* reported sighting a fleet in the north-east; Kempenfelt ordered the squadron to prepare for action, and sent the *Tartar* to investigate. It turned out to be a British convoy heading for Lisbon under the escort of two frigates. On the following evening, when he had reached a position about 180 miles west of Belleisle, Kempenfelt altered course to the eastward. 12 December dawned in thick weather with a rising sea and a strong south-easterly breeze. At about 7:30 a.m. Commander James Saumarez's fire ship *Tisiphone* sighted a fleet in the wind's eye, steering west. It was soon apparent that this time it really was their quarry.

De Guichen had sailed from Brest with a squadron of 12 ships of the line, covering two convoys comprising in all some 200 sail. That for the West Indies was escorted by Vaudreuil with five ships of the line; the other, destined for the East Indies, had an escort of four ships of the line, two of which were armed *en flûte*. The intention

6 Laughton (ed.), *Barham Papers*, Vol.I, p.352.
7 Laughton (ed.), *Barham Papers*, Vol.I, p.351.

'Richard Kempenfelt, Esqr.: Rear Admiral of the Blue Squadron of His Majesty's Fleet'. Mezzotint by Richard Earlom after Tilly Kettle. Anne S.K. Brown Collection)

was that de Guichen should sail with the two convoys as far as Madeira, where they were to separate and proceed to their respective destinations, while he sailed to Cadiz for a junction with the Spanish fleet. Vaudreuil's convoy, as British intelligence had reported, was carrying a large number of troops as well as artillery, munitions, equipment and provisions, intended for the planned attack on Jamaica. The East Indies convoy was to reinforce the French land forces in India, as well as Suffren's squadron which was engaged in a long running campaign there.[8]

8 Owen, 'Western Squadron', p.38.

By the time they were sighted by the *Tisiphone*, the French had reached a point some 150 miles west of Ushant. Surprisingly for so careful and vigilant a tactician as de Guichen, all but four of the ships of the line were sailing together with part of the convoy well in advance of the rest, and to leeward of them. The rest of the convoy was sailing on the same course to windward. Soon after 9.00 a.m. Kempenfelt ordered his two deckers, being the fastest ships of his squadron, to chase the enemy; the *Medway* and *Courageux* shook out their topsail reefs, set their topgallants, and tacked to the south south-west, while the *Edgar, Valiant, Agamemnon* and *Alexander* stood further west. The *Victory* also made more sail, and followed by the rest of the squadron, steered to cut off the enemy. Kempenfelt, in the letter which he wrote on 14 December to Middleton describing the action, looked back at what his thoughts had been at this moment:

> Had I waited for the slower sailing ships it would have been dark before we could have got near the enemy, and the convoy would all have escaped. Had we been sufficiently furnished with frigates and armed cutters, de Guichen might have returned to Brest, for then almost the whole of his convoy must have been taken. Had I that day known the superior strength of their squadron, and that it was such that I could not in prudence risk an action with, I should have made a general chase of it, and in that case very few of their transports would have escaped; for had any number of our ships been half an hour's sail ahead of us – and many would have been more than that, had the signal for the two decked ships continued out – they would have got in time between the convoy and the ships of war who have intercepted them.[9]

When his leading ships reported to Kempenfelt the disposition of the French men of war, it was at once clear to him that he had been presented with a superb opportunity. At 10.00 a.m., when he could see that de Guichen was forming line to leeward, he recalled his chasing ships and began to form line himself. Seeing that he did indeed have a chance of passing between de Guichen's line of battle and the bulk of the convoy, Kempenfelt now 'continued a pressed sail with a view of cutting them off'. At 11.30 a.m. he made the signal to prepare for battle.[10] The British line was led by Elliot in the *Edgar*, now followed by the *Medway* and *Union*. As they bore down, most of the ships in the convoy scattered, but the four ships of the line, headed by Vaudreuil in the *Triomphant*, 80, together with some of the transports, pressed across the head of the British line in an endeavour to regain de Guichen's main body. After more than an hour Elliot came up with the convoy. Three of Vaudreuil's ships had already crossed his bow, but the *Triomphant* was

9 Laughton (ed.), *Barham Papers*, Vol.I, p.357.
10 Owen, 'Western Squadron', p.39.

still to windward, and opened fire on the *Edgar* as she passed ahead of her. In his subsequent report of the battle, Kempenfelt described the encounter:

> The *Edgar*'s conduct on this occasion was masterly; she avoided being directly raked, by judiciously bearing up as the enemy passed her, and immediately after luffed to the wind, and brought her broadside at right angles with the enemy's stern, throwing in a well directed fire, which we could perceive was very effectual, the next morning we observed the *Triomphant* in the French line with main top mast and main yard gone.[11]

The *Medway* also engaged the *Triomphant*, while also firing her port battery at the convoy, and the *Union* was able to exchange broadsides with both the *Triomphant* and *Actif*, 74, the only two French ships of the line that got into action at all.

Once the *Triomphant* was out of the way, Elliot tacked in order to close with the transports. By now the rest of the squadron were among them, and had begun to take prizes. The *Arethusa* took three; the *Renown*, the other frigates, and the *Tisiphone* also took prizes on their own account, as well as taking possession of a number that had struck to Kempenfelt's ships of the line. Fourteen vessels were captured, and several sunk; but several more, which had struck, were not secured owing to the thick weather and approaching nightfall. The speed at which the engagement had begun had left some of Kempenfelt's ships some way astern, particularly the *Courageux* which had been on the wing of the squadron and had chased farthest from the main body. As Kempenfelt reported: 'By crowding sail to cut the convoy off from the line of battleships, some of our ships became very far astern, so that to form a line proper for action before dark would have been impossible. After collecting the ships together, I made sail on the same tack with the enemy'.[12]

For de Guichen, the engagement was a disaster; he was obliged to look on from leeward, powerless to do anything about it as the British ranged in amongst his convoy. The reason for his faulty deployment has never been explained; it may have been that he had the impression that the British squadron, which he knew to be at sea, would be encountered further to the north and that it would be from that direction that it would be met with. As it was the wind had backed south-southeast at midday, and thinking about it afterwards Kempenfelt wondered if his opponent might have done more:

> De Guichen was within an ace of suffering a most ridiculous disgrace – that of having all his convoy taken from him before his face. He, with the ships of war, was to leeward of the convoy; the weather was rather hazy,

11 Owen, 'Western Squadron', pp.39-34.

12 Laughton (ed.), *Barham Papers*, Vol.I, p.356.

> the convoy took us for part of their fleet, and I believe their ships of war for part of the convoy. We stood into the convoy upon the larboard tack. De Guichen was not above two points upon our lee bow; had he stood towards us on the starboard tack he would have fetched us, and by that manoeuvre obliged us to quit the pursuit of the convoy, to have tacked to close the rear ships we had separated from, to have got in proper form to have received him.[13]

As it was, at dawn on 13 December de Guichen's squadron could be seen in line, still to leeward, about eight miles off, in much the same position relative to the British squadron as on the previous evening. Kempenfelt formed his own line, and sent Captain Waldegrave in the frigate *Prudente* to reconnoitre. It was plain that the French superiority was so great that there could be no question of risking an attack. In any case, as Kempenfelt reported, the weather was by now so bad that the British could not have opened their lower deck ports to leeward; the French, to windward, might have been able to open theirs.

Kempenfelt sent the 50-gun *Renown* and the frigates *Arethusa* and *Monsieur* to guard the prizes, while keeping his battle line in position between them and the French. Gradually, the fleets drew apart, and by noon the French were some 10 miles off, and before dark they were out of sight. Next morning, Kempenfelt dispatched Saumarez in the *Tisiphone* to the Leeward Islands to give Hood the news of what had transpired; he arrived at St Kitts on 31 January 1782.

The *Agamemnon* and *Prudente* were now sent to pick up stragglers from the French convoy; they cruised for 12 days, and succeeded in capturing another five vessels which had been en route to join de Guichen. The 14 prizes taken by the squadron were sent home under the escort of the *Arethusa* and the *Medway*, bearing with them Kempenfelt's first report to the Admiralty and his letter to Middleton. There seems in fact to be some uncertainty as to the total number of prizes actually taken; Lacour-Gayet puts the figure at 24.[14]

At this point Kempenfelt had not yet decided to pack up and go home; but, learning from prisoners taken during the engagement that one incoming French West Indies convoy had already reached port, and that another Dutch convoy had also done so, he concluded that there was no point in staying out. Accordingly, leaving the *Renown* on station to inform any ships that might have been sent out to join him of what had occurred, he set his course for Spithead, arriving on 20 December. From there he reported his reasoning both to the Admiralty and to Middleton, concluding it made more sense to bring in his squadron for repairs than to stay out for little purpose. It would, though, as he pointed out, have been in his own interest to remain at sea somewhat longer in the hope of personal gain

13 Laughton (ed.), *Barham Papers*, Vol.I, p.357.

14 Lacour-Gayet, *La marine Militaire*, p.377.

'J.C. comte de Guichen: Lieutenant Général des Armées navales de France', engraving by Hardouin after Castelar (Anne S.K. Brown Collection)

from the taking of further prizes. Information from prisoners as to the French intentions were very contradictory; some of them said, correctly, that the plan had been for de Guichen to take the convoys as far as Madeira before heading for Cadiz; others claimed that his intention was to return to Brest. When Kempenfelt arrived at Spithead, he was met by fresh instructions from the Admiralty to continue his cruise with nine ships of the line, and try to intercept the French three deckers. He replied by giving his reasons for returning to port, and the Admiralty approved these. The *Arethusa* was sent out to look into Brest and to investigate the situation there, and Kempenfelt struck his flag and went on leave.

As it was, the unfortunate de Guichen's troubles were far from over. He endeavoured to collect together his scattered convoy, but on the night of 25/26 December he ran into a violent gale, which again widely dispersed his ships, the merchant vessels arriving at various ports on the French coast, particularly Royan. De Guichen's flagship *Bretagne* and the *Couronne*, carrying the flag of La Motte-Picquet, were both dismasted, and de Guichen took most of his squadron back to Brest for repairs; only the *Triomphant* and the 74-gun *Brave* succeeded in making their way to the West Indies, reaching Martinique on 30 January with five of the transports. It had been a comprehensive defeat, as Lacour-Gayet mournfully observed: 'The campaign which had begun for the British with the affair of the St Eustatius convoy had ended with a shattering revenge'.[15] It is said that de Guichen felt his disgrace so much that he wanted to strike his flag, but was not permitted to do so.

The operation had been extremely successful, wrecking the French attempt to launch a major offensive in the West Indies, but for various reasons there were many who did not so represent it. For the opposition in Parliament, the failure to send out a larger squadron was a valuable stick with which to beat the government. In the course of debates in the House of Commons on 20 December and 7 February, Keppel contended that the squadron in the Downs, as well as the ships waiting to sail with Rodney, could have been added to Kempenfelt's force. Charles James Fox considered that sending out Kempenfelt 'with only twelve sail of the line to encounter twenty' was a shameful and injurious step. Owen described the Admiralty's handling of the matter as being due to short-sightedness and a lack of political courage. The reasons for the Admiralty's decision were explained, rather unconvincingly, by Mulgrave, in the course of the debates in Parliament. He said that the Admiralty had had the 'strongest reasons' for supposing that de Guichen had no more than 13 ships of the line, and advanced the suggestion that the other six had been sent to join him when the French learned that Kempenfelt was at sea. This was palpably incorrect. Mulgrave went on to claim that only the ships comprising Rodney's squadron were available, and that it would have been 'a dangerous if not fatal measure' to have sent them. Howe wanted to know why, if Rodney's squadron was admittedly ready he was not sent out. Rodney and Hood, looking at the issues solely from their own perspective, took a different view, arguing that Kempenfelt should have been sent directly to the West Indies in order to intercept the convoy there. This raises the question of whether as a general rule it was better to seek the enemy at his point of departure or to wait for him at his destination.[16]

15 Lacour-Gayet, *La marine Militaire*, p.378.

16 Owen, 'Western Squadron', p.44.

In the memorandum that he prepared in response to the Parliamentary inquiries in the following year, Sandwich would put forward a number of points in the Admiralty's defence relating to the allegations about Kempenfelt's expedition. It was not, he claimed, possible to provide a larger force 'without breaking in upon all our arrangements for the East and West Indies and the North Sea'.[17] He contended that, in relation to the strength of de Guichen's fleet, 'the whole intelligence respecting the force and destination of this equipment was so contradictory that it was next to impossible to fix upon any precise number of ships of which it was likely to consist; and it was equally difficult to determine from the variety of the information received at what time it would probably sail'.[18] In any case, he said, since Kempenfelt was unencumbered with any convoy and all his ships were coppered, he ran little risk in meeting even a superior force. None of the Admiralty's arguments were particularly convincing; the truth was that it had been felt absolutely necessary to send out Kempenfelt with the strongest force that could be assembled, even if probably inadequate, and hope for the best. Having made the uncertainty of de Guichen's strength one of the main planks of the Admiralty's defence, Sandwich had effectively admitted that this was the case.

Middleton subsequently reflected on the issues that had been raised by the discussions about Kempenfelt's operation:

> Suffering Admiral Kempenfelt to sail with so small a force, when the ships fitting for the West Indies and others from the Downs might have joined him with advantage to other services, was an error that not only prevented that Admiral from attacking Mr Guichen to advantage, but lost us the island of St Christopher's. There were many blunders which concurred to this disappointment; and had a man of less activity than Admiral Kempenfelt been appointed to command, the squadron would not have got to sea in time for any service, nor have ventured an attack in the face of so superior an enemy. This happened under the former administration, and on the part of the Admiral was the most judicious attempt, except St Christopher's, of the war.[19]

Middleton's was an entirely reasonable judgment. Owen, concluding his account of Kempenfelt's operation, agreed with him:

> In the thick stormy weather, Kempenfelt had little enough time to gauge what was possible; it was not practicable to attack the greatly superior battle squadron, as he had evidently intended to do, but he took the one

17 Barnes and Owen (eds), *Private Papers of John, Earl of Sandwich*, Vol.IV, p.324.
18 Barnes and Owen (eds), *Private Papers of John, Earl of Sandwich*, Vol.IV, pp.338-339.
19 Laughton (ed.), *Barham Papers*, Vol.II, pp.75-76.

> chance that offered and boldly made the most of it; and he was valiantly supported by Elliot and by the ships of his squadron.[20]

Sir John Knox Laughton, in the entry he wrote for Kempenfelt in the Dictionary of National Biography, described his success as being 'perhaps the most dashing and brilliant feat of the whole war'.[21]

20 Owen, 'Western Squadron', p.45.
21 *Dictionary of National Biography*, vol 30, pp.395-396.

29

The Fall of Lord North's Ministry

Before the first news of Yorktown, which arrived in London at the end of November, the government's managers in the House of Commons were expecting a short and quiet sitting of Parliament before the Christmas recess. As a routine precaution, however, John Robinson was engaged in ensuring that sufficient of the government's supporters would be present, and he asked Sandwich for his help in securing the attendance of naval officers. This was not always convenient; the First Lord's response to one such request was that 'it is utterly impossible to call Commodore Stewart from his duty, as this is the very moment when the Dutch convoy will push down the Channel if they mean to try that experiment'.[1] At the same time, on the other side of the House, the leaders of the opposition were not very hopeful of their prospects for the opening of the session.

The news from North America changed all that. The opposition now regretted their lack of preparation for the session, and brought on a number of debates which provided an opportunity for the expression of sharp criticism of the government. Lord North was losing his nerve; on 21 December he seriously upset the King by the pessimistic terms in which he represented the situation, appearing to hint at the possibility of a complete surrender in America. The mounting crisis found the government supporters divided; some more or less adopted the position taken by the King and by Germain, to the effect that the war with the colonists must go on; some thought that the principal war effort should now be directed against France and Spain in the hope of strengthening Britain's bargaining position when it came to peace talks; and some were now prepared to abandon America at once.[2] Among the members of the Cabinet, Germain was alone in taking the first view. It took all North's political skill to devise a formula that for the moment papered over the gaps in the government's public position.

1 Ian Christie, *The End of North's Ministry 1780-1782* (London: Macmillan 1958), pp.267-268.
2 Christie, *End of North's Ministry*, p.277.

'The Right Hon.ble Lord North'. Unattributed Engraving. (NYPL)

Mulgrave gave it as his opinion, in a letter to Sandwich of 9 January, that it would be 'the exertions used in bringing forward the armaments at different periods' that would be of the greatest public interest:

> What the opposition will, I suppose, most attack will be application and objects of the armaments, because those, being matters of expediency, are most open to difference of opinion and criticism from events. The first is more immediately your business, as it affects your official conduct, and is where, if you have any false friends, you are most likely to be deserted; the other involves the whole Administration, and must be a common cause.[3]

The opposition's attacks upon the government were prompted not only by the news of Yorktown; they also, as Mulgrave had predicted, were based on a general criticism of Sandwich's management of the Admiralty, including, most recently,

3 Barnes and Owen (eds), *Private Papers of John, Earl of Sandwich*, Vol.IV, p.275.

the perceived failure to provide Kempenfelt with a strong enough force with which to attack de Guichen. The speeches on the Address of Thanks and the subsequent debates in both Houses of Parliament set out a wide range of complaints, and during December Sandwich sat down to prepare a detailed defence of his record at the Admiralty. He sent copies of this to the King, to the members of the Cabinet, and other political friends at the end of the month.

Apart from Sandwich, the most obvious target for the opposition was Germain. When Parliament reassembled on 21 January, North was confronted with an internal government crisis. One of his key supporters, the influential Henry Dundas, the Scottish Lord Advocate, had, before the Christmas recess, concluded that both Sandwich and Germain must go; now, he announced that if this demand was not met he would withdraw his support from the government. North was extremely reluctant to let Germain go, because he had no one else who could speak adequately for the government's American policy in the House of Commons. He told the King that Germain's removal would not be of permanent benefit, because the objections to him were stronger against his system than against his person. Nevertheless, Dundas was insistent. On 22 January he appeared briefly in the House of Commons with his colleague Richard Rigby; they declared that they would not attend as long as Germain remained in office.[4] In the face of this threat, North gave in; Germain was replaced as Secretary of State by Welbore Ellis on 31 January.

Sandwich's written review of his management of the affairs of the Admiralty made a powerful answer to his critics. It was published in full in Volume IV of Sandwich's edited papers, and dealt in considerable detail with each of the criticisms made of him, not only in respect of the preparations for war, but also the conduct of the war itself. It concluded with a firm defence of his record:

> Because we have not done more than ought to have been expected from us if we had been by a third superior to the enemy, we are supposed to have been negligent, or as some have said *treacherous*, because we have not conquered everywhere with a decided inferiority on our side. I own I think much more has been done than could have been expected, considering our losses by the hand of God and the unnatural combinations against us among the powers of Europe. Whatever may be the issue of this inquiry, I can put my hand upon my heart and say that I have done my duty with an honest intention and the best of my ability, and I have no doubt but that every impartial person (if such there is) will, on cool and unprejudiced consideration and after having made himself master of the subject, allow me some farther degree of merit than I think it decent to arrogate to myself.[5]

4 Christie, *End of North's Ministry*, p.294.
5 Barnes and Owen (eds), *Private Papers of John, Earl of Sandwich*, Vol.IV, p.301.

This document was convincing enough to persuade Rigby, who wrote to the First Lord that it 'very clearly evinces great attention on your part to the augmenting the naval force of this country'.[6]

The removal of Germain, so far as the government was concerned, might have been supposed to be enough; Charles Jenkinson, the Secretary at War, wrote to the King on 3 February to tell him that he understood that Dundas would 'be satisfied with one human sacrifice. This is the expression that was made use of. The whole transaction is very strange and humiliating'.[7] However, it was at once apparent that Germain's removal had by no means resolved the political crisis, and that the opposition intended to launch a sustained offensive against Sandwich. On 24 January Charles James Fox moved for an inquiry into the naval administration. To general surprise, he excluded from this inquiry any investigation of Sandwich's failure to provide adequate fleets, but said that it would be confined to his conduct of recent naval operations; the reason for this, he explained, was that it would make it too tedious and perplexing, and would be of little avail, as it would 'bring forward so many office witnesses, witnesses all under the patronage of the noble Lord himself'.[8] This manoeuvre wrongfooted Sandwich, who had made his development of the fleet a key part of the defence which he had prepared. Fox had skilfully chosen the ground which suited his attack best.

The first debate upon the inquiry, after a short postponement, took place on 7 February. Fox, moving the resolution of censure 'that there has been great mismanagement in the conduct of his Majesty's naval affairs in the year 1781,' based this on four specific allegations – letting de Grasse slip away unimpeded with reinforcements for the French fleet in North American waters; failing to prevent the loss of the St Eustatius convoy; despatching misleading information to the civic authorities in Bristol; and mismanaging the war against the Dutch. He also added a denunciation of the Admiralty for the way in which Kempenfelt had been sent out against de Guichen with a squadron of inadequate strength.[9] When the House divided, the government's majority rejecting the motion was 205 to 183, well below that to which it was accustomed, and North was severely shaken; Lord Hillsborough wrote that 'Lord North is worried to death and things wear a very uncertain aspect'.[10]

The opposition was beginning to scent victory. On 20 February Fox introduced another censure motion in practically the same terms as before. In preparation for this debate, both sides made the most strenuous efforts to ensure the attendance of every one of their supporters, and a total of 453 votes were cast when the

6 Barnes and Owen (eds), *Private Papers of John, Earl of Sandwich*, Vol.IV, pp.274-275.
7 Christie, *End of North's Ministry*, p.297.
8 Christie, *End of North's Ministry*, pp.305-306.
9 Christie, *End of North's Ministry*, pp.311-312.
10 Christie, *End of North's Ministry*, p.312.

House divided. Again, the motion was defeated; but the government's majority of 236 to 217 showed a further weakening of its position, the opposition having increased the number of members supporting their motion by 34. Two days later, a motion that the American war no longer should be pursued because it was not practical to reduce the colonists to obedience by force was lost by only one vote; on 27 February a similar motion was carried by 19 votes, and the writing was clearly on the wall.

On 6 March in the House of Lords, after an inquiry which lasted for several days, the Duke of Chandos moved 'that the immediate cause of the capture of the army under Lord Cornwallis in Virginia appeared to be the want of a sufficient naval force to cover and protect the same'.[11] In the course of the debate, Sandwich spoke at great length and in great detail, rebutting each of the charges laid against his administration, and the motion was defeated by 72 votes to 37.[12] This gave the government a short breathing space; but it was to prove very short indeed.

In the following two weeks the government's position steadily deteriorated, as the House of Commons continued to debate its American policy. On 8 March it only narrowly avoided defeat, and it was plain that as things stood it could no longer count on having a stable majority. In spite of this, Sandwich retained a lingering hope that 'if Lord North did not despond and talk of giving the thing up, matters would not yet be irretrievable'.[13] The Prime Minister still had the King's support; but he had by now had enough. On 19 March, following a letter which he had written foreshadowing his imminent resignation, he received from the King an emotional and reproachful response. Next day he visited the King again, whom he found in a calmer frame of mind, now realistically accepting that the administration had come to the end of the line. North at once asked him if he had not better state the fact at once. 'Well, you may do so', replied the King, and North went straight off to the House of Commons, which was about to debate yet another censure motion, and forestalled it by announcing the resignation of the ministry. The King continued to regard this as a betrayal; when Lord North went to take his leave formally, it is said that his words to his outgoing Prime Minister were: 'Remember, my Lord, it is you who desert me, not I you'.[14]

The consequences for the navy of the fall of the ministry were almost immediate. A new administration was formed under the Marquis of Rockingham, in which Keppel (who was elevated to the peerage) took office as First Lord at the head of an entirely reconstituted Board of Admiralty. His first task was to endeavour to carry into effect the long-held intention of the opposition that Howe should be appointed to the command of the Channel Fleet. This, however, proved not to be

11 Barnes and Owen (eds), *Private Papers of John, Earl of Sandwich*, Vol.IV, p.271.

12 Barnes and Owen (eds), *Private Papers of John, Earl of Sandwich*, Vol.IV, p.271.

13 Christie, *End of North's Ministry*, p.351.

14 Donne (ed.), *The Correspondence of King George the Third*, Vol.II, p.416.

entirely straightforward. The accession of the new government did not mean that the admiral would at once unconditionally agree to serve. Having a clear understanding of the strength of his bargaining position, Howe still insisted that he and his brother must be vindicated, and be rewarded by an expression of royal favour. The negotiations with Keppel concluded with the admiral's creation as Viscount Howe in the peerage of Great Britain – his existing title was an Irish one – and the appointment of Sir William Howe as Lieutenant General of the Ordnance. It was a stiff price, but Howe knew that he was pushing at an open door, and that the new government would be obliged to accept his terms.[15]

The next step for the new cabinet was to remove Rodney from his command in the West Indies. It was Keppel's duty to break the news; he wrote on 2 May:

> Reasoning upon the subject I am sure you will think unnecessary. It is enough for me to inform you as shortly as I am able that the King's servants have judged it for reasons of state that Admiral Pigot should immediately proceed to the West Indies and there take upon him the chief command of the fleet at present under your direction.[16]

It had been a difficult letter to write; unluckily for the government, news came on 18 May of Rodney's victory at Les Saintes, and a desperate attempt was made to stop Pigot before he sailed. It was too late, and Keppel was obliged to write again to Rodney with his congratulations on the victory, expressing the hope that the matter could be left for Rodney's 'quiet reasoning' when they met.

The appointment of Howe to the Channel Fleet meant, of course, the supersession of Darby, who had done nothing to deserve it. Not surprisingly, when invited to continue to serve but as second in command, he declined, and Barrington continued in that post, as did Kempenfelt as third in command, shifting his flag to the *Royal George* to make room for Howe in the *Victory*.

After Kempenfelt's return from his cruise against de Guichen, he and Middleton had been giving considerable thought to the future conduct of the war. They were in close touch with each other, and were agreed that in the current situation the existing strategy was seriously flawed. It was far from certain, for instance, that the planned reinforcement of the fleet in the West Indies would be sufficient to match the enemy there. Based on their discussions, Middleton wrote a memorandum to Sandwich, which he sent to him on Christmas Day; with an eye on the political situation, he also sent a copy to Shelburne. He endorsed it, grimly, with a comment wishing that it 'be submitted to all able sea officers unconnected with party or politics'.[17]

15 David Syrett, *Admiral Lord Howe* (Stroud: Spellmount, 2000), p.100.

16 Spinney, *Rodney*, p.408.

17 Laughton (ed.), *Barham Papers*, Vol.II, pp.37-41.

'Richd. Lord Viscount Howe, Rear Admiral of the White and Commander in Chief of the Fleet in N. America'. Engraving from the Hibernian Magazine, c. 1777. (Anne S.K. Brown Collection)

What was shocking about Middleton's paper was that it adopted the policies which the King and Germain had been pressing on the Cabinet for the last three years, and firmly recommended the strengthening of the fleet in the West Indies at the expense of the Channel Fleet. In the first draft of his paper Middleton included a characteristically aggressive comment on the existing policy:

> If the system of starving every other service to make up an insufficient western squadron is still to prevail, we shall not only lose island after island in sight of fleets that are too weak to protect them, but see every

> possession belonging to Great Britain, and the land forces that are placed there for their defence, seized by the enemy.[18]

Although he omitted this from the final draft, he was emphatic that the policy of putting the needs of a western squadron first must be discarded. At the same time, to protect military and commercial convoys, he proposed that they should assemble early in the year, before the Combined Fleet appeared, and be escorted by frigates, while inbound convoys should be directed to sail north about round Scotland. The squadron in the North Sea should be reinforced by all the three deckers not sent to the West Indies, since it would now become an area of key importance. These arrangements would leave the Channel Fleet with the sole responsibility of preventing invasion.

Sandwich was far from sure that this was right, but the members of the Cabinet reacted favourably. Two weeks later, Kempenfelt completed his own analysis of the strategic situation, dated 13 January.[19] A copy of this appears as Appendix III. In this document Kempenfelt spelled-out clearly the correct policy as he saw it; if a force sufficient to match the Combined Fleet could not be assembled in home waters, it would be better to reduce it still further to gain a superiority elsewhere. Inferior by sea, Britain must trust to her land forces to resist invasion. It should be noted, however, that Professor Rodger is still satisfied that Sandwich's policy of giving priority to the Channel Fleet remained correct, observing of the strategy put forward by Kempenfelt and Middleton that it 'was as unsound as ever in 1782, and decisive victory was still most likely in the Western Approaches'.[20]

At this time, as usual, the King was in belligerent mode. With an eye on the opposition's developing attacks in Parliament, he wrote on 14 January to urge the formation of a squadron strong enough to deal with de Guichen when he put to sea again:

> Lord Sandwich will have known yesterday that he returned on the 30th of last month to Brest; if he equips speedily a fleet of magnitude, and that Kempenfelt can give them a thorough blow, it will be more satisfactory than any other mode of defence when the inquiry takes effect.[21]

Meanwhile, there had been considerable activity on the part of the French. In February de Guichen did indeed come out with 14 ships of the line, and made for Cadiz, which he reached on 5 March. No attempt was made to prevent this, because in the event the Channel Fleet could not put together a force sufficient to

18 Laughton (ed.), *Barham Papers*, Vol.II, p.40.

19 Barnes and Owen (eds), *Private Papers of John, Earl of Sandwich*, Vol.IV, pp.80-82.

20 Rodger, *Insatiable Earl*, p.293.

21 Barnes and Owen (eds), *Private Papers of John, Earl of Sandwich*, Vol.IV pp82-83.

meet him. La Motte-Picquet had been detached from de Guichen's fleet with four ships of the line off Finisterre with the intention of raiding British convoys, but bad weather ultimately compelled him to return to Brest.

Towards the end of March intelligence reached the Admiralty that de Guichen, with five French ships of the line and an unknown number of Spanish ships, was to escort some Dutch East Indiamen to Lorient, and that a large force of troops for America was preparing to leave Brest escorted by 10 ships of the line under La Motte-Picquet. These movements were expected to take place in April, and Barrington was ordered on 5 April to take such ships of the Channel Fleet as were ready for sea to cruise between the latitudes of Ushant and Belle Isle as far to the west as he judged necessary to intercept them. He was to avoid action if he encountered a superior force.[22] His force consisted of 12 ships of the line and five frigates. His flag was in the *Britannia* and Kempenfelt was second in command, aboard the *Royal George*.

Barrington sailed from Spithead on 13 April, having been delayed by bad weather, and he cruised from about 50 to 70 miles south-west of Ushant between 16 and 20 April. At dawn on 20 April the frigate *Artois* sighted what appeared to be an enemy convoy, and reported this to Barrington, who at noon made the signal for a general chase. The convoy was headed for India, and consisted of 25 store ships and victuallers escorted by the *Protecteur*, 74, *Pégase*, 74, *Actionnaire*, 64 *en flute*, and two frigates. When the *Artois* first reported the convoy she was some 15 miles south-east of the British squadron, and it was difficult at first from the flagship to make out her signal. In a light southerly breeze, it was not until about 3.00 p.m. that the enemy came in sight of the *Britannia*. The French attempted to escape, first by trying to get across the bows of the British squadron and then, finding that impossible, making for the coast, but they were soon overhauled by the frigates and the faster ships of the line. By 7.00 p.m. the *Artois* was in amongst the convoy.

The leading ship of the line was the *Foudroyant*, 80, still commanded by Jervis. In the course of eight years she had gained the reputation of being 'the smartest and best ordered ship' in the Channel Fleet. As he approached the enemy just before dark Jervis could see that the convoy had been ordered to scatter, and he set his course to engage the men of war. He came up with the stern most ship, the *Pégase,* at 12:47 a.m., and captured her after a 50-minute action. In this engagement British losses were four men slightly wounded, one of whom was Jervis himself, while the *Pégase* lost 90 men killed and wounded. Meanwhile a dozen of the ships of the convoy had been taken before midnight. During the night the wind got up, and by dawn on 21 April it was raining and blowing hard, and Barrington only succeeded in weathering Ushant with difficulty. Several of his ships of the line were damaged in the mounting gale. Jervis was having difficulty in transferring

22 Owen, 'Western Squadron', p.47.

John Jervis, depicted in later life as Admiral Lord St Vincent. Engraving after William Beechey. (Anne S.K. Brown Collection)

the prisoners from the *Pégase*, and the *Queen*, 98, was sent to stand by him, but as night fell the *Foudroyant* lost touch with them both.[23]

Next day the *Queen* fell in with the *Actionnaire,* and chased her all day, finally catching up with her by 11:30 p.m. After a brief engagement, the *Actionnaire* struck. It was, however, extremely difficult for the *Queen* and her prize to make any headway in the face of an easterly gale. Ultimately, she met the frigate

23 Owen, 'Western Squadron', p.49.

Recovery on 28 April, sent her with the prize into Plymouth and headed for St Helens. En route on 4 May the *Queen* passed Kempenfelt, who had come out again to watch Brest, following a report that four ships of the line together with the *Protecteur*, which had returned safely with part of her convoy, were ready to sail. Kempenfelt had only seven ships of the line with him, but they sufficed to keep the French in port.

Barrington had taken the rest of his squadron back to port after the action with the convoy, reckoning that it would be better to get them refitted than remaining out. The news of his success was well received; it earned Jervis a knighthood. Barrington wrote of the *Foudroyant*'s action: 'My pen is not equal to the praise that is due to the good conduct, bravery and discipline of Captain Jervis, his officers and seamen on this occasion'.[24] As he read this report and considered the appropriate reward for Jervis, Keppel can hardly have failed to recall the support that he had himself received from Jervis at the time of his court-martial.

Howe wrote a warm private letter to Barrington on his success:

> I cannot, my dear Admiral, send off a letter in form without adding a private compliment of congratulation on the success of your late cruise. It has been happy in point of time, no less than creditable to the new Administration of our maritime affairs, and I hope the example of Captain Jervis will do us all good (or I ought rather speak as the one) who have been lying in rust for a length of time.[25]

24 Owen, 'Western Squadron', p.51.
25 Bonner-Smith (ed.), *Barrington Papers*, Vol.II, p.354.

30

Howe

Admiral Viscount Howe hoisted his flag aboard the *Victory* on 20 April. His immediate reaction was to conclude that the condition of the Channel Fleet was such that it was not ready for action, and two days later he wrote to the Admiralty: 'Their Lordships are already apprised of the deficiencies of men in this part of the squadron and as the state of the other ships fitting at this port is not in such progress that my present stay here can, as I conceive, be of any special utility, I propose to return to London'.[1] The challenges faced by the Channel Fleet were greater than ever; not only would it have to put to sea as soon as possible to cover the Western Approaches to the Channel, but also to provide cover in the North Sea against the Dutch. There were simply not enough ships of the line sufficient for both responsibilities.

The more immediate threat appeared to be materialising in the North Sea. The Dutch fleet under *Vice Admiraal* Hartsinck, apparently consisting of 11 ships of the line, had assembled in the Texel, and on 10 May Howe put to sea with nine ships of the line, and several smaller ships. He arrived off the Dutch coast on 16 May, where he received reports that Hartsinck had 13 ships of the line, of which only nine were operational.[2] It soon appeared that the Dutch did not intend after all to put to sea, and Keppel ordered Howe to return to Spithead. This was just as well; an epidemic of influenza had swept through some of Howe's ships. He left Ross with a squadron of nine ships to blockade the Dutch. Keppel observed that the 'Dutch war is a millstone round our necks', and it was certainly the case that the threat from the Dutch had developed into a serious problem at a time when the Channel Fleet was already severely overstretched.[3] The intention was that if needed Ross should at once re-join the Channel Fleet.

It was extremely likely that this would indeed be necessary. After the setback for de Guichen's convoy in December, there had been a considerable revival in

1 James, *The British Navy in Adversity*, p.367.
2 Syrett, *Howe*, p.101.
3 Syrett, *European Waters*, p.156.

the fortunes of France and Spain. In the West Indies, Dutch settlements had been retaken; on 14 February the Spanish had taken Fort Saint Philip and reconquered Minorca, suffering few casualties because the garrison had become widely afflicted with scurvy; and on 11 February de Guichen was able to leave Brest covering a convoy bound for the West Indies. This was first to sail for Cadiz, which it reached on 24 February.[4]

Such as it was, the Admiralty's intelligence was beginning to offer some alarming indications of potential enemy activity. It appeared that the French would have at least 14 ships of the line at Brest; that once the Combined Fleet had reassembled it might comprise as many as 62 ships of the line; and that the Dutch fleet could have 20 or 25 ships, although this number included several 50-gun ships.[5] It was abundantly clear that there would be a serious problem, since the most that the Channel Fleet could hope for was a total of 32 ships of the line once the current programme of refitting was completed.

After Barrington had returned from his successful cruise, Kempenfelt had sailed with a squadron of seven ships of the line, a frigate and two cutters, to take station off Brest in order to observe the French fleet, and to protect British trade. He remained at sea until 18 May before putting into Torbay; he then sailed again, taking up a position in the Western Approaches until the end of the month, without encountering any enemy. It was known that there was a squadron in Brest under La Motte-Picquet, but it was not clear to Howe or the Admiralty what the enemy's overall intentions might be.

The capture of Minorca had inspired the Spanish with renewed enthusiasm for an attack on Gibraltar. During the previous year a French engineer, the Chevalier d'Arcon, had put forward a project for an attack on the fortress which had impressed the Spanish government, which now put in hand arrangements for its execution. While these preparations were being made, de Guichen was sent on 17 March to cruise with a squadron of 12 Spanish and five French ships of the line off Madeira in quest of British convoys. It was the Spanish intention to keep de Guichen available for the attack on Gibraltar; the French, on the other hand, wished the cruise to last only into April, so as not to delay operations by the Combined Fleet in the Channel. So far as Gibraltar was concerned, the anxiety in Paris was that once it was taken, the Spanish appetite to continue the war would disappear. The plan for the Combined Fleet was that, as previously, it was to operate in the Western Approaches to the Channel, and that Córdova should be in command. In other words, as Lacour-Gayet pointed out, the same mistakes made previously were about to be repeated: 'one cannot fail to pity men of the valour of de Guichen and

4 Dull, *French Navy and American Independence*, p.267.
5 Syrett, *Howe*, p.100.

La Motte-Picquet, condemned to impotence by a plan so bad and a commander so incapable'.[6]

For Vergennes, seeking to put together a strategy that might be effective in persuading the Dutch to join actively in the naval war against Britain, the Spanish insistence that their fleet be employed against Gibraltar was intensely frustrating. The 24 additional ships of the line which they wished to commit would add nothing to the operations against the fortress, 'but could help induce the squadron to stand up to the English, encourage a reaffirmation of the Dutch principle of cooperation, and make the new English ministry feel more deeply the need for reasonable sacrifices for peace'.[7]

In the end Vergennes got his way, and on 4 June Córdova and de Guichen sailed from Cadiz with 32 ships of the line. The change in the Spanish attitude appears to have been brought about by a personal approach by Louis XVI's brother, the Comte d'Artois, to Carlos III, asking that he might take part in the successful conclusion of the siege of Gibraltar. Immediately following this, the Spanish King agreed that 27 of his ships of the line could go north.[8] The intention now was that they should be joined by other units from Rochefort and by the squadron at Brest, and also by a Dutch squadron of 10 ships of the line. This, it was hoped, would give the Combined Fleet a total of 54 ships of the line, far more than the Channel Fleet could muster.

On its way northward the Combined Fleet encountered on 24 June a British convoy en route to Canada, and captured 19 vessels. A few days later La Motte-Picquet brought his squadron out from Brest to join the Combined Fleet, bringing it to a strength of 40 ships of the line; the hoped-for Dutch contingent did not appear.

Meanwhile the Admiralty, in order to get some reliable information as to the enemy's movements, had ordered Howe to send out a small squadron to reconnoitre off Cadiz to see what could be ascertained of the Combined Fleet's movements. This consisted of the *Vigilant*, 64, and three frigates. Mindful of the temptations to which frigate captains were subject, each of them was expressly instructed to keep the squadron's mission in mind:

> The special purpose of these instructions is to acquire such material and timely information as may be of the greatest moment in the conduct of his Majesty's service. You are not to suffer your ship to be unnecessarily engaged with the enemy subjecting you thereby to be disabled or disappointed in the execution of that more important trust.[9]

6 Lacour-Gayet, *La marine Militaire*, p.382.

7 Dull, *French Navy and American Independence*, p.277.

8 Dull, *French Navy and American Independence*, pp 280-281.

9 James, *The British Navy in Adversity*, p.368.

This squadron sailed on 24 June. Without waiting for the receipt of any further intelligence about the Combined Fleet, the Admiralty ordered Howe to put to sea with the ships immediately available, since it was expected that a large convoy from Jamaica escorted by a squadron under Vice Admiral Sir Peter Parker would any day arrive at the entrance to the Channel. Howe sailed from St Helens on 30 June, having with him 22 ships of the line, Barrington and Kempenfelt being second and third in command respectively. During the course of 1 July the fleet met two neutral ships, each of which told of encountering the Combined Fleet. One reported seeing 56 ships, large and small, some 48 miles west of Ushant; the other had sighted a large fleet 300 miles south-west of the Lizard. Next day, another report indicated that the Combined Fleet might put into Brest. If it had, Howe told the Admiralty, he would return to Spithead, but would otherwise continue westward.

On 5 July Howe received a report that the Combined Fleet had been sighted off Ushant. He now knew where he stood in relation to the enemy; but on 11 July the sloop *Cormorant* joined him with the news that the Jamaica convoy was now approaching from the west, and was expected to make landfall in Ireland. At dawn on the next day, 45 miles south-east of the Scillies, Howe, whose fleet comprised 25 ships of the line, sighted the Combined Fleet to the westward. At this time there was a north-west wind, and the enemy was to windward, and hence between the Channel Fleet and the convoy. It was a dangerous moment. Reckoning, as he said later, that it was 'proper to avoid coming to battle with them as then circumstanced,' but knowing that he must get between the Combined Fleet and the convoy, he took a brave decision. It required considerable nerve and skill to do so, but as the enemy formed line of battle, he stood to the northward, passing between the Scilly Isles and Land's End. At the same time, he sent the *Cormorant* back to the west to warn Parker and the Jamaica convoy of the situation, instructing that the merchant ships be sent into Irish ports.[10]

Córdova and de Guichen were baffled by the Channel Fleet's disappearance. Few fleet commanders would have attempted such a bold manoeuvre as to take a large fleet through such a relatively narrow passage. La Motte-Picquet, whose squadron of eight ships of the line headed the Combined Fleet, was unable to overtake Howe, even though he was prepared to tackle the Channel Fleet with just his own squadron. He wrote later:

> I did all that was humanly possible to engage the enemy, even at the risk of being overwhelmed or captured, but it was useless. The enemy fleet continued to be less than two leagues away, and a large part of it was very strung out. If we had sailed faster, the English fleet would have been destroyed in these waters. What a day! We were thwarted by the slowness

10 James, *The British Navy in Adversity*, p.369; Syrett, *Howe*, p.102.

> of the Spanish vessels. My officers and men had shown the greatest ardour, and I shall regret for the rest of my life that I was unable to make use of it.[11]

Howe, after his escape, remained to the north of the Scilly Isles, waiting for further news of the Jamaica convoy. Getting none, and being forced off his station by a northerly gale, he decided to return eastward 'in quest of the enemy' with a view to attempting to draw them away from their position off the Scillies.[12] In fact the Combined Fleet had itself been driven to the southward; upon discovering this on 2 August, and also that the Jamaica convoy had safely entered the Channel, Howe made first to Torbay and then Spithead, which he reached on 14 August. The threat from the Combined Fleet was at an end; Córdova was now ordered to take his fleet back to Spain to deal with an attempt to relieve Gibraltar, which the Spanish reckoned, correctly, must soon be made.

It was certainly true that the British had recognised the urgent need to resupply Gibraltar; but even as Howe was returning to Spithead, another threat materialised in the North Sea with which it was urgently necessary to deal. In yet another illustration of the ongoing problem of trying to do too many things at once with insufficient resources, the Admiralty had to face a fresh indication that the Dutch were preparing to send the fleet to sea. News arrived that Hartsinck had at last sailed, and Commodore Hotham was ordered into the Downs with eight ships of the line with orders to intercept the Dutch squadron, and to protect an incoming Baltic convoy. Three more ships of the line were sent after him, followed by five more under Vice Admiral Mark Milbanke, who took over the command.[13]

When the first news reached London that the Dutch fleet was at sea, the Cabinet decided that Howe was to proceed into the North Sea 'with 20 or 30 ships of the line in quest of the Dutch squadron'.[14] The threat was being taken extremely seriously; Howe was to go just as soon as sufficient ships were ready for sea to seek out Hartsinck's squadron either at the Texel or, if necessary, off the Naze of Norway. Keppel explained to Howe that the Dutch must be dealt with, since otherwise 'essential naval supplies from the Baltic would be cut off, and the Dutch would be in a position to blockade London and every other port on the north coast, and put an end to our coastal trade and every other branch of commerce'. This sounds alarmist, but as Keppel emphasised: 'If we fail getting the ships safe from the Baltic our next year's equipping the fleet must also fail, if relief does not get soon to Gibraltar that garrison must fall'.[15]

11 Lacour-Gayet, *La marine Militaire*, p.384.

12 Syrett, *Howe*, p.103.

13 James, *The British Navy in Adversity*, p.370.

14 Syrett, *Howe*, p.104.

15 Syrett, *Howe*, p.104.

Fortunately, the Dutch threat evaporated on 25 August when it was learned that Hartsinck had returned to port, having seen a convoy, part of which was for the East and part for the West Indies, safely through the North Sea. Nevertheless, it was essential to be sure that he did not re-emerge, and 10 ships of the line were sent into the North Sea to look into the Texel. If the Dutch appeared not to have any immediate intention of putting to sea, the squadron was to return at once to Spithead, where preparations had begun for the relief expedition to Gibraltar.

On 29 August the Royal Navy suffered a disastrous and irreparable loss. The *Royal George*, at anchor at Spithead, while undergoing the replacement of a lead pipe on her starboard side, suddenly went down, taking with her Kempenfelt and some 800 other men, women and children. The work being undertaken required that the vessel be given a 'parliament heel,' which entailed moving shot and cannon to her larboard side in order to expose the pipe.[16] In her comprehensive account of the tragedy, Hilary Rubinstein has shown that the decision to undertake this was taken with Kempenfelt's approval; that when he discussed it with William Nickelson, the master attendant at Portsmouth dockyard, he reversed the decision; but that subsequently Kempenfelt, and his flag captain Martin Waghorn, decided after all to proceed with the repair.

The work had begun during the morning watch. A combination of factors caused the vessel's list to larboard steadily to increase. Acting Lieutenant Philip Durham, later to become a distinguished admiral and himself commander-in-chief at Portsmouth, described the events that followed in an account which he wrote in 1842, in which he claimed that he 'heard the men who were boring the hole for the stopcock call out, "Avast, avast heeling! She is quite high enough; the ship is rising out of the water"'. When Waghorn was told of the situation, he summoned the drummer, although according to Durham it was he who did so:

> The captain then ordered the ship to be righted, and I called the drummer, and ordered him to beat to quarters, and for this purpose the guns were begun to be run out on the weather side, when the ship took a sally or tremulous motion ... Looking up aloft, I saw that the masts continued to fall over.[17]

Everything now happened very quickly. Aboard the ship there were hundreds of women and children, as well as dealers who had come on board to sell goods to the crew, and there was an almost instant panic. Among them, and among the crew, there were few could swim, and in any case there was not time for many of them to come on deck. The commanding officer of a 50-gun ship anchored about half a mile north-east of the *Royal George* described what happened:

16 Rubinstein, *Catastrophe at Spithead*, p.85.
17 Rubinstein, *Catastrophe at Spithead*, pp.95-97.

> [S]he turned over suddenly, her masts went underwater and continued so for some time; the starboard side of her bottom was then above water, on which many hundred men and some women had scrambled, and were making sad lamentations ... This continued as long as the air in the hold supported the ship in that position, but as the water forced the air out, she sank from under them, and then the masts came up again, and as the ship lay on the larboard side they inclined to the south (towards the Isle of Wight) at an angle of about 45 degrees, and the maintop was then eight or ten feet above water.[18]

Waghorn, who survived the sinking, said a few days later that he had gone down to tell Kempenfelt of the need to right the ship, but before he could get to the admiral's door, the ship went down almost at once. Some 910 members of the crew were on board, and of these 331 men survived. The number of civilian casualties was never accurately assessed, but it appears to have been in excess of 300, of which some 60 were children. How Kempenfelt actually met his death is uncertain, though one account suggested that he had left his cabin to give orders to right the ship; another suggested that he was still in his cabin and unable to reach the deck as the ship sank. There were also several other accounts of his fate.

That afternoon Howe urgently reported the shocking news to the Admiralty:

> It is with inexpressible concern that I have occasion to inform you of the loss of the *Royal George*, which ship, being upon the heel this morning, suddenly overset, filled and sank. The captain is much bruised, and some few of the people (I fear not many) have been saved; but I have not the satisfaction to hear that the rear admiral is among the number. Much as this misfortune is to be lamented, I esteem the loss of that officer the most interesting circumstance attending it, as regards the detriment to the King's naval service. A fresh wind and lee tide prevents me, by this express, to add any particulars respecting this unhappy event.[19]

The subsequent court martial of Waghorn and his company concluded that 'the ship was not over heeled' and that 'the captain, officers and ship's company be acquitted of all blame on account of the loss of the ship'. The verdict went on to express the opinion 'that some material part of her frame gave way, which can only be accounted for by the general state of the decay of her timbers'.[20] Rubinstein concludes that there will probably never be a satisfactory answer to why Kempenfelt and Waghorn took the decision which they did; possibly they had been misled into

18 Rubinstein, *Catastrophe at Spithead*, pp.98-99.

19 Barrow, *Richard Earl Howe*, pp.138-139.

20 Rubinstein, *Catastrophe at Spithead*, p.143.

assuming that a minimal degree of heel would suffice, but if so 'Waghorn should surely have aborted the operation as soon as he learned that the initial degree of heel was insufficient'.[21]

The blame for the ship's condition has been laid by critics of his tenure at the Admiralty at Sandwich's door; Admiral James, for instance, noted that 'it was the irony of fate that Kempenfelt, who had done so much to reform abuses in the Navy, should have fallen victim to the shortcomings of corrupt administration'.[22] David Syrett has expressed the view that the tragedy 'probably resulted from corrosion of the iron fastenings caused by the ship's copper bottom'.[23] This certainly seems not unlikely.

The loss to the Navy was immense. In addition to Kempenfelt's achievements as a fighting admiral, his influence extended to a wide range of the navy's functions. He was noted for the care of his men, the divisional system to enhance officer responsibility, and the enunciation of tactical principles which were adopted later by such as Howe, St Vincent, Duncan and Nelson. One example of Kempenfelt's strategic thinking, written in the light of his experience of the cruise against de Guichen, appears in the letter or to Middleton of 6 January 1782 reproduced as Appendix III. Yet perhaps he was most celebrated for his development of the signalling system based on that which Howe had put forward. During the war he also contributed to a marked improvement of gunnery and the development of ordnance, as Admiral James described:

> For this, and for many improvements in training and discipline Richard Kempenfelt was mainly responsible. He was a man of remarkable vision and knowledge, coupled with tireless energy. His ideas on discipline and ship management permeated a large number of the personnel… He was an unsparing critic, but, like Hood, the letters containing his inmost thoughts were written to men who could be relied not to divulge their contents. He had greater trials to bear than Hood.[24]

Kempenfelt, like Middleton, was devoutly evangelical; he wrote religious verse, and was pious, temperate, benevolent, honest and brave; he would have had so much more to give, and stands out as the most thoughtful of the Navy's leaders of the time.

Meanwhile at Gibraltar, the Spanish were preparing their assault. D'Arcon's scheme for the capture of the fortress was based on the use of floating batteries. Designed with a roof of thick hides, and with wooden sides of great thickness,

21 Rubinstein, *Catastrophe at Spithead*, p.173.
22 James, *The British Navy in Adversity*, p.372.
23 Syrett, *European Waters*, p.161.
24 James, *The British Navy in Adversity*, pp.419-420.

they were equipped with a system intended to deal with red-hot shot fired by the defenders. A thousand guns, afloat and on shore, took part in the attack, which was launched on 13 September. Including the personnel of the Combined Fleet anchored off Algeciras, it is estimated that 100,000 men took part in the attack.[25] There was, however, not much confidence among the allied high command in the effectiveness of d'Arcon's batteries. The Duc de Crillon, in command of the land forces, and Córdova were both sceptical, while d'Arcon himself had wanted to carry out more tests before committing his creations to action. He was overruled by Crillon, and the attack went ahead. The launching of a daytime assault took the garrison by surprise, but it quickly brought its artillery into action, and there was a prolonged and fierce exchange of fire. The floating batteries, although at first undamaged by many hits, found it difficult to elevate their guns to reach the target. Gradually, however, as the use of red-hot shot built up it began to cause havoc among the floating batteries, which were unsupported by the ships of the French and Spanish fleets. One after another caught fire, and then they were attacked by a flotilla of gunboats under Captain Roger Curtis. By noon next day five of the batteries had blown up, three had burnt to the water's edge and two more were in flames. The attack had proved a disastrous failure.

The delay in despatching the fleet on its vital mission might have been fatal to the chances of holding the fortress. Middleton was of the opinion that its departure had been unnecessarily delayed, and expressed his views in characteristically pungent terms in a letter, written on 11 September but not in fact sent, to Lord Shelburne, who had become Prime Minister in July following the death of Rockingham. In this, he pointed out that he had received the Treasury order to provide for Gibraltar as early as 26 July; that the winds continued westward until 4 September, but by the next day had gone round to the east:

> On the 6th the river ships arrived at Spithead. Why the whole did not meet off the Isle of Wight on the 6th and sail immediately is a matter of enquiry. If they had, their passage to Gibraltar would have been secured, and their arrival almost certain by the 20th. The wind has now changed, the consequences, in every point of view, are fatal. Can a nation whose public business is managed in this way possibly succeed? Is it not necessary to make enquiry in the Cabinet by calling for returns from the ships' officers, and see where the fault lies. Every neglect of service since I have been in office has originated in London.[26]

It was on 11 September that Howe sailed from Spithead with the entire Channel Fleet, consisting of 35 ships of the line, several frigates and 130 victuallers,

25 James, *The British Navy in Adversity*, p.373.
26 Laughton (ed.), *Barham Papers*, Vol.II, p.66.

store ships, transport and cargo vessels. A hundred of these were in three individual convoys, for the West and East Indies and Portugal respectively, and the remainder were for the relief of Gibraltar. Two regiments of infantry to reinforce the garrison were carried aboard warships. If the Combined Fleet interfered, it was left to Howe's 'judgment and direction to determine what measures to pursue upon such an event'.[27] After unloading the troops and supplies, Howe was to return to England, en route detaching six ships of the line for the West Indies and two or three more to cruise in the Bay of Biscay.

One day, when lying to to collect the convoy, Howe convened a meeting of his subordinate commanders and his captains. He had been turning over in his mind the problem of facing a greatly superior fleet. One possible solution which had occurred to him was a night attack. Turning to Barrington, he said:

> It is a thought suddenly come across me, and as we have no better employment just now, we may as well discuss the question. I should therefore, my dear Admiral, like to know your opinion on this point, and also that of the several captains; and if you please we will follow the practice of courts martial, and begin with the youngest.

The captains, not wishing to stand out against what might be a cherished idea of their commander, generally spoke in favour, until Jervis expressed his opinion. He must, he said, give a dissenting voice to the suggestion, and declare most decidedly against any such night attack. Such confusion might be created that friends might fight with each other instead of the enemy, and it would deprive the fleet of making use of the new signals. Barrington then said that he entirely agreed, adding that he preferred daylight, if for no other reason than that it could be seen who did and who did not do his duty. 'Give us daylight, my Lord, by all means, that we may see what we are about'. On this, the discussion concluded.[28]

The fleet made poor time due to contrary winds, arriving off Cape St Vincent on 9 October. From there, Howe sent a frigate to Faro to pick up intelligence from the British consul, which returned next day with news that the Combined Fleet was anchored in the Bay of Gibraltar, with 50 ships of the line, information which was then confirmed by several neutrals. That evening, however, a fierce westerly gale scattered the Combined Fleet, driving ashore four vessels, including the ship of the line *San Miguel*, 70, which was captured by the British. Two more ships of the line were driven away to the eastwards into the Mediterranean.

Early on 11 October the Channel Fleet and the relief convoy entered the Straits of Gibraltar. The westerly gale was still blowing, however, and only four of the storeships were able to get into Gibraltar; the rest, and the whole of the Channel

27 Syrett, *European Waters*, p.161.
28 Barrow, *Richard Earl Howe*, pp.145-146.

Fleet were driven eastward some 50 miles into the Mediterranean. Howe sent the convoy to wait for the moment off the African coast until the situation was clarified. On 12 October Captain Curtis came out to report to Howe what had happened to the Combined Fleet. Although it had been disarranged by the effects of the gale, it still retained a considerable numerical superiority. Next day Córdova put to sea to pick up the two ships that had been driven into the Mediterranean and to seek out and attack the relief convoy. The Combined Fleet reached Malaga, where it was becalmed. When the wind picked up again, it had come round to the east, enabling the Channel Fleet and the convoy to enter Rosia Bay. Between 14 and 17 October all the storeships discharged their cargo, and the troops disembarked from the warships; some 1,500 barrels of gun powder from the fleet were landed.

On 19 October, with the wind still in the east, Howe was ready to commence his return journey to England. As the fleet put to sea the Combined Fleet was sighted to the north-east. The Channel Fleet at this time was between Europa Point and Ceuta, with insufficient room to form line of battle, so Howe passed through the Straits into the Atlantic, followed by the enemy. Howe laconically described the action off Cape Spartel which followed:

> The British fleet being formed to leeward to receive the Spaniards, they were left uninterruptedly to take their own distance, at which they should think fit to engage. They began their cannonade at sunset, on the van and rear, seeming to point their chief attack on the latter; and continued at a considerable distance, and with little effect, until ten at night. It was returned occasionally from different ships of the fleet, as their nearer approach at times afforded a more favourable opportunity for making any impression on them. The enemy hauling their wind, and the British fleet keeping on all night with the full sail directed before the commencement of their fire, the fleets were now much separated.[29]

The engagement had been indecisive, but the losses were not trifling, suggesting that it was harder fought than many supposed. British losses were recorded as 68 killed and 208 wounded, while the Combined Fleet lost 60 killed and 320 wounded.[30] Repairs to the British ships were at once put in hand; a number of these had suffered damage to their masts. The Combined Fleet now stood away west-northwest; Howe was disinclined to follow, and he set his course for home, arriving at St Helens on 14 November.

Admiral Mahan reckoned that 'the services rendered to his country by Howe on this occasion were eminently characteristic of the special qualities of that great

29 Barrow, *Richard Earl Howe*, pp.150-151.

30 Mahan, *Major Operations*, p.232.

officer'.[31] Howe had certainly displayed great competence during his command of the Channel Fleet, but he was perhaps fortunate in being opposed by such a diffident enemy. A French naval historian has described his conduct of the operation to relieve Gibraltar in glowing terms:

> The qualities displayed by Lord Howe during this short campaign rose to the full height of the mission which he had to fulfil. This operation, one of the finest in the War of American Independence, merits praise equal to that of a victory. If the English fleet was favoured by circumstances – and it is rare that in such enterprises one can succeed without the aid of fortune – it was above all the commander-in-chief's quickness of perception, the accuracy of his judgment, and the rapidity of his decisions, that assured success.[32]

31 Mahan, *Major Operations,* p.232.

32 E. Chevalier, *Histoire de la Marine Francaise pendant la guerre de l'independence Americain* (Paris: Hachette et Cie, 1877), p.358.

Epilogue

After the battle of Cape Spartel, there were to be no more fleet actions by the Channel Fleet. Once it had returned to St Helens, where it arrived on 14 November, Howe went ashore. In London, he became immersed once more in the political life of the country. Somewhat surprisingly, he next found himself on 30 January 1783 as First Lord of the Admiralty. This followed Keppel's resignation from Shelburne's government over the proposed terms of the peace treaties now in course of negotiation to end the war. During the debates in the House of Lords on these terms, Howe had supported Shelburne's position, declaring that the 'peace was necessary as our Fleets were in wretched decayed condition'.[1] His appointment to the Admiralty was in the nature of a stopgap; the government was falling to pieces, but it was essential that a naval figure of authority was in place to oversee the process of demobilisation, which was already giving rise to unrest aboard the fleet at Portsmouth. Howe's term of office as First Lord was brief; when a new coalition government took office on 10 April, led by North and Fox, Keppel was restored as First Lord of the Admiralty.

During the closing months of the war, after Sandwich had been replaced by Keppel, there had been no significant change of policy. The prolonged attack on Sandwich, culminating in 30 separate calls for papers in the House of Commons debates, each in respect of a separate ground of complaint about the First Lord's handling of the naval war, had really been an attack on the man rather than his policy. In the documents and notes for speeches which he prepared in his defence, Sandwich put forward a detailed answer to each of the charges made against him. Although for many years these cut no ice with historians, who almost uniformly condemned him for incompetence and corruption, they amounted to a comprehensive answer to his critics. The editors of his papers point to the difficulty of making a fair judgment, remarking that most of the questions arising about his stewardship of the Admiralty 'can be answered only with the full knowledge of eighteenth century methods and conditions of government and administration'. They go on to quote the words of George Selwyn, a supporter of the government but on familiar terms with Fox, who wrote after the great debate in the Commons:

1 Syrett, *Howe*, p.109.

> Our majority was but *mince*; but it was a popular question, because Lord Sandwich is not a popular man. But I have lived long enough to have remembered other ministers less popular, if possible, and who have been since reverenced, and by the most respectable among those who had traduced them.[2]

Professor Rodger concluded his outstanding biography of Sandwich by observing that his reputation had unfairly suffered by being associated solely with the American War, and that 'for his enemies then, and those that have taken their part since, he became a personification of folly and wickedness'. He went on to quote Lord North's summary in 1782 of Sandwich's career as a public man in 1782: 'He has certainly been a very diligent and a very able, and a very faithful servant; his situation naturally drew upon him many enemies, and made him the object of persecution on the part of the opposition, but Lord North believes that his merit will be known when he is gone'.[3] In his biography, Rodger has demonstrated that merit beyond question, while at the same time providing a remarkably comprehensive picture of the Admiralty and its management of the Royal Navy during a critical period in its history.

Although, when the peace came, it found the Royal Navy in some respects perhaps in a stronger position relative to its enemies than at any time previously during the war, it had never been able to attain the degree of maritime superiority without which Britain never could have defeated the colonists or successfully obtained command of the sea. Always in a situation of numerical inferiority, it proved impossible in practice to devise a consistent and effective strategy for Britain to win a decisive victory over her enemies. The threat of invasion was real; Kempenfelt might assign to the land forces the task of resisting invasion, but the British Army was not strong. It was all too clear that if the enemy got ashore, Britain would be in serious trouble. As it was, the threat never materialised, but this was almost entirely a matter of good fortune.

The navy had lost Kempenfelt; but there was a continuum of talent that would stand it in good stead when the country found itself once more at war with France a decade later. Some of its leaders, who had held fleet or squadron command in the American War, would do so again, such as Howe, the brothers Hood, and Cornwallis. Behind them, too, came some of the navy's rising stars, who would prove to be among the greatest names of British naval history, who had already begun to distinguish themselves in individual commands. These included such as Jervis, Duncan, Keith, Nelson, Collingwood, Saumarez and Pellew. The Royal Navy's extraordinary tradition of victory was to prove safe in their hands.

2 Barnes and Owen (eds), *Private Papers of John, Earl of Sandwich*, Vol.IV, p.272.
3 Rodger, *Insatiable Earl*, p.330.

Appendix I

The British Fleet at the Battle of Ushant, 27 July 1778

Van Division		
Monarch	74	J. Rowley
Hector	74	Sir J. Hamilton
Centaur	74	P. Crosby
Exeter	64	J.N.P. Nott
Duke	90	W. Brereton
Queen	90	L. Prescott; flag Vice Adm. Sir R. Harland
Shrewsbury	74	Sir J. Ross.
Cumberland	74	J. Peyton
Berwick	74	K. Stewart
Stirling Castle	64	Sir C Douglas
Centre Division		
Courageux	74	Lord Mulgrave
Thunderer	74	R. Walsingham
Sandwich	90	R. Edwards
Valiant	74	J. Leveson Gower
Bienfaisant	64	J. MacBride
Victory	100	J. Faulkner; flag Adm. Keppel; R. Adm. J. Campbell Capt. of the Fleet
Foudroyant	80	J. Jervis
Prince George	98	Sir J. Lindsay
Vigilant	64	R. Kingsmill
Terrible	74	Sir R. Bickerton
Vengeance	74	M. Clements
Rear Division		
Worcester	64	M. Robertson

Elizabeth	74	F.L. Maitland
Robust	74	A. Hood
Formidable	98	J. Bazeley; flag Vice Adm. Sir H. Palliser
Ocean	90	J. Laforey
America	64	Lord Longford
Defiance	64	S.G. Goodall
Egmont	74	J.C. Allen
Ramillies	74	R. Digby
Outside the Line		
Six Frigates		

Appendix II

The French Fleet at the Battle of Ushant, 27 July 1778

Blue and White Squadron		
Dauphin Royal	70	de Nieuil
Amphion	50	de Trobriant
Éveillé	64	du Botderu
Bien-Aimé	74	d'Aubenton
Couronne	80	Huon de Kermadec; flag *Lt Gén.* du Chaffault
Palmier	74	de Réals
Indien	64	de la Grandière
Glorieux	74	de Beausset
Vengeur	64	d'Amblimont
White Squadron		
Réfléchi	64	Cillart de Suville
Ville de Paris	90	de Peynier; flag *Chef d'Esc.* de Guichen
Actif	74	Estienne d'Orves
Magnifique	74	de Brach
Bretagne	110	D. Parscau; flag *Lt Gén.* d'Orvilliers, du Pavillon *major d'escadre*
Fendant	74	de Vaudreuil
Actionnaire	64	de Proissy
Orient	74	Hector
Artésien	64	des Touches
Blue Squadron		
Sphinx	64	de Soulanges
Robuste	74	Longueville; flag *Chef d'Esc.* Comte de Grasse
Roland	64	de l'Archantel
Zodiaque	74	de la Porte-Vezins

Saint Esprit	80	M. Roquefeuil; flag of *Lt Gén*. Duc de Chartres with *Chef d'Esc*. La Motte-Picquet
Intrépide	74	Beaussier de Chateauvert
Solitaire	64	de Briqueville
Conquérant	74	de Monteil
Diadème	74	de la Cardonnie
Outside the Line		
Triton	64	de Ligondès
Saint Michel	60	M de Genouilly
Fier	50	Turpin de Breuil
Seven Frigates		
Detached (Separated from fleet night of 23/24 July)		
Duc de Bourgogne	80	de Rochechouart
Alexandre	64	de Trémignon

Appendix III

Kempenfelt's Ideas of 13 January 1782 about the Mode of Carrying on the War

When the enemy's force by sea is superior to yours and you have many remote possessions to guard, it renders it difficult to determine the best means of disposing of your ships.

When the enemy's designs are known, in order to do something effectual, you must endeavour to be superior to them in such parts where, if they should succeed in their design, they would most injure you.

If your fleet is so divided as to be in all places inferior to the enemy, they will then in all places have the probability of succeeding in their attempts.

If a squadron of sufficient force cannot be formed to face the enemy at home, it would be more eligible to let the number of that squadron be yet less, that thereby you may be enabled to gain a superiority elsewhere.

When inferior to the enemy, and you have only a squadron of observation to watch and attend upon their motions, such squadron should be composed of two-decked ships only, as to answer its purpose it must have the advantage in sailing of the enemy, otherwise in certain circumstances, they may be forced to action or to give up some of their heavy sailers.

It is highly expedient to have such a flying squadron to hang about the enemy's large fleet, as it will prevent their dividing into squadrons for intercepting your trade or other purposes, or spreading and extending their ships for a more extensive view. Such a squadron will be always at hand ready to profit from any accidental separation or dispersion of their ships from strong gales, fogs, or other causes. They may intercept supplies, intelligence, etc. to them. In fine, such a squadron will be a check and restraint upon their activity or motions, and thereby may prevent much of that mischief they otherwise might do.

When the enemy are near the Channel, I should suppose the best situation for such a squadron would be to keep without them to the westward, as more favourable to protect your ships coming into the Channel. The squadron will also be more at liberty for its operations to approach or keep a distance from the enemy as they may find convenient, and not liable to be forced into port and blocked up.

When the enemy perceive your design of keeping the North Sea free by a stout squadron for your trade to return home that way, it may be supposed they will detach from their Grand fleet as many ships as the inferiority of your Western squadron will allow to endeavour, in conjunction with the Dutch, to turn in that sea the balance of power to their side. But probably they will not penetrate into this scheme of ours time enough to prevent its good effects this ensuing summer, and other objects they may have in view to attempt with their Grand fleet may divert their attention from it.

The enemy I conceive have at this time two grand designs against us: the one, the conquest of our West India islands; the other at home, not confined merely to the interception of our trade, but to favour by the superiority of their fleet a formidable descent upon Great Britain, and I should suppose the blow would be directed where it would be most felt by us, either against the Metropolis or Portsmouth, I should rather think the latter is more practicable from the nature of the navigation.

They will with some reason conclude that one of their designs will succeed, knowing that we cannot by our naval power guard against both, and that if we employ a force sufficient to defeat their design in one place, we must necessarily leave the other exposed to them.

It may be (or might have been) in our power to send such a force of ships to the West Indies as would frustrate their designs there, but at home I imagine, with our utmost exertions, we must remain inferior by sea, and trust our defence from a descent to our land forces.

As our ships are now all coppered, they are always ready for service; therefore, when the enemy's fleet at the end of the campaign returns into port, which hitherto has been always early in the fall, you are then at liberty to send what number of ships you might think proper to act offensively or defensively in the West Indies during the winter months, and have them again at home in sufficient time for the summer service.

There is greater advantage upon such occasions in letting your ships slip out single, as their voyage is thereby rendered much shorter, and your design a secret.

Source: Barnes and Owen (eds), *Private Papers of John, Earl of Sandwich*, Vol.IV, pp.80-82.

Bibliography

Adkins, Roy and Lesley, *Gibraltar: The Greatest Siege in British History* (London: Little Brown, 2017).

Anon., *The Defence of Vice Admiral Sir Hugh Palliser* (London: T. Cadell, 1779).

Allen, Gardner W, *A Naval History of the American Revolution* (New York: Houghton Mifflin, 1913).

Barnes, G.R., and Owen, J.H. (eds), *The Private Papers of John, Earl of Sandwich* (London: Navy Records Society, 1936).

Barrow, Sir John, *The Life of Richard, Earl Howe* (London: John Murray, 1838).

Barry, Quintin, *Crisis at the Chesapeake* (Warwick: Helion & Co, 2021).

Baugh, D.A., 'Why did Britain Lose Command of the Sea During the War for America?' in Black, J.R., and Woodfine, P. (eds), *The British Navy and the Use of Naval Power in the Eighteenth Century* (Leicester: Leicester University Press, 1988).

Black, Jeremy, *Natural and Necessary Enemies* (London: Duckworth & Co, 1986).

Blandemor, Thomas (ed.), *The Trial of the Honourable Augustus Keppel* (London: Wilkes & Co, 1779).

Beatson, Robert, *Naval and Military Memoirs of Great Britain from 1727 to 1783* (London: J Strachan, 1804).

Billias, George A. (ed.), *George Washington's Generals and Opponents* (New York: William Morrow & Co, 1969).

Bonner-Smith, D. (ed.), *The Barrington Papers* (London: Navy Records Society, 1937).

Broomfield, J.H., 'Lord Sandwich at the Admiralty Board: Politics in the British Navy, 1771-1778' in *The Mariner's Mirror* (February 1965), pp.7-17.

Broomfield, J.H., 'The Keppel-Palliser Affair, 1778-1779' in *The Mariner's Mirror* (August 1961), pp.195-207.

Butterfield, H., *George III, Lord North and the People 1779-1780* (London: G. Bell & Sons, 1949).

Callender, Geoffrey, *Sea Kings of Britain: Keppel to Nelson* (London: Longmans Green, 1939).

Cavaliero R., *Admiral Satan: The Life and Campaigns of Suffren* (London: I.B. Tauris, 1994)

Chadwick, Rear Admiral French Ensor (ed.), *The Graves Papers* (New York: Naval History Society, 1916).

Chevalier, E., *Histoire de la Marine Francaise* (Paris: Hachette et Cie, 1902).

Christie, Ian R., *The End of North's Ministry 1780-1782* (London: Macmillan, 1958).

Clark, William and Morgan, William James (eds), *Naval Documents of the American Revolution* (Washington DC: US Navy Dept., 1961).

Clowes, W. Laird, *The Royal Navy: A History* (London: Sampson Low Marston & Co, 1898).

Cock, Randolph, '"Avarice and Rapacity" and "Treasonable Correspondence" in "an Emporium for All the World": The British capture of St Eustatius, 1781', in *The Mariner's Mirror* (August 1981), pp.265-278.

Corbett, Julian S. (ed.), *Signals and Instructions 1776-1794* (London: Navy Records Society, 1908).

Corbett, Julian S. (ed.), *Fighting Instructions 1530-1860* (London: Navy Records Society, 1905).

Corbett, Julian S., *Some Principles of Maritime Strategy* (London: Longmans Green & Co, 1911).

Cornwallis-West, G., *The Life and Letters of Admiral Cornwallis* (London: Holden, 1927).

Corwin, Edward S., *French Policy and the American Alliance* (Princeton New Jersey: Princeton University Press, 1916).

Creswell, John, *British Admirals of the Eighteenth Century* (London: Allen & Unwin, 1972)

Donne, W. Rodham (ed.), *The Correspondence of King George the Third and Lord North* (London: W Clowes & Sons, n.d.).

Dull, Jonathan, *The French Navy and American Independence* (Princeton New Jersey: Princeton University Press, 1975).

Dull, Jonathan, *The French Navy and the Seven Years War* (London: University of Nebraska, Press 2005).

Edler, Friedrich, *The Dutch Republic and the American Revolution* (Baltimore, Maryland: Johns Hopkins Press, 1911).

Fabel, R.F.A., *Bombast and Broadsides: The Lives of George Johnstone* (Tuscaloosa: University of Alabama Press, 1987).

Gardiner, Leslie, *The British Admiralty* (London: Blackwood, 1968).

Graham, G.S., *Empire of the North Atlantic* (Toronto: University of Toronto Press, 1966).

Graham, G.S., *The Royal Navy in the War of American Independence* (Greenwich: National Maritime Museum, 1976).

Gruber, I.D., *The Howe Brothers and the American Revolution* (New York: Atheneum, 1972).

Hamilton, C.I., *The Making of the Modern Admiralty* (Cambridge: Cambridge University Press, 2011).

Hamilton, Sir R. Vesey, and Laughton, Sir J. (eds), *Recollections of James Anthony Gardner* (London: Navy Records Society, 1906).

Hamilton, Sir R. Vesey (ed.), *Letters and Papers of Sir T. Byam Martin* (London: Navy Records Society, 1903).

Hannay, David (ed.), *Letters Written by Sir Samuel Hood* (London: Navy Records Society, 1895).

Harding, Richard, *Sea Power and Naval Warfare 1650-1830* (London: UCL Press, 1999).

Hodges, H.W. (ed.), *Select Naval Documents* (Cambridge: Cambridge University Press, 1922).

Holland, L.E., 'The Development of Signalling in the Royal Navy' in *The Mariner's Mirror* (February 1953), pp.5-26.

Holmes, Michael, *Augustus Hervey: A Naval Casanova* (Bishop Auckland: Pentland Press, 1996).

Hood, Dorothy, *The Admirals Hood* (London: Hutchinson, 1940).

Holmes, Michael, *Augustus Hervey* (Bishop Auckland: Pentland Press. 1996).

James, Rear Admiral W.M., *The British Navy in Adversity* (London: Longmans Green, 1938).

Jenkins, E.H., *A History of the French Navy* (London: Macdonald & Janes, 1973).

Kennedy, Paul M., *The Rise and Fall of British Naval Mastery* (London: Macmillan, 1983).

Knight, R.J.B., 'The Royal Navy's Recovery after the Early Phase of the American Revolutionary War' in Andreopoulos, George J., and Selesky, Harold F. (eds), *The Aftermath of Defeat* (New Haven: Yale University Press, 1994).

Knight, R.J.B. (ed), *Portsmouth Dockyard Papers, 1774-1783: The American War* (Portsmouth: City of Portsmouth, 1987).

Knox, Dudley W., *The Naval Genius of George Washington* (Boston: Houghton Mifflin, 1932).

Lacour-Gayet, G., *La marine Militaire de France sous le règne de Louis XVI* (Paris: Honoré Champion, 1905).

Larrabee, Harold, *Decision at the Chesapeake* (London: Kimber, 1965).

Laughton, Sir John (ed.), *Journal of Rear Admiral Bartholomew James* (London: Navy Records Society, 1896).

Laughton, Sir John (ed.), *Letters and Papers of Charles Lord Barham* (London: Navy Records Society, 1908).

Laughton, Sir John, *From Howard to Nelson* (London: Lawrence & Bullen, 1899).

Lavery, B. (ed.), *Shipboard Life and Organisation, 1731-1815* (Aldershot: Navy Records Society, 1998).

Le Fevre, Peter and Harding, Richard (eds), *Precursors of Nelson: British Admirals of the Eighteenth Century* (London: Chatham Publishing, 2018).

Lewis, Charles Lee, *Admiral de Grasse and American Independence* (Annapolis Maryland: Naval Institute Press, 1945).

Longmate, Norman, *Island Fortress* (London: Grafton, 1993).

Mackay, Ruddock F., *Admiral Hawke* (Oxford: Clarendon Press, 1965).
Mackesy, Piers, *The War for America* (London: Longmans Green, 1964).
Mahan, Admiral A.T., *Major Operations of the Navies in the American War of Independence* (London: Sampson Low Marston & Co, 1913).
Mahan, Admiral A.T., *Types of Naval Officers* (London: Sampson Low & Co, 1904).
Marcus, G.J., *A Naval History of England: The Formative Centuries* (Boston: Little Brown & Co, 1961).
Martelli, George, *Jemmy Twitcher* (London: Jonathan Cape, 1962).
McIntyre, Captain D., *Admiral Rodney* (London: Peter Davies, 1962).
Middleton, Richard, 'Naval Resources and the British Defeat at Yorktown 1781' in *The Mariner's Mirror* (February 2014), pp.29-43.
Miller, N., *Sea of Glory: A Naval History of the American Revolution* (Charleston: David Mackay, 1974).
Owen, J.H., 'Operations of the Western Squadron 1781-1782'in *The Naval Review* (1927, XV:1), pp.33-53.
Padfield, Peter, *Maritime Supremacy and the Opening of the Western Mind* (London: John Murray, 1999).
Parkinson, C. Northcote, *Edward Pellew, Viscount Exmouth* (London: Methuen, 1934).
Patterson, A. Temple, *The Other Armada* (Manchester: Manchester University Press, 1960).
Pears, Richard, *King George III and the Politicians* (Oxford: Oxford University Press, 1954).
Pengelly, Colin, *Sir Samuel Hood and the Battle of the Chesapeake* (Gainesville Florida: University Press of Florida, 2009).
Perrin, W.G. (ed.), *Naval Miscellany* (London: Navy Records Society, 1928).
Ranft, B. McL. (ed.), *The Vernon Papers* (London: Navy Records Society, 1958).
Richmond, Admiral Sir Herbert, *The Invasion of Britain* (London: Methuen & Co, 1941).
Richmond, Admiral Sir Herbert, *National Policy and Naval Strength* (London: Longmans, 1928).
Richmond, Admiral Sir Herbert, *Statesmen and Sea Power* (Oxford: Clarendon Press, 1946).
Robison, Rear Admiral S.S. and Robison, Mary, *A History of Naval Tactics from 1530-1930* (Annapolis Maryland: Naval Institute Press, 1942).
Rodger, N.A.M., 'Image and Reality in Eighteenth Century Naval Tactics' in *The Mariner's Mirror* (August 2003), pp.280-296.
Rodger, N.A.M., *The Admiralty* (Lavenham: Terence Dalton Ltd, 1979).
Rodger, N.A.M., *The Command of the Ocean* (London: Allen Lane, 2004).
Rodger, N.A.M., *The Insatiable Earl* (New York: W.W. Norton & Co, 1993).
Rodger, N.A.M., *The Wooden World: An Anatomy of the Georgian Navy* (London: Collins, 1986).
Rubinstein, Hilary, *Catastrophe at Spithead* (Barnsley: Seaforth Publishing, 2020).

Rutherford, G, 'The Capture of the *Ardent*' in *The Mariner's Mirror* (February 1941), pp.106-131.
Shea, J.G. (ed.), *The Operations of the French Fleet under the Count de Grasse in 1781-1782* (New York: Da Capo Press, 1864).
Sherrard, O.A., *A Life of Lord St Vincent* (London: Allen & Unwin, 1933).
Spinney, David, *Rodney* (London: Allen & Unwin, 1969).
Sulivan, J.A., 'Graves and Hood' in *The Mariner's Mirror* (May 1983), pp.175-194.
Syrett, David, *Admiral Lord Howe* (Stroud: Spellmount, 2006).
Syrett, David, 'The Organisation of British Trade Convoys During the American War, 1775-1783' in *The Mariner's Mirror* (February 1976), pp.169-181.
Syrett, David (ed.), *The Rodney Papers* (Aldershot: Navy Records Society, 2007).
Syrett, David, *The Royal Navy in American Waters 1775-1783* (Aldershot: Scolar Press, 1989).
Syrett, David, *The Royal Navy in European Waters during the American Revolutionary War* (Columbia South Carolina: University of South Carolina, 1998).
Talbott, John E., *The Pen and Ink Sailor* (London: Frank Cass, 1998).
Tilley, John A, *The British Navy and the American Revolution* (Columbia South Carolina: University of South Carolina Press, 1987).
Tracy, N., *Navies, Deterrence and American Independence* (Vancouver: University of British Columbia Press, 1988).
Trew, Peter, *Rodney and the Breaking of the Line* (Barnsley: Pen & Sword, 2006).
Tunstall, Brian (ed. Tracy, Nicholas), *Naval Warfare in the Age of Sail* (London: Conway Maritime Press, 1990).
Valentine, Alan, *Lord George Germain* (Oxford: Clarendon Press, 1962).
White, Captain Thomas, *Naval Researches; or, a candid inquiry into the conduct of Admirals Byron, Graves, Hood, and Rodney* (London: Whittaker Treacher & Arnold, 1830).
Willis, Sam. *Fighting at Sea in the Eighteenth Century* (Woodbridge: Boydell Press, 2008).
Willis, S., *The Struggle for Sea Power* (London: Atlantic Books, 2015).
Wilson, Ben, *Empire of the Deep* (London: Weidenfeld & Nicolson, 2013).
Woodman, Richard, *Britannia's Realm* (Stroud: History Press, 2009).

General Index

Index of Ships

From Reason to Revolution – Warfare 1721-1815

http://www.helion.co.uk/series/from-reason-to-revolution-1721-1815.php

The 'From Reason to Revolution' series covers the period of military history 1721–1815, an era in which fortress-based strategy and linear battles gave way to the nation-in-arms and the beginnings of total war.

This era saw the evolution and growth of light troops of all arms, and of increasingly flexible command systems to cope with the growing armies fielded by nations able to mobilise far greater proportions of their manpower than ever before. Many of these developments were fired by the great political upheavals of the era, with revolutions in America and France bringing about social change which in turn fed back into the military sphere as whole nations readied themselves for war. Only in the closing years of the period, as the reactionary powers began to regain the upper hand, did a military synthesis of the best of the old and the new become possible.

The series will examine the military and naval history of the period in a greater degree of detail than has hitherto been attempted, and has a very wide brief, with the intention of covering all aspects from the battles, campaigns, logistics, and tactics, to the personalities, armies, uniforms, and equipment.

Submissions

The publishers would be pleased to receive submissions for this series. Please contact series editor Andrew Bamford via email (andrewbamford@helion.co.uk), or in writing to Helion & Company Limited, Unit 8 Amherst Business Centre, Budbrooke Road, Warwick, CV34 5WE

Titles

No 1 *Lobositz to Leuthen: Horace St Paul and the Campaigns of the Austrian Army in the Seven Years War 1756-57* (Neil Cogswell)

No 2 *Glories to Useless Heroism: The Seven Years War in North America from the French journals of Comte Maurés de Malartic, 1755-1760* (William Raffle (ed.))

No 3 *Reminiscences 1808-1815 Under Wellington: The Peninsular and Waterloo Memoirs of William Hay* (Andrew Bamford (ed.))

No 4 *Far Distant Ships: The Royal Navy and the Blockade of Brest 1793-1815* (Quintin Barry)

No 5 *Godoy's Army: Spanish Regiments and Uniforms from the Estado Militar of 1800* (Charles Esdaile and Alan Perry)

No 6 *On Gladsmuir Shall the Battle Be! The Battle of Prestonpans 1745* (Arran Johnston)

No 7 *The French Army of the Orient 1798-1801: Napoleon's Beloved 'Egyptians'* (Yves Martin)

No 8 *The Autobiography, or Narrative of a Soldier: The Peninsular War Memoirs of William Brown of the 45th Foot* (Steve Brown (ed.))

No 9 *Recollections from the Ranks: Three Russian Soldiers' Autobiographies from the Napoleonic Wars* (Darrin Boland)

No 10 *By Fire and Bayonet: Grey's West Indies Campaign of 1794* (Steve Brown)

No 11 *Olmütz to Torgau: Horace St Paul and the Campaigns of the Austrian Army in the Seven Years War 1758-60* (Neil Cogswell)

No 12 *Murat's Army: The Army of the Kingdom of Naples 1806-1815* (Digby Smith)

No 13 *The Veteran or 40 Years' Service in the British Army: The Scurrilous Recollections of Paymaster John Harley 47th Foot – 1798-1838* (Gareth Glover (ed.))

No 14 *Narrative of the Eventful Life of Thomas Jackson: Militiaman and Coldstream Sergeant, 1803-15* (Eamonn O'Keeffe (ed.))

No.15 *For Orange and the States: The Army of the Dutch Republic 1713-1772 Part I: Infantry* (Marc Geerdinck-Schaftenaar)

No 16 *Men Who Are Determined to be Free: The American Assault on Stony Point, 15 July 1779* (David C. Bonk)

No 17 *Next to Wellington: General Sir George Murray: The Story of a Scottish Soldier and Statesman, Wellington's Quartermaster General* (John Harding-Edgar)

No 18 *Between Scylla and Charybdis: The Army of Elector Friedrich August of Saxony 1733-1763 Part I: Staff and Cavalry* (Marco Pagan)

No 19 *The Secret Expedition: The Anglo-Russian Invasion of Holland 1799* (Geert van Uythoven)

No 20 *'We Are Accustomed to do our Duty': German Auxiliaries with the British Army 1793-95* (Paul Demet)

No 21 *With the Guards in Flanders: The Diary of Captain Roger Morris 1793-95* (Peter Harington (ed.))

No 22 *The British Army in Egypt 1801: An Underrated Army Comes of Age* (Carole Divall)

No 23 *Better is the Proud Plaid: The Clothing, Weapons, and Accoutrements of the Jacobites in the '45* (Jenn Scott)

No 24 *The Lilies and the Thistle: French Troops in the Jacobite '45* (Andrew Bamford)

No 25 *A Light Infantryman With Wellington: The Letters of Captain George Ulrich Barlow 52nd and 69th Foot 1808-15* (Gareth Glover (ed.))

No 26 *Swiss Regiments in the Service of France 1798-1815: Uniforms, Organisation, Campaigns* (Stephen Ede-Borrett)

No 27 *For Orange and the States! The Army of the Dutch Republic 1713-1772: Part II: Cavalry and Specialist Troops* (Marc Geerdinck-Schaftenaar)

No 28 *Fashioning Regulation, Regulating Fashion: Uniforms and Dress of the British Army 1800-1815 Volume I* (Ben Townsend)

No 29 *Riflemen: The History of the 5th Battalion 60th (Royal American) Regiment, 1797-1818* (Robert Griffith)

No 30 *The Key to Lisbon: The Third French Invasion of Portugal, 1810-11* (Kenton White)

No 31 *Command and Leadership: Proceedings of the 2018 Helion & Company 'From Reason to Revolution' Conference* (Andrew Bamford (ed.))

No 32 *Waterloo After the Glory: Hospital Sketches and Reports on the Wounded After the Battle* (Michael Crumplin and Gareth Glover)

No 33 *Fluxes, Fevers, and Fighting Men: War and Disease in Ancien Regime Europe 1648-1789* (Pádraig Lenihan)

No 34 *'They Were Good Soldiers': African-Americans Serving in the Continental Army, 1775-1783* (John U. Rees)

No 35 *A Redcoat in America: The Diaries of Lieutenant William Bamford, 1757-1765 and 1776* (John B. Hattendorf (ed.))

No 36 *Between Scylla and Charybdis: The Army of Friedrich August II of Saxony, 1733-1763: Part II: Infantry and Artillery* (Marco Pagan)

No 37 *Québec Under Siege: French Eye-Witness Accounts from the Campaign of 1759* (Charles A. Mayhood (ed.))

No 38 *King George's Hangman: Henry Hawley and the Battle of Falkirk 1746* (Jonathan D. Oates)

No 39 *Zweybrücken in Command: The Reichsarmee in the Campaign of 1758* (Neil Cogswell)

No 40 *So Bloody a Day: The 16th Light Dragoons in the Waterloo Campaign* (David J. Blackmore)

No 41 *Northern Tars in Southern Waters: The Russian Fleet in the Mediterranean 1806-1810* (Vladimir Bogdanovich Bronevskiy / Darrin Boland)

No 42 *Royal Navy Officers of the Seven Years War: A Biographical Dictionary of Commissioned Officers 1748-1763* (Cy Harrison)

No 43 *All at Sea: Naval Support for the British Army During the American Revolutionary War* (John Dillon)

No 44 *Glory is Fleeting: New Scholarship on the Napoleonic Wars* (Andrew Bamford (ed.))

No 45 *Fashioning Regulation, Regulating Fashion: Uniforms and Dress of the British Army 1800-1815 Vol. II* (Ben Townsend)

No 46 *Revenge in the Name of Honour: The Royal Navy's Quest for Vengeance in the Single Ship Actions of the War of 1812* (Nicholas James Kaizer)

No 47 *They Fought With Extraordinary Bravery: The III German (Saxon) Army Corps in the Southern Netherlands 1814* (Geert van Uythoven)

No 48 *The Danish Army of the Napoleonic Wars 1801-1814, Organisation, Uniforms & Equipment: Volume 1: High Command, Line and Light Infantry* (David Wilson)

No 49 *Neither Up Nor Down: The British Army and the Flanders Campaign 1793-1895* (Phillip Ball)

No 50 *Guerra Fantástica: The Portuguese Army and the Seven Years War* (António Barrento)

No 51 *From Across the Sea: North Americans in Nelson's Navy* (Sean M. Heuvel and John A. Rodgaard)

No 52 *Rebellious Scots to Crush: The Military Response to the Jacobite '45* (Andrew Bamford (ed.))

No 53 *The Army of George II 1727-1760: The Soldiers who Forged an Empire* (Peter Brown)

No 54 *Wellington at Bay: The Battle of Villamuriel, 25 October 1812* (Garry David Wills)

No 55 *Life in the Red Coat: The British Soldier 1721-1815* (Andrew Bamford (ed.))

No 56 *Wellington's Favourite Engineer. John Burgoyne: Operations, Engineering, and the Making of a Field Marshal* (Mark S. Thompson)

No 57 *Scharnhorst: The Formative Years, 1755-1801* (Charles Edward White)

No 58 *At the Point of the Bayonet: The Peninsular War Battles of Arroyomolinos and Almaraz 1811-1812* (Robert Griffith)

No 59 *Sieges of the '45: Siege Warfare during the Jacobite Rebellion of 1745-1746* (Jonathan D. Oates)

No 60 *Austrian Cavalry of the Revolutionary and Napoleonic Wars, 1792–1815* (Enrico Acerbi, András K. Molnár)

No 61 *The Danish Army of the Napoleonic Wars 1801-1814, Organisation, Uniforms & Equipment: Volume 2: Cavalry and Artillery* (David Wilson)

No 62 *Napoleon's Stolen Army: How the Royal Navy Rescued a Spanish Army in the Baltic* (John Marsden)

No 63 *Crisis at the Chesapeake: The Royal Navy and the Struggle for America 1775-1783* (Quintin Barry)

No 64 *Bullocks, Grain, and Good Madeira: The Maratha and Jat Campaigns 1803-1806 and the emergence of the Indian Army* (Joshua Provan)

No 65 *Sir James McGrigor: The Adventurous Life of Wellington's Chief Medical Officer* (Tom Scotland)

No 66 *Fashioning Regulation, Regulating Fashion: Uniforms and Dress of the British Army 1800-1815 Volume I* (Ben Townsend) (paperback edition)

No 67 *Fashioning Regulation, Regulating Fashion: Uniforms and Dress of the British Army 1800-1815 Volume II* (Ben Townsend) (paperback edition)

No 68 *The Secret Expedition: The Anglo-Russian Invasion of Holland 1799* (Geert van Uythoven) (paperback edition)

No 69 *The Sea is My Element: The Eventful Life of Admiral Sir Pulteney Malcolm 1768-1838* (Paul Martinovich)

No 70 *The Sword and the Spirit: Proceedings of the first 'War & Peace in the Age of Napoleon' Conference* (Zack White (ed.))

No 71 *Lobositz to Leuthen: Horace St Paul and the Campaigns of the Austrian Army in the Seven Years War 1756-57* (Neil Cogswell) (paperback edition)

No 72 *For God and King. A History of the Damas Legion 1793-1798: A Case Study of the Military Emigration during the French Revolution* (Hughes de Bazouges and Alistair Nichols)

No 73 *'Their Infantry and Guns Will Astonish You': The Army of Hindustan and European Mercenaries in Maratha service 1780-1803* (Andy Copestake)

No 74 *Like A Brazen Wall: The Battle of Minden, 1759, and its Place in the Seven Years War* (Ewan Carmichael)

No 75 *Wellington and the Lines of Torres Vedras: The Defence of Lisbon during the Peninsular War* (Mark Thompson)

No 76 *French Light Infantry 1784-1815: From the Chasseurs of Louis XVI to Napoleon's Grande Armée* (Terry Crowdy)

No 77 *Riflemen: The History of the 5th Battalion 60th (Royal American) Regiment, 1797-1818* (Robert Griffith) (paperback edition)

No 78 *Hastenbeck 1757: The French Army and the Opening Campaign of the Seven Years War* (Olivier Lapray)

No 79 *Napoleonic French Military Uniforms: As Depicted by Horace and Carle Vernet and Eugène Lami* (Guy Dempsey (trans. and ed.))

No 80 *These Distinguished Corps: British Grenadier and Light Infantry Battalions in the American Revolution* (Don N. Hagist)

No 81 *Rebellion, Invasion, and Occupation: The British Army in Ireland, 1793 -1815* (Wayne Stack)

No 82 *You Have to Die in Piedmont! The Battle of Assietta, 19 July 1747. The War of the Austrian Succession in the Alps* (Giovanni Cerino Badone)

No 83 *A Very Fine Regiment: the 47th Foot in the American War of Independence, 1773–1783* (Paul Knight)

No 84 *By Fire and Bayonet: Grey's West Indies Campaign of 1794* (Steve Brown) (paperback edition)

No 85 *No Want of Courage: The British Army in Flanders, 1793-1795* (R.N.W. Thomas)

No 86 *Far Distant Ships: The Royal Navy and the Blockade of Brest 1793-1815* (Quintin Barry) (paperback edition)

No 87 *Armies and Enemies of Napoleon 1789-1815: Proceedings of the 2021 Helion and Company 'From Reason to Revolution' Conference* (Robert Griffith (ed.))

No 88 *The Battle of Rossbach 1757: New Perspectives on the Battle and Campaign* (Alexander Querengässer (ed.))

No 89 *Waterloo After the Glory: Hospital Sketches and Reports on the Wounded After the Battle* (Michael Crumplin and Gareth Glover) (paperback edition)

No 90 *From Ushant to Gibraltar: The Channel Fleet 1778-1783* (Quintin Barry)

No 91 *'The Soldiers are Dressed in Red': The Quiberon Expedition of 1795 and the Counter-Revolution in Brittany* (Alistair Nichols)

No 92 *The Army of the Kingdom of Italy 1805-1814: Uniforms, Organisation, Campaigns* (Stephen Ede-Borrett)